Global Societies
An Introduction

Edited by **Akwasi Osei & F. Odun Balogun**

Excerpts taken from
*Global Perspectives: A Handbook for
Understanding Global Issues*
by Ann Kelleher and Laura Klein

PEARSON CUSTOM PUBLISHING
75 Arlington Street, Suite 300, Boston, MA 02116
A Pearson Education Company

Contents

Part III   Global Marketplace

Preface

The necessity to produce this text has been forced on us by the reality of our times. Ours is a time when the world, as is now universally acknowledged, has become a global village, within which the human population in all its diversities live much closer and share much more in common than was possible half a century ago. Thanks to the highly advanced level of modern communication and transportation, people of the world now live virtually as next-door neighbors and are subject to the same modern human experiences. No matter where in the world we are located today, chances are that we watch the same television programs, use industrial products made by the same multinational companies, treat our ailments with drugs marketed by the same pharmaceutical companies, and wear clothes made by the same designers. For this same reason, what happens to one part of the world—be it economic depression, disease epidemic or war—quickly affects the rest of the world.

Under these circumstances, the citizens of the world can no longer afford to think and act locally. The continuation of our very existence requires that now every child think in global terms. The necessity to educate the world to this awareness rests with all the tiers of the educational ladder, and the university is certainly the place to take this responsibility seriously. Ensuring that students who graduate from colleges and universities come out of these institutions as globally aware, if not as global citizens, is the goal of Global Studies and textbooks such as ours.

In assembling the essays that compose this book, we sought contributions that provide historical insight into how the global village came into being, what its manifestations are in the present, and in what directions we are headed in the future. Thus, the essays here are in four sections: Part I: The Global Past; Part II: The Global Present; Part III: The Global Marketplace; and Part IV: Future Global Trends.

It is to be expected that contributions such as these would not all have the same uniform perspectives on issues of globalization. For instance, Valle's view of history is essentially logocentric, as if history begins with writing. Balogun's contribution, on the other hand, assumes the opposite: that orality predated writing, which is relatively a modern technology. The focus in Balogun's contribution, however, is on the claim that "because of its nature, origin, history, methods and purpose, literature perhaps more than any other discipline helps us to discover our common humanity."

Also, we clearly see the female immigrant's bias in contributions taken from *Becoming American,* represented here by Brintrup, Danticat and Hammad. These three women writers give individual narratives of their experiences and conditions of immigration and integration into the American society. They explore the problematic concept of naturalization and provide fascinating perspectives on what it means for a Third World citizen to become the citizen of an industrialized nation such as America. Umerah-Udezulu discusses the differences in feminist theories and the circumstances that made it possible between 1966–2002 for about fifty women to successfully beat male domination to participate in the global politics as chief political leaders of their states.

One of the central questions of our times is the debate about the need—or otherwise—of preserving the diversity of world cultures. Drohan and Freeman demonstrate how one language, English, has come to dominate global communications. The question thus arises as to whether or not this is a negative development of global relationships, as Kelleher and Klein allude to in their contributions. Long Yingtai makes a similar point in respect to world dominance. She believes that everything has been overly commercialized, that western influence has invaded the rest of the world, and 99% of this influence is from the United States. Thus globalization is effectively Americanization.

The contribution by Shariff suggests that even though the global economy has grown immensely, and that international trade has grown fifteen times more, the majority of the world has not shared in the fruits of globalization and wealth creation. In other words, globalization has losers and gainers. This sentiment is shared by Rosenberg in her *New York Times* article, and is also illuminated by Hagos' assertion that the Third World lives on the margins of the global village. Agbango, who also notes this negative tendency in globalization, asserts that "the global village is controlled by the global elite." He believes that the potential global conflicts that may be provoked by the increasingly widening gap between the rich minority global elite and the mass of the global poor could be averted if educational institutions all over the world "create avenues for effectively learning about our world and about how we can make it a better place to live in."

Ackah remarks that criminality is a common human trait which, under current trends of globalization, has acquired global dimensions and has become a menace. The persistence of international crises and wars in spite of the economic gains of globalization is the concern of Kofi Annan, the current Secretary-General of the United Nations, who argues that "if globalization is to succeed, it must succeed for poor and rich alike. It must deliver rights no less than riches. It must provide social justice and equity no less than economic prosperity and enhanced communication. It must be harnessed to the cause not of capital alone, but of development and prosperity for the poorest of the world." To achieve this goal, Annan recommends at both the local and intergovernmental levels the practice of "the politics of good governance, liberty, equity and social justice."

In his contribution, Stephen Kobrin contemplates the economic and political implications of the fast-developing culture of electronic money for national and international governance in the era of electronic commerce, a byproduct of globalization. He points out, for example, that "in a digital economy it will be difficult, or even impossible, to link income streams with specific geographic locations" and this will problematize the issue of political and economic jurisdiction in national and international relations and politics.

Globalization, according to Lester Thurow, is producing what he calls "the third industrial revolution," the second having been produced by the invention of electricity. A significant aspect of this third industrial revolution, in Thurow's view, is the manner it limits the ability of governments to "restrict—or even control—economic activity." In the globalized economy, companies now make their products where they can produce them at the cheapest cost. The consequence of this trend for the American economy, in Thurow's opinion, is that the majority of Americans are experiencing falling wages, while "the top 20 percent of the population has seen its earnings and wealth rise rapidly." This is the future trend that Thurow predicts for the American economy.

The team of Halal, Kull and Leffmann, on the other hand, defines the present era as the age of "Technology Revolution" and provides futuristic prognoses of innovations in all scientific and technological fields. They predict, for instance, that "gene therapy will be eradicating inherited diseases by 2013" and that "growing genetically similar or cloned organs is likely by 2018."

The promise of genetics is the subject of Coates, Mahaffie and Hines, who in their joint contribution assert that "genetics will be a key enabling technology of the twenty-first century, rivaling information technology, materials technology, and energy technology in importance." The team discusses, among other sub-themes, genetics and global development in various fields such as agriculture, industry, economy and health.

The contributions by Kelleher and Klein introduce the issue of the conflicting diversity in human perceptions as a result of the differences in backgrounds, histories and ideological convictions. They emphasize the power of subjectivity in perception, which, compounded by the diversities in ethnic cultures, creates the multiple conflicts that afflict humanity. They believe that "to create a peaceful and cooperative world, people must come to understand the differences that exist between cultures and respect the depth of those differences." In the economic section, they identify the wide gap between the developing world and the industrialized nations, and examine the merits of the two approaches to development: industrialization and basic needs strategy.

Kraig Wheeler discusses the revolution in the contemporary method of scientific investigation, showing that the traditional method of disciplinary separation has been overtaken by the interdisciplinary mode of scientific investigation which merges scientific disciplines. Wheeler argues that the latter approach, which "extends beyond the limits of institutional and national boundaries," produces faster and more spectacular results than the former. He points out, for instance, that in the last decade, scientists who utilize the interdisciplinary approach dominate in the list of those who have won the Nobel Prize in the field of science.

As we can see, Global Studies is not only a necessary area for those who wish to understand our times, but also a field that can provide the needed knowledge about how to promote ideal relationships within and between cultures and nations. In other words, it holds the key to the future of humanity and of our planet. It is, however, also a complex discipline that requires an interdisciplinary approach because it involves all aspects of human living. Furthermore, the issues that it raises can be interpreted differently, depending on the ideological orientation of the interpreter. It is hoped, however, that the essays assembled here will provide some illumination for young minds grappling with the complex nature of today's world.

We wish to thank the individuals and institutions who have granted us permission to use copyright materials:

Indiana University Press for essays in *Globalization and the Challenges of a New Century* contributed by Kofi Annan; Madelaine Drohan and Alan Freeman; Stephen Kobrin; Lester Thurow; William Halal, Michael Kull and Ann Leffman; and Joseph Coates, John Mahaffie and Andy Hines;

Prentice Hall for extracts from *Global Perspectives* by Ann Kelleher and Laura Klein;

Hyperion for essays in *Becoming American: Personal Essays by First Generation Immigrant Women* by Edwidge Danticat, Suheir Hammad, and Lilianet Brintrup;

The Editors of *Zhaobao*, Singapore United Morning News, for Long Yingtai's essay.

Part 1

The Global Past

Introduction to the Modern World

Ann Kelleher and Laura Klein

The past is prologue.

—*William Shakespeare*

Every man takes the limits of his own field of vision for
the limits of the world.

—*Arthur Schopenhauer*

Since the focus of this book is the contemporary world, it is necessary to review
briefly the major perceptions of reality and themes of history that have created modern life. All people have local knowledge of what the world is and how it functions.
This is necessary for daily life. To understand the complexity of the modern world,
however, individuals have to recognize that their view of the world is both limited
and historically created. People living under different circumstances have different,
but no less certain, understandings of the nature of the world, and their understanding, like all others, differs from the perceptions of their ancestors. This chapter outlines some basic issues and events that define the modern world.

PERCEPTIONS OF THE WORLD

Earth is home to all humanity and, as such, might be expected to be universally
understood in a common way, but it is not. Differences about the nature of Earth are
more apparent than the similarities. Some authors have described the world as small,
while others write that it is vast. In fact, people experience both. In daily living, the

scale can be as small as one-on-one encounters. Through travel and learning, the scope of interaction can increase to planetary proportions. The world is "us," but it is populated by a variety of people. The world seems constant, but it is always changing. Given these contradictions, people inevitably explain what goes on in the world very differently. Seeking such explanations becomes more difficult because we are a part of what we want to understand. Even the maps used to image the world are distinct from one another. To some, topographical features compose the world; to others, the world is made up of political units or states; and to still others, the world consists of the different peoples inhabiting it. All three characteristics, and others, together define the world as we know it.

The Physical World

The map used by those who see the world as the physical planet Earth reflects a topography that has no boundaries or place names. It is a unified reality divided only by natural features. It emphasizes mountains, deserts, rivers, oceans, and lakes. No purposeful human creations show on this map. In this context, human differences and constructions seem insignificant and transient. This does not mean, however, that geographical realities are unchanging or protected from human agency. The physical maps drawn of Earth's distant past are different from those of the present. Some of these differences are evolutionary. Volcanoes have developed, erupted, and created islands and mountains. Rivers have moved and glaciers advanced and retreated. Even the continents themselves have broken apart or moved together over time. Other changes, the ones caused by humans, are more revolutionary in nature. Deserts have grown in size, rivers have been dammed, forests have been cut, and lakes and oceans have been polluted.

The Political World

People who see the world politically place an overlay on the physical map. Their map boasts a series of lines that differentiate the states of the world. This representation predominates on the walls of many American classrooms. It implies that the significant differences among people and places are political. South America is divided into Ecuador, Colombia, Brazil, and so on, rather than by the Andes Mountains and the Amazon River. Like the topographical map, the political one changes over time, but the rate of change is far more rapid. A political map of the world ten years old is terribly out of date. New states have been created from the division of old ones; others have been produced from the end of colonial relationships. The political map of the world a thousand, or even five hundred, years ago would show vast areas unclaimed by states. Unlike the topographical map, the political one is made and changed solely by human agency.

The Ethnic World

Cultural maps of the world have, until recently, been found mainly in the offices and classrooms of anthropologists. These maps divide the world into *culture areas* or portions of the world where the people within the boundaries are more culturally alike than those outside the lines. These are collections of related cultures, whose people share similar beliefs, customs, languages, and skills. On these maps, South America is divided into Amazonian Indians, highland Quechua and Aymara (Inca), and urban Mestizos, among others. These maps no longer are considered esoteric due to the growing awareness of the role ethnicity plays in world affairs. These maps, too, are rapidly changing. The cultural map of five hundred to a thousand years ago would include the Incan peoples and indigenous Amazonians but Mestizos did not yet exist. Immigrants from Europe and Africa would soon appear and create new cultures in the region. Migrations from region to region have created significant population shifts throughout human history. Humans have moved and adapted to new environments and new cultures. These maps change, like political maps, through human actions.

Each map is a valid image of reality but none is complete. The world is a complex interaction of physical, political, and cultural elements. When change occurs in one sphere, changes in the others often follow. At any point in history, these elements intersect to form a reality. It is no wonder that people living at that time believe that their world must be both permanent and proper.

EMERGENCE OF THE MODERN WORLD

It follows that the world as we know it is a historical way station on a very long road. Particular events that occurred in specific places over hundreds of years have lead to the present situation and will influence the future. Things could have occurred differently, but they did not. It is important to look to the past to understand how the modern world came to be. By doing so, it will appear that the modern state system that seems so obvious and permanent is, in fact, recent and changeable. The division of the world into state-controlled areas is relatively new and strongly influenced by a historically dictated European colonial model. History is not uniformly moving in one direction, however, and over time states have divided into noncentralized, often ethnically defined units just as such units have centralized into states. History suggests that continued changes in the world system are to be expected.

The World in 1350

It is hard for modern people to consider a past when their states did not exist or existed on the periphery of global events. As historians look deeply into the past, all states disappear. In order to understand the modern world, it is necessary to understand what came before it, to look briefly at the world before the contemporary system was developed. Even in this brief review, it should become clear that the world system of the past was as complex and volatile as the present one and that its history challenges common assumptions about the stability of social and political systems. Further, because the world as we know it has changed dramatically within only several hundred years, it is reasonable to expect equally dramatic changes in the future.

This review has as its starting point the mid-fourteenth century. At this time, continents that were often pictured as uncivilized by Europeans in later centuries, were indeed the centers of civilizations. Every continent had seemingly stable, stratified, and economically sophisticated trading societies with elaborate art and architecture during these years. Soon, however, European exploration and colonialization would begin, creating the new power centers that continue to define the current world system. Even today, people who are descended from the great civilizations of this earlier time continue to remember their historical antecedents, with pride, as highly developed at a time when European society was seemingly more primitive.

In 1350, elaborate civilizations with classical arts and monumental architecture could be found throughout the world. By this time, China had been for centuries an elaborate state with sophisticated forms of education, art, economy, and social organization. Since 1279, the Yuan Dynasty had been established by the Mongol conquest. By 1350, revolts had begun that would lead to the Ming Dynasty in 1368. Chinese scientists had already developed nautical knowledge and ship-building technologies that were unknown in Europe. In the Americas, a number of civilizations thrived. Among the best known are the Mayans in the Yucatan of Mexico, whose elaborate cities with pyramids and temples were regional centers of religion and trade. The Aztecs, who the Spanish conquerors would first meet, had just built their capital at Tenochtitlan, in present-day Mexico City. South Americans had similar cultures to those in the north with one major civilization coalescing in the mid-fourteenth century. The culture of the Incas was just developing and their empire would grow to control all its neighbors. Incan building expertise was unsurpassed in the world at the time. Another kingdom, called Chimor, however, was expanding to contest Incan power. Chan Chan, the great city of the region, continued to thrive.

International trade was important for many of the civilizations of the time. Africa was home to a number of complex societies in 1350. In the north, for example, the city of Timbuktu was a center for trade and learning within the Mali Empire. As a university center it ranked among the finest in the world. Its trade depended on the gold and salt it exchanged for goods made from leather, cotton, iron, and copper from trading partners in the region. To the south the walled city of Great Zimbabwe, in what is currently the country of the same name, was an advanced trade center with goods from the Middle East and Asia passing through its markets. In Southeast Asia, Islam spread and a number of trade cities became prominent. One, the Malacca state on the Malay Peninsula, was on its way to dominating the important East-West trade routes. In the still isolated Americas, trade routes ran for thousands of miles. Mexican trade traveled far to the north, as Mexican artifacts and architectural styles found in archaeological sites in the southeastern United States and along the Mississippi River have documented. The people, now known as Mississippians, had a complex class system and long-range trade that extended far south. They built cities with elaborate architecture, including large earthen pyramids, long before Europeans reached the New World.

This was also a time of international political expansion. By 1350, Islam was on the rise. The Ottoman Empire, which would grow to conquer most of the Middle East, northern Africa, and southeast Europe, was expanding rapidly. In India, Turkish raiders were overtaking the existing principalities in the north. In Africa, the Songhai Empire was expanding and soon would annex Timbuktu. To the east, Ethiopia was a flourishing Christian empire. Throughout the Americas, the Incas, Aztecs, and their rivals vied for political and economic control of their agricultural neighbors.

In Europe, the fourteenth century was a period of near-constant political and social turmoil. French and English monarchs, who headed the most politically organized societies, began the so-called Hundred Years' War (1337–1453), which was actually a series of intermittent battles, peasant uprisings, and revolts by regional princes. For most Europeans, the fourteenth century was a time of poverty. The Black Death (now known as the bubonic plague), which reached Europe in 1347, killed millions of people and lowered the average life expectancy in England from thirty-four to seventeen years at the height of the disease (Tannenbaum 1965:37–38). Also during this time, technologies from distant lands, such as gunpowder and the compass from China, spread to Europe. If the fourteenth century was not the pinnacle of European civilization, the fifteenth century would be a new beginning. Europe would emerge a century later, with the centralized political systems and technological innovations in transportation and weapons of war to begin centuries of exploration and dominance.

European Expansion (1400–1900)

Exploration   Europeans still did not know much about the world's other civilizations by the end of the fifteenth century, but they did know about some of the riches that came from Asia. The spices of "the Indies," used for food preservation and medicines, were traded to Europe at high prices. Europeans wanted a direct route to Asia that would eliminate the Ottoman Empire and other middlemen and, therefore, cut costs. With improvements in sailing ships and navigation devices, Europeans were ready to move out of Europe to trade on their own terms.

The Portuguese and Spanish were the masters of early exploration. Prince Henry the Navigator (1394–1460) of Portugal, who established a school for navigators, led his country's push to exploration. In 1445, Portuguese crews discovered that slaves and gold were available in coastal Africa. By 1498, Vasco de Gama reached India, and Portugal claimed the sea route to Asia. Lisbon replaced Venice as the city for Far Eastern trade, but it soon was challenged by Dutch cities. Spain looked for a western route to the Indies. Funded by Queen Isabella of Castile, Christopher Columbus reached the Caribbean in voyages between 1492 and 1502. The Indies seemed at hand in 1513, when Balboa first saw the Pacific Ocean. Yet, it remained for Ferdinand Magellan to sail from Spain, around South America, and to the Philippines in 1519.

For the most part, this early era of exploration was economically motivated, and many trade ports were established. Settlement and conquest were in the futures of Asia and Africa, but many people in the Americas suffered. Spain used the Caribbean for farming and mining and its local people as forced laborers. This practice, combined with several epidemics, led to their near-total extinction. On the mainland, Spain's goals, often termed "Gold, God, and Glory," also led to disaster. By 1521, Hernando Cortés had conquered the civilizations of Mexico. In the name of religion, all books and artifacts considered "pagan" were destroyed. Beautiful items made of gold or silver were melted down for their metal value. By 1536, the Incan civilization had suffered a similar colonial experience at the hands of Francisco Pizarro and Diego de Almargo.

France and England had less success than the Spanish and Portuguese in the early period of exploration. Their agents searched for a northern route west to Asia, the so-called Northwest Passage. Failing that, the French and English made conflicting claims on North America that they would settle by war. The people on this continent had no gold and silver artifacts. Their riches remained to be exploited through settlement by farmers and trappers.

Colonialization   Europe changed dramatically during the first two centuries of exploration. The Reformation wars, economic growth, and technological advances changed the face of the continent. Spain faded into relative obscurity as a European power but kept its extensive American possessions. Similarly, Portugal, held on to the Asian colonies and Brazil but became a small power in Europe. France and especially England and the Netherlands thrived with resources from their colonies and the growth of their commercial classes.

In the Americas by the eighteenth century, the Caribbean plantation system was in full operation with African slaves providing the labor. British colonies on the East Coast of North America were growing, as was the French settlement of Quebec. The French claimed a vast amount of land, but much of it was populated by Native Americans who traded with French trappers. English settlers, many with African slaves, however, populated the British colonies. Native people there had been decimated by epidemics brought by the settlers, and the survivors were pushed off of their farmlands.

By the nineteenth century, the situation in North America had again undergone dramatic change. A peace in 1763 sealed Britain's defeat of France in North America and left the French with only their islands in the Caribbean. In 1776, however, the Europeans in the thirteen colonies began their successful bid for independence, and only Canada and some Caribbean islands remained for Great Britain. At nearly the same time, the India Act brought India into the British colonial fold.

The late nineteenth and early twentieth centuries were marked by imperialism, when European states completed their conquest of virtually all the world. The Industrial Revolution provided both the means and the cause for increased expansion. Industrializing Europeans needed raw materials and new markets. Also, as nationalism grew stronger, national pride was built in part by colonial success. A paternalistic missionary zeal played a role as well. The perceived needs to bring Christianity to pagans and civilization to people considered "inferior" were often used to rationalize colonial enterprises.

While European states achieved colonial hegemony over most countries in Asia and forced open trade with Japan and China, the subjugation of Africa tells the story of direct colonialism. Before the 1880s, Europe's interest in sub-Saharan Africa focused largely on the slave trade. This had allowed the colonies in the Americas to thrive and earned prosperity for many Europeans and Americans. Attitudes about slavery changed, however, and it was now considered morally reprehensible. Virtually all contact with tropical Africa was on the coast. Despite five hundred years of exploiting the resources of Africa, Europeans knew practically nothing about its interior lands or people.

With the British occupation of Egypt in 1882, the European division of Africa and direct rule over its peoples had begun. At the Berlin Conference in 1884–1885, representatives of the interested states convened to divide the continent. The public rationales for the conference included bringing an end to the slave trade and ensuring free navigation and trade in the Congo River basin. European explorers were moving inland, and King Leopold II of the Belgians had established the Congo Free State in the center of the continent controlling trade on the Congo River. Delegates at the Berlin Conference affirmed Leopold's claim to the Independent State of the Congo and shortly afterward he began ruling it as a personal possession. It was later deeded to Belgium, in 1908. Other European states were given smaller colonies in central and western Africa.

Shortly after the conference, East Africa was similarly divided up. In the south, the British took control of South Africa in 1902, after fighting the long and bloody Boer War with the white settlers since 1899. By the end of the first decade of the twentieth century, virtually all parts of tropical Africa had been claimed by France, Great Britain, Italy, Spain, Portugal, Belgium, or Germany. The division of the continent had been accomplished by European states in their own interest, with no consideration given to the claims of the native people. By the First World War, few places on Earth remained without the stamp of a European state on them. Those few peoples who maintained their independence were often tied economically or militarily to Europe. Culturally, Christian missions had spread throughout the world and converted millions to their faith and an admiration of European culture. For a time at least, Europeans had succeeded in gaining control of the world.

DEFINITION OF THE MODERN STATE

Europeans used their version of the state to achieve worldwide dominance. Its highly centralized organizational structure was capable of concentrating large-scale human and material resources over very long periods. During the colonial era, the European state spread worldwide and became the primary institution for people to interact internationally. Since states have been, and many people think still are, the most powerful decision makers affecting international events, learning about current world issues begins with analyzing the nature of the modern state. Four primary characteristics define a state: *territory, government,* a *loyal population,* and the *recognition of other states.*

Territory   This element of a state may seem obvious at first, but the notion of a precise border existing between independent political units is a relatively recent one. Many empires did not control land so much as populations, often leaving their boundaries inexact because they did not matter very much. As long as subject peoples paid their taxes, fought when conscripted, and did not rebel against the ruling elite, they were allowed to keep their cultural identity and regulate the activities of their daily life, such as education, religion, property inheritance, and ownership. Resources were considered more important than the direct control of individuals or specific pieces of land. Empires usually did not consider territory a symbol of their power or prestige, and therefore, as something worth fighting over. The importance of territory became much more prevalent as the modern state developed in Europe, a place where many peoples and separate political jurisdictions existed in a confined space.

Government   All persons living on the territory of a modern state relate to the government directly. Before the modern state, empires and feudal systems considered most of their subject peoples as existing in groups whose leaders spoke for them and saw to it that the rules the government imposed were obeyed. Those in political power were far away, often physically as well as perceptually. The governments of modern states, in contrast, consider their people as citizens and indivisible parts of the whole population.

Government is defined as the one institution in a society that has the legitimate claim to exercising decisive authority over its population. It requires payments and regulates certain categories of behavior. It can even deny liberty and, in extreme cases, life if a person violates specified laws. Governments have a virtual monopoly on force and the right to make and enforce laws, which everyone must obey. Thus, governments are highly centralized, powerful institutions. The key to their effectiveness lies in the word *legitimacy*. A government achieves legitimacy when its people believe that it is justified, that its laws ought to be obeyed, and that its rule conforms to commonly accepted political values. Such political values have changed over the centuries. A currently prevailing one accepts a government as legitimate if it represents the will of its population as expressed through elections. A former idea causing consent to governmental authority was the idea of a God-given hereditary monarchy. If major segments of a population begin to consider the government as illegitimate, it is forced to rule solely on the basis of its monopoly of force. Inevitably, this type of government becomes oppressive and authoritarian. The situation can become dangerous if people avoid compliance or initiate rebellion. In either case, a government only relying on force has less ability to make enforceable decisions than one that is perceived as legitimate by its people. Legitimacy, therefore, is needed for effective rule.

*A **Loyal Population***   Citizens generally identify with the modern state, at least to some extent. Their feeling of loyalty, called *patriotism*, is distinguished from *nationalism*, which is an individual's identity with an ethnic group based on several shared characteristics, such as language, history, and religion. Empires did not always expect or demand to be the primary focus of identity and loyalty for most of the peoples they ruled. These attitudes were required only of members of the governing elite. The modern state that evolved in Europe, however in its most developed form, fused nationalism and patriotism, at least as ideals. Each state was assumed to have one dominant cultural group, hence the designation *nation-state*, which was the term used for decades. The "nation" part has been dropped in recent years because virtually every state in the world today includes more than one cultural group.

Distinguishing between cultural nationalism and state patriotism helps clarify one of the most significant causes of current conflicts. The clash of identity between the two occurs because, generally, one cultural group controls the government, society's most powerful institution. This creates a situation whereby the dominant group, either consciously or unconsciously, discriminates against other groups. In the 1990s, for example, over forty countries have cultural groups wanting some form of political representation separate from their existing governments, including the Scottish Nationalist Party in the United Kingdom and the French-speaking Quebeçois Party in Canada.

Recognition of Other States   The recognition of other states can become significant when a government changes hands by way of revolution. If most countries of the world fail to recognize the new government as legitimate, economic and political difficulties can result. North Korea provides a case in point.

States thus become weaker when one or more of the four characteristics of a state are questionable. Government leaders strive to make policies that attempt to strengthen their control over territory, legitimate rule, instill their patriotism, and gain respect from other states.

TRENDS OF THE POST WORLD WAR II WORLD

Events in today's world occur in the context of the modern international system. Therefore, adequately explaining the causes of, and responses to, international issues depends on knowing how the current international system functions. That system is defined as the organizations and processes that people use to interact across state borders. The modern state is the most powerful institution in the international system and it has a major impact on many others, such as the United Nations, by setting their policies. States have changed in their relationships with each other and with international organizations during the decades since World War II (1939–1946). The war altered how the world works. The international organizations and trends comprising the current international system were either established after the war or transformed because of it. Four of the most significant general trends since World War II include US leadership, the Soviet challenge, the end of colonialism, and the world's increasing interconnections.

These four trends continue to provide the context for world events, although each has undergone substantial change. The United States is still the world's most powerful state, but it operates in an increasingly complex international environment and needs positive economic and political relations with other states to retain its leadership. Other actors in the international system, states in the developing world, other industrial states, Russia as successor to the Soviet Union, and international organizations have different interpretations of current world issues. In order to understand at least some of the reasons for their varying points of view and their roles in international events, it is necessary to review the trends in the international system since World War II.

US Leadership

The United States emerged from World War II as a hegemony—a dominant world power. It was the only great power that had not been physically and psychologically devastated by the war. Its economy and confidence were at an all-time high. Internationally, the United States used its preponderance of power to establish the international system's institutions and rules. These organizations can be divided into two categories: economic institutions, such as the World Bank, and political institutions, such as the United Nations. The general principles underlying these organizations are derived from the US diagnosis of World War II's fundamental causes. The United States believed its prescriptions would be the best antidotes for a war-prone world.

According to the thinking of US policy makers, as well as many others around the world, the most devastating war in human history had primarily two underlying causes, one economic and the other political. The Great Depression of the 1930s hit only Germany harder than the United States. Each state's setting higher tariffs to protect its own economy only made the downturn worse for all states and ensured the Depression's spread worldwide. In fact, the highest tariff in US history was passed in 1932. Each state reacted with some degree of political change, but the changes in Germany proved to have devastating consequences. Hitler's Nazi Party, a particularly degenerate and racist version of fascism, came to power in Germany in 1933. Its hypernationalism extolled the state as the ultimate good, demanded absolute obedience to the government and its dictator, and predicted that the "master race" of Germans would control the world by eliminating "inferior" peoples. To the fascists, war benefited society since it destroyed the weak. Virtually every analysis of the causes of World War II cited Nazi policy at the top of the list.

The United States and its allies were convinced that following the war, the international system had to be structured so as to foster worldwide economic prosperity, and to identify, plus weaken, potentially aggressor states. Economically, expanding international trade through open markets was essential to each state's prosperity, which, in turn, provided the conditions for stability and peace. Politically, the sobering experience of World War II convinced the world's great powers that international security required mutual effort: Leading states had to adopt internationalist policies and work together in responding to aggressors before they grew into major threats to the peace.

Three institutions were established in the 1940s to organize the international economy. Called *international governmental organizations (IGOs)* because states compose the membership, together they were designed to stabilize the international economy and ensure economic growth. The International Bank for Reconstruction and Development, called the *World Bank*, offered economic aid in the form of loans to countries whose projects were approved. This IGO was originally planned to assist in European recovery, but recipient countries changed over the years as former colonies achieved independence in the 1950s and 1960s. Loans for economic development rather than rebuilding became the World Bank's task, a much more massive undertaking. Whereas Europe already had the prerequisites for healthy industrial economies, the newly independent states did not.

The *International Monetary Fund (IMF)* provides member states with loans to restore international confidence in a country's currency if its value plummets. Like the World Bank, the IMF first helped Europe but, over time, its loans shifted primarily to newly independent, less industrialized countries. Both the World Bank and the

IMF have weighted voting, which means that those countries paying the majority of the institutions' annual assessments have the majority of the votes. Thus the contributors, not the borrowers, control policy making and the terms of the loans tend to reflect those of commercial international banks.

The General Agreement on Tariffs and Trade (GATT), the forerunner of the present-day *World Trade Organization (WTO),* was assigned the task of lowering tariffs and other barriers to trade. The mechanism devised to achieve increased trade through lower tariffs is called *most-favored nation status.* In practice, this consisted of an agreement between two states to lower their tariffs with each other to match the lowest that each charged any trading partner in a specific product category, such as clothing or automobiles. Over time, as more and more states granted most-favored nation status to each other, tariffs around the world were reduced substantially.

As the worldwide political IGO, the *United Nations* began in 1945 with the adoption of the UN Charter. Initially, its main task was tackling threats to security; however, because the founding states understood peace to be linked to economic factors, several specialized agencies were created to address related issues, such as the Food and Agricultural Organization. The two main UN bodies—the *General Assembly* and the *Security Council*—have different roles. The General Assembly provides a forum in which each member state has one vote and there is no weighted voting. The UN Charter gives the Security Council the key role in responding to threats to world peace. Some Council members have more power than others. Of the fifteen member states in the Security Council, five have permanent seats and the other ten are elected to two-year terms by the General Assembly. The United States, the United Kingdom, France, Russia, and China are permanent members, chosen because they were the winners in World War II. Each of these five members has a veto over any resolution passed by the Security Council.

The United States has thus used its leadership to establish international institutions capable of coordinating economic and political relations among the world's countries. This has proven farsighted for reasons US policy makers did not realize at the time; namely, that one state's dominance would not continue for long and that a common framework had to be in place for debating and dealing with the world's problems. The next three post–World War II trends challenged US leadership and redefined major global issues.

The Soviet Challenge

Within only months after the end of World War II, differences between the United States and the Soviet Union began to surface. For example, the states argued over what factions should come to power in Eastern European countries. By the late 1940s, the differences had crystallized into a superpower rivalry. Another geographically large, resource-rich state with a sizable multiethnic population and major military power was challenging the United States for world leadership. Two characteristics combined to make the adversarial relationship more intense and the consequences of war more threatening than earlier competition, such as that between France and Great Britain in the 1700s. First, the US versus Soviet rivalry introduced a new and devastating military threat—nuclear weapons. Second, the struggle was explained in terms of deep ideological divisions that gave form and focus to policy making. People used these *ideologies* or sets of interrelated ideas, to give meaning to events and to legitimize political institutions.

Probably because of the threat of nuclear war, the post–World War II superpower competition proved to be unlike other historical periods of intense state rivalries. No war was fought between the two main antagonists directly, which is why the term cold war was used. Wars relevant to the rivalry occurred often, but they have been called proxy wars because the parties involved were clients of the superpowers. During the Vietnam War, for example, North Vietnam's weapons were supplied mainly by the Soviet Union. The US rejoinder came as it supported the insurgents in Afghanistan who were fighting the Soviet Union. The antagonists divided Europe into two rival military alliances. The North Atlantic Treaty Organization (NATO), organized by the United States, faced off against the Soviet Union's Warsaw Pact.

With elaborate networks of alliances and aid recipients, the foreign policies of both states became fixated on each other. Both the Soviet Union and the United States interpreted everything that happened in the world in terms of their rivalry. International relations analysts have defined this period as *bipolar* because the world had two main centers of power. The enemies confronted each other for over forty years, until the Soviet Union dissolved in the 1990s because of decisions made by its own people. Its member republics became independent states without a war, a rare event historically.

Russia, the republic that controlled the now-defunct Soviet Union, inherited its permanent seat in the Security Council and its status as one of the world's leading states. Yet, Russia does not command the Soviet Union's economic, military, or ideological power. The fact that it cannot act as a counterweight to the United States has fundamentally changed world politics. The United States is freer to act in international conflicts when it chooses to become involved. The US and (to a large extent) European economic and political system has become the prevailing world standard.

The End of Colonialism

From World War II on, a steady stream of newly independent states took their places in the United Nations. The number of UN members grew particularly in the 1960s, when decolonialization spread to most of Africa. Fifty states had founded the United Nations in 1945, and by 1955 UN membership had grown to seventy-five. These numbers increased to 117 members by 1965, 141 by 1975, 157 by 1985, and 185 by 1995. With a large majority in the General Assembly, the states in Africa and Asia, often supported by those in Latin America, began asserting their priorities, especially their need for economic development.

The newly independent states did not see the world as bipolar but as *multipolar;* that is, as comprised of many power centers. The terms *First World, Second World,* and *Third World* were coined in part to reflect their disagreement with the prevailing bipolar perception of the international system. The First World represented the already industrialized states in the West with their free-market economies and multiparty politics. The Second World reflected the Soviet Union and its Eastern allies with their one-party systems and government-controlled economies. The Third World referred to the rest of the world's states with their lower levels of industrialization, higher levels of poverty, and vulnerability to actions taken by the more powerful countries.

Leaders in Third World states thought that by coordinating their policies they could become another power center. Their first attempt to do so occurred as early as 1955, at a conference in Bandung, Indonesia. The attending countries initiated the Nonaligned Movement (NAM) to differentiate themselves from the United States and its allies, and the Soviet Union and its allies. Subsequently, Third World states followed this political initiative with a coalition designed to bring their economic plight to the world's attention. This network, called the Group of 77, grew to include 130 states by the 1990s. It established the UN Conference on Trade and Development (UNCTAD) as an organization focused solely on Third World issues.

It was not until 1973 that less industrialized states scored some success in negotiations with the First World. The Organization of Petroleum Exporting Countries (OPEC) used an embargo of oil to triple the price paid for a barrel of crude oil. In the heady atmosphere this produced, Third World states passed a series of resolutions in the General Assembly reflecting their interests, such as recommending more foreign aid. None of the resolutions were implemented, and by the early 1980s OPEC's negotiating position had been undermined by the world's oil glut. Yet during the 1970s, Third World countries had managed to focus attention on the different set of problems they faced and to redirect some World Bank and IMF resources. The less industrialized states became more than just places where the Soviet Union and the United States could play their bipolar game by proxy.

Increasing Interconnections

As the numbers of states and IGOs have increased, so too have *nongovernmental organizations (NGOs)*. These private agencies link people across international borders in a wide variety of ways, such as by occupation, religion, personal interest, and issue activism. A sample listing of NGOs would include professional groups, such as the International Skeletal Society with pathologists and orthopedists as members, the Catholic Church and the World Council of Churches, Rotary International, Amnesty International, Care International, and the International Red Cross. In addition, the number of businesses with overseas affiliates has exploded over the years. Currently, about three hundred IGOs and five thousand NGOs channel international contacts among governments, groups, and individuals.

The proliferation of organizations has greatly contributed to the complexity of the international system. No longer are most international interactions bilateral ones in which states deal one-on-one with each other. More and more states, even the most powerful ones, engage in multilateral diplomacy within the framework of IGOs as an established way to address issues. Common positions are negotiated, resolutions are passed, and actions are taken in cooperation with other states. Also, whether using bilateral or multilateral relations, states are no longer the primary channels for international interaction. People have created ever-expanding networks of NGOs and businesses, each with its own priorities, policies, and communication links.

The explosive expansion of international activity in the decades since World War II continues today. It is a necessary reaction to the ever-accelerating globalization of issues, institutions, and interaction processes, whether economic, ecological, linguistic, social, philosophical, or political. The pace of technological innovation shows no sign of abating and, together with population growth, continues to shrink the psychological and actual space among people of the world. The increased speed of communication and transportation can be applied peacefully, as in email, or during war, as with missiles, for example. International decision-making networks aim to foster the former and forestall the latter. The international scope, importance, and complexity of issues facing the planet's peoples demand cooperative and coordinated responses. No longer can one state or even a small group of states manage, much less negotiate, solutions to the world's problems.

Gold, God, Glory . . . Globalization:
The Foundations of Contemporary Global Connections

Akwasi Osei

In the last decade of the twentieth century, the major theme that dominated most aspects of human interactions was that of invasive and extensive global connections. This trend is set to continue and perhaps dominate the twenty-first century. In every aspect of human endeavor, it is easy to see deepening relations—both cooperative and antagonistic—among cultures, civilizations, countries and continents. For the most part, this has gone under the rubric of *globalization*: the increasing consolidation of the world's economy under market forces alongside increasing democratization. This is in reality only a part of human endeavors which have from millennia brought different cultures together into differing relationships. The present manifestation continues the practice of the last five centuries when a true global system emerged with the imperatives of European efforts to expand its borders in all ways: economically, culturally, and politically. In other words, since roughly the middle of the fifteenth century, in seeking "gold," European nations imposed their "god" on much of the world, thereby creating for their "glory" huge empires which formed the basis of the contemporary global system. (Ali Mazrui, in *The Africans*, #04)

Nations and cultures have always interacted with each other. Venturing further afield from one's habitat has always been a natural human disposition. What sets the last five hundred or so years apart was the creation of a hierarchy of world cultures under the imperial and colonial control of European powers. The gradual appropriation of others' lands, cultures and political lives distinguished this era of European "universalism." Empires were built, whole civilizations were annihilated, and anti-human ideologies created to maintain the fledgling system.

This paper argues that the interactions between much of the world and Europe since the middle of the fifteenth century created dependencies and interdependencies which established the basic structure of the modern global system. Further, that this globalism has tended to favor certain social formations over others. From whichever perspective one judges the past, the pre-1450 world had several centers of power in which indigenous cultures were clearly in control more or less of their own areas. There was no global power that reached all corners, despite empires that reached many miles beyond their borders. Post-1450, however, it was clear that the globe was on a different path as organized Europe gradually extended its power. All corners of the globe became integral to each other's development, non-development, and under-development. In the twenty-first century, we are a global neighborhood where some are more equal than others. Like all neighborhoods, however, the interdependency in the midst of inequality continues to challenge residents' understanding of how they have to live together and maintain that neighborhood. What has been the nature of these relationships in living in this community? Who has occupied what position in these relationships?

By examining the establishment of contacts across the Atlantic world, this paper will seek answers to such major questions in an effort to demonstrate that the close connections linking the cultures around that great ocean resulted in stratified, tangible, concrete relationships. These close Atlantic connectivities expanded into other parts of the world, eventually cementing together a European-dominated global system.

THE PRE-1450 AD GLOBAL SYSTEM

The last five hundred years were of course built upon several millennia of human inter-action. From its beginnings in Africa, humanity spread out around the world. Whether foraging for food, seeking shelter, or combing for clothing, peoples have always found it necessary to venture farther afield. In virtually all areas of the globe, cultures rose and fell for all the possible reasons: ambition, conquest, greed, implosion and size.

The centers of learning and growth were all over. On the African continent history records major civilizations dating back 5000 years. Classical historians cor-rectly recorded that ". . . there is always something new out of Africa" (Davidson, 1993). The continent seemed to have always held an attraction to cultures from across the globe. Nubia, Egypt, Meroe, Napata, Zimbabwe, Abyssinia, and Ghana were among some of the more established cultures that eventually influenced areas far beyond their borders (Davidson, 1993). Empires big and small rose and fell across the length and breadth of the continent through 1400 AD. At its height in the fifteenth century, for instance, the Songhai empire was twice the size of present-day United States, and was known all around the world.

In Asia several cultures had already shown the world various levels of sophis-tication in travel, trade and forms of thought. The Chinese, for instance, flourished initially under several distinct dynasties, overtime being united under a centralized system. This was achieved under the Qin and Han dynasties which propelled China beyond its borders across other parts of Asia, Africa and Europe. (Bentley and Ziegler, 2003). In what is now India, several Hindu states which had developed from millennia and practiced several different modes of worship fell victim to incursions and raids by Muslim Turks bearing an even newer religion, Islam.

In what became known as the Americas, there flourished some of the world's stable empires. The Olmecs are considered to be the first complex society in this area. They influenced other cultures in their wake, among them the Mayans, the Teotihuacán, the Aztecs and the Incas. Centuries of steady growth and development attended these societies: they were sophisticated, they managed complex social and political systems, engaged in agricultural production, and carried on long-distance trade. The world of the Arawaks, Caribs and others truly made this an "old world" even as they and their lands came to be dubbed the "New World" by the Europeans who came in the fifteenth century.

European society centered on the Greek city states and the Roman empire. The Greeks especially left a rich legacy of philosophy and culture which influenced the rest of the continent. At its height, the Roman empire had political control over areas as far from its center as present-day Iraq to the east, and present-day Britain to the north.

By the middle of the fifteenth century, all across the globe, peoples had created viable societies. Further, most of these societies had also established contacts by building relationships through trade, exchange and communication. As merchants traversed land from east to west and seafarers connected many societies from the Atlantic to the Indian Ocean, cultural exchanges also took place, primarily through the spread of various faiths, Islam, Buddhism, and Christianity. These commercial, cultural and civil connections were to be taken to a much higher level after 1500.

THE POST-1450 GLOBAL SYSTEM

In the 1995 film, *Pocahontas,* there is a scene in which English sailors, on a voyage across the Atlantic to the "New World," sing the following words:

> . . . we sailed the open sea for Glory God and Gold and for the Virginia Company; For the new world is like heaven; We will all be rich and free; Or so we have been told by the Virginia Company . . . (*Pocahontas*)

This new, activist impulse represented a much more purposeful opportunity on the part of Europe for wealth acquisition, cultural imposition and political expansion. Relationships among Europe and the rest of the world became more systematic, more complex, and more decisive. The underlying motivation in the song was in essence, the tripartite imperative: the economic (Gold), the cultural (God), and the political (Glory). Europe needed and wanted riches and resources, it had the technology to get them, it had ideas as to where they were, and therefore went ahead to get them, at all costs. This aggressive attitude would come to have a lasting effect on other peoples of the world in the ensuing centuries. In effect, it laid the groundwork for a systematic Globalism, one which had its roots in earlier years, but had a different quality to it. It is important to state that undergirding these motivations was the use to which European mariners put all the seafaring technology that was available at the time:

> The most important navigational equipment on board vessels were magnetic compasses and astrolabes . . . The compass was a Chinese invention that had diffused throughout the Indian Ocean basin in the eleventh century. (Bentley and Ziegler, 2003, 611)

In addition, adding a rudder onto the stern—another Chinese invention—and using square and other sails—which had been used by other sailors centuries before—enabled these new ships to take on dangerous seas and their potentially devastating winds. It is this combination of need and desire to acquire and to impose, coupled with the use of new technology in support of these desires, which pushed this new global exploitation, exploration and expansion which touched all the areas of the world very deeply. Europe benefited the most; the rest of the world benefited much less, or not at all, and for yet others, it was annihilation, slavery, destruction, and death.

ENCOUNTERING THE ATLANTIC

The Portuguese and the Spanish were the first Europeans to sail forth in this new dispensation. They went around the continent of Africa, making contact with both indigenous peoples on islands of Madeira, Cape Verde, Fernando Po (Ringrose, 2001), and on the mainland on the coasts. These new relationships centered on trade in commodities such as gold, ivory, and cotton which previously had made their way to Europe by other means, including the Trans-Saharan trade. There was now a need for direct access to these items. In addition, these voyages came to have an air of permanency and finality to them. Everywhere the Europeans went, they encountered local socioeconomic systems from which they tried to extract as much as possible. The indigenous peoples did indeed trade with the Europeans, in the best sense of the word. There was mostly a mutuality of interests. For instance, along the coast of Africa, Portuguese and Spanish adventurers established contacts which resulted in more or less equal exchanges with the different coastal peoples from the Senegalese coast all the way to the southernmost tip of the continent. In what became known as the Gold Coast, Don Diego d'Azambuja established trade and other political links with the Fanti (Thompson, 1987). There was so much gold that the Portuguese called the place "El Mina," the mine. Pedro de Sintra went to Sierra Leone, and Prince Henry (the Navigator)'s men were all over the west coast. Two of his men, Nina Tristao and Antam Goncalves, were so overwhelmed with all they saw that there are reports they kidnapped about twenty people from those areas back to the Iberian Peninsula.

Among the adventurers to the west coast of Africa was one Christopher Columbus. According to Ivan Van Sertima (1976), it was well established that Columbus, on one of the trips, picked up evidence of well-endowed lands on the other side of the waters.

THE COLUMBUS EFFECT

On his return to Europe, Columbus went about trying to line up commercial support for his scheme to take this possible alternate route to Japan. Essentially, he calculated that since the earth was a sphere, one could get to Asia easier by sailing west. His calculations, and conjectures, were not conventional, however, and he found few potential investors to finance him. In fact, he was onto something. Little did they know that these conjectures, actually based on the information from what had been done previously, was about to change the course of global interactions profoundly. Columbus would be getting to Asian lands quicker by going west. Or so he thought.

With the support of the Spanish imperial court, he finally set out to test his theories. His encountering of land months later set in motion a veritable wave of conquistadores in his wake whose actions had a sense of proprietariness to their activities. Indeed the planting of the flag and the cross were telling representations of European intentions: the need for "gold," aided by their "god" and appropriating land and adding to the greater "glory" of Europe. Long after Columbus, men such as Cortes, Pizarro and Cabral gave concrete meaning to the holy trinity of gold, god and glory. As Columbus noted in a letter to his sponsors back in Spain, "Gold is most excellent. Gold is treasure, and he who possesses it does all he wishes to in this world, and succeeds in helping souls into paradise."

This encountering of cultures around the Atlantic took on a different coloring. The seemingly unlimited supply of vast real estate with its mineral and agricultural potential in the Americas turned the newcomers into a new type of imperialists. Relations between the peoples turned conflictual. The indigenous peoples sensed in these newcomers a different resolve.

The growing imperial rivalry between Spain and Portugal led to a Europeanized sense of ownership of these new lands, as evidenced by their signing the Treaty of Tordesillas in 1494. This treaty divided the world along a north-south line such that all land to the west belonged to Spain, and all to the east belonged to Portugal. Thus pacified, Spain and Portugal proceeded to prosper, and before long, the expropriation of indigenous land was enjoined by other European powers— the Dutch, the British, the French, the Swedes, the Danish—all across the area. With expropriation came the need for labor to farm and to mine.

The indigenous peoples resisted their enslavement to do the work. This resistance led to the decimation in their ranks. Further, a sizeable chunk of the indigenous population fell victim to the new diseases that the newcomers brought with them. Indeed, the world witnessed a holocaust, an aboriginal holocaust.

The new empires sought to use their brethren—convicts, peasants, indentured, hired help—on the land. This did not last, as the system could not guarantee a steady stream of labor. It was at this juncture that the centuries-old relationship between earlier European societies and the Africans was about to change. From a few Africans who had found their way to the European mainland centuries before, and from a concentration of commodities such as ivory, gold and textiles, we entered into a new era where the needs of Europe gradually became the dominant impulse and shaper of the changing relationship between the Atlantic communities. This need for labor led to an increase in kidnapping and snatching of able-bodied Africans for sale and subsequent enslavement for work in this "new world."

In a sense, Columbus' accidental and erroneous arrival in the "Indies" gradually led to a situation whereby the future of Africa became linked up with American lands and European commercial interests. This was a triangular trade pattern that connected the Americas, Europe and Africa. The former European incursions around Africa to the Indian Ocean and beyond all became a part of this larger, global network.

THE TRADE IN HUMANS

At the root of this relationship was the economic imperative, and at its root was the trade in human cargo. This trade, and the system of slavery it established around the world, held the globe together like glue.

The need for labor in these new lands was overwhelming. The patterns that resulted from this need changed the existing patterns of interaction among peoples. Initially, the indigenous populations were pressed into service. They resisted, and coupled with their susceptibility to new diseases, their numbers were almost wiped out. After a failed attempt to use imported labor from Europe—convicts, hired help—the experiment failed as a result of low numbers.

The attention was then turned on the continent of Africa, where, at least fifty years prior, the Portuguese and the Spanish had established themselves in trade with Africans. That relationship among the principals was for the most part one of equals. There was an equal exchange in gold and other precious metals, ivory, pepper, gum, and other commodities. Occasionally, the Europeans got involved in local rivalries, leading to periodic warfare.

Prior to 1492, therefore, we do not witness the wholesale buying and selling of humans in Africa, except in the east, and parts of the west where the spread of Islam contributed to a mass of different African peoples taken to the north and east to present-day Middle East.

By the beginning of the sixteenth century, the demand for labor from the Americas had changed this relationship from one of reciprocity to one of gradual unequal exchange. By 1510, Africans were being sold into slavery in large numbers; humans gradually became the item of choice. Indeed, it is important to note that this trade in humans was the major economic enterprise in the world between 1500 and 1850s. Slavers were European, and later American, merchants. European home governments chartered companies to trade: the Royal African Company, the Dutch East Indian Company, the French West Indian Company, among others. In other words, the trade in humans was a response to *external* factors; what Africa "exported" was dictated by European needs.

The destination was the New World, and the profits repatriated to Europe. Indeed, the trade in humans shepherded capitalism (Williams, 1942). Major seaports flourished all over Europe such as Birmingham, Bristol, Bordeaux, Nantes, and Seville. Ancillary business such as shipbuilding, insurance and banking accompanied the trade.

The processes that led to this take-off in industrial development in Europe, and later the United States, were also the same that led to a veritable decline in the fortunes of Africa and the rest of the world. They are two sides of the same coin. There was, for instance, an enormous transfer of wealth from Africa, the Americas, and the Caribbean to Europe, a transfer made possible by this truly international venture. Europe's monopoly in the trade, enhanced by military means, and technology—ships, guns—in effect paved the way as it seized control and used global waterways to take over vast landholdings across the world. This accumulation of wealth allowed Europe later to expand its cultural and political imperatives: colonies, empires, and the spread of perhaps the most fundamental cultural trait, language. This is essentially the reason that, globally, the "major" languages of culture and commerce are European languages. As Basil Davidson has stated,

> Through these four centuries, the balance of gain was all one way. In any effective sense there was . . . no sharing of wealth and achievement. To Europe the trade with Africa was always an enrichment; and this enrichment could and did help Europe into new and more productive forms of society and government . . . (Davidson, 1980, 284)

By the late nineteenth century, European peoples ". . . parlayed their advantageous position into global hegemony . . . " (Bentley, 802), effectively in control of most of Africa, Asia, the Americas, and "even tiny Pacific islands." This is the era of imperial domination. This relationship, built since the fifteenth century, was cemented by imperialism and colonization.

In other words, the colonized and the colonizers were part and parcel of the same historical process. From a global perspective, therefore, peoples of the world were part of a connected whole based on a hierarchy of cultures that had European culture at the center and all others on the periphery. However one explains the connections and relationships of the world's peoples—whether it was in conflict or in cooperation—this has been the underlying feature of the global political system. Of course, imperialism and colonialism were to bring their own dynamics as the colonized sought to be independent for most of the twentieth century

THE TWENTIETH CENTURY/PRESENT

Whether it was war, anti-colonial struggles, global ideological battles, or cultural exchange, historical developments in the twentieth century could not escape global interconnections and interdependencies. During World War I and World War II, the problems of a few European nations affected the entire world. In both wars, the majority of the world on all continents became enmeshed in conflicts that had nothing to do with them. After WWII, an effort was made to inject some humanism into the imperial and colonial enterprise. The colonizers supported the idea of the self-determination of subject peoples, eventually leading to the formation of the United Nations. This world body trumpeted the better side of cooperation, even as its leaders did all they could to hold on to their economic and political advantages.

In spite of this, the march toward independence and self-determination continued apace. By 1989, as the former Soviet Union fell apart, the United Nations had over 191 nations. Most of these were previously colonies of Europe. One of the major contentions of the global system is that former colonies have had to sit as "equals" in international fora. The theory is that all are equal, but the reality is that some are more equal than others. The practical effect of this imbalance has been that at any one time, this heavily connected global system is always—and simultaneously—in conflict and cooperation.

We are at a time in history when national boundaries are at the mercy of advanced technology, and peoples are indeed much more closely aligned with each other. The world has never been this much connected across borders. We live in a global neighborhood, and living in such an environment requires neighbors to respect each other, share resources, and be wary of the effects that our actions have on others. This is difficult because as we have seen, the nature of the global interactions has been one of inequality. It is difficult to practice sharing in such a relationship.

This is the challenge of the twenty-first century: How are we going to address this imbalance in political, social and cultural inequality? Is Globalization going to maximize these inequalities and thereby deepen cultural divides on a global scale?

Rather than *Globalization*, perhaps we need to practice *globalism*, the idea that ". . . we share one fragile planet the survival of which requires mutual respect and careful treatment; . . . and the belief that the condition of our neighbor, no matter how far away, affects each of us and thus demands our attention." (Mark Ritchie, *http://www.itcilo.it/english/actrav/telearn/global/ilo/globe/kirsh.htm*). The first step in this direction is a total respect for, and acceptance of, the diversity in different cultures of the world.

REFERENCES

Bentley, Jerry and H. Ziegler. (2003). *Traditions and Encounters: A Global Perspective on the Past*. Second Edition. New York: McGraw Hill.

Chinweizu. (1975). *The West and the Rest of Us: White Predators, Black Slavers, and the African Elite*. New York: Vintage Books.

Davidson, Basil. (1993). *African Civilization Revisited: From Antiquity to Modern Times*. Trenton, NJ: African World Press.

Davidson, Basil. (1987). *The Lost Cities of Africa*. Revised Edition. Boston: Back Bay Books.

Davidson, Basil. (1980). *The Atlantic Slave Trade*. Revised and Expanded edition. Boston: Little Brown and Co.

Kelleher, Ann and Laura Klein. (1992). *Global Perspectives: A Handbook for Understanding Global Issues*. Upper Saddle River, NJ: Prentice Hall.

Mazrui, Ali. (1985). *The Africans #04: Tools of Exploitation*.

Ringrose, David. (2001). *Expansion and Global Interaction, 1200–1700*. New York: Longman.

Mark Ritchie, *http://www.itcilo.it/english/actrav/telearn/global/ilo/globe/kirsh.htm*.

Pocahontas, The Movie, directed by Mike Gabriel and Eric Goldberg.

Rodney, Walter. (1982). *How Europe Underdeveloped Africa*. Washington, DC: Howard University Press.

Thompson, V. B. (1988). *The Making of the African Diaspora in the Americas, 1441–1900*. New York: Longman.

Van Sertima, Ivan. (1976). *They Came Before Columbus*. New York: Random House.

Williams, Eric. (2003). *Capitalism and Slavery*. Chapel Hill, NC: University of North Carolina Press.

Out of the Global Past:
A Brief History of the Interaction Between the World's Peoples

James E. Valle, Ph.D.

IN THE BEGINNING

In the long life of our planet, extending back some 4.6 billion years, the time of humankind has been brief indeed. Our earliest hominid ancestors, the Australopithecines, first appeared in Southern Africa approximately 5.5 million years ago. Subsequent examples of hominids, Homo Hablis and Homo Erectus, followed at long intervals. Finally, some 130,000 years ago the first modern human appeared, apparently originating in Southern Africa. Although most of their existence was passed in an epoch of intense glaciation, these men and women were able to populate all but one of the continents of the Pleistocene World, Africa, Asia, Europe, Australia, and the Americas. In so doing, they slowly evolved into different cultures, Africans, Europeans, Asians, and Australians, each adapting to a specific natural environment. They also created the basis of human culture, the mastery of fire, the making of tools, the invention of articulate speech, and self-expression through painting, sculpture, and decorative art. When the intense cold of the Ice Age ended, perhaps 10,000 years ago, our human ancestors numbered about six million individuals widely scattered across the surface of the Earth, but fully prepared to take advantage of the warm post glacial climate of the Holocene Epoch.

Since the retreat of the glaciers, virtually all of humanity's historical experience with the arts of civilization has taken place. By 8000 BC, a town supported by an agricultural field system had arisen on the site of present-day Jericho. Further east, along the arc of the Fertile Crescent, more towns arose slowly expanding into cities as the people dug irrigation canals and erected levees to control the floodwaters of the Tigris and Euphrates Rivers in present-day Iraq. Eventually, elaborate city-states emerged supported by an agricultural base and featuring walled fortifications, monumental structures, a populace divided into social and occupational classes, permanent royal governments, and a diversified economy featuring both barter and foreign trade. By 4000 BC, these urban civilizations were present in lower Mesopotamia and along the Nile River Valley. All that remained to do was to evolve systems of writing to record their annals so that History could begin.

The earliest forms of writing, Sumerian cuneiform and Egyptian hieroglyphs, were in place by 3000 BC and recorded the deeds of the first persons to emerge as actors in Human History. Narmer, the Pharaoh who united Upper and Lower Egypt, and Sargon, the Lugal (King) who organized most of the Fertile Crescent into an Empire ruled from his capital, the city of Akkad, are the first of our ancestors to have names that we can cite today. The chronicles of their lives, although incomplete, clearly show that they inhabited a world that featured trade, diplomacy, war, dynastic consolidation, empire building, and heroic deeds. It also contained greed, treachery, violence, slaughter, decadence, oppression, and pillage; indeed, all the components of human creativity and folly that we are still familiar with in our own time.

From this relatively small nexus of fertile land located near where the African and Eurasian landmasses touch on each other the idea of civilization diffused outwards in several directions, eastwards to the Indus River Valley, southwards towards Nubia and Axum, northwards to Persia and Mycenaean Greece, and eventually to Cambodia, China and Western Africa. In each of these places, civilizations would arise, each unique in terms of its language, its religion, its social customs, its philosophical speculations, and its artistic and architectural achievements. Nevertheless, all of these diverse empires would share the same basic structural elements as the Mesopotamian city-states. Separated from each other by vast distances, they managed to establish tenuous linkages by land and sea to barter for or purchase valued products and commodities. In this way, Egyptian glassware, Chinese silks, Indian spices, African ivory, Greek pottery, and Roman gold and silver found their way to destinations thousands of mile from their places of origin. The civilized culture of the Ancient World probably reached its peak in the First Century AD with four prosperous empires, Roman, Nubian, Vedic, and Chinese, trading along the Great Silk Road and the connecting sea-lanes.

THE RISE OF EMPIRES AND NATIONS

In the time-honored manner of all such entities, these major empires were decidedly expansionist and their restless urge to conquer and subjugate brought them into contact with a wide variety of cultures, the Celtic and Germanic peoples of Northern Europe, the Huns and Mongols of Central Asia, Bantu peoples of Africa, sea peoples of Southeast Asia, and the warriors of the Arabian Peninsula. Often successful at first, the imperial peoples eventually learned to their dismay that conquest could be a two-way street. The Roman Empire was eventually swept from end to end by Hunnish and Germanic invaders and its Western half went into eclipse in 476 AD. The Vedic civilization of ancient India was taken over by Arians from Persia and later by conquering Muslims. The sophisticated culture of China could not resist the

Mongol onslaught led by Genghis Khan In 620 AD Muhammad formally launched the Islamic faith with a theology that virtually guaranteed rapid expansion outwards from Arabia. It would eventually dominate a vast sweep of territory from the Atlantic Coast of Spain and Morocco to the waters of the Indian Ocean. In this way, the Medieval World grew out of the civilizations of the Ancient World, destroying some of them at least partially, but preserving the essence of civilization itself. Meanwhile, across the wide waters of the Atlantic Ocean, other civilizations were emerging, apparently spontaneously and in isolation from Eurasia. The Mayan peoples of Central America had mastered the problems of sustaining cities in the jungles of the Yucatan Peninsula and the Guatemalan lowlands by 1 AD. In Central Mexico, Olmec and Toltec cultures maintained their kingdoms until they were taken over by the more powerful and aggressive Aztecs. Along the littoral of the Andes Mountains, the Inca civilization began to erect elaborately sculpted stone cities, some at elevations above the ten-thousand-foot level.

By the middle of the Fourteenth Century (circa 1350), this Medieval World was essentially complete. The human population of the World, once so tiny, had by now grown to approximately 750,000,000. Trade between the Orient and Mediterranean World was constantly expanding, dominated by the Muslim caliphates at Baghdad, Damascus, and Cairo who acted as middlemen. Key inventions such as the compass, gunpowder, instruments for finding latitude at sea, paper, and block printing emerged from China and traveled along the Silk Road and the sea lanes of the Indian Ocean to remote Western Europe where they sparked a technological revolution, first in warfare and later in the art of ocean navigation. Here technological innovation was accompanied by political change leading to the gradual emergence of five maritime nations, the first of their kind in human history. Spain emerged from several smaller kingdoms of the Iberian Peninsula because of a crusade against Muslim domination that had gone on for centuries but was essentially complete by 1492. Portugal had consolidated itself even earlier while England and France had finally given up claiming each other's lands and crowns and settled into recognized separate identities. Further north, the several states of the Netherlands were beginning to come together in the conviction that they shared a common destiny. These maritime kingdoms were something new in the World. Each one featured a compact territory, a population that shared a common linguistic and ethnic identity, more-or-less agreed-upon boundaries, a unified royal government, and an intensely ethnocentric view of the outside World. Although their political philosophies were monarchial and authoritarian, there was scope for individual initiative, a sense that upward mobility was possible and, above all, an economic system that rewarded successful business ventures.

The World had seen empires before, but these entities were to be its first nation-states, its earliest examples of what we today call a "country." And they were hungry. Relatively modest in size and population—the Netherlands had less than a million inhabitants and England's population was under five million—the maritime states stood at the outermost edge of the Old World. The vast wealth of Asia was ten thousand miles to the East with all of Islam in between. Fortunes stood to be made by any nation or individual that could find a way to link Europe directly with the Far

East and open a channel for highly prized trade goods, silk, spices, sugar, chinaware, and jade to come into the European market in quantity and without paying off the Muslim middlemen.

It was the Portuguese who led off in this great trading venture. Having mastered the use of the compass and learned to construct fast, seaworthy ships that were capable of long voyages carrying men armed with muskets and cannons, they began to explore southwards down the West Coast of Africa looking for a way around the continent to gain access to the Indian Ocean. It actually took more than fifty years, but in 1493 Bartholomew Diaz rounded the Cape of Good Hope and proved that a sea route to the Orient was possible. The Spanish, recognizing that the Portuguese were searching for a passage around Africa, decided to try something different. In 1492 they concluded the last phase of their reconquest by capturing the Islamic kingdom of Grenada. Flush with their victory, King Ferdinand and Queen Isabella decided to back an expedition under the leadership of a Genoese navigator, Christopher Columbus, who claimed that he could reach the Orient by sailing Westward across the Atlantic. Misunderstanding the true size of the Earth, Columbus claimed that he could reach the Coast of China, or perhaps Japan, after a voyage of some two thousand miles, difficult but not impossible given the ships of that day. The cost of the expedition would be modest, but the potential rewards were enormous, certainly enough to enrich anyone who backed the voyage. Columbus himself modestly asked for only one-tenth of all the riches he might generate. Acting quickly, the Spanish monarchs authorized the voyage and in August of 1492 Columbus' fleet of three small ships departed from the modest port of Palos on the voyage that would break down the isolation of the Americas and mark the beginning of Modern History.

THE COLUMBIAN REVOLUTION

There has been much speculation among contemporary historians as to whether Columbus is a hero or a villain. His voyages set in motion a chain of events that played out over hundreds of years. The results have been favorable for some peoples and catastrophic for others, and the ecological impact on the Caribbean Basin and the rest of the Americas has been truly profound. Perhaps it is best to review briefly just what Columbus himself thought about his achievement. For starters, he was entirely focused on finding a sea route that would link the civilizations of Asia with the seaports of Spain. He never accepted the reality that he had in fact encountered a new and hitherto unsuspected landmass (from his perspective), not even after he had made four Trans Atlantic voyages and conducted extensive explorations. He was willing to believe that he had landed on islands located off the coasts of India, China, or Japan inhabited by peoples who were somehow less civilized and organized than these imperial entities. He was prepared to claim these outlying islands for Spain, Christianize and enslave their peoples, exploit whatever riches they possessed, gold, silver, precious stones and the like, and to found cities and towns that would facilitate Trans Atlantic trade. He expected to be made Governor-General of the "Indies," Admiral of the Ocean Sea (the Atlantic), and to receive his one-tenth share of the profits to be realized from trading with the "Orient." He dreamed of using a large part of his anticipated fortune to finance a new crusade to liberate the Holy Land from Muslim domination, and he expected to share his fortune and responsibilities with his immediate family, particularly with his brothers Bartholomew and Diego.

None of this came to pass, mainly because Columbus persisted in his basic error to the end of his days and because his brothers turned out to be hopelessly incompetent assistants. By 1519, he was dead and his successors now realized they had stumbled upon what was, to them, a "new" World. They were also keenly aware that a vast and mysterious landmass lay just to the West of their modest headquarters in Havana, Cuba. In that year, an obscure mercenary soldier named Hernando Cortez set sail from Cuba for the coast of Mexico to search for a magnificent kingdom rumored to lay somewhere within a vast continent. He fully expected to locate this splendid entity, claim it for the Spanish Crown, install himself as its ruler, convert its people to Catholicism, and appropriate a vast treasure of gold and precious stones. He had no real factual evidence to justify these expectations and his expeditionary force was pitifully small—475 soldiers, a notary, and a priest. They were so doubtful that once they had landed on the Mexican coast, Cortez burned his ships at the water's edge to discourage anyone from deserting the expedition.

After an epic march inland over deserts and mountain ranges, the Spanish soldiers, now accompanied by thousands of Indian allies, passed into the Valley of Mexico and beheld a splendid city apparently floating in the midst of a vast lake. It was Tenochtitlan, the seat of the Aztec Empire, a civilization of some two million inhabitants, rich in gold and plunder and waiting to welcome Cortez as the fulfillment of a prophecy that their all-powerful God, Quetzalcoatl, was about to pay them a visit. Thus began a complicated cycle of conquest, subjugation, rebellion, retreat, reinforcement, reconquest, and resubjugation. Spanish muskets and edged weapons clashed with obsidian swords and flint-tipped javelins. Armored conquistadores on horseback, backed by cannons and savage wolfhounds, hacked their way through masses of Aztec infantry amazing both their enemies and their Indian auxiliaries. By 1521 the Spaniards were firmly in control of the Valley of Mexico and busily engaged in reaping the first installments of gold and silver that would, in time, become the largest mass transfer of wealth the World had yet seen.

Cortez' accomplishment was not to stand alone. In 1573 Francisco Pizzaro and his four brothers led an even smaller expedition into the Andes Mountain of Peru and duplicated Cortez' feat by overthrowing the civilization of the Incas. As before, there was the initial shock of encounter and conquest, rebellion, treachery, retreat, and reconquest, but in the end the result was the same, a new Spanish viceroyalty and another enormous haul of treasure. Reasoning that what had already been done twice could be done again, fresh waves of conquistadores set out on further expeditions. Some like Cabeza de Vaca and Hernando de Soto explored vast stretches of the American Southwest before returning to Mexico gaunt and clothed in tattered rags. Others, such as the violent and unstable Aguirre, went slowly mad trying to cut their way through the green hell of the Amazon jungle. In the end, Spain was endowed with an empire that stretched from north of the Rio Grande River to the frigid reaches of the Tierra del Fuego. This empire with its forts, its three viceroyal seats of power, its bishoprics, its missions, and its presidios sent annual fleets of treasure ships back to the mother country. The Spanish had revealed to the other maritime states of Europe the possibilities and the potential rewards of imperialism, and they followed suit.

THE CLASH OF CULTURES

Ironically, it would be the Portuguese who actually realized Columbus' dream of reaching the Orient by sea. In 1498, five years after Diaz had doubled the Cape of Good Hope, Vasco da Gama led a small Portuguese squadron around Africa and into the Indian Ocean. He eventually made landfall at the port of Calicut on the southern tip of India, loaded his ships with trade goods, and made his way back to Lisbon. Portugal's elation moved the Spanish to protest their exuberant claims to be masters of the Indies and, finally, the Pope was obliged to intervene. By the terms of the Treaty of Tordesillas, a line was drawn down what was supposed to be the middle of the Atlantic Ocean. Everything East of the line was awarded to Portugal and everything West of it went to Spain. A later Portuguese landing on the eastward bulge of South America would give them Brazil while Magellan's encounter of the Philippines gave Spain a possession in the Orient, but for the moment, the World was neatly divided between the two Iberian powers and they proceeded to make the most of their respective hemispheres.

As more powerful fleets of Portuguese warships and numerous trading vessels undertook the long voyage into the Indian Ocean, they entered into a complex political and economic venue. The Muslims had long dominated this part of the World. Arab dhows traded along the East Coast of Africa from Mogadishu to Dar-es-Salaam and Sofala exchanging manufactured goods for timber, ivory, gold, and slaves. The entire Sub-continent of India was mostly under the rule of the Mogul Empire, a small clique of Muslim sultans holding sway over tens of millions of Hindus. Muslim trading posts and enclaves dotted the strategic Straits of Malacca and whole communities of Islamic merchants inhabited the seaports of China. This was the world of Sinbad the Sailor and the adventurer and writer Ibn Batutta.

The Portuguese were well equipped to penetrate this Muslim stronghold. Under their talented and energetic Admiral and Governor-General, Alfonso de Albuquerque, the massive Portuguese galleons, with their long tiers of cannons firing on the broadside, took on the Arab dhows and rowing galleys, winning battle after battle. Putting armed men ashore on the Coast of India, they shot their way into Goa to establish a trading enclave of their own. Quickly mastering the Straits of Malacca, they established trading posts for the collection of precious spices and penetrated the seaports of China proper to load silk, carved jade, and fine porcelains. The profits they reaped when they carted these goods back to Europe exceeded the cost of ships and crews so that each additional voyage undertaken became almost pure profit. Although the teeming populations of India and China could not be conquered and governed by the Portuguese as readily as the peoples of the Americas could be dominated by the Spaniards, gunpowder weapons and ocean-capable sailing ships allowed them to come and go as they pleased, establish enclaves and bases, and beat down any opposition—that is to say, any opposition from the empires of the Oriental seas.

European opposition was a different matter. The huge hauls of gold and silver carted home to Spain by the annual treasure fleets and the rich cargoes of spices and oriental luxuries brought back by the Portuguese excited the envy of the other European maritime states. The Papal Line of the Demarcation, created in a moment of supreme hubris, could not protect the interests of the Iberian powers forever, especially after the Reformation made England and the Netherlands Protestant nations. By the middle of the Sixteenth Century, the English and the Dutch were sending their own battle fleets to the Caribbean and the Indian Ocean with the French following close behind. There was a mad scramble to explore and claim still more land in the Americas, Africa, Southeast Asia, and the islands of the Pacific, indeed, any place that could be reached by a sailing ship. Some navigators, like the naturalized Englishmen John Cabot and Henry Hudson, even penetrated Arctic seas. These later explorers encountered peoples and vast landscapes where they eventually created little replicas of London, Amsterdam, or Paris. This was the beginning of a tidal wave of immigration from the Continent of Europe that would ultimately total some fifty-two million souls and repopulate entire continents and sub-continents.

In addition to the quest for precious metals and luxury trade goods, the Europeans embarked on another series of ventures. There was a growing demand in their homelands for agricultural commodities that could not be cultivated in Europe's cool temperate climate. Sugar, rice, indigo, cotton, tobacco, tea, coffee, and cocoa grew splendidly in the tropics and sub-tropics and commanded premium prices when landed in a European port. These were the classic plantation crops of the era, requiring the clearing and planting of Caribbean islands, coastal mainlands, and fertile tropical highlands. They also required massive amounts of labor, but if everything could be put in place the profits were enormous. There are records of Caribbean sugar plantations that made one thousand percent profits in a single year of operation. To meet the demands for labor, European debtors and convicts were transported overseas as indentured servants and later a massive trade in African peoples ultimately transferred some ten million persons to the Americas.

The practice of raiding the continent of Africa for slaves dates back to the Egyptian civilization. In the Medieval World, the various Muslim caliphates had been the most active slave traders distributing Africans to places as far apart as Cordova, Spain and the coast of India, with many going to the Persian Gulf and the Arabian Peninsula. By 1450 the Portuguese had initiated a small traffic in slaves from the West Coast of Africa into Europe, but the institution never flourished there because of the abundance of peasant labor. Starting around 1550, the Spanish and Portuguese both began to realize the potential that existed for plantation crops and especially sugar in the Caribbean Basin and along the coast of Brazil. From that point on, an extensive trade in humans was carried on from West African fortress cities to what was then known as the West Indies. A highly profitable triangular trade grew up with ships coming out from the Iberian ports loaded with manufactured products and trade goods, which they exchanged for slaves at Elmina or Accra or some other African port. The slaves were then transported across the tropical Atlantic—the dreaded Middle Passage—to the Coast of Brazil or the sugar islands of the Caribbean. Here they were traded for bulk cargoes of sugar or spices and the ship returned to Europe. At each port visited on this voyage, the ship earned a profit often enough to repay the entire coast of its construction. Each subsequent voyage undertaken was almost pure profit and a stout ship might last for twenty or more years in this trade.

Of course, this kind of wealth generation quickly attracted the attention of the other European maritime powers. After a brief period of trying to persuade the Spanish and Portuguese to share the traffic with them, the British, Dutch, and French sent naval forces of their own to seize sugar islands and mainland enclaves touching off two centuries of rivalry and warfare along the "Spanish Main," the Caribbean coastline from Venezuela to Mexico, and the Caribbean. Formal naval expeditions, motley collections of buccaneers and privateers, and bands of outright pirates clashed and struggled with the entrenched Spanish and with each other as well as seeking an ever greater share of the wealth being generated by the gold and silver mines and the tropical plantations. Every island became a fortified enclave and European monarchs willingly sacrificed whole battle fleets to ship worms and entire armies to yellow fever for the sake of gaining just one more sugar island. Attempting to capture the annual Spanish treasure fleet became a national pastime for the Dutch and English.

Under the then prevailing theories of mercantilism, an economic system dedicated to national enrichment by the accumulation of gold reserves, each European power attempted to create a closed system of commerce between itself and its colonies and then to expand that system by raiding its neighbor's colonies in an unregulated war of all against all. Although this led to incredible waste and unnecessary destruction, the turnover of wealth was so enormous that the entire Continent of Europe gained capital at an unprecedented rate, capital that was to underwrite the Industrial Revolution and usher in still another phase of Colonialism.

IMPERIALISM AND TRADE

In the decades prior to the invention of James Watts' double-acting steam engine, first introduced in 1775, most of the European powers had been content to assemble empires made up of small islands in the Caribbean, Indian Ocean, or Southeast Asia or, alternatively, to establish enclaves on the coasts of Africa, India, or China to facilitate the trade in the luxury of goods they sought. Only Spain and Portugal sought to actively administer vast tracts of territory in the Americas. The great empires of the Middle East, the Indian sub-continent, and mainland China at first resisted, but then adjusted themselves to the tiny European enclaves. Imperial China felt secure in its sense of cultural superiority to the "long-nosed barbarians." The Emperor was preoccupied with the historical problems of invasion by Central Asian steppe nomads and challenges to his authority by regional warlords. Conceding a series of trading enclaves in remote coastal cities seemed a small thing to do and there was gold and silver specie to be earned in selling products which China had in abundance and which the Europeans desperately wanted. True, the skill and deadly efficiency with which the Europeans deployed their muskets and cannons was disturbing, but Chinese subtlety and superiority was thought to be more than a match for crude force of arms.

In South Asia there was a different dynamic. The Indian sub-continent constituted a vast mass of Hindu peasants and their Mahratta princes, ruled over by a small but powerful Muslim upper class presided over by the Mogul Emperor whose seat of power was Delhi, far from the coastal cities the Europeans were interested in. The Hindu-Muslim relationship was clouded by suspicion, oppression, envy, and occasional violence. In this setting, the Europeans, with their deadly gunpowder weapons, were seen as a force that might tip the delicate balance of power, either firmly cementing Muslim rule or providing the lethal edge needed for the Hindu maharajas to overthrow it. Inexorably, the Europeans found themselves drawn into the vortex of Indian power politics simultaneously maneuvering between the contending indigenous powers while endeavoring to eliminate each other from the game. At the Battle of Plassey in 1747, a private army belonging to the British East India Company and consisting of English troops and indigenous auxiliaries decisively defeated an opposing force of French soldiers and their local allies. This victory set the stage for the eventual British conquest of all of India which was accompanied by the classic tactic of "divide and rule" in which Muslim and Hindu princes were played off against each other until both were firmly under the control of the Honorable East India Company.

The Continent of Africa offered a far different challenge to pre-industrial imperialism. Enormously large in size, much of Africa consists of nearly impassable dessert, dense tropical rain forest, or semi-arid grassland. Diseases such as malaria, dengue fever, sleeping sickness, and river blindness made penetration into the interior by Europeans virtually impossible. Although caravan routes linked them to the Islamic World, entire kingdoms and inland empires were effectively out of reach of the Europeans who were effectively confined to trading at coastal enclaves. Initially, they were dependent on the Africans themselves to round up and deliver the trade goods—palm oil, ivory, and gold, and later people— to coastal trading posts. Only in the far southern tip of Africa, where the climate was temperate and there was a strategically important harbor, was it possible to plant a substantial European colony of settlement. Capetown and Table Bay changed hands from the Dutch to the French to the British, slowly expanding its population of European inhabitants who derived their importance as a harbor of refuge and replenishment on the long sea route between the North Atlantic and the Orient.

One resolute people was able to resist the blandishments of the Europeans and maintain their aloofness to the colonizing process. The opening of Japan, or "Chipangu" as Columbus called it, had been one of the main objectives on all of his four voyages between 1492 and 1504. Not long after Magellan's circumnavigation of the World was completed in 1521, Spain had established a foothold in the Philippines while Portuguese navigators arrived off the coast of China. From these two bases, the Spanish and the Portuguese were soon locked in a race with each other to open up Japan and incorporate her into their respective trading systems. At first, the Japanese were receptive and quickly mastered the use of European firearms, but soon they grew wary. Disturbed by the inroads of Catholic missionaries and upset by the destabilization of their complex political structure through the introduction of new weapons, they ultimately opted to expel all of the foreigners from their islands, destroy every vestige of their technology, forcibly reconvert all those who had become Christian back to the official Shinto faith, and close their ports to foreign trade. Only one small window on the outside world was kept open. A single Dutch trading ship was permitted to make one voyage a year between the Dutch East Indies and the minor port of Nagasaki. This almost total isolation lasted virtually intact until the arrival of the American Commodore Matthew Calbraith Perry in 1855 and prevented Japan from becoming a victim of the European imperialist system that engulfed the rest of the World.

Today, Japan's luck seems doubly fortunate in the light of what was to come after the advent of the Industrial Revolution. Trading in precious metals, spices, and luxury goods had left Europe awash in capital wealth and this windfall craved further avenues of investment. Watts' steam engines made possible the concentration of manufacturing activity in factories equipped with power-driven machinery. It also held the potential for revolutionizing ocean navigation in the form of steamships and facilitated the development of railroads. Intellectually, Europe was ripe for these revolutionary inventions because of a series of internal changes that had taken place in parallel with its colonial adventures.

First, there had been the Renaissance, which lasted from 1200 to 1550 and opened European minds to the potential for individual achievement in the arts and sciences. Next came the Protestant Reformation, a long and painful interlude that demonstrated the limits of a culture and political order based mainly on religious doctrines. This was followed by the scientific and philosophical breakthroughs of the Enlightenment, which showed that human knowledge was dynamic rather than static and capable of being infinitely expanded. Finally, there came the American and French Revolutions of 1776 and 1789 with their ideas of the Rights of Man and the role of the citizens in politics and government. This heritage made the European World more reception to rapid technological and economic progress, quicker to apply new ideas and artifacts, and more ruthless and direct in solving practical problems than the other great cultures of the early 1800's. From this point on, it would be Western culture that defined what was "modern" by confronting and controlling civilizations which had no choice but to adapt to European culture which victimized them.

THE INDUSTRIAL REVOLUTION

Strengthened by the Industrial Revolution which produced even more wealth than the previous patterns of trade and plunder, the European maritime states, now joined by Germany, Italy, and Russia, made the Nineteenth Century the absolute peak of the Colonial and Imperial Epoch. To feed the European industrial complex, it was now necessary to trade extensively in cotton, wool, jute, coal, metallic ores, hides, timber, grains, livestock, nitrates, and an enormous variety of manufactured goods. These were crude commodities compared to the glamorous luxury imports of the past. To procure them in bulk, it was necessary to expand colonial empires from mere coastal enclaves to embrace huge tracts of territory and millions of indigenous peoples.

The classic example of the new imperialism of the Nineteenth Century was British India. Chartered and sanctioned by the home government, the British East India Company steadily expanded its power and authority until it exercised effective control over the entire sub-continent. An army of English officers commanding mixed cadres of British and Indian troops (sepoys) established order and imposed British concepts of law and justice, determinedly uprooting ancient cultural and religious practices that clashed with British sensibilities. A secure road system basically free of banditry and confiscatory tolls was soon followed by an extensive railroad network and telegraph system. Whole districts were converted to the production of cash crops like cotton and tea intended for export to Britain. Jute fiber for the production of rope and burlap sacking replaced the food crops that had once supported a self-sufficient peasantry. Tens of millions of those peasants were obliged to raise industrially oriented crops for export while purchasing their food grains and finished clothing from British traders. On top of this, they commonly paid land taxes and rental remittances to the new overlords. All of this control and domination was accomplished by some 9,000 British civil servants and approximately 90,000 soldiers who enforced British raj (rule) over 250 million Indians on behalf of an island nation located on the other side of the World. This is not to say that there was no resistance on the part of Indian princes and their peoples. In 1857 a mutiny broke out that was so severe that it put the entire colonial enterprise in jeopardy. The British government was obliged to set the East India Company aside and take India under its direct control, but in the end the combination of European technology, military tactics, a belief in its cultural supremacy, crushed all opposition.

The Nineteenth Century experience in China was a variation on what happened in India. The Manchu Dynasty, while weak and corrupt, remained in nominal command of a civilization that was simply too immense to be swallowed up by any colonial power. In any event, not one but several imperialist states were intent on penetrating China and tapping an enormous trade potential. Throughout the Nineteenth Century, would-be traders arrived, joining the long-established Portuguese. The British set the stage, creating enclaves at Shanghai and Hong Kong. When they settled down to trade, they found that the Chinese wanted nothing to do with their goods. What they wanted was for the British to pay for highly valuable Chinese luxuries in gold and silver specie. This would have initiated trade on the basis of an adverse balance of payments, in effect diverting British wealth into Chinese coffers, but the Chinese were adamant. They had been draining Europe since the days of the Roman Empire and, secure in the conviction that they were the World's most advanced and sophisticated culture, they saw no reason to stop now.

Stymied at what seemed to be a reversal of the usual balance of trade, the British hit upon an evil but ingenious solution. They undertook the large-scale cultivation of opium in India and imported the addictive drug into China, reasoning that they could quickly engender a raging demand for the narcotic. Opium profits would then underwrite the purchase of Chinese goods for export to Europe with money left over. When the Chinese Emperor, alarmed at the effect that opium was having on his people, attempted to put a stop to its importation and expel the British merchants, England responded by sending steam-powered gunboats armed with the latest cannons to sink the Chinese customs junks while detachments of British soldiers stormed the harbor and river forts and slaughtered their garrisons. The classic Chinese weapons, swords, bows, and arrows, firecrackers, and stink bombs were of little use. After three years of fighting, the Imperial Court at Beijing signed a treaty with the British essentially permitting them to do as they pleased in China. This Treaty of Nanking, dating to 1843, served as the precedent for other European powers, France, Germany, Russia, and eventually even Japan to penetrate into China while claiming the privilege of "extraterritoriality," namely that Chinese law did not apply to Europeans.

Like the Indians, the Chinese struggled against this fate. In 1856 a renegade warlord, having converted to a bizarre interpretation of Christianity, touched off the Taiping Rebellion in an attempt to depose the now disgraced Manchus. He only succeeded in sparking the most costly and devastating civil war in human history. The first attempt to build a railroad in China ended in a huge riot when traditional religious leader determined it violated the sacred principles of Feng Shui. As late as 1900, a secret society, the Harmonious Fists, abetted by the Manchu Dowager Empress, attempted to drive the foreigner out of Beijing as a prelude to ridding all of China of Western influence. This so-called Boxer rebellion proved to be the last attempt of the Chinese to restore the traditional civilization of classical China to its native soil. After its collapse, the Chinese empire came to terms with European powers.

THE SLAVE TRADE AND THE IMPERIAL SCRAMBLE

The final frontier of the new imperialism of the Nineteenth Century was the interior of Africa. By 1800 the slave trade was past its peak and headed for eventual abolition. The heart of the continent was still a mystery to the Europeans. Even such basic facts as the source of the Nile and the full extent of the Congo River were unknown. Hundreds of indigenous cultures had never been visited by Europe's four centuries of activity there. Men like the medical missionary David Livingston, Henry Morton Stanley, the ethnic geographer Richard Burton, and the soldier of fortune Cecil Rhodes saw an opportunity to extend British glory and fortunes. Islamic Northern Africa was attracting the attention of the French and Italians while the extreme south was slowly filling up with the descendants of Dutch and British settlers. As exploratory expeditions slowly began to fill up the supposed blank areas on European maps of Africa, areas which had been known to other cultures for centuries, the European powers began to scramble for territories they could claim and colonize. The competition became so heated that they eventually hit upon a novel approach to the problem of overreaching and overlapping claims. In 1884 all of the "interested" powers met in Berlin, Germany, laid out a blank map of Africa, and proceeded to divide it up among themselves! When they were done, all of the continent, with the exception of Liberia and Ethiopia, was the property of one or another of the European nations. Everyone got into the act, even the Belgians and the Italians. In classic European style, the boundary lines marched across the landscape in arrow-straight lines, followed river courses, or were determined by the extent of effective exploration or administration by one of the powers. No Africans were consulted and the lines made little sense in terms of indigenous cultures, lands, or political divisions. They did delimit colonies that in many cases were only workable in the European context, as places to establish ports, build railroads into the interior, establish mines, trading posts or plantations, and create a network of military garrisons and police stations. Advances in tropical medicine made it possible for Europeans to survive long enough to complete a tour of duty as a soldier or colonial administrator while the application of Western technology opened up the continent to all sorts of lucrative economic exploitation.

As was the case elsewhere, there was resistance. The French were obliged to create a special force, the Foreign Legion, to police the vast body of the Sahara Desert. Belgian troops undertook ruthless pacification campaigns in the Congo. British expeditionary forces confronted the militant Zulu and Matabele peoples in a series of pitched battles while Italian imperial ambitions were at least temporarily stopped cold by an Ethiopian army at Adowa in 1889. Nevertheless, the Europeans were always able to save themselves in the end by the judicious application of divide and rule tactics and modern firepower, now including the Maxim machine gun, repeating rifles, and lightweight precision artillery firing exploding shells. The construction of roads and railroads came next as "trade followed the flag" and some fertile sections of southern and eastern Africa even attracted settlers from Europe eager to establish plantations and deal in tropical commodities. Africa and various islands of the South Pacific put the finishing touches on the so-called "Imperial Scramble." By 1914 it was virtually complete as far as Europe was concerned, although Japan would attempt to duplicate Western imperialism during the next three decades.

Having reached its peak, European imperialism began to unravel almost immediately afterwards. The great weakness of the European imperial cycle had always been the disunity of Europe itself. They had constantly warred among themselves. At the end of the Thirty Years War in 1684, contemplating vast devastation in the very heart of the continent, the European states sought to moderate and regulate their internecine warfare by adopting codes of International Law governing war, trade, diplomacy, and travel. This ushered in the era of the Competitive State System wherein each European nation sought to outmaneuver the others by raiding colonies, constructing alliances, manipulating balances of power, and frequently resorting to short, sharp tactical wars utilizing professionalized armies and navies. It was a classic struggle of all against all, cold, calculating, cunning, and essentially amoral and it did very little to foster trust or cooperation. Occasionally, it resulted in massive global conflicts and each conflict became an opportunity for colonies to break away and declare their independence.

It was the people of the thirteen British colonies of North America who first exploited this weakness. Britain and France engaged in a titanic struggle for both mastery in Europe and possession of overseas territory in a war of seven years' duration between 1756 and 1763. Britain emerged victorious but bankrupt and sought to recoup her losses by taxing her colonies. This drove the Americans to revolt and, aided by a vengeful French government, they achieved independence and the opportunity to craft a new constitutional system of government for the United States based on rational Enlightenment principles. By 1788 this system had elected its first congress and president.

Next came a cataclysmic quarter century of incredibly violent warfare which was triggered by the French Revolution in 1789 and lasted until the final defeat of Napoleon in 1815. In the ensuing chaos, the French colony of Haiti liberated itself in a massive slave revolt. The vast Spanish territories, four viceroyalties stretching from North of the Rio Grande to the Argentine pampas, were cut off from their mother country when Spain was invaded and occupied by French troops. Forced to fend for themselves, creole elites devised their own liberal constitutions and established fledgling nations. When Spain was finally restored to sovereignty, it proved impossible to re-impose colonial discipline and by 1824 there were twenty-two new Latin American republics. It is perhaps ironic that in the Americas, colonies were winning independence even as Asia and Africa were becoming more firmly colonized.

WORLD WARS AND EUROPEAN DECLINE

After the conclusion of the Napoleonic Wars, Europe took a break from large-scale conflict for about a century, but the essential patterns of diplomacy and warfare were never altered. Suspicion was still rife and armed conflict was still very much an option in the practice of statecraft. Virulent rivalry between France and a newly united Germany led to an accumulation of tensions that resulted in the gradual division of the major European powers into two hostile alliances. In 1914 a relatively minor event triggered World War I, a massive conflict on the continent which spilled over into the colonies. When it was done, there were ten million European dead, victor and vanquished alike were in desperate financial straits and the myth of European racial and intellectual superiority had been dealt a major blow. These facts could not be hidden from the rest of the World because hundreds of thousands of colonial soldiers had witnessed it with their own eyes. The British dominions of Canada, Australia, New Zealand, and South Africa had seen their men sacrificed under incompetent English generals. Indian, Senegalese, Kenyan, Algerian, Somali, and West Indian troops had carried the brunt of battle alongside white soldiers, watched them do manual labor and shared both victories and defeats. When they returned home, it was with the conviction that they were owed something for their sacrifices and that their colonial overlords were no longer invincible supermen.

Capitalizing on these revelations, the "white" dominions pressed successfully for full home rule and Ireland split violently but successfully away from England. In India, an Oxford-trained barrister turned nationalist, Mohandas K. Gandhi, asked his people a fundamental question. How can a small cadre of Englishmen, thousands of miles from home, rule over a vast sub-continent with hundreds of millions of inhabitants? The answer was simple: Because they let them. Thus was born the tactic of passive resistance aimed at making Imperialism impossible by withdrawing cooperation from the imperialists. At the Versailles Peace Conference in 1919, held to conclude World War I, the United States had introduced the concept of national self-determination for the peoples of Eastern Europe who had been cast loose from the defunct internal empires of Germany, Russia, and Austria-Hungary. They would now form their own countries and govern themselves. Did this glittering new idea not extend to the peoples of Asia, Africa, and the Caribbean as well? The European colonial powers denied it and, backed by a huge stock of arms and equipment left over from the war, they clamped down hard on rebels and independence movements, but it was an uneasy process. In 1922 Gandhi's Indian Congress Party drafted a declaration of independence quoting directly from the American document of 1776. They used the railways, the telegraph line, and the newspaper presses introduced by the British to knit together all of India to resist British rule. As his campaign intensified, Gandhi's tactics, his imprisonments, his boycotts, strikes, and demonstrations became the stuff of headlines around the World. The rest of Asia, Africa, and the Caribbean began to consider their options.

Meanwhile, the European tradition of competitive states was far from dead. The victor nations of World War I remained uneasy and the vanquished powers seethed with frustration. New totalitarian ideologies, Fascism and Communism, took over in the nations most wounded by the war. Although professedly different in quality and ultimate goals, both of these governing philosophies stressed vengefulness, secretiveness, unscrupulous pursuit of power, military might, and a willingness to stoop to mayhem and murder on a massive scale. Mussolini's Italy, Hitler's Germany, and Stalin's Russia were turbulent and dangerous neighbors located in the very heart of Europe. In the Pacific, a newly industrialized Japan nerved itself to begin the process of enlarging its own empire by force of arms. China and the Asian colonies of the established empires were Japan's main targets. Throughout the 1930's, the tensions escalated and by the end of the decade, another world war was in progress.

THE AMERICAN CENTURY

As measured in the loss of human life and massive property destruction, the Second World War was larger than the first by several orders of magnitude. Seven major world powers went into it between 1939 and 1941, but only two were still standing by the time it ended in August 1945. The three fascist states—Germany, Italy, and Japan—were in ruins, totally defeated. Britain and France had come out on the winning side, but both were bankrupt and coping with serious casualties and property damage. Russia had born the brunt of Germany's onslaught with 22 million of its people dead and its most developed industrial regions thoroughly wrecked. Its only assets were a massive land army and a huge tactical air force with which it now dominated the eastern half of Europe. Only the United States remained a true world power. Undamaged at home and enjoying the prosperity of a vastly expended economy, the United States possessed an Army, Navy, and Air Force second to none in size and quality, produced fully half of the entire World's industrial output, and owned half of the World's negotiable wealth. No nation or empire had ever been in quite this position before. It was an opportunity to reshape the world.

Having come late to the practice of great power politics, the United States was resolved to use its opportunity to chart a different path. At the Bretton Woods Conference of 1944, a global free trading company was hammered out with all major currencies pegged to the American dollar. A World Bank and an International Monetary Fund were established to monitor reconstruction and allocate resources. Postwar relief and rehabilitation plans were sketched out. A General Agreement on Trade and Tariffs would regulate competition and break up closed imperial trading blocs. The aim was to eliminate intense economic rivalry as a future cause of war. At San Francisco and later in New York, the United Nations (UN) organization was chartered and put in motion to create a forum for the World's nations to meet and settle disputes, cope with political crises, and accomplish important humanitarian goals. The UN would also deal jointly and collectively with aggressive behavior on the part of individual nation states. Once again, the intention was to head off future wars caused by political or ideological rivalry. Overall, the goal of the United States was to lay to rest the old competitive state system by eliminating as many of its friction points as possible. It was a bold venture taken at a time when the main competitive states had no choice but to follow suit.

And where did the peoples in the colonies fit into this grand scheme? The United States itself was the product of a colonial revolt, a stunningly successful one, the first of its kind in modern history. Although it had acquired a small colonial empire as the result of the Spanish American War of 1898, the United States had never been a wholeheartedly imperialistic nation, mainly because its vast interior landscape contained most of the resources necessary for industrial development and its internal market was large enough to absorb most of its manufactures. Consequently, American policy makers took a dim view of Europe's colonial systems and actually advocated that they be liquidated. This profoundly shocked the Europeans, but they slowly began to realize that the war had done fatal damage to both their prestige and their economic and military power.

This trend first became obvious in Southeast Asia. The Japanese had driven the Dutch out of the East Indies, the French out of Indochina, and the British out of Malaya and Burma. Although they had, in the end, proven to be even harsher masters than the Europeans, the Japanese had at least proven that Asian people could defeat Europeans in battle. When they surrendered, the Japanese went home, but left behind most of their weapons which quickly fell into the hands of nationalist insurgents. Returning Dutch and French colonial administrators found themselves facing well-armed rebellions, which made it impossible for them to regain their former dominance. Following the example of the Americans, who had granted Philippine independence in 1946, the Dutch pulled out quickly, making the new nation of Indonesia a reality.

The French proved more stubborn. Straining their damaged post-war economy to the utmost, they dispatched significant naval and ground forces to Indochina in a desperate attempt to hold on, but a determined Viet Minh guerilla movement under the leadership of the Marxist Ho Chi Minh initiated a long grim struggle that eventually wore them down to the point where a catastrophic military defeat could be inflicted at Dien Bien Phu. By 1954 French power in Indochina was irrevocably broken. While acknowledging France as a major ally in Europe, the United States declined to give them the direct help needed for them to recover and hold former colonies. Another disastrous experience in Algeria simply confirmed the verdict of Viet Nam. The days of the French Empire were over.

The British had a similar wrenching experience. Fighting a decidedly uphill battle with Germany and its Axis partners during World War II, they had relied heavily on their empire for resources and troops; however, to secure its loyalty, they had been forced to make promises. Virtual equality was promised to the white dominions and major concessions leading towards eventual independence were granted to India. In the immediate post-war years, Britain was so bankrupt that it could hardly sustain itself through the harsh winters of 1946 and 1947. Holding onto a restless and determined sub-continent was out of the question. After partitioning the land into two nations, India for the Hindus and Pakistan for the Muslims, the British departed in almost unseemly haste. The French and British experience in Asia made a profound impression on African and Caribbean independence leaders.

China took a different path. Never fully occupied by colonial powers but, nevertheless, at their mercy, the Chinese had bitterly resented the "Unequal Treaties" and the extraterritorial claims imposed upon them in 1843. Realizing that the traditional imperial system could not cope with modern invaders, they had overthrown the Manchus and created a republic in 1911 under Sun Yat-Sen. The republic eventually evolved into a nationalist government which seemed modern in theory, but was corrupt and ineffective in practice. Marxist revolutionaries under the leadership of Mao Zedong challenged the Nationalists ideologically and in actual combat, sustaining their rivalry even when China was subjected to a full-scale invasion by Japan in 1931 and again in 1937. After the departure of the Japanese in 1945, Mao's Communist forces soon overcame the Nationalists and by 1949 China was firmly under the control of one powerful and determined authoritarian regime which abrogated all existing treaties and concessions to the European nations and effectively closed the nation to any foreign penetration.

COLONIALISM AND IMPERIALISM COLLAPSE

As the two largest ex-colonial entities, India and China were faced with a dilemma that would torment all the Asian, African, and Middle Eastern peoples that would follow their path to independence in the 1950's, 1960's, and 1970's. How should they reconcile their traditional civilizations, stretching back into antiquity, with the modern concepts of politics, government, society, and above all, technology which the Europeans had, however imperfectly, exposed them to? In debates with his colleagues in the Congress Party, Gandhi had proposed that all of the British infrastructure, railroads, telegraphs, telephones, and even hospitals should be rooted out of India. He wanted to see his native land restored to cultural harmony, self-sufficiency, and intellectual wholeness as a uniquely Hindu civilization. His comrade, Jawaharlal Nehru, contended that there was no way that such a transformation could be accomplished. He pointed out that Gandhi himself had traveled on the trains, printed anti-British pamphlets on modern presses, and coordinated his many demonstrations and protests with telegrams and telephone calls. In Nehru's view, India had no choice but to forge ahead and become a modern nation and somehow reconcile what was best in the ancient Hindu traditions with European parliamentary democracy and scientifically based technology.

Mao Zedong had no such hesitation. He was prepared to root out all of China's ancient customs and traditions and to drive relentlessly toward a modern military-industrial society along the lines laid down by Marxist-Leninism, which he took to be the most progressive of all political ideologies, never mind its European origins. Under Mao's leadership, Buddhism, Taoism, and Confucianism were ruthlessly suppressed, railroads were laid down, and highways built without regard to the teachings of Feng Shui. The hereditary aristocracy of Mandarins and landlords was liquidated or driven into permanent exile. Universities were founded to teach science and engineering and the Red Army was put to work mastering the art of modern warfare with tanks, artillery, and jet aircraft. Soviet Russia, which had gone from an agrarian peasant society to a great power in twenty years under Stalin's leadership, would supply the model and, incidentally, some of the technology as well. The human cost of this endeavor was enormous, but Stalin had willingly paid it and Mao, with six hundred million people under his command, was determined to pay it also.

A somewhat similar problem gripped the Middle East. The Muslims themselves were no strangers to imperialism. Indeed, in the Fourteenth and Fifteenth Centuries they had presided over the World's largest and richest empire, stretching from Spain to India. Faced with the European challenge, they had become static and their technology obsolete, but they did manage to resist European domination even while falling under the control of the Ottoman Turks. After two centuries of dynamism, the Ottomans had become moribund in their own turn and their empire effectively collapsed at the end of World War I leaving the Middle East with a confused legacy of incipient nationalism coupled with a semi-colonial system of mandated European rule under the auspices of the League of Nations. To add further to the confusion, enormous reserves of oil were uncovered throughout the region during the 1920's and 1930's, oil which proved a vital necessity during World War II. The post-war British and American consensus was that the Middle East should be organized into nations which would extract the oil with the assistance of Western corporations and live on the proceeds of its sales to the industrialized countries of Europe and North America. Complicating this arrangement were two factors. One was the State of Israel was founded as a refuge for Jews who had fled Europe in the wake of the Nazi Holocaust and the other was the religious imperatives of Islam with its vision of a unified Muslim World free from the taint of modern secular social practices.

Founded by Zionist pioneers and supported by the West for reasons that seemed exceptionally valid at the end of World War II, Israel revealed the fundamental weakness of the Islamic world by resisting all efforts to dislodge it and by inflicting humiliating defeats in 1949, 1958, 1967, and again in 1972. No Muslim state or combination of states seemed capable of defeating this small but determined nation in their midst. The oil bonanza provided another complex of intractable dilemmas. Oil was not distributed equally throughout the Muslim World. Some of the new states were awash in it and others, including those with the most people, had virtually none. The oil was so vitally important to the global economy that it forced Saudi Arabia, Iran, Iraq, Kuwait, and other Persian Gulf peoples into close commercial and cultural contact with the consuming nations. How much of Islamic culture and religious practice could be successfully maintained and kept "pure" in the face of continual contact with secular businessmen and technicians? Worse, the oil was the property of the Middle Eastern states, but it was of overwhelming strategic importance to the rest of the World. It has been necessary to strike a very delicate balance between the need to respect the national sovereignty of the oil-exporting states and the need to keep that oil flowing and defend it against threats emanating from invasion or sabotage. By their very nature, delicate balances are difficult to justify to a determined opponent and they also convey a subtle cultural insult implying gross weaknesses on the part of one party and indulgence on the part of the other. The Iranians acknowledged both of these dilemmas when they deposed their Shah, expelled all foreigners, and pro-claimed an Islamic theocratic republic in 1979. Even with these drastic measures in place, they have not escaped the need to sell oil in order to survive.

The last great expanse of the colonial world to gain its independence has been Africa and the Afro-Caribbean islands. During the 1950's, Africa was home to five colonial regimes, British, French, Belgium, Portuguese, and Spanish. Only two indigenous states were independent, Liberia and Ethiopia, and there was one other strange entity determinedly going it alone, the white-ruled Union of South Africa on the far southern tip of the continent. Ethnically and linguistically, Africa was more complex than any other continent. In laying out their colonies, the Europeans had chosen to essentially ignore this complexity except for the opportunities it offered for divide and rule tactics. In order to give shape and order to African independence struggles, it was necessary for each colony's insurgents to struggle against their own metropolitan power. English-speaking Africans like Jomo Kenyatta and Kwame Nkrumah waged their fight against the British. French-educated leaders like Felix Houphouet-Boigny tackled the French, and anti-Belgian nationalists like Patrice Lumumba fought to redeem the Congo from Belgium. Although pan-Africanists had dreamed of a single united continent emerging from colonialism on the pattern of India or China, what actually emerged was a large collection of individual nations based mainly on the previous colonial jurisdictions, inheriting the cities, railroads, mines, and other infrastructure left behind by the Europeans and also incorporating the incredible variety of tribal and linguistic peoples that had been haphazardly thrown together to facilitate divide and rule policies.

Although they recognized the challenges that independence on these terms presented, the first generation of modern African leaders set out to make their European model states work. They wanted true independence, democracy, and the benefits of modernization. Unfortunately, these have proven to be elusive goals. In the absence of industrial development, political independence did not guarantee economic independence. The colonial economy had been based on the extraction of low-priced raw materials and commodities which were shipped to the Northern Hemisphere for processing into manufactured goods. A certain amount of these manufactures were then returned to the colonies to be sold at relatively high prices. This had the dual effect of disposing of surplus production at a profit and transfer-ring yet more wealth from the colonies to the manufacturing nation. Although the colonial powers had contributed a considerable amount of infrastructure to their empires in the form of roads, railroads, ports, and communications facilities, nearly all of it had been intended to facilitate this pattern of trade. As newly independent states, the ex-colonies found themselves locked into the old economic relation-ships. To break out of it and modernize, they would have to find a way to engage in manufacturing themselves. However, this required vast amounts of capital invest-ments and the Northern Hemisphere powers had eighty percent of the World's liq-uid assets, the most experienced and aggressive corporations, virtually all of the recognized brand names for products ranging from cars to soap, and they were in the forefront of continual technological innovation and change. It is ironic that once they were shorn of their colonial possessions, the European states became even more prosperous than they had been before because now they were free of the burden of administration and, thanks to American-sponsored alliance systems, no longer engaged in military rivalry and competition with each other.

THE COLD WAR

The alliance systems that characterized the post-World War II era grew out of a broadly based phenomenon known as the Cold War. During the Second World War, the United States and Soviet Russia had been allies against Hitler's Germany. Indeed, by engaging approximately seventy-five percent of all German ground forces, the Soviet Union had been the key to victory over the most dangerous of the Axis Powers. The alliance had never been an easy one, however, because the United States and the Soviet Union represented radically different social and economic philosophies. America was the champion of democratic institutions and a Free Enterprise system of economics with a strong bias towards individual civil rights. The Soviet Union was committed to a Communist political ideology that stressed the authority of a totalitarian dictatorship, socialist economics, and the subordination of individuals to the collective interests of a mass society. Each viewed the other with suspicion. The liberation of occupied Europe from 1944 to 1945 had resulted in a division that passed right down the middle of the continent. To the West were states freed by the United States and its democratic allies. To the East were nations that had been taken from the Germans by the Soviet Union. The Cold War began in earnest a few years later when it became obvious that the Soviet Union intended to impose its socioeconomic system on the Eastern European states and take them into its permanent sphere of influence.

To be fair, it must be admitted that the United States had done somewhat the same thing in Western Europe. It had insisted that the European states completely root out fascist elements, organize parliamentary democracies, and coordinate their programs of post-war reconstruction with a view towards establishing a unified European economy. American intelligence services worked vigorously to counter Communist influence in Western Europe, and eleven billion dollars of Marshall Aid Plan funds went a long way towards restoring economic and social stability. After the Russians engaged in a series of aggressive moves in Greece, Berlin, and Czechoslovakia, the United States formed its European allies into a collective security pact, the North Atlantic Treaty Organization (NATO), which combined European military assets into a joint force under an American commander aimed directly at the Soviet Union. Stalemated in Europe, Russia and her new ally China began to probe elsewhere forcing the United States to fortify occupied Japan and establish a chain of military bases throughout Southeast Asia, the Middle East, and the Eastern Mediterranean. This "Containment Policy" ushered in a bi-polar World wherein the United States and its allies squared off against the Soviet Union and its allies and satellites in a deadly competition that featured large conventional armed forces, a growing stockpile of nuclear weapons, vicious propaganda campaigns, and rivalries in every aspect of cultural and economic life, including Olympic sports.

A significant part of this superpower competition involved an attempt to win over the hearts and minds of Asian, African, and Latin American ex-colonial peoples. The preferred tools for accomplishing this goal would be aid programs, technical missions, huge construction projects, the training of university students, lucrative trade agreements, and information services and libraries. Each move in this direction on the part of one superpower elicited a countermove by the other. There were coups, assassinations, proxy wars, sabotage, and other forms of violence. Bribes were administered and unpopular dictators were sustained in office in exchange for promises of cooperation. The two rival superpowers took stock of their strategic goals and interests and their desire to outmaneuver their opposition and acted accordingly. It was hard to escape the conclusion that the newly formed nations of the Southern Hemisphere were simply pawns in a gigantic power struggle that would last for forty years and cost trillion of dollars and rubles.

THE NON-ALIGNED MOVEMENT

To counter this manipulation, President Sukarno of Indonesia organized a conference at Bandung in 1955 to which he invited representatives from Africa, Asia, Latin America, and the Caribbean. Virtually every delegate represented a nation that was non-European, ex-colonial, underdeveloped economically, and not firmly aligned with either superpower. After intense discussion, the delegates agreed to form a new bloc of states that would enable them to steer an independent course. They were determined to promote their own economic and political interests and advocate their own unique causes which they assumed were not identical with those of the superpowers. They intended to demand a more equal distribution of the World's wealth and to avoid being dominated or controlled. Most of all, they had no wish to become embroiled in a superpower rivalry which seemed dangerous to the whole world. Defining the capitalist West as the "First World" and the socialist states as the "Second World," they declared themselves to be the "Third World."

Since its inception, spokesmen for the Third World have worked tirelessly to promote its agenda before various World forums. In the United Nations General Assembly, the Afro-Asian bloc nations and the Latin American republics collectively outnumber the developed countries several times over. They have pressured the World Bank (WB) and the International Monetary Fund (IMF) to make loans and credits available. They have created regional organizations such as the Organization of African Unity (OAU, now the African Union) and the Organization of American States (OAS) to work jointly on promoting the welfare and security of their respective continents. They have harnessed much of the United Nations' permanent bureaucracy to the task of ameliorating the suffering of Third World peoples and they have contributed peacekeeping forces to contain armed conflicts and prevent ethnic rivalry from degenerating into warfare. They have not been uniformly successful in all of the endeavors, of course, but they have seen to it that their interests are not easily ignored and that their plight does not go undocumented and unreported.

As the Third World, now calling itself the "Group of 77," slowly became more influential, the Second World eventually suffered a monumental collapse. Overstrained by forty years of incredibly expensive and totally unproductive rivalry with the capitalist democracies, the Soviet Union began to experience a slow slide into economic ruin. Taking over from a succession of stagnant elderly rulers, Premier Mikhail Gorbachev attempted to take the pressure off his ailing economy by liquidating the Cold War. As he negotiated nuclear disarmament agreements and liberalized the conditions of trade and political dependency within the Communist Bloc, he came face to face with an unpleasant reality. The Second World was itself a colonialist and imperialist entity made up of subject peoples held together by a Muscovite metropolitan state! Indeed, it was the last colonial empire left on Earth and when Gorbachev and his politburo lost the will to dominate it, it signaled the beginning of the end. Eight Eastern European nations bolted, shattering the Warsaw Pact military alliance that had threatened Western Europe for four decades. Next, the Soviet Union itself devolved into fifteen ethnic states as peoples whose cultures stretched back to medieval times at last saw the opportunity to form their own nations. By 1992 all that was left of the Soviet superpower was tens of thousands of nuclear warheads, obsolescent steel mills geared to turning out armor plate for tanks, a population facing declining standards of health, nutrition and general welfare, and an economy being systematically looted by gangsters and profiteers. In its own way, the Cold War had been as destructive to the loser as any armed conflict.

ECONOMIC GLOBALIZATION

Since the end of the Cold War in the early 1990's, a new global regime has slowly evolved and, in fact, continues to take shape. The United States is now the sole remaining superpower in both the military and the economic spheres. It alone possesses armed forces that have a truly global capability with state-of-the-art technology. Its economy is the world's largest with a gross national product (GNP) exceeding nine trillion dollars a year. It is committed to free trade, the globalization of production and consumption, the support of multi-national corporations and ever larger trade associations, and the continual fine-tuning of the global economy utilizing the procedures and institutions first established at the Bretton Woods Conference in 1944. The European states have moved steadily towards full economic integration with a common currency and the elimination of traditional cross-border controls. If they succeed, they will ultimately form an industrial and commercial bloc that would exceed that of the United States in both size and productive capacity. Japan duplicated the post-war experience of the European states. When it no longer had to support a large military establishment and was free of the need to administer its admittedly short-lived colonial empire, Japan experienced an unleashing of its productive capabilities that allowed it to catapult to economic greatness with a GNP second only to that of the United States. After an interval, other Asian nations, the so-called "Four Tigers," followed Japan's lead specializing in the production of consumer goods, especially light manufactures and consumer electronics for export. With China now moving down this same path, the potential for economic growth in

Asia is truly awesome. For the advanced industrial nations, it is evident that the road to prosperity lies in the direction of free trade and the cultivation of markets, rather than in the conquest and administration of colonial empires.

Unfortunately, this post-Cold War prosperity has largely eluded many nations of the Third World. Although they see a modest improvement in overall economic growth and a slow upward creep in standards of living, the gap between them and the developed nations continues to widen. A seemingly intractable complex of problems and issues—lack of investment capital, low productivity, the near absence of social services, high rates of illiteracy, insufficient infrastructure, and corrupt or incompetent government—frustrates efforts to foster sound economic development. Small gains in economic progress are often eaten up by runaway population growth. The old colonial practice of combining different ethnic groups makes the administration of the resulting new nations difficult. The European model nations that emerged from the colonial independence struggles seem not to be well suited to deal with African and Asian ethnic complexities. In Latin America, large nations like Brazil and Argentina hover on the brink of an economic take-off into modern industrialism only to be thwarted by internal mismanagement and the accumulation of enormous external debt. Orthodox capitalist remedies for these problems imposed by the World Bank (WB) and International Monetary Fund (IMF) bear down so heavily on already impoverished populations that they are often abandoned or repudiated before any real change is effected. The flow of investment capital into the underdeveloped World is frequently offset by the return flow of debt service payments and principal back to the developed nations. Meanwhile, direct aid from the rich nations to the poor nations has never come up to expectations and seems to be consistently declining in real terms.

At the beginning of the Twenty-first Century, old-fashioned colonialism and imperialism are thoroughly discredited. The ideological struggles of the previous mid-century between democracy, communism, and fascism largely resolved in favor of democracy. Free trade, the globalization of economic activity, and the primacy of the capitalist business model constitutes the dominant organizing principle sponsored by the wealthiest nations, the so-called G-7 plus Russia. A northern tier of highly developed states confronts a vast southern tier of countries that are painfully aware of their inferior economic prospects and status. It has been suggested that the problem of the new century will be how to bridge the economic chasm between the hemispheres so that a decent life can be provided for all of Earth's citizens.

BOOK-LENGTH READINGS FOR *OUT OF THE GLOBAL PAST*

Barratt-Brown, M. *The Economics of Imperialism.* London, Penguin Books, 1974. A useful primer on the economics of classical imperialism.

Calloway, C.G. *New Worlds for Old: Indians Europeans and the Remaking of Early American.* Baltimore, MD, Johns Hopkins University Press, 1997. The European penetration of the Americas is emphasized.

Davidson, Basil. *Africa in World History.* New York, Macmillan Publishing Co., 1991. A sweeping account of the role of the African Peoples in World History.

Dunbabin, J.P.D. *The Cold War: The Great Powers and Their Allies,* Vols. I and II. New York, Longman, 1994. A synthesis of the entire cold war experience.

Fairbank, J.K. *The Great Chinese Revolution, 1800–1985.* New York, Harper and Row, 1986. An overview of China in transition.

Hollister, C. Warken. *Medieval Europe, A Short History.* New York, McGraw-Hill, Inc. Includes a useful discussion of the relationship between Christendom and Islam at the time of the Crusades.

Leakey, Richard E. *The Making of Mankind.* New York, E.P. Dutton, 1981. An account of human origins from the first hominids to the dawn of civilization.

Masselman, George. *The Cradle of Colonialism.* New Haven, CT, Yale University Press, 1963. The struggles between the European maritime states and the mercantile system are detailed.

Nanda, B.R. *Gandhi and His Critics.* New York, Oxford University Press, 1985. Discussion of Gandhi's tactics and character.

O'Meara, Patrick, Howard D. Mehlinger and Matthew Krain (Eds.). *Globalization and the Challenges of a New Century, a Reader.* Bloomington, IN, University of Indiana Press, 2000. A series of essays to bring the issues of globalization up to date.

Tinker, H. *Men Who Overturned Empires: Fighters, Dreamers, and Schemers.* Madison, WI, University of Wisconsin Press, 1987. Profiles African and Asian leaders.

Weinberg, G. *A World at Arms: A Global History of World War II.* New York, Cambridge University Press, 1994. A readable overview of World War II.

Wilford, John Noble. *The Mysterious History of Columbus.* New York, Alfred A. Knopf, 1991. A modern interpretation exploring all aspects of Columbus' life and legacy.

SHORT READINGS FOR *OUT OF THE GLOBAL PAST*

Fernandez, Ernesto Filipe. "Columbus, Hero or Villain?" *History Today,* May 1992. (From *Western Civilization,* Vol. 1, 8th Ed., 1995.)

Huntington, Samuel. "The Many Faces of the Future." (From *Global Issues,* 17th Ed., 2001/02.)

James, Lawrence. "The White Man's Burden?" *History Today,* August 1992. (From *Western Civilization,* Vol. II, 8th Ed., 1995.)

Mee, Charles L., Jr., "The Fateful Moment When Two Civilizations Came Face to Face," *Smithsonian,* October 1992. (From *World History,* Vol. II, 5th Ed., 1998.)

Tharoor, Shashi, "Are Human Rights Universal?" *World Policy Journal,* Winter 1999/00. (From *Global Issues,* 17th Ed., 2001/02.)

Part II

The Global Present

do for final due

The Politics of Glob...

Kofi Annan

I speak to you at a time of global turmoil, of economic crisis, political challenge and conflict throughout much of the world. To cast a glance on the map of the world is to be not only concerned, but humbled. Concerned, of course, because long-simmering *intra*-state conflicts have in recent months intensified and been joined by *inter*-state tensions from Africa to Asia.

Humbled, because we all perhaps have been surprised by the swiftness with which these crises have accumulated in the space of twelve months. Any belief that either the end of major ideological competition or the revolutionary process of economic globalization would prevent conflict has been revealed as utterly wishful thinking. And yet, since these crises and conflicts are the product of human folly and human evil, I am convinced that they can be solved by human wisdom and human effort. But if we are to solve them, we must rededicate ourselves to addressing the *political* roots as well as the economic roots of the problems now gripping much of the world. That is why I have chosen to speak to you today about the politics of globalization.

To many, it is the phenomenon of globalization that distinguishes our era from any other. Globalization, we are told, is redefining not only the way we engage the world, but how we communicate with each other. We speak and hear often about the economics of globalization—of its promise and its perils.

Rarely, however, are the *political* roots of globalization addressed in a way that would help us understand its *political* consequences—both in times of progress and in times of crisis. Rarely, indeed, are the *political* aspects of globalization recognized by either its friends or its foes.

Reprinted from "The Politics of Globalization," address delivered at Harvard University, Cambridge, Mass., September 17, 1998, by permission of the Weatherhead Center for International Affairs.

...day, globalization is rapidly losing its luster in parts of the world. What as a currency crisis in Thailand fourteen months ago has, so far, resulted in a tagion of economic insolvency and political paralysis. Globalization is seen by a growing number not as a friend of prosperity, but as its enemy; not as a vehicle for development, but as an ever-tightening vise increasing the demands on states to provide safety-nets while limiting their ability to do so.

At a time when the very value of globalization is being questioned, it may be prudent to revisit the role of politics and good governance in sustaining a successful process of globalization. Before doing so, however, let me say that great efforts are being made in every part of the world to contain and reverse the negative impact of globalization.

The fundamental recognition that lasting prosperity is based on legitimate politics has been joined by a growing appreciation of the need to maximize the benefits of the market while minimizing its costs in social justice and human poverty. To do so, regulatory systems must be improved in every part of the world; solid and sustainable safety-nets must be crafted to shield the poorest and most vulnerable; and transparency must be advanced on all sides.

Globalization is commonly understood to describe those advances in technology and communications that have made possible an unprecedented degree of financial and economic interdependence and growth. As markets are integrated, investments flow more easily, competition is enhanced, prices are lowered and living standards everywhere are improved.

For a very long time, this logic was borne out by reality. Indeed, it worked so well that in many cases underlying political schisms were ignored in the belief that the rising tide of material growth would eliminate the importance of political differences.

Today, we look back on the early 1990s as a period of savage wars of genocide in Bosnia and Rwanda that cruelly mocked the political hubris attending the end of Communism. Soon, we may well look back on the late 1990s as a period of economic crisis and political conflict that with equal cruelty mocked the political hubris attending the heyday of Globalism.

In time, these twin awakenings—rude as they have been—may be recalled as a form of blessing in disguise, for they will have reminded us that any peace and every prosperity depend on legitimate, responsive politics.

They will have shown beyond a doubt that the belief in the ability of markets to resolve all divisions neglected the reality of differences of interest and outlook; differences that *can* be resolved peacefully, but *must* be resolved politically.

In a sense, it may be said that politics and political development as a whole suffered a form of benign neglect during globalization's glory years. Extraordinary growth rates seemed to justify political actions which otherwise might have invited dissent. Autocratic rule which denied basic civil and political rights was legitimized by its success in helping people escape centuries of poverty. What was lost in the exuberance of material wealth was the value of politics. And not just any politics: the politics of good governance, liberty, equity and social justice.

The development of a society based on the rule of law; the establishment of legitimate, responsive, uncorrupt government; respect for human rights and the rights of minorities; freedom of expression; the right to a fair trial—these essential, universal pillars of democratic pluralism were in too many cases ignored. And the day the funds stopped flowing and the banks started crashing, the cost of political neglect came home.

Throughout much of the developing world, the awakening to globalization's down side has been one of resistance and resignation, a feeling that globalization is a false God foisted on weaker states by the capitalist centres of the West. Globalization is seen, not as a term describing objective reality, but as an ideology of predatory capitalism.

Whatever reality there is in this view, the perception of a siege is unmistakable. Millions of people are suffering; savings have been decimated; decades of hard-won progress in the fight against poverty are imperiled. And unless the basic principles of equity and liberty are defended in the political arena and advanced as critical conditions for economic growth, they may suffer rejection. Economic despair will be followed by political turmoil and many of the advances for freedom of the last half-century could be lost.

In this growing backlash against globalization, one can discern three separate categories of reaction. All three threaten to undermine globalization's prospects. All three reflect globalization's neglect of political values. All three call for a response at the global level to what is, at root, a global challenge.

The first, perhaps most dangerous reaction, has been one of nationalism. From the devastated economies of Asia to the indebted societies of Africa, leaders in search of legitimacy are beginning to view globalization, and its down side, as a process that has weakened them vis-a-vis their rivals and diminished them in the eyes of their allies. Globalization is presented as a foreign invasion that will destroy local cultures, regional tastes and national traditions.

Even more troubling, political leaders are increasingly seeking to sustain popular support amidst economic difficulties by exploiting historic enmities and fomenting trans-border conflict. That these steps will do nothing to improve their nations' lot—indeed just the opposite—must be evident even to them. But the costs of globalization have given them a rhetorical vehicle with which to distract their peoples' attentions from the penury of tomorrow to the pride of today.

The irony, of course, is that globalization's promise was based on the notion that trading partners become political partners, and that economic interdependence would eliminate the potential for political and military conflict. This notion is not new. In the early years of this century, the rapid expansion in trade and commerce even led some to predict an end to conflict. However, no degree of economic interdependence between Germany and Britain prevented the First World War. But this lesson was soon forgotten.

It was assumed that the political nature of inter-state relations had been transformed by a quantum leap similar if not equal to that which has revolutionized technology in the information age.

The fallacy of this doctrine—that trade precludes conflict—is not simply that nations and peoples often act out of a complex web of interests that may or may not favour economic progress. Power politics, hegemonic interests, suspicion, rivalry, greed, and corruption are no less decisive in the affairs of state than rational economic interests. The doctrine also underestimates the degree to which governments often find that the relentless pace of globalization threatens their ability to protect their citizens. Without addressing this concern, globalization cannot succeed.

The second reaction has been the resort to illiberal solutions—the call for the man on the white horse, the strong leader who in a time of crisis can act resolutely in the nation's interests. The raw, immediate appeal of this idea seems most apparent in newly liberalized nations with weak political systems, incapable of reacting with effectiveness or legitimacy in the face of economic crisis.

As central power disintegrates and breadlines grow, there is a growing temptation to forget that democracy is a condition for development—and not its reward. Again—and again falsely—democracy is seen as a luxury and not a necessity, a blessing to be wished for, not a right to be fought for.

Here, too, there is an irony: the proponents of globalization always argued that greater trade would naturally lead to greater prosperity, which in turn would sustain a broad middle class. As a consequence, democratic rule would take firm and lasting root, securing respect for individual liberties and human rights. This, too, proved to be overly optimistic.

Some of globalization's proponents believed too much in the ability and inclination of trade and economic growth to foster democracy. Others, too little in the importance of democratic values such as freedom of speech and freedom of information in sustaining firm and lasting economic growth. Traders will trade, with or without political rights. Their prosperity alone, however, will not secure democratic rule.

In all the debates of the post-Cold War years about whether political liberalization should precede economic liberalization or vice versa, one question was left out. What if, regardless of which comes first, the other does not follow? What if economic liberalization, however profitable in the short term, will never beget a political liberalization that is not already integral to economic progress? What if political liberalization, however desirable on its own, is no guarantee of economic growth, at least in the short term?

These are the questions that globalization's friends must face—and answer—in *political* terms, if they are to win the argument against those who would seek solutions in tyranny. Freedom itself is too valuable, its spirit too important for progress, to be bargained away in the struggle for prosperity.

The third reaction against the forces of globalization has been a politics of populism. Embattled leaders may begin to propose forms of protectionism as a way to offset losses supposedly incurred by too open an embrace of competition, and too free a system of political change. Their solution is for a battered nation to turn away and turn inward, tend to its own at whatever cost, and rejoin the global community only when it can do so from a position of strength.

In this reaction, globalization is made the scapegoat of ills which more often have domestic roots of a political nature. Globalization, having been employed as political cover by reformers wishing to implement austerity programs, comes to be seen as a force of evil by those who would return to imagined communities of earlier times.

Notwithstanding its flaws and failed assumptions, this reaction is a real challenge with real power. Those who would defend the policies of openness, transparency and good governance must find ways to answer these critics at two levels: at the level of principle and at the level of practical solutions which can provide some kind of economic insurance against social despair and instability.

The lesson of this reaction is that economic integration in an interdependent world is neither all-powerful nor politically neutral. It is seen in strictly political terms, particularly in times of trouble, and so must be defended in political terms. Otherwise, the populists and the protectionists will win the argument between isolation and openness, between the particular and the universal, between an imaginary past and a prosperous future. And they must not win.

If globalization is to succeed, it must succeed for poor and rich alike. It must deliver rights no less than riches. It must provide social justice and equity no less than economic prosperity and enhanced communication. It must be harnessed to the cause not of capital alone, but of development and prosperity for the poorest of the world. It must address the reactions of nationalism, illiberalism and populism with political answers expressed in political terms.

Political liberty must be seen, once and for all, as a necessary condition for lasting economic growth, even if not a sufficient one. Democracy must be accepted as the midwife of development, and political and human rights must be recognized as key pillars of any architecture of economic progress.

This is, undoubtedly, a tall order. But it is one that must be met, if globalization is not to be recalled in years hence as simply an illusion of the power of trade over politics, and human riches over human rights. As the sole international organization with universal legitimacy and scope, the United Nations has an interest—indeed an obligation—to help secure the equitable and lasting success of globalization.

We have no magic bullet with which to secure this aim, no easy answers in our common effort to confront this challenge. But we do know that the limitations on the ability of any state or any organization to affect the processes of globalization call for a global, concerted effort.

If this effort is to make a genuine difference, it is clear that the creation of lasting political institutions must form a first line of response. Such steps must, however, be combined with a clear and balanced acceptance of the roots of the precipitous collapse of so many economies. To some extent, this collapse was rooted in flaws and failures of already existing economies characterized by unsound policies, corruption and illiberal politics.

However, we must not be blind to the fact that irresponsible lending practices and aggressive investment policies pursued by outsiders played their part, too. Without improvements in these practices, we cannot expect political reform to succeed in creating the basis for lasting economic growth. All sides matter; all sides must play a role.

I have argued today that politics are at the root of globalization's difficulties, and that politics will be at the heart of any solutions. But where will solutions be found? In the heyday of globalization, it was assumed that all nations, once secure in prosperity, would turn to multilateral institutions out of maturity; today, I believe, they may turn to those same institutions out of necessity.

The challenge facing the United Nations is to ensure that the difficulties facing globalization do not become an impediment to global cooperation, but rather give such cooperation new life and new promise.

We will do so in two key ways: by emphasizing in all our development work the importance of civil society and institutional structures of democracy at the national level; and by seeking to strengthen the effectiveness of multilateralism in sustaining free economies while securing genuine protection for the poorest and most vulnerable of our world.

After World War II, there was a recognition that ultimately, economic problems were political and security problems. There was a recognition that prosperity and peace are *political* achievements, not simply natural consequences either of trade or of technological progress.

We owe the wisdom of this view and the consequences of its implementation to one man in particular, Franklin Delano Roosevelt. In his fourth inaugural address, President Roosevelt—a founder of the United Nations and surely the greatest Harvard Man of this century—made a passionate plea for global engagement:

"We have learned that we cannot live alone, at peace; that our own well-being is dependent on the well-being of other nations, far away. We have learned that we must live as men, and not as ostriches, nor as dogs in the manger. We have learned to be citizens of the world, members of the human community."

In this era, we have learned our lessons, too: that democracy is the condition for true, lasting and equitable development; that the rewards of globalization must be seen not only at the centre, but also, at the margins; and that without free, legitimate and democratic politics, no degree of prosperity can satisfy humanity's needs nor guarantee lasting peace—*even* in the age of Globalization.

Ethnicity and Global Diversity

Ann Kelleher and Laura Klein

The first step to understanding global issues is reviewing the diversity of the world's peoples. It is this diversity that often makes it difficult to resolve common world problems. An examination of the differences, or perceived differences, between people is essential to understanding the world situation. While defining these differences, cultural identity is a significant underlying factor that is often overlooked by analysts who use states as their main (or only) frame of reference. Cultures, ethnic groups, genders, and class play a role in the decisions that individuals make about their lives. The decisions that governments make are equally influenced by these and other concerns. Therefore, in order to fully understand international debates it is important to know which identities within a state are privileged and which are discriminated against.

All people, both leaders and followers, within any political system are informed not only by their state imperatives, but also by their different values and views of reality. Thus, the well-educated leader of one country can diametrically disagree with the equally well-educated leader of another country, and neither will yield to the other's understanding. Bitter disputes, many of which may lead to war, may be based on claims to land or resources that seem insignificant to outsiders. Many will die to preserve their country's rights to seemingly trivial places or things. When contemporary people of European descent study their history they look at the children's crusades, the Inquisition, and witchcraft trials with utter bewilderment. Time has so changed European traditions that the past has become a different, and somewhat distasteful, culture to modern Europeans.

It is clear that cultural beliefs are very powerful. Some people will fight to the death to maintain them, while others will deeply disagree with these same beliefs and be unable to support them. This is the reality of the world today, as it has been throughout human history. To create a peaceful and cooperative world, people must come to understand the differences that exist between cultures and respect the depth of those differences. People may not like one another but, if they are going to work together, they must agree to disagree on what they cannot resolve and find solutions to their conflicts, which must be resolved or violence will result.

This chapter introduces significant ethnic changes and cultural distinctions in the contemporary world in order to begin to explain why people value various economic, political, and environmental issues differently. It rejects the assumptions of the Victorian theory of Social Darwinism, which still echo in some arenas. The assumptions that the most technologically advanced societies are chosen by nature to rule the world and that less complex societies are doomed to extinction are now repudiated. Different societies adapt to different environments and succeed or fail in those contexts.

The case study involving the Inuit of Nunavut, presented at the end of this chapter, illustrates many of the concepts introduced in the chapter and provides a case for further analysis. It is an important case because it presents the contemporary effort of one state, Canada, to deal with the ethnic variation within its boundaries without resorting to force or state disintegration. The development of a new territory with an ethnically defined legislature can offer, if successful, a new model for other states with similar ethnic enclaves.

CULTURE: THE DEFINITION OF HUMANITY

> In 1990 a group of American college professors, who taught a variety of international courses, traveled to Thailand in order to learn more about the people of that country. They found themselves sitting in a rural village asking questions of the residents. The group leader asked the townspeople if they had any questions for the Americans. The first question came from a soft-spoken woman who asked: "Did you plant your rice fields before you left home?" None of these urban American professionals knew how to answer the question.

The incident in Thailand demonstrates the existence of two contrasting truths of humanity. The first is that all humans share a common heritage: a *human culture* that allows us to understand the basic needs and capabilities that all people share. The second is that different groups of people have developed their own ways of dealing with these human problems in their own environments: *specific cultures* that the members of particular societies share. Americans and Thais both understand the need for people to provide sufficient nutritious food for their families, but the way they obtain that food is radically different. "How can these people leave their fields in the summer?" the Thai woman wonders. The Americans recognize the importance of this question but ponder, "How do we explain that we talk and write in the winter and earn enough to pay for a year's food?" Each is capable of understanding the other, but the explanations are not simple because they are embedded in complex cultural systems. Each needs to translate the questions and answers for the other, not only in linguistic terms but in cultural ones as well.

Culture

As the vignette implies, culture is central to understanding human life on the planet. That is why the first concern must be to define culture, a term that has so many different meanings. Natural scientists see a culture in a Petrie dish. Some artists find culture in opera and classic literature, but not in rap or comic books. In this book, the term *culture* is used as defined by cultural anthropologists. Traditionally, anthropologists begin by quoting the first academic definition, offered by Edward Tylor in 1871. According to Tylor (1871:1), culture is "that complex whole which includes knowledge, belief, art, morals, law, custom, and any other capabilities and habits acquired by man [*sic*] as a member of society." The strength and utility of this historical definition rest in the fact that cultures are indeed complex, patterned, and learned.

Children learn the culture shared by the adults in their world. There is nothing biologically innate in culture. The Thai child learns how to grow rice and other related social traditions, from eating habits to religion to gender rules. Reared in another culture, the same child might adopt very different traditions and might never eat rice. The culture that children learn involves a complex mix of skills, beliefs, and facts that allow them to function successfully as adults in their respective societies.

As cultural traits are developed, they are integrated so that they support one another. The term *holism* is used to mean that all traits of a culture influence all others. Therefore, the religious beliefs of a culture complement the economic system, and the political system is supported by the kinship system. In traditional Inuit culture, for example, the importance of hunting and gathering in the economic system is reinforced by the political focus on consensus and dispute resolution, the centrality of nuclear families, and the importance of animal spirits in religion. A change in any one element would change all the others.

While culture shapes human society, it is located in the minds of individuals and encompasses every aspect of life. Culture, therefore, consists of patterns of belief and guidelines for behavior learned by individuals as they become full members of a society. Individuals can learn a second culture, but usually not to the same level of completeness as the one they learned in childhood.

Cultural Change

One of the most common observations made about the modern world is that it changes constantly. Most people laud some changes, from new medical breakthroughs to improved technology for special effects in films, as progress. Other changes, such as social shifts in family composition or immigration patterns, are publicly condemned as destructive of morality. At the same time, the seemingly exotic areas of the world are presented as unchanging realities. This perception is not true. In fact, change is inherent in all human cultures. Since culture is the adaptation of society to environment, changes in environment, both physical and social, always trigger changes in cultures. Cultural change, then, is necessary for continued human survival. Logically, there are two categories of cultural change: *internal* and *external.*

Internal Change Internal cultural changes are those that are created by people within a society that is changing. In the end these changes can be seen as evolutionary, but in the short term, they appear as *inventions*. Important inventions are new ideas or techniques that are constructed from the mass of collected knowledge and are adopted as valuable by members of the society. Successful innovations are those which are seen as useful or desirable within the contexts of their specific culture. Internal changes are negotiated by the members of a society and ultimately sustain the flavor of the culture itself. This is not necessarily true, however, of changes from external sources.

External Change   External changes are those that are invented or promoted in one culture and introduced, from the outside, to another culture. In the most benign fashion, these changes are voluntary. Innovations from one cultural area of the world are seen as desirable and other cultures clamor to adopt them. These innovations can be trivial—such as new music styles from the Caribbean, new fruits from the tropics, or new soft-drink flavors from Europe—or important—such as new drug therapies from France or new computer technology from the United States. Exposed to new cultural traits through everyday living, individuals adapt those that fit their lives and tastes.

More broad-based and philosophical innovations can also be adapted voluntarily. The recent adoption of the capitalist model by former communist countries is a clear example. After decades of foreign pressure to overthrow communist regimes, the changes came from within. Trade agreements between countries that are ideologically divergent, such as the United States and China, also demonstrate the ability of vastly different cultures to integrate their respective practices voluntarily. Such agreements represent the victory of economic needs over political dogma. Many external changes, then, are the result of the open and welcomed diffusion of desired ideas and material goods.

Some external changes, however, are not welcomed and are *involuntary*. Within the historic context of colonialism, it is easy to find cases of nations with superior military technology that forced their ideas and methods on colonized nations. Often these changes were defined by the stronger state as being "for the good" of the colonizing nation. The spread of Christianity and British social customs in the colonies of Great Britain during the nineteenth century illustrates this well. While there is clearly no evil in the practice of Christianity or the playing of cricket, the fact is that these specific practices were impressed by the colonizer without respect for the culture of the colonized people. The traditional religions and rituals were often outlawed in the colonized nation and any practitioners were punished. Those who adopted British customs, in contrast, were rewarded with employment and material goods. Some who adopted the new traditions also adapted them into their own culture. Today one can find variations of Christianity around the world. In Mexico, saints are reminiscent of older gods and in New Guinea variations of cricket include war and sex dances.

Other social practices and restrictions were mandated as well. In the nineteenth century, several African nations allotted political offices to women. In the state of Buganda, for example, the women of the royal family had courts with judicial roles. Under the British, who ironically were then headed by Queen Victoria, the offices of the women were eliminated while those of the men were maintained. At the same time, the military and punishment for capital crimes were placed in the hands of the British governor so that Europeans controlled all forms of physical force. The male leaders were allowed to remain in office but their powers were substantially truncated. Such imposed changes instilled dependency on the colonial states.

Culture and Economic Adaptations

At first, it might appear that the variations among societies and cultures are so vast that any attempt at generalization would be fruitless. It is possible, however, to group cultures into four categories that describe the cultural and economic bases of most societies: *gathering* and *hunting, agriculturalism, pastoralism,* and the *state.*

These categories can be called evolutionary in the sense that they proceed from simple to complex technology but not in the sense of Social Darwinism. The categorization does not assume the moral superiority of more complex stages nor does it argue that contemporary cultures in the simpler stages are backward or ancestral to their more complex contemporaries.

Gatherers and Hunters   There are few self-reliant groups of gatherers and hunters left in the world today. Small enclaves can be found in the arctic, the deserts, and the tropics, but even these exist encapsulated within a modern state. In the past, however, independent foragers thrived across the globe. This was the original way of life for all humanity. The economic base of this simplest form of human society is the gathering of wild plants and hunting of wild animals for food. Economics within this system takes the form of *generalized reciprocity.* People in bands share with one another. They give without the expectation of equal or immediate return. All benefit from the successes of any one individual. People only go hungry if no one is able to find food. Once the plants and animals of one area are depleted, the people are forced to move their camps to a new place. The only goods they can own are those they can carry. This means that bands need large areas of land and individuals own little wealth.

The social implications of this economic system are profound and repudiate some of the assumptions held by citizens of state societies. Social classes do not exist in such societies since all individuals own roughly the same material goods and perform the same tasks according to their age and gender. There are no designated leaders in bands and, while some individuals may be more admired or liked than others, group decisions are made by consensus and all people are given a say. Competition within and between bands is minimal. In short, gatherers and hunters lead generally egalitarian lives in small groups in which cooperation is the essential ideal.

Agriculturalists   One of the most important innovations in the history of humanity was the domestication of various staple plants. Once established, dependence on domesticated plants allowed populations to grow well beyond the capabilities of foraging societies. Additionally, farmers can settle in permanent towns where they can own, work, and defend their fields. Outside of the family, generalized reciprocity gives way to balanced reciprocity where equal return is expected for each gift. Differences in wealth develop between those families with good lands that have access to more food and better trade goods and those that do not. Permanent homes allow for the collection and storage of material goods.

Members of agricultural societies, or tribes, own personal possessions and some are wealthier and more prestigious than others. Raiding between groups is common in this type of society because of political issues as well as the fact that people have things worth stealing. Poorer clans and communities become dependent on the generosity of richer ones in times of need. This dependency often leads to differences in status and prestige. Equality is not an ideal in most tribes. Social rank becomes an issue and some people are born into a better life than others. There is still some flexibility, however. While tribes, unlike bands, recognize leaders in their groups, tribal leaders are rarely permanent and there is no office of chief in simple agricultural societies. Outstanding individuals in war or peace are recognized and followed.

Pastoralists   Whereas agriculturalists depend on domesticated plants, pastoralists depend on domesticated animals. Some pastoralists, including the Nuer, Dinka, and other people of eastern Africa, are farmers as well, but they consider farming secondary in status to herding cattle. Others, such as the hill tribes of Afghanistan, the Sami of northern Europe, and the Bedouins of the Middle East, have traditionally depended almost entirely on their herds for food. In these tribes, nomadic movement is the norm. Herds, generally owned by clans, are moved over hundreds of miles to graze on ever-new fields. These groups, unlike bands, however, have the use of animals to help with transportation and heavy work. Horses, camels, and in the case of the Sami, reindeer, allow for a far different trek from that of the bands. Domesticated animals also provide security not found with hunting. Barring catastrophic accidents, a relatively stable food source can be relied on to feed a relatively large population.

Like the agricultural tribes, differences in wealth among pastoralists are clear and dictate differences in status. Ownership of large herds and the rights to rich grazing areas confer high status on members of the clan. Prestige as well as power are important issues here. Wealthy individuals wield both influence within their family groups and power in their relations with others. Raiding is common in these societies. Herds are more easily stolen and maintained than fields and the heroics of warriors on horseback belong to the romance of human history.

State Organization   The development of primitive state organization over five thousand years ago was a major turning point in human history, as was the creation of the modern state much later. In this system, political organization takes precedence over economic organization as a defining feature. Most *primitive states*, like most tribes, are dependent on agriculture as the major source of food. A major difference, however, is that states employ economic specialization and market exchange to an extent well beyond that of any other stage of social organization. Among clans one would find farmers growing a variety of foods for their own needs with some surplus for trade; among states one is more apt to find individual farmers growing crops for the market. Additionally, bilateral nuclear families, rather than clans, become the primary kin groups. Among other things, this means that the support of a wide array of kin is gone. Individual families become far more vulnerable than ever before.

The primary legal identity of an individual in a state is based on political or geographic designation. Rather than say "I am the son of Zarn" or "I am a member of the Dingo clan," people in states announce that they are "from Sydney" or "a Canadian." Their rights, privileges, and obligations stem more directly from their citizenship than from their personal relationships.

This does not mean that all people in a state are equal within the system. One of the hallmarks of the state is a class system. Certain groups of people are considered inherently better and more privileged than others. Individuals who are born into urban families that are close to the centers of power are likely to hold important offices as adults. Individuals born into peasant families are fated to be peasants. Specializations of many kinds based on education, status, gender, age, and many other factors are common in states.

The core criterion of a state is a centralized political organization. Leadership becomes defined by offices that must be filled. Laws and courts, which decide disputes, are formalized and dictate the behavior of citizens. All this must be paid for and the participants must be fed and this is made possible through taxation. Police and military forces support the order and power of the leaders.

Warfare is common in state systems. Competition for land and scarce resources between states can become fierce. Expanding populations demand new sources of food, minerals, and land. Before the expansion of modern states throughout the world, primitive states could expeditiously overrun less powerful tribes. In more recent times, similarly powerful states face off with far more deadly results.

Industrialism changes the productive focus of the state system from the farm to the factory. The goods produced by urban workers and the mechanism to create those goods owned by the elite define the wealth of a society. The difference in financial and social status differential between the urban rich and poor mirrors that previously found in the urban elite-peasant relationship.

Cultures, Subcultures, and Other Classifications

People speak about American culture, French culture, Bantu culture, Kurdish culture, and the like with a general understanding that the people in each of those cultures differ in distinctive ways from the others. More important, perhaps, is that all Americans (here meaning from the United States) identify as Americans and clearly recognize that they are *not* French, Bantu, or Kurds. At the same time, not all Americans are identical and each has additional distinctive social identities. Some Americans are upper-class males of African heritage who use Spanish as a mother tongue, while others are middle-class Navajo women who speak Diné as well as English. The United States, of course, is a state that prides itself on the wide diversity of its citizens. Still, even more culturally homogeneous nations such as Japan and Saudi Arabia see significance in certain human variations.

Ethnic Groups   Literally, *ethnic group* means "culture" or "cultural group," but commonly the term is used to specify cultural groups that are minorities in a larger, heterogeneous nation. Ethnic groups include *indigenous people*, those who first lived on this land and no longer control it, but also include later migrants to the country. Apache and Tlingit, then, are ethnic groups in the United States but so are the Amish, Cuban Americans, and Cajuns. Individuals descended from each ethnicity are American citizens and fully invested in the country. Some have left the traditions of their ancestors so far behind that they no longer identify with the group at all. Most, however, recognize a common identity with others of similar descent and share traits from language to marriage customs to food that are important to them.

For the most part, as many American towns can demonstrate, a mixture of ethnic groups enriches a community. New Orleans, New York, and Santa Fe are very different cities due, in large part, to the peculiar mixture of prominent ethnic groups that each city boasts. Internationally, the national cultures of Latin American states enjoy a dynamism based on the blending of native, African, and European cultural elements. The variety of foods, language, celebrations, and ideas broadens the lives of everyone who lives there.

Unfortunately, this ideal synthesis is not always the reality of multicultural states. In some cases, ethnic identities take priority over the state identity and ethnic rivalries erupt. Antagonism toward, or isolation from, citizens of different heritage ensues. Sometimes this dissension springs from events that occurred long in the past and/or far from the current site. For example, tales of the Armenian Massacre or the Irish potato famine remain important issues in American Armenian and Irish ethnic communities. Often differences in religion (Jews in Nazi Germany, Muslims in contemporary Europe, and B'hais in Iran), in language (Spanish speakers in the U.S. Southwest and French speakers in Canada), or in physical appearance (African Americans and Asians in West Africa) are used to characterize the value or nature of the individuals within those groups.

In some cases, as the preceding examples suggest, the differences between ethnic groups can cause minor social discord, threaten the integrity of the state, and even lead to genocide—the extinction of an entire ethnic group. The relative powers of those who hate and those who are hated anticipate the results. In areas where the power is not overwhelmingly one-sided and where there is no overriding authority restricting it, long-term ethnic antagonisms, such as those in Eastern Europe and parts of Africa, can result in civil wars with extensive bloodshed.

Indigenous Peoples   One category of ethnic groups, *indigenous peoples,* has become conspicuous in headlines. For the first time, guidelines for the treatment of First Nations issues are actively being discussed in the international arena. News stories report that rock stars appear at concerts with Native Amazonian people demanding their rights and health professionals plead their case in hopes of gaining indigenous knowledge of tropical drugs and treatments. Indigenous peoples represent the last groups of colonized people from the era of European colonization who remain under the control of foreign societies. The United Nations declared the 1990s as the "Decade of Indigenous Peoples."

Indigenous cultures, or *First Nations*, are those traditional societies that have been enveloped by a nation-state with a distinctively different cultural base. They are the original people of an area who have lost political control over their ancestral lands and do not fully recognize the moral authority of the state government to dominate them. The best recognized indigenous cultures include the Native Americans of both North and South America, the aboriginal people of Australia, the Sami of Scandinavia, the San (Bushmen) of the Kalahari, the Ainu of Japan, and Native Hawaiians. They differ from most other ethnic groups by maintaining a prior claim to the land controlled by the state. They differ from other colonized peoples because the colonizers have settled in large numbers and, after generations, have stayed. The colonizers will not return to their native land because they now define this land as their home.

"Races"   *Race*, the category of human diversity that would be mentioned first by many people, is probably the one most poorly understood. Americans will assert that there are four human races color-coded as white, black, red, and yellow or by geographic heritage as European, African, American, and Asian. Upon reflection, others might include people from Australians to Hispanics.

Few Americans realize that they echo the scientific classification of race that has been widely discounted by the anthropologists and biologists who study human diversity. At this point in human development, all people from Aachen to Zimbabwe belong to the same race: *Homo sapiens sapiens*. The only other possible race of modern humans, *Homo sapiens neanderthalensis*, became extinct some thirty thousand years ago. The physical variations seen in people around the world are minor, and scientifically they do not have the depth of true racial differences seen in other animals. One of the reasons for this is that animals that develop races have had geographically isolated populations that have reproduced within these isolated groups. Over time, adaptations to particular environments became dominant in specific populations and not in others. Over even more time unique species could have developed. The history of *Homo sapiens* is, however, such that there have never been these types of truly isolated populations. Asia, Africa, and Europe formed an extenuated, but common gene pool with no barriers to breeding at their borders. The Americas and the Pacific have been populated in biologically recent times and did not have time to form new races before they were reintroduced to the Old World.

It is obvious that people are physically different and that groups of people can look different from others. The scientific reticence at using categories like race is not based on any denial of human physical diversity, but quite the opposite, the recognition of the complexity of that diversity. The popularly held racial classifications emphasize a few physical traits, largely skin tone, hair color and texture, and nose shape. They tend to ignore the more biologically significant traits such as blood types and genetic markers. Many American children would argue that dark skin (high melanin) means Africa and, indeed, dark skin is often found in parts of sub-Saharan Africa. Not all people of African heritage have dark skin (see the San or Pygmies as examples) and many people among those with the darkest skin tone come from Australia or Melanesia, far from the so-called "Dark Continent." Aboriginal Australians are not Africans, but many of the former have darker skin than many of the latter.

Most specialists in human physical variation today look at clines, and not *biological races*. *Clines* are the frequencies of particular genetic traits in different parts of the world. The percentages of blood types in different regions are examined, as are the frequencies of particular diseases. Traits like propensity to diseases are emphasized, rather than hair, skin, or eye color because the former makes a difference to human welfare and potential while the latter group of traits should not.

However, in spite of the biological reality, many societies do classify people in categories that are based on perceived physical differences. What most people do not realize is that the classification of these so-called *social races* differs around the world and over time. The US Census questionnaire has changed racial categories several times and today strays from the color-code classification by adding Hispanics to the list. Other countries recognize a different collection of races. Brazilians are said to recognize forty different races. Under apartheid in South Africa, white, black, Asian, and colored were the primary categories. A person with a mother of European heritage and a father descended from sub-Saharan Africans would be called "colored" there. If he moved to the United States, he would be called "black."

If race is such a difficult concept to concretize, how does it retain such power in the modern world? One answer may be found in a brief review of the history of racial categories. Americans now speak of the Hispanic race, although it would be difficult to define what is physically distinct about Hispanics. This is because the category, in fact, depends on language and culture, not biology.

A century ago similar races existed in America; for example, the Irish race and the Jewish race. Popular and academic literature of the time used these races as givens. Caricature of simian-looking Irish and hook-nosed sinister Jews portrayed these types. There is no Irish or Jewish race today (outside of the philosophies of extreme hate groups) because these were social categories of a particular time when a majority of Euro-Americans who held cultural prejudices against these groups wished to distance themselves from them. To label a group as a different kind of human using scientific jargon allows others to discriminate against them in a manner that social differences could not justify. Better education or equal opportunity, the argument often goes, would not make them the equals of the superior race because their inferiority is inbred and not easily modified. This argument allowed many groups to justify slavery while at the same time claiming to value the human soul or spirit. In many societies around the world, those ethnic groups most despised by the majority are categorized as inferior races.

Genders Sex might appear to be a physical universal without the difficulties of the term *race*. As mammals, the breeding strategy of *Homo sapiens* is based on the sexual reproduction of males and females. It would, therefore, appear that male and female should be unified categories. But purists would note that normal frequencies of hermaphroditism, variety in sexual preferences, and genetic varieties beyond XX and XY are found in all populations and, therefore, that an exclusive male-female dichotomy is not the full biological story. For the most part, however, categorizing men and women as different physically is basic biology. However, the extension of beliefs about male-female differences beyond the primary sexual ones is open to disagreement. In fact, the dispute over the biological reach of sex is widely interpreted in ways compatible with cultural beliefs. Societies that believe that women are incapable of particular types of work outside of the home, for example, assert that they are biologically incapable of doing such work without harm. It was this type of explanation in the United States of the mid-nineteenth century that lead Sojourner Truth, a former slave, to assert in a now-famous speech for women's rights that she had done all the hard physical jobs and, as she put it, "ain't I a woman."

Gender, distinct from sex, is the term used in the social sciences, as a cultural definition. Different societies define the proper roles and the assumed capabilities of men and women differently. In some societies, there are more than two genders. In India the Hijra form is a third gender category that anthropologist Serena Nanda (1990) asserts is "neither man nor woman." Real Hijras either are natural hermaphrodites or undergo surgery to remove external sex organs. Their ideal role in society is to be followers of the goddess Maia, and they are called upon to dance at weddings and childbirth celebrations in order to bring the blessing of fertility. Less ideally for the Hijras, many are employed as prostitutes in the cities. In Native America, the Navajo recognize *nadles* as a third gender of people who have the blessings of both males and females and who often have special supernatural abilities. The classification of berdache (Williams 1986), or more properly "those of two spirits," in other Native American groups is also recognized as a (normal) third gender. While the vast majority of people around the world are labeled as man or woman, additional categories are recognized in some cultures.

A more obvious variation can be found by looking at the definitions of man and of woman in different societies. Most Americans would identify a fully veiled woman as a Muslim from the Middle East and a figure in a football uniform as an American male. Similarly, they would assume a person identified as a Roman Catholic priest is a man and one identified as a hula dancer is a woman. However, these visual intercultural assumptions are often more complex. In the nineteenth-century plains of North America, a farmer was clearly defined as a male by the Euro-American settlers. Equally clearly, the Native American residents defined a farmer as a female. In each culture the role of farmer was sex-linked but in opposite ways. Each found the gendered concepts of the other absurd and even distasteful. This became an issue, and one little understood by the US government when it attempted to "civilize" the Plains Indians by making them farmers. The resistance to farming by native men in this area was taken as a sign of laziness and backwardness. At the same time, no effort was made to help native women develop their farms because nondomestic work by women was not taken seriously within the equally cultures-bound gender expectations of Euro-Americans. Over time, such differences in gender expectations in North America have often led to the disenfranchisement of native women in economics and politics (Klein and Ackerman 1995).

Only recently have the issues of women's rights as intrinsic to human rights been genuinely argued in the United Nations and other international bodies. The widespread impact of varying rights being granted to men and women in different states had often been ignored in discussions of global issues. However, overwhelming data demonstrate that women and children are more often found in poverty than men throughout the globe and this mandates new research and calls for new programs.

Some cultural issues, such as the so-called female circumcision in some African and Asian societies, have become international disputes. In this tradition girls have some of their sexual organs surgically removed or altered in a coming-of-age ceremony. As a result they are recognized as women and are ready for respectable marriage. Many from other parts of the world are appalled by this practice and call it genital mutilation. The United States has granted an African woman, who fled her county to avoid the procedure, refugee status based on the argument that if she were returned to her country she would be forced to undergo the operation. Most argue that these operations often endanger the health of the women, while others point out that the procedure permanently destroys the women's pleasure in sexual relations. Both contend that good health and sexual pleasure are basic human rights, which are being denied.

Diplomats and many citizens from countries that practice female circumcision argue that others are meddling in an important family and gender tradition that is private. They assert that outsiders are ethnocentrically judging them. They assert that surgeries that are more hygienic should be the solution to health problems and point to a parallel to male circumcision as performed in the West. Moreover, they argue that moral behavior and female submission are important in their states and that the surgery supports proper female behavior.

Clearly, there are very different interpretations of human rights and gender status at work here. The issues have become more complex because of immigration. The movement of people who demand the surgery to western countries have made the issues important in many states which had never needed to address them before. Countries like the United States and France now have laws banning the genital operations. Immigrants are forced to either adapt to the customs of their new countries or seek, often dangerous, illegal surgeries. As all countries become increasingly heterogeneous, conflicting concepts of gender and individual rights can only generate more controversy between and within countries.

Classes   A final global category, and one that has no biological base but great human consequence, is social hierarchy or *class*. National and international decision makers are drawn from the upper classes and reflect upper-class understandings and goals. While as noted, bands and tribal societies maintained relative social equality, states by their definition do not. With the dominance of the state form come almost global-class strata. Poverty tied to powerlessness and great wealth tied to great power prove true not only when dealing between states, but within them as well.

Stratification is a difficult concept for Americans because it conflicts with the deeply held ideal of human equality and the fictive identification of the United States as a classless society. Even so, class is an element of American society and the ideal of equality is taught to children as equal opportunity rather than equal results. Therefore, there can be rich and poor, powerful and powerless, as long as all people have the right to reach the high positions. Every child, or boy it was said until recently, can grow up to be the president. The fact that this is not, and has never been, true is a painful cultural contradiction that many Americans would like to change.

Most states do not recognize all their citizens to be equal. In fact, people are valued, paid, and respected according to the social status they hold. Some obtain their status by birth. Royalty and the wealthy elite, for the most part, are born into families that already have royal titles or wealth to pass on. This type of position is often called an *ascribed status*. The opposite, an *achieved status*, is one that is earned by the actions of an individual. For example, in England, Queen Elizabeth II holds an ascribed status while the prime minister has earned an achieved status. The next monarch of England is expected to be the son of the reigning queen, while the next prime minister almost certainly will not be a child of the current one. Some societies are more fluid with respect to social movement than others, and an individual, not born in it, can become part of the wealthy elite by earning vast amounts of wealth and socially learning the correct behavior of the group. Some nonroyals may even marry into the royal family and earn the title of princess or prince. For the most part, however, most citizens of states change little from the status or class of their parents.

One of the problems in the contemporary world is the pervasiveness of the underclass, which is linked to ethnic background. In many countries, minority ethnic groups deprived of opportunities to rise in the social system have remained subservient, dependent, and poor through centuries. While slavery as an institution has been internationally prohibited, servitude remains. The roles of Indonesian servants in Saudi Arabia, Gypsies (Romi) in Europe, and Koreans in Japan all, in different ways, reflect an ethnic group stratification.

Reactions to Diversity

Human diversity is a reality of everyday life and, while it is increasing in most societies, it has been an issue throughout history. This history has not been a uniformly peaceful one, however. Many countries have celebrated human diversity, but in others it has been the reason for legal discrimination, war, human slavery, and even genocide. The following concepts can help explain why.

The most common reaction to cultural diversity is *ethnocentrism*, which involves judging the customs of another culture according to the one's own standards. This can be as simple as judging other's food preferences, declaring, for example, that eating dog or rancid whale skin is disgusting and that eating pig or "spoiled" cow milk (that is, sour cream) is natural. On a more serious level, members of one religion might declare the practices of another immoral or illegal. These cultural differences being condemned need not be very different than those followed by the critics. In fact, seemingly minor differences are often more severely condemned than extreme ones. For example, in largely Christian jurisdictions, laws exist against snake handling in the religious services of minority Christian denominations in parts of the southeastern United States. At the same time, the use of poisonous snakes in some Native American religious ceremonies in the Southwest are protected by law. Ethnocentrism, then, appears throughout societies at different levels of cultural diversity.

Ethnocentrism is difficult to combat because there is a positive reality that helps cause the negative outcome. Universally, children are reared to appreciate and adapt the culture of their parents. As they learn, they are enculturated so that they can function as full members of their society. They learn that their religion is true, their customs are good, and their political system is just. The child, who does not learn this, does not fit in. It should be of little surprise, then, that when they are adults these individuals see other religions as false, other customs as inappropriate, and other political systems as unjust. In a homogeneous setting, this would cause little trouble but in a heterogeneous world, it creates problems when groups interact.

Cultural relativity is the term used to describe a form of solution to this problem. Cultural relativity suggests that the actions of people within each culture should be evaluated according to the rules of that culture. The person who eats a dog in Vietnam, then, is evaluated differently than an American who might do the same in the United States. A concern often voiced is that cultural relativity taken to its logical extreme would allow for moral anarchy. Would the murders of thousands, or millions, as has occurred in even recent history be acceptable because the nation that allowed these deaths deemed them appropriate? From the perspective of most religious and ethnic systems the answer would surely be no. Politically, the United Nations asserts that there are universal human rights that supersede any national values.

The balance between ethnocentrism and cultural relativity is a delicate one. Patriotism, putting the well-being of one's state before one's own, is an admirable trait but it is a form of identity that gives priority to the state. Is nationalism good if one's government causes deaths or denies freedom to other peoples? However, accepting people as different but still as human, is far more difficult than popular slogans suggest. Where extreme ethnocentrism exists, it may be impossible to understand people from other cultures and hence to deal with them successfully in business or diplomacy. Extreme cultural relativism makes it impossible to raise issues of human rights violations or environmental ruin beyond the boundary of one's own culture.

Racism and *sexism* further hinder world cooperation, within countries and worldwide. When individuals judge other individuals based on perceived biological differences, it tends to distort their understanding of the world. Africa became "the Dark Continent" in European minds and Africans became defined as a different and inferior type of people. As "inferior" people, they were perceived as needing the benefits of European civilization and consequently colonialism. The slavery of Africans was justified by this assertion of innate difference. Likewise, differential immigration laws, which encourage and discourage migration throughout the world, are often based on racist assumptions.

Similarly, sexism allows people to use their perceptions of appropriate gender behavior to judge other nations. The images of veiled and draped Islamic women are used by other societies as evidence of the "backwardness" of some Arab countries without understanding the meaning of Purdah or female seclusion. At the other extreme, women who traditionally wear little clothing (such as those in the Pacific Islands) and those who wear sexually alluring clothing (Latin or Caribbean women during Carnival), are used as evidence of the "backwardness" of those cultures. Even the presence of women in high political office is used by some to indicate the weakness of such a "henpecked" country. At the same time, countries with few women in high political office are taunted as medieval. Concerns over human rights, as noted earlier, are confused by sexism.

Governmental responses to human diversity within domestic borders have historically taken many forms—from acceptance to forced conformity to reservations to genocide. Recently, governments have seen a need to deal with the increasing diversity in new ways that conform to international standards of human rights. In many states, the treatment of indigenous peoples has become the test case. Because indigenous peoples have historically been treated brutally and now are among the most powerless people in contemporary states, their treatment can be seen as proof of a country's commitment to human rights and its openness in dealing with human diversity.

The Imperatives of Globalism

George A. Agbango, Ph.D.

THE DEBATE ON GLOBALIZATION AND GLOBALISM

Globalism is not a new phenomenon. It is as old as the development of the human species. It has taken different forms over different periods of human development. For example, in the 15th century, Prince Henry the Navigator of Portugal expanded the horizons of Europe when he established a school of navigators and charged them to explore the unknown waters of the Atlantic Ocean off the coast of Africa. When Christopher Columbus landed on the islands of the New World in 1492, it was a major global feat that later led to greater interaction between Europe, Africa, and the Americas. The last great global transformation occurred in the late 19th Century and the early part of the 20th Century. By 1871, Germany was unified and Japan was rapidly modernizing after the Meiji Restoration in 1868. The major global players at the time rushed to acquire territories. There was a yearning desire to build empires and to extract from colonies enough resources to build great civilizations that would last for thousands of years. These developments upset the balance of power in Europe and led to the First World War. The two world wars weakened the European powers and helped the Soviet Union and the United States to emerge as the dominant players in world affairs in the post-World War II era.

For fifty years, the North Atlantic Treaty Organization (NATO) and the Warsaw Pact, under the hegemony of the United States and Soviet Union respectively, dominated the global scene. The struggle for global hegemony by the two superpowers (the United States and the Soviet Union) gave rise to the Cold War. The Cold War policies of these two powers were not healthy for global peace and stability.

By the late 1980's, the United States had become the world's largest debtor nation thanks to *Reaganomics* (the defective economic policies of President Ronald

Reagan). Reagan's "trickle-down" economic policies led to mounting budget deficits for the United States. Meanwhile enormous amounts of money were spent on the arms race. The Soviet Union was not better off either. In a recent interview of Mikhail Gorbachev in Washington, DC, by a reporter following the death of President Reagan, Gorbachev remarked that both the Soviet Union and the United States lost the Cold War. Apparently both countries benefited from the end of the Cold War. But history will record that the rather naïve and exuberant young Mikhail Gorbachev brought about the premature collapse of the Soviet Union because of his rapid economic, political, and social reforms.

As we enter the 21st Century, the world is witnessing a new wave of global transformation in many areas and dimensions of human endeavors. At the beginning it appeared that a unipolar world would emerge with the United States as the undisputed leader. That didn't happen. The United States is certainly at the center of affairs but the world is unwilling to accept its complete domination of global affairs. The United States' domestic constituency is also unwilling to allow it to assume more global responsibilities. In the end, we have a multipolar system.

There are many advantages of this emerging trend. There is less rivalry and less tension because former adversaries now work together to resolve global problems. However, this opportunity for cooperation was threatened by the recent Bush doctrine of preemptive strike. Generally, the struggle for global hegemony is replaced by regional efforts for global cooperation in a very competitive business environment. The tragedy is that whereas some countries and/or regions have excelled in this competition, others are left behind in abject poverty and squalor. According to Francis Fukuyama:

> Globalization of the world economy has created new modes of marketing and production that have different organizational requirements. No one at this point knows what the corporation of the early twenty-first century will be like. Whatever that form of organization turns out to be, however, will be discovered most quickly by societies that have a strong tradition of social cooperation. Conversely, societies that are riven with strong barriers of distrust, based on class, ethnicity, kinship, or other factors, will face extra roadblocks in their adoption of new organizational forms.[1]

It is not surprising, therefore, that many developing countries are experiencing roadblocks in their efforts to catch up with the global transformation. Consequently, many scholars see globalization as the free flow of commerce across borders, making the world one big market. According to Ellen Grigsby:

> . . . globalization refers to internalization—that is, a loosening of ties that might have held people, things, and symbols to a single place and thus bracketed in their mobility, influence, and exposure to people, things, and symbols in other places. With globalization, more permeable boundaries replace more closed boundaries. For example, a product becomes global or globalized when its influence becomes international in reach because it has found borders to be penetrable, not rigid and closed.[2]

---

[1]Francis Fukuyama, *Trust: The Social Virtues and the Creation of Prosperity,* New York: The Free Press, 1992, p. 318.
[2]Ellen Grigsby, *Analyzing Politics,* Third Edition, Belmont, CA: Thomson Wadsworth, 2005, p.263.

Other scholars contend that globalization is synonymous with modernization and/or western domination. Violent street demonstrations have disrupted meetings of organizations such as the International Monetary Fund (IMF), the World Bank, and the World Trade Organization. The demonstrations were clear manifestations of the anger of the world against the naked rape and marginalization of the poor developing nations by the wealthy ones vis-à-vis the latter's negative trade policies, practices and politics.

In some countries, globalization is seen as humanity's greatest enemy because it corrupts cultures. A few years ago, the Iranian government ordered people who had satellite disks to get licensed. Having secured their registration, the Iranian government effectively censored what their citizens could watch. The fear that uncensored foreign programs could ruin their culture was at the center of this policy. Similarly, Sam Nujoma, President of Namibia, in September 2002, ordered the state-owned television stations to censure foreign films and programs and to eliminate those that will corrupt the youth of his country. The United Nations Association of Canada offers another viewpoint here about globalization:

> Globalization, contrary to popular belief, is not only about the economy, it is also about culture, immigration/emigration, human rights, the environment, and much more. Basically it's the idea that our planet is getting smaller because countries are more and more open to each other . . . Today we automatically think of the Internet as one of the causes of globalization. However, looking back in time, at the beginning of the century airplanes seemed to shrink the planet drastically by making the transatlantic voyage so much shorter. However, many feared the impacts of such innovation.[3]

To the business tycoon in Hong Kong, globalization means the ability to rapidly transfer monies from one end of the globe to the other. Of all the arguments that have been advanced by scholars to describe globalization, the one that most captures the concept is that presented by Haleh Afshar and Stephanie Barrientos. They write:

> The term 'globalization' has been used to define various aspects of global expansion in the past decade. It has been associated with key areas of change, which have led to a marked transformation of the world order . . . globalization has been associated with the trend towards increasing economic liberalization. This has been reflected in freer trade and more deregulated labour, goods and financial markets. Combined with this has been an increasing dominance in global capital and financial deepening as capital movements across countries have been facilitated by removal of regulation and national barriers. Transnational corporations, which have benefited from the removal of national constraints on their activities, now occupy an increasingly dominant position. Within the developing world, the process of economic liberalization has been heralded by the International Monetary fund (IMF) and World Bank, which have imposed the new economic order on more vulnerable debt-ridden countries through conditionality in their programmes. At the technological level, globalization has been facilitated by the innovation of mass rapid transportation and the global communication networks, leading to information revolution. The overall result has been the emergence of a global consumer society with a tendency to greater cultural homogenization.[4]

[3]See http://www.unac.org/youth_sd/youth_e/Globalization%20Final%20ENGhtml.htm, a United Nations Association of Canada Website.
[4]Haleh Afshar and Stephanie Barrientos, *Women, Globalization and Fragmentation in the Developing World,* New York: St. Martin's Press, 1999, p. 1–2.

On the other hand, globalism is the philosophy that no nation is an island in a true sense of the word. All nations are interdependent in this shrinking world, which is caused by the forces of human interaction in areas such as:

- Trade and commerce (the rise of free market systems)
- Travel and migration of labor
- Ecological systems and the environment
- Population change and demographic rearrangements
- Information revolution
- Political reforms and citizen participation
- The United Nations and global cooperation
- Widening gap between civilizations and cultures

THE INFORMATION TECHNOLOGY

A few years ago, at the height of the O.J. Simpson trial, I traveled to Ghana to investigate the Impact of British Colonial Rule on the Traditional Institutions of the Kusasis of Northern Ghana. The Kusasis occupy the remote northeastern corner of Ghana. One evening, in Zebilla, I saw a group of people huddled around a black-and-white TV set in a drinking bar. They watched the O.J. Simpson trial, which was being beamed worldwide by CNN. From time to time, they argued about the pending verdict. The group was evenly divided. Some thought O.J. Simpson was framed and others thought he must have known who murdered the victims. There, in Zebilla, some 10 thousand miles away from the scene of the trial, some citizens of the world were passing judgment on a murder trial about which they had no direct connection.

Such is the world of the media today. Information is telecast across the globe in a matter of seconds. Political activities such as the mass civilian action that forced President Marcos out of office in the Philippines were replicated in Yugoslavia where Milosovic was forced to concede defeat. In October 1999, in the Ivory Coast, a military general (Robert Guei) who tried to nullify a popular election was run out of the country by sheer mass civilian power. As the terrorist attacks on the United States on September 11, 2001, were beamed to the people of the world in a matter of minutes, world leaders sent prompt expressions of support to America in its time of need. Subsequently, the collective effort by the United Nations in fighting global terrorism led to the quick defeat of the Taliban government in Afghanistan. These events represent the era we live in. We, indeed, live in a global village.

E-commerce has led to rapid transfers of monies across the globe. More importantly, it has reduced the market place to the size of a computer screen from which one can trade and transact commercial activities without leaving one's home. A Canadian may sip his coffee while communicating over the Internet with his investment banker in Taiwan. Gone are the days when the Internet was the preserve of the CIA. The CIA no longer has monopoly over the Internet. Every second, millions and millions of people establish contact all over the world via the Internet. Information flow has become very rapid and, in many countries, cannot be curtailed by governments. Indeed, while the growth of TV usage and home fixed-line telephone connections have remained fairly stable over the years, computers in use, cellular phone subscriptions, and internet host computers is rising at an extremely fast pace.

In November 2000, Filipinos were determined to remove their President from office on allegations that he used his official residence to gamble. The organizers of these groups called for demonstrations and in a matter of minutes people burst out into the streets to demonstrate. What was their secret weapon of communication? They used cellular phones that received coded messages. If they cannot use the government-controlled press and the media to rally their supporters, they can at least use their phones. And they did so effectively. This could not have happened some ten years ago. It is estimated that nearly 2,000 organizations used the Internet to organize the demonstrations that crippled the annual conference of the World Trade Organization in Seattle several years ago. Through the TV, Internet communication, and other fast forms of communication, the world is rapidly shrinking. This is good in many respects, but there are also many disadvantages.

TRAVEL, IMMIGRATION AND DEMOGRAPHIC CHANGE

During the rise of the iron curtain over Eastern Europe, free travel was restricted for many people in the Soviet bloc. That is now a thing of the past. It is relatively easy for people to travel around the world now, more than before. Our shrinking world has exposed the relatively affluent and attractive societies of the world to the people of regions that are relatively deprived: what Frantz Fanon would call the "wretched of the earth." Such exposures have become pull factors and have triggered large-scale migration of people from the less privileged parts of the world to the "lands of great opportunities."

As the populations of countries increase (particularly in Western Europe and North America), the need for curriculum change has become more obvious. Multi-cultural education and the teaching of tolerance in an inclusive society have become the much-needed tools of the global village. India recently hit the billion-person mark and, together with China, it provides a great market for global commerce. These two countries are likely to attract greater international attention for commerce than ever before. The world that does business with these two giants must understand their cultures and national policies. The continent of Africa, with its great reserves of natural resources, will largely play a great role in global trade and it too, must be understood. Africa has abundant oil reserves, precious minerals such as gold, diamond and uranium, as well as numerous forest products and cash crops. The gateway to Africa's vast resource reserves is the understanding of its cultures and peoples. Nations that must do business with African countries, therefore, must have personnel trained in African politics, culture, and geography.

TRADE AND COMMERCE

The ability to move liquid assets across continents and oceans in a matter of seconds via the Internet has changed the nature of commerce. It has been reported that "the leading GIS software company, ERSI, grew from fewer than 50,000 clients in 1990

to more than 220,000 in 1999."[5] Records show that these technologies have contributed in large measure to the rapid growth of the global economy. Experts estimate "the worldwide market for information and communications technologies at
$1.83 trillion in 1997 and commerce over the Internet at $7-15 billion in 1998. The
boom in Internet businesses helped push the net worth of the world's people from
$463 billion in 1989 to beyond $1 trillion in 1999."[6]

ECOLOGICAL SYSTEMS AND THE ENVIRONMENT

Without revisiting the Malthusian Theory about population growth and population
explosion, we are faced with a new concern. This concern has little to do with food
production. It has more to do with an increasing global population that continues to
increase its consumption of global resources, which, unfortunately, are exhaustible
and sometimes irreplaceable. It has been estimated that between 1950 and 2000, the
"world population increased from 2.5 billion to 6.1 billion, a gain of 3.6 billion."[7]
There are serious implications of such uncontrolled population growth. Resources
such as fresh water, fisheries, forests, and rangelands are becoming scarcer and will
someday reach a point of complete depletion if steps are not taken to halt the reck-
less rate of consumption.

According to Lester Brown, "As population grows, the shrinking per capita
supply of each of these natural resources threatens not only the quality of life but, in
some situations, even life itself."[8] India, for instance, is beginning to face water
problems. The country's aquifers are yielding less and less water supply as the water
tables fall. Studies have revealed that as China's economy grows so also does its
water use rise to levels "far beyond the sustainable yield of aquifer recharge."[9]

The 1992 United Nations-sponsored conference on the environment in Rio de
Janeiro (Brazil) may have achieved very little in terms of securing global agreement
and cooperation to preserve our environment. However, it did draw global attention
to the predicament of our earth. Participants agreed that the world's ecosystem is
deteriorating. Scientists at the conference also were in agreement that there is the
need to arrest the environmental degradation of the earth—particularly when melt-
ing ice in the tundra—due to global warming—revealed the corpse of a dead ances-
tor who had lain buried for centuries.

In a fast-growing world that has become smaller because of the high level of
technological development, diseases can spread rather quickly. The HIV/AIDS epidemic is now no longer an African, a Thai, or an American problem. It is a global

---

[5]Molly O'Meara, "Harnessing Information Technologies for the Environment," in Lester Brown et al, *The State of the World 2000,* New York: W.W. Norton & Company, 2000, p. 123.
[6]Ibid. Also see International Data Corporation (IDC), *Digital Planet* (Vienna, VA: World Information Technology and Services Alliance, 1999); U.S. Department of Commerce, *The Emerging Digital Economy II* (Washington, DC: June, 1999); and Kerry Dolan, "200 Global Billionaires," *Forbes,* 5 July 1999.
[7]Lester R. Brown, "Challenges of the New Century," in Lester R. Brown et al, *The State of the World 2000,* New York: W.W. Norton & Company, 2000, p. 5.
[8]Ibid.
[9]Ibid. p.7. Also see Lester R. Brown and Brian Halweil, "China's Water Shortage Could Shake World Food Security," *World Watch,* July/August 1998.

problem that demands a global solution. Even Egypt can no longer claim ownership of the Nile Valley mosquito. New Yorkers are equally concerned about the effects of the bites of this mosquito, which may have been brought ashore in a jetliner. The Ebola virus is no longer confined to the tropics. It can be alive and well in temperate America. These are some of the imperatives of globalism.

POLITICAL REFORMS AND CITIZEN PARTICIPATION

With globalization comes the problems of nation building. The rebellion of East Timor nationalists and the ruthless suppression of these nationalists by pro-Indonesian forces stunned the entire world. World public opinion was clearly on the side of the East Timorese. It was not surprising therefore that the United Nations had to intervene and to press for a lasting solution to the people of East Timor's struggle for self-determination. Yet, it took the media in a fast-growing global village to mobilize the necessary moral and political support for the people of East Timor, and this partly secured them their freedom.

Elsewhere in Africa, conflicts along ethnic and class lines have resulted in genocide. The genocide in Liberia, Sierra Leone, and Rwanda should not have happened. The cleansing of ethnic Albanians in Kosovo by Serbian forces should not have happened. But these events did take place under the watchful eyes of the global community in a shrinking global world. These are the challenges that face the people of this re-configured world.

Global political transformation is also witnessing legal precedents, which will dictate the behavior of global political leaders. The attempt by Chilean nationals in Europe to have the former dictator and leader of Chile, Augusto Pinochet, tried for the murder of Chileans by his secret police during his reign was a historic landmark.[10] It sent shockwaves across the world. Suddenly, most world leaders realized that their actions in office could be the subject of legal actions when they leave office.

In Senegal, the former President of Chad, Hissene Habre was arrested and tried for crimes he committed against his people while in office. Unlike Pinochet, who was humiliated but not jailed, Habre found himself locked up in jail. Pinochet escaped serving jail-time in Britain (thanks to Margaret Thatcher's strong lobbying which saved him from further suffering and humiliation), but he returned to Chile only to face the same charges leveled against him. The onetime strongman of Chile became an accused criminal in a country where he once was the first among equals. Such is the nature of the new global village. And cooperation between the United States and Russia has sent a clear message that dubious world leaders can no longer play the West against the East and hide under the umbrella of a superpower while creating havoc and threatening global peace and stability. The rising tide of democratization dictates that " . . . all states everywhere must become more democratic and secure 'good governance' over their people."[11]

[10]Kay Lawson, *The Human Polity,* New York: Houghton Mifflin Company, 1997, p.249. See Tina Rosenberg, "Overcoming the Legacies of Dictatorship," *Foreign Affairs,* Spring 1995, p.134.
[11]Haleh Afshar and Stephanie Barrientos, *Women, Globalization and Fragmentation in the Developing World,* New York: St. Martin's Press, 1999, p.1.

In mid-2004, the United Nations Security Council debated a United States draft resolution requesting sanctions be imposed on Sudan unless the latter takes decisive steps to end the violence in its Darfur region caused by the Arab militia, which has been accused of causing widespread atrocities against civilians. According to a British Broadcasting Corporation news report, "US Secretary of State Colin Powell said that Sudan had 'days' to stop the violence or face possible sanctions. Some one million people have fled their homes and at least 10,000 killed since two rebel groups took up arms last year."[12] This, again, is evidence that all nation-states are under greater global scrutiny in this era of globalization. A country must either conform to international norms or risk being a pariah nation—not even the United States is excluded from this requirement since many world leaders were quick to condemn the torture of some Iraqi prisoners under United States care in Iraq in early 2004.

THE GREATEST CHALLENGE TO GLOBALISM

The global village is controlled by a global elite. This global oligarchy is often oblivious of the plight of the global masses. The global elite speak the same language and they have common tastes and common habits. The danger is that the global elite may be so consumed by their economic, social, and political successes and achievements that they may ignore the plight of the less privileged of their societies. This could be a great source of conflict in the 21st Century. There are nearly two billion people who have no access to good drinking water, education, housing and suitable health services. Women and children form the bulk of this neglected population. Haleh Afshar succinctly argues that:

> Changes in the global political economy since the 1980s have had a dramatic effect on the lives of women, who have become increasingly integrated as players in the world's production and consumption processes. Women have been affected by globalization in the most diverse aspects of their lives and in the furthest reaches of the world.[13]

In many societies, social and economic deprivations have led to civil wars. Children and women have been disproportionately affected by these wars. In Sierra Leone and Liberia, for instance, children were drafted into the war. Very often, these kids are drugged, intimidated and given guns to terrorize their own people in the name of liberation. Consequently, the child-soldiers (constituting generations of future leaders of these countries) have been mentally marred by their participation in the bloody wars. In many parts of Africa (Liberia, Sierra Leone, the Ivory Coast, Sudan, Uganda, the Democratic Republic of the Congo, and Rwanda) the rehabilitation of these child-soldiers is a global concern *and* a national responsibility.

Another visible area where there is great disparity between the developed and the developing world is in the area of access to the communication superhighway.

[12]BBC NEWS World Edition of Friday July 9, 2004 captioned, "Sudan warns US against 'new Iraq.'" See http://news.bbc.co.uk/2/hi/africa/3880237.stm
[13]Haleh Afshar and Stephanie Barrientos, *Women, Globalization and Fragmentation in the Developing World,* New York: St. Martin's Press, 1999, p.1.

There is a great disparity in the distribution of networks. Internet network for the whole of Africa, for instance, is about 0.4 of the total global network. Compare this to 64% for the United States and Canada, and 24% for Europe. If the world is to benefit from the resources of the global village, then it is in the global interest to support those countries that cannot afford to have these facilities.

In my travels in Africa, I have come across schools that have no typewriters, let alone computers. Comparatively, some American high schools have better computer labs than most African universities. In this situation, there are, therefore, clear policy options for developing countries—particularly African countries. They must invest in computer technology. They have to choose between equipping their educational institutions with much-needed technology and investing in presidential jet-planes for the enjoyment of their political elite.

CONCLUSION: THE CHALLENGE TO EDUCATIONAL INSTITUTIONS

Educational institutions hold the key to the survival of the human race. Yes, universities have used their chemistry, biology and physics laboratories to develop the technology for making war weapons. Fortunately, universities can do more than that. The United Negro College Fund campaign slogan states that, "the mind is a terrible thing to waste." If so, universities, as citadels of learning and charged with the responsibility of training young minds, must create opportunities for effective learning. The global village needs more doctors, nurses, engineers, farmers, masons, and teachers, to mention a few. Consequently, universities must do the following:

- Train people to become good citizens of the global village.
- Develop curricula that present a holistic approach to learning.
- Provide opportunities for practical training in survival skills in the workplace as well as in the community.
- Establish mechanisms for appropriately rewarding students for community service.
- Teach students languages that can enhance communications across groups and nationalities.
- Teach the history of the many cultures and civilizations of the world so that they may be tolerant of each other.

As John Donne once wrote:

> No man is an island, entire of itself; every man is a piece of the continent, a part of the main. If a clod be washed away by the sea, Europe is less, as well as if a promontory were, as well as if a manor of thy friend's or of thine own were. Any man's death diminishes me, because I am involved in mankind; and therefore never send to ask for whom the bell tolls: it tolls for thee.[14]

Therefore, if educational institutions adequately prepare their students to become useful citizens of the world, they will become the proper keepers of the world and they will be mindful that whenever a bell tolls, it tolls for all humanity.

[14]M.H. Abrams, general editor, *The Norton Anthology of English Literature,* 7th edition, Volume 1, New York: W.W. Norton & Company, 2000, p. 1278.

Some ten years ago, a group of professors in the United States came together to form the Global Awareness Society International (GASI). The aim of the organization is to promote global understanding, peace, and cooperation. At GASI's annual conference in New York City, the organization adopted the Guiding Principles of the organization. These principles attest to what humankind can do individually and collectively to make the world a better place. In presenting these principles to the august gathering of scholars in New York for adoption, the founder of the organization, Chang Shub Roh[15], opined that our generation has a duty to give to succeeding generations a world better than we found it. The following principles were adopted for the organization:

- All global citizens are equal, yet unique as human beings in the global community.
- Every global citizen has the right to be respected by others and the obligation to respect others.
- A global citizen has the right to be educated for self-enhancement and to contribute as a useful citizen, utilizing one's knowledge, skills, technology and talent.
- Every global citizen has the right to the satisfaction of basic human needs. The advantaged citizen has an interest in assisting the disadvantaged in the global world.
- Every global citizen has the right to be protected by and to provide protection to others.
- A global citizen has the right to his/her own belief system, but also the responsibility to be respectful of other belief systems.
- Each global citizen has the right to pursue and enjoy his/her own cultural life style and happiness, and to help others to undertake the same.
- As global citizens, we share the joys, happiness, sorrows and pain of human life in the world, whatever the cause.
- Citizens of the globe have the opportunity to contribute, in their own way, to the welfare of the family, community and nation-state, and strive for harmony and peace throughout the world.[16]

These principles are laudable. They are essentially a reaffirmation of the United Nations' Universal Declaration of Human Rights. In an era of globalization and globalism, organizations such as the Global Awareness Society International have a vital role to play in the promotion of peace, harmony, and respect for human dignity. The imperatives of globalization, therefore, are far-reaching and very rewarding. Our survival depends on our ability to maximize our potential for the common good. That is the greatest legacy than we can bequeath to future generations.

---

[15]Dr. Chang Shub Roh is a retired sociology professor. He emigrated from Korea to the United States shortly after the Korean War. His vision of a global village at peace with itself led to his founding of the Global Awareness Society International, which has chapters in the Americas, Europe, Africa, and Asia.
[16]See *The Global News,* Volume 200, Issue 02, p.6.

On the Margins of the Global Village

Asgede Hagos

"News is that which comes from the North, South, East and West, and if it comes from only one point of the compass, then it is a class publication, not news."

—*Benjamin Disraeli, 1855*

INTRODUCTION: THE MEDIA'S POWER AND REACH

The Western mass media's global reach today has been unprecedented and there is every indication that it will continue to grow quickly. It is also interesting to note that the new communication technology has helped transform the old media systems in the field. For example, the Internet, in addition to creating a virtual world never seen or even imaged before, has transformed all other channels of mass communication, forcing them to compete for audience and advertising dollars in cyberspace as well.

In fact, the ongoing explosion in communication technology is making Marshall McLuhan's theory of "the global village" more and more acceptable. The assumption of McLuhan's theory is that technology, especially mass communication technology, will "shrink" the world and its peoples together. Today, global satellites can deliver instantaneous information—in all its forms—to almost any part of the world. Thanks to satellite telecommunication systems, the latest world cup soccer games were watched live by billions of people worldwide. Thomas Friedman, summing up his experience as a Pulitzer Prize-winning correspondent for the *New York Times* covering several areas of the globe, said, "I gradually realized that what was driving the rise and power of markets, what was reshaping how nations and individuals interacted with one another, and what was really at the heart of globalization, was the recent advances in technology—from the Internet to satellite telecommunications" (2000, 22).

However, this technology and the rest of the modern resources of communication, including the news agencies, are under the firm control of only one part of the globe, the Northern Hemisphere, the home of the industrialized nations. News agencies, which account for most of the information that flows across the globe—though, as we will see later, mostly in one direction—are based in the North and are run and controlled by people who know very little about the societies and cultures of the Southern Hemisphere. In other words, most world news is being disseminated from such news centers as New York, Washington, D.C., London, and Paris, where the major world news agencies—the Associated Press, United Press International, Reuters, and Agence France-Press—are headquartered. Thus, the developing regions of the world are seriously disadvantaged by the prevailing pattern of information flow, from the Northern Hemisphere to the developing regions in the South.

The relationship between the northern and the southern portions of the globe can also be viewed from a structural schema in relation to "the global village"—the Center and the Periphery, the former representing the industrialized nations of the West and the latter the developing regions of Africa, Asia, and South America and the Middle East. The Center-Periphery dichotomy attempts to explain the imbalance in the interaction between the hemispheres, an imbalance that encourages exploitation of the regions on the margins of the system.

Western press coverage of the major developing regions of the world has been characterized largely by neglect. In fact, the level of coverage of these regions by the dominant news organizations ranges from minimal to nonexistent, except for occasional stories by correspondents who fly in and out of the capitals of the developing nations when crises—war, famine, etc.—strike, especially if the disasters have implications for Western interests in these areas. In other words, though there is a great deal of information that flows from the Center of "the global village," mostly in the form of cultural products from the industrialized nations to the Periphery, there is very little that goes in the other direction. As a result, the ongoing communication revolution that is "shrinking" the globe also ironically tends to increase the gap between the North and South. Kennedy argues that "the relative lack of capital, high technology, scientists, skilled workers and export industries in the poorer countries makes it difficult for them to take part in the communication and financial revolutions" (2000, 347).

McPhail describes the new relationship between the developed, industrialized nations and the developing, less-industrialized Third World countries as "electronic colonialism" or as the electronic version of the empires the West had controlled in Africa, Asia, South America and the Middle East (1987). The interaction between the two hemispheres, which is multi-dimensional in nature and includes cultural, political, and economic aspects, is characterized mostly by dependency and exploitation. However, it is less of an interaction and more of a one-way transfer not only of information, goods and services, but also of social values and beliefs from the Center to the Periphery, done under "the free flow of information" doctrine.

Kamara argues that "media program export statistics unequivocally establish Western domination of global communication at all levels: satellite technology, news agency coverage, and general programming" (1996, 50).

Such imbalance and neglect have serious implications for the visibility of the developing nations because the media giants have the power to reconstruct reality. There is no question that the high-technology-driven Western media represent a very powerful global institution, which is at the leading edge of the most fundamental changes taking place in the world today. This power is rooted in the media's capacity to reconstruct reality and their ability to deliver images of that reality to billions of people almost instantaneously and in such a vivid way. Their power to set the agenda for media consumers as individuals and as members of society determines whether a region, a nation or an issue will get attention at all, and how much attention. Their power to frame, define and shape reality is mostly through a selection process based primarily on ideological orientation. Studies during the last quarter-century (Gandy 1982; Dorman et al. 1987; Linsky 1987; Mowlana 1986) have shown that these channels of information have the power to frame the issues that define the developing world, its people and the people's struggles for freedom. For example, "The *New York Times* coverage is one of the most robust predictors of the levels of aid the United States offers to foreign disaster victims . . . and the levels of development aid the United States offers are closely tied to the salience of countries on U.S. network television newscasts" (van Belle 2000, 25).

Below, we will discuss the implications of the media's growing influence and the institutional processes that make this possible.

IMPLICATIONS FOR AFRICA

The Western mass media's unprecedented reach and power across the globe have grave implications for the visibility and acceptability of any country, any region, and any part of the globe, especially those on the margins of the global economic and political systems. The amount of Western media attention—or lack of it—tends to determine how much international aid, say, Sudanese refugees receive in Chad. The kind of press coverage that Africa and Africans get greatly influences the investment climate in the continent.

Studies conducted during the last decade show the 1992 U.S. intervention in Somalia and its withdrawal a little over a year later from that Horn of Africa nation were very much media driven. Lawrence Eagleburger, who served as secretary of state in the first Bush administration, which launched the intervention, said, "Television had a great deal to do with President Bush's decision to go in the first place" (Seib 2002, 43). In the debate that preceded the intervention, the elite press gave the Somalian humanitarian crisis a great deal of attention. The number of stories in the two leading elite newspapers in the country, the *New York Times* and the *Washington Post,* jumped from 186 in 1991 to 1,025 in 1992 (Moeller 1999; also see Seib 2002, 41). Then in October 1993, when the Western media showed the body of a dead American soldier being dragged by Somalian militia members through the streets of Mogadishu, the capital, following a gruesome battle, calls for immediate withdrawal came from many sectors of the American political elite and the U.S. press. Three days after the incident, a decision was made to withdraw all U.S. troops from Somalia. "Television's ability to bring graphic images of pain and outrage into our living rooms has heightened the pressure both for immediate engagement in areas of international crisis and immediate disengagement when events do not go according to plan," said Madeleine Albright when she was U.S. ambassador to the UN, before she became Clinton's secretary of state (Sharkey 1993, 18).

We see here not only television pictures driving U.S. foreign policy, but also the crisis-oriented nature of the little media attention African nations have been getting over the years. In addition to showing the active role the Western media play in international relations, the Somali story provides a good example of how the media's neglect of the developing nations is occasionally broken by crisis-driven bursts of attention. However, after the cameras leave and the correspondents return to their mostly Europe-based bureaus a few days, in some cases a few hours, after they arrive, the attention level reverts to what has become "normal" for these nations: none to minimal.

The media gatekeepers, those who control access to "the global village," attribute the neglect of the developing regions by the press to the public's lack of interest in news about peoples half a world away. Proximity is one of many news values that are supposed to govern news gathering and writing practices and marketing strategies in Western journalism. However, the ideological orientation or world outlook of the gatekeepers plays an even greater role in determining whether an issue, a nation or region will get media attention at all.

This pattern of neglect may have far-reaching effect not only on the people being pushed to margins, but also those in the Center of "the global village." The September 11, 2001, terrorist attacks on the World Trade Center and the Pentagon generated a great deal of international news in the Western press, especially in the U.S. press; this in turn was expected to generate new interest in foreign news among Americans. However, a study conducted by the Pew Research Center for the People and the Press about nine months after the attacks shows that this has not been the case. The man who conducted the Pew survey, Andrew Kohut, told the *Washington Post,* "There hasn't been the transformation that the political scientists had hoped for. The modest increase comes from the ranks of those who are already interested in international news" (Kurtz 2002, A13). Furthermore, the modest increase, as the research organization's biennial news survey indicated, didn't extend beyond America's war against terrorism and the Israeli-Palestinian conflict. Other major foreign news stories seemed to "attract no greater attention than in the past."

The Pew study concluded that the increase of international news coverage generated by the attacks as well as the war on terrorism has little or no impact on the American public's news consumption habits. But, why didn't the additional coverage result in a surge of interest in international news? The survey revealed that most Americans have trouble understanding foreign news or following international news events. This is what the Pew researchers found: "The survey offers powerful evidence that broad interest in international news is most inhibited by the public's lack of background information in this area . . . Overall, roughly two-thirds (65%) of those with moderate or low interest in international news say they sometimes lose interest in these stories because they lack the background information to keep up" (http://people-press.org).

However, these results should not be surprising, given the almost total neglect of most of the developing regions of the Third World by the Western mass media and other key Western institutions, especially the state. And we will see below how such a legacy of lack of attention adversely affects a whole continent's attempt to gain international visibility, approval and support. But, here we will examine the role of the press in its interplay with another powerful Western institution, the state, and examine how the two viewed the struggles for freedom in three African territories, one in the south, one in the east, and the third in the west.

Of the regions on the periphery of "the global village," Africa has been the most disadvantaged. During the last three decades, scholars have shown how regions like Africa, the most central of them all, have been pushed to the margins. The U.S. press, for example, despite having larger news holes than other world presses, is said to have consistently shown neglect of Africa and Africans. A 1989 study based on a 62-day investigation of daily prime-time television coverage of sub-Saharan Africa represented less than one percent of the total number of stories in all three American networks. All of the stories relating to the continent were crisis-oriented, and were about one country, South Africa, which was on the brink of fundamental changes as apartheid was coming to an end, creating an uncertain future for the minority white population in that country. However, there were many other equally momentous changes in other parts of the continent, but Western interests determine Western media attention. Kamara says there was no coverage of the rest of the more than 400 million population of sub-Sahara Africa during the 62-day study period (1996, 51). A similar study conducted about a decade earlier indicated similar inadequacy in the coverage of the developing regions of the globe. The news capitals of Africa are not Nairobi, Lagos, or even Cairo, which has had telegraph cable facilities since the 1860s. Chances are that what a Rwandan knows about a war in neighboring Burundi, or a Kenyan hears about horrific massacres in Rwanda, are dispatches from the giant news agencies beamed back to Africa via the British Broadcasting Corporation, the Voice of America, or Radio France Internationale from the news centers of the world.

Several writers (Challenor 1977; McHenry 1974; Skinner 1986) have also invariably indicated that the continent is not only the most neglected, but also the most sensationalized and stereotyped major region of the world. The little coverage of the continent in the Western media is not only spasmodic and crisis-oriented, but it also reveals a tinge of crude cynicism. The portrayal of Africa in the media as "the region where nothing works" is partially rooted in the racist ideology deeply ingrained in Western culture. A BBC correspondent who covered the 1994 Rwanda genocide which claimed close to a million lives wrote, "The fact that this was an act of systematically planned mass murder, a final solution of monstrous proportions, was too often lost in the rush to blame the catastrophe on the old bogey of tribalism. This was not just lazy journalism, it was an insult to the nearly one million dead" (Kean, 1995, T4). Anthropologist Elliot Skinner said the U.S. press's frequent use of terms like "tribalism," "tribal jealousies" and "tribal hatred" to explain complicated

African problems such as power struggles between social elites or liberation move-ments, which represent the highest and most violent stage in the process of decolo-nization, is a way of portraying Africans as "primitive people ruled by primeval forces" (See Artis 1970, 48). In its attempt to justify colonialism, this is what *Time* magazine wrote in the years following Congo's independence: "A single life, or even a hundred, may not appear to mean much more in the grim reckoning of Africa. The tribes butchered each other for centuries before the white man arrived" ("The Congo Massacre" 1964, 19). *Time*, ironically calling itself the newsweekly, editori-alized about Africa and Africans in its news columns without restraint. During the same year in 1964 *Time* correspondent Robin Mannock, who said he wanted to stay in Africa because he was "interested in abnormal psychology" (See Auer 1964, 19), gave two possible reasons to explain why African nations strongly condemned the landing of a group of white mercenaries in the Congo as an invasion of a sovereign nation: "Red influence" or insanity, with the latter being the more probable. "The sane part of the world could only wonder whether Black Africa can be taken seri-ously at all or whether, for the foreseeable future, it is beyond the reach of reason" ("The Congo Massacre" 1964, 19).

INSTITUTIONAL BASES OF NEGLECT

Though the Western mass media represent a powerful force on their own, they don't work in a vacuum, independent of the other institutions in the society, at both the national and international levels. For example, the institutions of the press and the state complement each other in the making and implementation of foreign policy (Cater 1959; Cohen 1963; Altschull 1984; Cook 1995). The two institutions operate within a shared cultural and ideological environment. In his 1959 landmark book *The Fourth Branch of Government*, Douglas Cater said, "The reporter is the recorder of government, but he is also a participant . . . [and] . . . helps to shape the course of government" (1959, 7). Timothy Cook, writing four decades later and reaffirming Cater's assessment of the relationship between the two institutions, concluded, "Indeed I will claim that the American news media today are not merely part of politics: they are part of government" (1997, 3).

As a result, the extent and nature of the impact on a region or nation can have even more lasting effect when the press works in tandem with other key institutions in the marginalization process. We see this in action in the interplay between the U.S. press and the U.S. government in relation to Africa. Writing a quarter of a cen-tury ago, former U.S. ambassador to the U.N. Donald McHenry stated, "Africa remains the unchallenged occupant of the bottom rung of American foreign policy priorities" (1974,148). The statement is as true today as it was then. We can also say the same thing of U.S. press coverage of the continent; it was the most ignored region in the American newsrooms a quarter of a century ago, as it is today. Con-fined to the periphery of the system, "the continent is still viewed by the West and, as a result, portrayed by its media outlets, not as an independent actor in interna-tional relations, but as an inconsequential extension of the former colonial powers in all phases of that relationship" (Hagos 2000, 5).

Below we describe and explore the nature of the interplay between the U.S. government and the American elite press in relation to a key African issue, the national liberation movement, considered to be on the cutting edge of change in the continent because it represents the last and often violent stage in the process of decolonization. To conduct the study, content analysis was used as the chief methodological tool of inquiry to analyze editorials from two elite newspapers, the *New York Times* and the *Washington Post*, as well as documents from the official organ of U.S. foreign policy, the *U.S. Department of State Bulletin*, over an eight-year period (January 1977 to December 1984). The study period covers two consecutive U.S. administrations—one Democratic, one Republican; one liberal, the other conservative. Three movements were selected from across the continent—one in the south (South Africa), one in the east (Eritrea), and the other in the west (Western Sahara).

A close examination of the data reveals that, despite the portrayal of its own role as a neutral link and disinterested medium of information, the press is an active participant in the foreign policymaking process. There is a strong interplay between the press and the foreign policymakers, which becomes evident when the two sides try to influence the policy agenda. The findings also show an interplay of support when the two institutions work in harmony. This is particularly evident when the state senses danger. Though sometimes the press disagreed with the policymakers on policy tactics and style, it did not seem to challenge the basic assumptions of U.S. foreign policy and the two institutions seemed to agree on most of the key issues raised in the present study. The positions of the press and the policymakers on Africa's national liberation movements seemed to be similar. Both failed to see the internal dimensions to these struggles and viewed them as products of an external communist conspiracy.

U.S. diplomacy in Africa during this period was widely viewed as an effort to preempt the efforts of the national liberation movements, and some of the policymakers and the editors were very open about it. Some of these movements, most of which started in the 1960s, had begun to come of age and showed that they had the military muscle to take state power. In fact, the main reason why Washington showed such a high level of interest in Africa during the study period had to do with these national liberation movements.

The data clearly shows that, despite occasional disagreements on tactics and style, the journalists and officials seemed to have uniformity of views on these movements throughout the study period. Consider the following six areas of agreement:

First, both the press and the state seemed to have the same perception of the nature and motivation of these movements These national liberation movements were widely viewed as being too radical, probably communist and Soviet-inspired and bent on destroying Western interests. The documents show that the editors and policymakers failed to fully grasp the socioeconomic and political factors that lead to armed struggle. The press and the officials tended to attribute their existence to external factors—more specifically, the Soviet Union and other communist forces. They subtly and sometimes not so subtly portrayed these movements as part of an international communist conspiracy, a depiction that came through in several ways in both the documents and editorials. They failed to recognize the internal factors that defined these movements. Nelson Mandela, at his trial in the early 1960s, after the ANC came to the painful conclusion that armed struggle was the only way for black South Africans to determine their own destiny, told the court that he was fully aware of how risky it was to militarily confront the South African regime. The three movements of South Africa, Eritrea, and the Western Sahara were willing to face three of the largest and best-equipped armies in Africa because they knew they could depend not on Russian guns, but the will and fortitude of their respective peoples to endure and sacrifice in order to win a basic right—the right to self-determination. Andrew Young, who was praised for bringing an understanding of Third World issues, especially African, and sensitivity to his job as Carter's ambassador to the U.N., told the World Conference in Lagos in 1977: "Too often . . . the armed struggle is advocated most vigorously by those who are thousands of miles away and whose only contribution to the struggle is the rhetoric of bitterness and frustration" (*Bulletin* October 1977, 447). The assumption that the liberation movements were foreign-controlled showed a total ignorance on the part of the U.S. policy makers about the liberation forces' reason for existence. The Eritrean liberation movement was probably the best example to show that to have a Russian weapon did not necessarily mean control by or even influence of the Soviet Union or its satellites. They successfully turned captured Soviet weapons, supplied to the Ethiopians, against the enemy. The triumph of the Eritrean struggle against formidable enemies, including sub-Saharan Africa's largest army and one of the best equipped in the continent that had the full backing of the Soviet Union and its satellites, is a testament that the assumption of both the policy makers and editors was wrong.

Second, both institutions misrepresented the political essence of these movements and the distortion emanated from the editors' and officials' common framework of what they perceived to be the reality in Africa. Both editors and policymakers persistently misrepresented the political essence and justness of the liberation movements' causes and demands. Such misrepresentation usually begins in the news coverage of the continent in general and the movements in particular. It soon finds its way into the editorial pages of the press. Since the method, and sometimes even the nature of the distortion of the political content of these struggles, varies from movement to movement, it is very hard to generalize on how it becomes evident. However, it invariably starts when the coverage presents the armed struggle as the source of the chaos that war causes while portraying the governments in power as the legitimate authorities trying to reassert law and order (Paletz and Entman 1981). For example, the Ethiopian army was described as being "in firm control of Asmara" but the Eritrean fighters "are choking off its 250,000 residents from food, water and fuel." The Eritrean struggle was consistently portrayed as "imperiling" Ethiopian unity. Throughout the years it carried the labels of "secessionist," "Marxist" and "Moslem-led." The people's right to self-determination—the very core of the political content of the struggle—was never mentioned in its proper context in the documents or the editorials. There was not even a hint of the fact that the struggle was in response to the forcible annexation of the former Italian and British colony by Ethiopia. The same was true of the Western Saharan movement, which both the policymakers and the press tried to push to the back burner. In South Africa, the ANC, instead of being taken as the key political actor that it was in the struggle for change in its country and the region in general, was portrayed as a group of rebels who wanted to force their will through violence when non-violent means were possible. This perspective is firmly rooted in the counterinsurgency tradition of the United States. One of the main goals of U.S. foreign policy, starting from the Truman Doctrine, has been the suppression of insurgent movements. At about the beginning of the study period, the U.S. government was training counterinsurgency forces in 34 countries (Finney 1975, 1).

Third, policy statements about social justice, human rights and human dignity notwithstanding, their positions on the three movements were politically motivated. A careful reading of the documents and editorials also reveals that, despite pro-nouncements of social justice, human rights and even self-determination, the posi-tions of both sides on these movements were mostly politically motivated. Apartheid is primarily a human rights issue. However, though both the Carter and Reagan administrations repeatedly promised that there would not be any compromise on the question of social justice in South Africa, their respective policies basically repre-sented an effort at "preemptive diplomacy" to avert or at least forestall a revolutionary and potentially violent change in this highly sensitive region. The data also show the same attitude in the other regions. For example, despite its highly publicized and high-profile human rights campaign, the Carter administration was almost solely guided by political expediency in its responses to the human rights tragedy in Eritrea. The press also followed the same lines. In 1975, when the Eritrean liberation movements, in a major show of force which rattled the Ethiopian occupation army in Eritrea, the now-defunct *Washington Star*, in an editorial, urged American policy-makers to resupply the Ethiopian army to make sure that the Eritreans would not succeed. "The emergency of a radical Eritrea on the Red Sea giving Moslem control of both sides of that body of water, would further threaten access to the Israeli port of Elath" (12 February 1975, 26). The view that Eritrea's independence would pose a threat to Israel has had a continuous adverse impact on the Eritrean struggle's effort to find access to the Western media. The *New York Times* also advocated against U.S. support of the Eritrean struggle because it would be "resented" by Ethiopia and the rest of Africa (3 February 1978, A22). The same expediency was also at work in dealing with the Western Saharan case.

Fourth, both were consistent in their opposition to armed struggle as a means to change the status quo. At the heart of Washington's attitude toward these libera-tion movements was the issue of armed struggle, with all its implications of vio-lence. Armed struggle is that stage of the conflict on which oppressed and struggling peoples embark after trying and failing to achieve freedom and liberation through non-violent political means. The South Africans, Eritreans and West Saharans set out to achieve their freedom through protracted armed struggle after attempting to win it without resorting to violence. For example, Carter's U.N. Ambassador, Andrew Young, said many times that one of the primary goals of his frequent visits to Africa during the early years of the administration was to convince black Africans that armed struggle was not the desired way to win freedom and independence. The officials and the press were also consistent in their opposition to armed struggle as an option to achieve liberation. Young, who was praised for his sensitivity to the needs and interests of Africans, repeatedly said he was opposed to such a method as a means of achieving freedom. His reasoning was that "armed struggle . . . exacts a cruel price from the people . . . the leadership that will be lost in a prolonged struggle . . . [and] the infrastructure that will be destroyed in extended military conflict" (*Bulletin* July 1977, 55-58). It is true that armed struggle exacts a high price, especially at the initial stages when the people have not acquired the weapons they need to defend themselves from the dictators they are trying to overthrow. It was lack of a rational alternative that made them choose the violence option. The alternative offered by the American policymakers was not viewed as being realistic.

The prevention of further radicalization of the continent, one of the two important policy goals of both administrations, had its target in these movements, which had already shown that they could take over state power by force if necessary. In the documents and editorials the issue became even more focused within the context of the discussion on apartheid after Zimbabwe achieved its independence. The *Washington Post,* in an editorial, said that among black South Africans there was a great happiness at that country's triumph and "an appreciation of the key role that armed struggle played in positioning [Robert Mugabe] both to gather popular favor and to enter the elections he finally won." The recognition that armed struggle forced the white minority in Zimbabwe to give up power had sent shock waves among white South Africans. The paper said that though making easy comparisons between what was still Rhodesia and South Africa was unwarranted, in view of the fact that the latter has the resources and larger population base at least to delay and make costly such an eventuality, "Rhodesia/Zimbabwe is probably the closest thing there is to a model of change for South Africa." However, the editors said that whites in South Africa "don't need to be told long-distance, by people who will not have to share the consequences, to embrace either revolution or reform. They seem, finally, to be on the way to making their own choice. For the effort, they deserve our respect." The paper applauded a proposal made by Prime Minister P.W. Botha to hold "a state conference," which was to include non-whites, to discuss the country's future in the wake of the developments in Zimbabwe. "His initiative is forcing a fateful debate on whether whites should move beyond compromises meant merely to buy time and divide non-whites on racial, tribal or economic grounds, or whether they should move deliberately to grant equal rights to all South Africans" (18 March 1980, C6). The *Washington Post* reiterated this message in another editorial a little over two months later which was prompted by a series of hit-and-run attacks in the urban areas targeting economic installations that symbolized white South Africa's resistance to sanctions. "The latest raids cannot fail to sharpen the question before white South Africans of whether it is better to stand firm or to accelerate reform. Since the eventual security of whites cannot be guaranteed under either approach, it seems wise for outsiders not to offer advice too glibly" (5 June 1980, A18). The paper then urged the South African regime to release prominent black political leaders, first among them being Nelson Mandela because, the editors believed, intransigence on the part of Pretoria would only force black South Africans to press armed struggle, thereby making it easier for communism to take root in the region. Equating armed struggle with Soviet weaponry and, in turn, the view that whoever carries Soviet weapons carries communist ideas are evident throughout the study period.

Fifth, both tried to use the movements as a bogeyman to push U.S. policy goals especially in southern Africa. Both the press and the policymakers tried to use armed struggle to undermine the causes of armed struggle. As we will see below, both administrations tried to use these movements as bogeymen to frighten the white minority regimes in southern Africa into taking the path of reform the Americans recommended and pursued to the extent they could, their differences in approaches notwithstanding. They tried to use the liberation movements as a straw man to scare the racist regime in Pretoria into softening its intransigence on U.S. demands for racial reform, which was at the heart of the American policy to avoid a race war in southern Africa and prevent the further radicalization of the continent. Especially the press frequently used this stick to prod South Africa into accepting Washington's views that the apartheid regime had either to accept a meaningful change, and fast, or accept apocalypse. In other words, they tried to use armed struggle as a weapon in an attempt to preempt the goals of armed struggle. Armed struggle was addressed as either what happens if the white South Africans don't accept the reform suggestions from the West, especially the United States, or as the undesirable alternative in resolving the crises that characterized many regions in the continent, but especially southern Africa. When the ANC escalated attacks in response to the South African regime's decision to allow "Coloreds" and Asians limited political participation while continuing to exclude the black majority population, the *Washington Post* went into its familiar argument. "Why did the ANC escalate now? . . . . It is in the business of armed rebellion . . . . In another sense, the raids are a tribute of sorts to the efforts undertaken by the ruling white minority to forestall armed struggle and revolution by timely reform" (5 June 1980, A18). The *New York Times* quickly condemned the results of the "state conference," which established the State President's Council, giving "the Coloreds" and Asians an advisory role while the majority of blacks were given a separate Advisory Council, as an invention of yet "another color-coded political institution" which "institutionalizes a hierarchy of color with the obvious purpose of perpetuating white dominance." The *New York Times* added that "the sad truth is that the new 'reform' further confirms Prime Minister P.W. Botha's retreat from his early promises to bring South Africa's blacks to a position of greater economic and political influence. Without such an evolution, no peaceful development seems conceivable" (21 May 1980, A34). In fact, a month later, the newspaper called upon the United States to "speak forcefully to South Africa." The editors went on to criticize the prime minister for reneging on the promises he had made when he took office in 1978 and for "resorting to the same tactics of suppression" used by his predecessor, John Vorster. "Therefore," the newspaper concluded, "there is in fact a high American interest in a peaceful evolution in South Africa. When Pretoria betrays that prospect, it should hear about it from Americans, publicly and privately, in very forceful ways" (20 June 1980, A30).

Practically all of the members of Carter's foreign policy team stressed the need for the minority regime to move quickly toward reform to prevent the inevitability of armed struggle and to defend Western interests against communism. One of them,

Anthony Lake, Carter's director of policy planning staff, told the regime, quoting President Kennedy, "Those who make peaceful evolution impossible will make violent revolution inevitable" (Bulletin 12 December 1977, 843). The *Washington Post* said "moderate" African leaders also believed that it was a choice between armed struggle and reform in southern Africa. In 1976, when Kissinger met with Vorster, the Washington newspaper in an editorial stated that President Nyerere of Tanzania, who played "the crucial black African role," had "forced upon Mr. Kissinger the choice of going all-out for a diplomatic solution or coming under a direct demand from black Africa to support armed struggle" (26 September 1976, A22).

Lastly, both seemed to agree on approaches that tried to marginalize and undermine the leaderships of these movements. In the search for solutions to the political crises that the movements represented, the national liberation forces were viewed not as part of the solution but part of the problem, of which the Soviet Union and its surrogates were the main actors. As a result, the policy makers did everything they could to undermine the leaderships of these movements and totally marginalize them by promoting "moderate" alternatives more acceptable to Washington. Secretary of State Cyrus Vance said that the main challenge the foreign policy team faced in South Africa was two-sided: to overcome the mistrust that black Africans felt toward the U.S. intentions in the region and also to present "a credible alternative to armed struggle" (Vance 1983, 256-257). Though this was nothing new in American policy for this or any other region, the issue of finding alternative leadership to that of ANC in South Africa, for example, was given unprecedented attention. Both administrations promoted leaders and forces opposed to the liberation movement. One of the first African notables invited to Washington a few months after Jimmy Carter took office was Inkatha Party leader Gathsha Buthelezi, who was well known at the time for his opposition to the ANC and economic sanctions. Also invited to Washington early during the Carter administration were Joshua Nkomo and Bishop Abel Muzorewa, who were known as "moderate" leaders. In their continuous search for peace, American policymakers also solicited advice from other "moderate" African leaders, the South African head of state, as well as European leaders. The Reagan administration continued the same approach and reached out to many of these leaders, though it was not successful in its attempt to "sell" its constructive engagement strategy for South Africa. It also extended help to other moderate leaders in Sudan, Somalia and Kenya in response to a regrouping of radical, pro-Soviet nations in the region. The policymakers' effort to nurture a black moderate leadership and marginalize the leadership of the national liberation movements was fully supported by the elite press that kept expressing its "dismay" at the South African regime's suppression of moderate South African leaders.

The attitude of the two administrations toward national liberation movements was rooted in their respective policies on regional conflicts. Carter's policy on these conflicts constituted a key part of his African policy and it was one of the two most important aspects of U.S. stance on global security, the other being American relations with the Soviet Union. The administration followed a six-point approach in dealing with regional conflicts as in southern Africa and the Horn of Africa, but here again the main motivation seemed to be the prevention of communist forces from influencing the final outcome of these conflicts. The first point in Carter's strategy, for example, was "to engage in diplomatic activity to help resolve conflicts before outside involvement escalates." Most of the rest of the strategy, however, was a pledge to "strive for genuine self-determination rather than seeking to impose made-in-America solutions," not to rely on unilateral diplomacy, and to recognize and support the United Nations' role and African initiatives in mediating these conflicts. It was also designed "to minimize American military involvement in African conflicts" (*Bulletin* December 1977, 842–845).

The Reagan administration's policy on regional conflicts had basically the same underpinnings, but added an important dimension to them: the Reagan Doctrine, which advocated directly helping "anti-communist" insurgents (*Bulletin* August 1981, 58). The Reagan strategy highlighted two significant tactical objectives which were present but not emphasized in the Carter plan. They sought to insulate South Africa from the increasing violence sweeping across southern Africa and justify the policy of constructive engagement. Ronald Reagan's policy approach was based on South Africa as a deserving partner in all areas of relations with the United States. The other objective, which was meant to reinforce the first, was to ensure that the neighboring countries did not give sanctuary and any other help to the South African liberation movement. It was intended to deprive the armed struggle of the rear base that kept it going, since establishing permanent bases was virtually impossible in South Africa, unlike in Angola, Mozambique or any other country in the region, for that matter. During the early months of the Reagan administration, the State Department repeatedly denied that the new strategy would in fact exacerbate regional tension in the continent. "Our preferred choice is to foster and help implement, where we can, diplomatic solutions to Africa's conflicts. In southern Africa as in the Horn of Africa, we seek a reduction of regional tensions. Those who characterize this administration's goals differently are, simply put, wrong" (*Bulletin* August 1981, 58). But, the scheme to reduce tension was to be at the expense of the ANC. Reagan's Undersecretary of State Eagleburger said, "To succeed in southern Africa, we must define a coherent regional strategy" aimed at defending the South African state and curbing any across-border activities of the ANC or any group opposed to the white minority Pretoria regime (*Bulletin* August 1983, 9).

The administration used the well-recognized principle of national sovereignty to base the strategy on. Members of the Reagan foreign policy team pushed the policy line that the region was made of sovereign states that should be respected. "Respect for international boundaries and renunciation of the use of violence across them are central to any framework for international security. There can be no double standards for either South Africa or its neighbors. The obligations of statehood, in southern Africa as elsewhere, are basic and reciprocal." It also reaffirmed the principle that all states have a duty to refrain from tolerating or acquiescing in organized activities within their territory by guerrillas or dissidents planning acts of violence in the territory of another state. This applied equally to South Africa and its neighbors. The policy was based on the premise that "regional security cannot rest solely on the activity, the vision, or the influence of outsiders. . . . It is up to the governments directly concerned . . . to make the basic choice between the temptations of violence and the challenge of coexistence" (*Bulletin* August 1983, 10).

Highlights of that strategy could be seen in the accords with Angola and Mozambique—both directed against the national liberation movements; the press gave the credit to the Reagan administration. The nonaggression pact between South Africa and Mozambique and a "disengagement" accord between South Africa and Angola were aimed at curbing the military capacity of, and reducing the operational theaters of the liberation movements in the region, especially the ANC. However, despite the success in securing pacts between South Africa and two of its neighbors, the Reagan approach only exacerbated regional tension.

Part of Washington's consistent attempt during the study period was to try to place itself in a position where it could have some leverage in the shaping of the final resolution of these conflicts by ensuring that "moderate" African leaders were well positioned to take over when the right time came. The general assessment of both the editors and officials was that the conflict in South Africa was reaching a boiling point. The death of Steven Biko, leader of the militant student movement, erupted into a mass uprising centering on Soweto. However, in its attempts to solve the political crises as well as human tragedy which had resulted in the death of millions of South Africans, Eritreans, West Saharans as well as Ethiopians, Washington decided to go around the leaderships of these movements, with the policymakers going to extreme lengths to cultivate alternative leaderships to these movements and their leaders.

How successful was the Carter policy on regional conflicts? The administration did not have many victories in Africa, but it pointed to its contribution to the resolution of the Shaba crisis. "We cannot and do not claim credit for the resolution of the Shaba affair . . . . But the fact that Shaba did not evolve into a major crisis is evidence that our policy was mature and correct" (*Bulletin* December 1977, 845). The Shaba incident involved Katangan insurgents crossing into Zaire from Angola in the spring of 1977, representing a serious threat to one of America's staunchest "moderate" leaders in the continent. The Carter administration, in response, deployed U.S. transport aircraft to airlift a contingent of Belgian, French and Moroccan troops, among others, to repulse the rebels and save Mobutu from his own people. The incident is a good example of the extent that the American administrations were prepared to go to save the pro-Western so-called moderate African leaders. This was even truer when the threat came from revolutionary groups that used protracted armed struggle as a primary means to bring about change no matter how badly it was needed. Paletz and Entman showed that the media fully supported the American policy in dealing with the Shaba incident (1981, 226).

CONCLUSIONS

In the end, both administrations had nothing to show for their policies toward regional conflicts. None of the conflicts was any closer to resolution as a result of either administration's policy. In a way, that is not surprising because the solutions proposed by the policymakers were "made in America," their policy pledges notwithstanding, in total disregard of the internal dynamics of these liberation movements. The approaches the policymakers proposed and tried to implement and those suggested by the press were far from what the political, economic and social realities in the respective territories demanded. For example, Washington's strategy to try to go around the leadership of the movements was not the right one, and this became evident years later when Washington found out that it couldn't play a constructive role in the resolution of these conflicts without dealing with this leadership. In 1991, for instance, the United States accepted the Eritrean People's Liberation Front leadership—also reflected in the U.S. media—as one of the key actors in the Horn of Africa and brought the warring sides to a negotiating table in London which ended with the EPLF declaring a provisional government in Eritrea and a coalition of democratic forces forming an interim government in Ethiopia. In South Africa, Nelson Mandela and the ANC came to be accepted as the genuine representatives of black South Africans. However, if the U.S. media had performed their watchdog function and questioned, as they should, the respective administration's policies with regards to Africa in general and the national liberation movements in particular, the outcome may have been different.

This interplay in which the powerful Western institutions reinforce their respective agendas leaves the developing regions and nations voiceless on the world stage, without alternative communication and information systems. Whether world public opinion will hear the stories of the peoples of the southern part of the globe is likely to depend on others. When, occasionally, these stories pass the media gatekeepers in New York, Washington, London, and Paris, they tend to reflect the views of the gatekeepers rather than the reality they are supposed to represent.

An end to this cycle of neglect and distortion does not seem to be in sight because the one-sidedness, the imbalance in information flow, between the developed, industrial nations and the developing, Third World nations is likely to continue for some time, leaving the latter on the margins of the political and economic systems of the world. As a result, the relationship between these two spheres of the globe is characterized by inequality, dependency and exploitation.

BIBLIOGRAPHY

A. Books

Altschull, J. Herbert. 1984. *Agents of Power: The Role of News Media in Human Affairs.* New York: Longman.

Arno, Andrew and Wimal Dissanayake (eds.). 1984. *The News Media in National and International Conflict.* Boulder, CO: Westview Press.

Artis, William Jr. 1970. "Tribal Fixation," in *Columbia Journalism Review,* fall 1970, pp. 48–49.

Auer, Bernhard M. 1964. "Letters from the Publisher," in *Time*, December 4, 1964, p. 19.

Bloomfield, Richard J. 1988. *Regional Conflict and U.S. Policy: Angola and Mozambique.* Algonac, MI.: Reference Publications, Inc.

Cliffe, Lionel; Davidson, Basil. 1988. *The Long Struggle of Eritrea for Independence and Constructive Peace.* Trenton, NJ: The Red Sea Press, Inc.

Cohen, Bernard C. 1963. *The Press and Foreign Policy.* Westport, CT: Greenwood Press.

Cook, Timothy. 1997. *Governing with the News: The News Media as a Political Institution.* Chicago: The University of Chicago Press.

Disraeli, Benjamin. Speech, House of Commons, March 26, 1855, in Dictionary of Quotable Definitions, 1970, s.v. "News."

Dorman, William; and Mansour Farhang. 1987. *The U.S. Press and Iran: Foreign Policy and the Journalism of Deference.* Berkeley: University of California Press.

Duignan, Peter; and L.H. Gann. 1984. *The United States and Africa: A History.* Stanford, CA: Hoover Institution Press.

Finney, John. 1975. "U.S. Teams Train Forces in 34 Lands," *The New York Times*, February 20, 1975.

Friedman, Thomas L. 2000. *The Lexus and the Olive Tree.* New York: Random House.

Gandy, O. 1982. *Beyond Agenda-Setting: Information Subsidies and Public Policy.* Norwood, NJ: Ablex.

Gans, Herbert J. 1980. *Deciding What Is News: Study of CBS Evening News, NBC Nightly News,* Newsweek *and* Time. New York: Vintage Books.

Hawk, Beverly G. (ed.). 1992. *Africa's Media Image.* New York: Praeger.

Heise, Juergen Arthur. (1979). *Minimum Disclosure: How the Pentagon Manipulates the News.* New York: W.W. Norton & Company.

Iyengar, Shanto; and Donald Kinder. 1987. *News That Matters.* Chicago: University of Chicago Press.

Jackson, Henry F. 1982. *From the Congo to Soweto: U.S. Foreign Policy Toward Africa Since 1960.* New York: William Morrow and Company.

Kamara, Musa. 1996. "Western Free Flow of Information Doctrine in a Borderless World Threaten Developing Nations' Cultures and National Identities," in *African Communication,* Spring 1996, Vol. 1, No. 1, pp. 42-54. Bowie State University, Bowie, MD 20715.

Keane, Fergal. 1995. "Spiritual Damage," in *Guardian,* October 27, 1995, T4.

Kennedy, Paul. 2000. "Preparing for the 21st Century," in *Globalization and the Challenges of a New Century: A Reader,* by Patrice O'Meara, Harold D. Mehlinger, and Mathew Krain (eds.). Bloomington: Indiana University Press.

Jakobsen, Peter Viggo. 2000. "Focus on CNN EFFECT Misses the Point: The Real Media Impact on Conflict Management Is Invisible and Indirect," in *Journal of Peace Research,* March 2000 v37, i2, p. 131 (13).

Linsky, Martin, Jonathan Moore, Wendy O'Donnell and David Whitman. 1987. *How the Press Affects Federal Policymaking.* New York: W.W. Norton and Company.

MacArthur, John R. l993. *Second Front: Censorship and Propaganda in the Gulf War.* Berkeley: University of California Press.

MacKuen, M.J.; and S. L. Coombs. 1981. *More Than News.* Beverly Hills, CA.: Sage Publications.

McLuhan, M. 1964. *Understanding Media: The Extensions of Man.* New York: McGraw-Hill.

McPhail, T. L. 1987. *Electronic Colonialism: The Future of International Broadcasting and Communication.* (2nd ed., rev.). Beverly Hills, CA: Sage.

Merrill, John. 1983. *Global Journalism.* New York: Longman.

Moeller, Susan. 1999. *Compassion Fatigue.* New York: Routledge.

Mowlana, Hamid. 1986. *Global Information and World Communication: New Frontiers in International Relations.* New York: Longman.

Nielson, Waldemar A. 1969. *The Great Powers and Africa.* New York: Praeger.

Ogene, F. Chidozie. 1983. *Interest Groups and the Shaping of Foreign Policy.* New York: St. Martin's Press.

O'Heffernan, Patrick. 1991. *Mass Media and American Foreign Policy: Insider Perspectives on Global Journalism and the Foreign Policy Process.* Norwood, NJ: Ablex Publishing Corporation.

Paletz, David L.; and Robert M. Entman. 1981. *Media Power Politics.* New York: The Free Press.

Pew Research Center. 2002. "Public's News Habits Little Changes by September 11," at http://people-press.org

Reston, James. 1979. *The Artillery of the Press: Its Influence on American Foreign Policy.* New York: Harper & Row, Publishers.

Rivers, William L. 1970. *The Adversaries: Politics and the Press.* Boston: Beacon Press.

Rystrom, Kenneth. 1983. *The Why, Who and How of the Editorial Page.* New York: Random House.

Switzer, Les. 1985. *Media and Dependency in South Africa.* Athens, OH: Ohio University Center for International Studies.

"The Congo Massacre," in *Time,* December 4, 1964, pp. 28–32.

Ungar, Sanford J. 1978. *Africa: The People and Politics of an Emerging Continent.* New York: Simon and Schuster.

Vance, Cyrus. 1983. *Hard Choices: Critical Years in America's Foreign Policy.* New York: Simon and Schuster.

Van Belle, Douglas A. 2000. *Press Freedom and Global Politics.* Westport, CT: Praeger

B. Documents and Newspapers

The New York Times. Editorials.

   1977. 27 February; 15 March; 15 April; 17 and 23 May; 21 August; 15, 23 September; 3, 11, 13, 14, 19, 23, 27 and 29 October; 5 November; 2, 3, 6, 14, 23 and 30 December.

   1978. 5 and 19 January; 3 and 15 February; 10 March; 25, 22 and 25 April; 12 and 14 July; 19 November; 5 December.

   1980. 21 May; 20 June; 16 December.

   1981. 28 January; 22 and 25 March; 8 July; 3 September; 12 December.

   1982. 4 February; 24 May; 19 September; 3 and 20 October.

   1983. 26 May; 14 June; 25 June; 19 July; 11 September; 5 November.

   1984. 2 March; 1 June; 2 September; 18 November; 1 December.

United Nations General Assembly Resolution 390 (V), Dec. 2, 1950.
_____.289-A(IV), Nov. 21, 1949.

United Nations, General Assembly. (VII). *Final Report of the U.N. Commissioner to Eritrea.* (General Assembly Records, 15A/2188, 1952.)

United States Department of State Bulletin, No. 550, Jan. 16, 1950.
_____. No. 560, March 27, 1950.
_____. No.576, July 1950.
_____. No. 577, July 24, 1950.
_____. No. 594, Nov. 20. 1950.

U.S. Department of State Bulletin. Vols. 79 to 84, No. 2094, January 1977-December 1984 inclusive.

The Washington Post. Editorials.

1976. 13 June, 11 November.

1977. 5 and 14 March; 25 April; 8 May; 9 and 20 June; 12 July; 15 and 24 August; 15 September; 21, 26 and 29 October; 1 November; 2, 4, 8 December.

1978. 13 and 31 January; 2 February; 1, 3 11 March; 12 April; 4 May; 22 September.

1979. 14 and 31 March; 15 April; 2 and 27 May; 17 June and 27 October.

1980. 18 March; 5 June.

1981. 22 March; 14 April; 6 July; 18 August; 6 and 16 September; 2 November.

1983. 10 and 17 March; 27 June; 18 July; 13 and 29 October.

1984. 31 January; 13 March; 8 October; 2, 23, 27 and 29 November; 4, 9, 14, 16, 18 and 31 December.

C. Essays and Articles in Edited Books or Collections

Bagdikian, Ben H. 1989. "The Lords of the Village," in *The Nation,* June 12, 1989, pp. 805–820.

Bering-Jensen, Henrik. 1992. "African in the Balance," in *Insight,* August 9, 1992, pp. 6–26.

Bray, Charles W. 1974. "The Media and Foreign Policy," in *Foreign Policy,* 16, fall 1974, pp. 109–126.

Cutler, Lloyd. 1984. "Foreign Policy on Deadline," in *Foreign Policy,* 56, fall 1984, 113–128.

Emerson, Rupert. 1958. "The Character of American Interests in Africa," in *The United States and Africa.* New York: The American Assembly, Columbia University.

Galtung, Johan; and Mari H. Ruge. 1965. "The Structure of Foreign News," in *Journal of Peace Research,* Vol.1, No. 65.

Harwood, Richard. 1974. "Did Newspapers Muff the Job of Informing on Vietnam?" in *Of the Press, By the Press, For the Press, and Others, Too,* by Laura Longley Babb. Boston: Houghton Mifflin, pp. 79–81.

James, C.L.R. 1971. "Colonialism and National Liberation in Africa," in *National Liberation,* Vol. 8, No. 3, pp. 102–136.

Larson, J.F. 1986. "Television and U.S. Foreign Policy: The Case of the Iran Hostage Crisis," in *Journal of Communications,* 36(4), 108–130.

Mandela, Nelson. 1982. "Why We Had to Act," in *The African Liberation Reader, Vol. 2,* pp. 37–40.

McCombs, Maxwell; and Donald Shaw. 1972. "The Agenda-Setting Function of the Media," in *Public Opinion Quarterly,* No. 36 (Summer, pp. 176–187).

Mowlana, Hamid. 1984. "The Role of the Media in the U.S. Iranian conflict," in *The News Media in National and International Conflict,* by Andrew Arno & Wimal Dissanayake (eds.). Boulder, CO: Westview Press, pp.71–100.

Noble, Gil. 1974. "Who Controls Media Information?" in *Freedomways,* Fourth Quarter, 1974, pp. 317–319.

Payne, William. 1966. "Press Coverage of Africa," in *Africa Report,* January, 1966, pp. 44–48.

Peterson, S. 1980. "International News Selection by the Elite Press: A Case Study," in *Public Opinion Quarterly,* 45, pp. 143–63.

Rothchild, Donald. 1988. "Africa's Ethnic Conflicts and Their Implications for United States Policy," in *Africa: In the 1990s and Beyond,* by Robert I. Rotberg (ed.). Algona, MI: Reference Publications,Inc.

Sharkey, Jacqueline. 1993. "When Pictures Drive Foreign Policy," in *American Journalism Review,* December 1993, pp. 14–19.

Staniland, Martin. 1983–84. "Africa, the American Intelligentsia, and the Shadow of Vietnam," in *Political Science Quarterly,* Vol. 98, Nov. 4, Winter 1983–84, pp. 595–616.

Stokke, O. 1971. "The Mass Media in Africa and Africa in the International Mass Media," in *Reporting Africa.* Uppsala, Sweden: Scandinavian Institute of Africa Studies.

Wriston, Walter B. 1988. "Technology and Sovereignty," in *Foreign Affairs,* Vol. 67, No. 2, 67–75.

D. Unpublished Materials

Brown, William J. 1988. "U.S. Foreign Policy with Iran: Portrayals by American Newspapers and the Tower Commission Report." Presented at the International Communications Association's 38th Conference, New Orleans, May 31, 1988.

Malek, Abbas. 1989. "News Media and U.S. Foreign Policy: The Case of the Chemical Warfare in the Persian Gulf." Paper presented at the Third Annual Colloquium on Communications and Culture, Dubrovnik, Yugoslavia, Sept. 22–27, 1989.

Theorizing Women's Access to Power in the Global State:
Interplay of Gender and Class

Ifeyinwa E. Umerah-Udezulu

The purpose of this chapter is to develop an alternative interpretation of how women in the global system have managed to emerge and fare as political leaders. It starts by evaluating the various feminist perspectives in the literature, reviews the numbers of women who have officiated over the highest echelons of national decision-making, and presents the experiences of four women government leaders of the Third World. 1966 to 2002 saw an unprecedented number of women governing their countries. A total of 50 women have acted in one capacity or the other as the heads of their national governments. While some women presided as presidents, others fared as prime ministers (Table 1).

In explicating the state, two major frameworks, the Marxist and classical (realist) approaches, prevail. For Marxist analysis, conflict is the basis of explaining the global state system. The state is seen as an instrument of the ruling class, which monopolizes the power structure at the expense of the proletarian majority whose labor power sustains the society. The workers are exploited through the use of their labor to such an extent that they become destitute, while the elite or the capitalists get richer. Therefore, the gap between the worker and the owner regarding the means of production (land, labor, and capital) keeps widening to such an extent that the frustrated and exploited workers revolt to establish a stateless society. The opposing viewpoint, the classical view, holds that states as the unit level of analysis are rational egoists. The state is self-centered and altruistic at the same time. Although the state is neutral, it acts to protect its national interests as it mediates among divergent interests in the world system.

The theoretical inadequacies in these two major frameworks lie in the fact that gender is not seen as central to the state and is ignored by state-centered authors.

The prevalent discourses are androcentric. One cannot successfully evaluate the state without taking into account the majority of the states' population, who are women. Women as a group in the contemporary global system comprise nearly 50% of the world's population. According to the United Nations, even though women surpass men in most regions, men exceed women in parts of Asia. The ratio of women to men is 99 to 100 depending on regional reference. In light of their numerical strength, women's place in the system should be addressed and cannot be reduced merely to interests and classes. The presence of women in the state system includes these dimensions of interest and class, but also exceeds them, embracing gender and ethnic differences in the society. However, conventional analyses hold that only class and interest are vital to state power.

FEMINIST THEORIES OF THE STATE
AND WOMEN IN GENERAL

For many years there have been demands for a change in the way that state-centered theorists explain the state. People subscribing to the women-centered ideas argued that gender issues be included in the debate. For instance, Theda Skocpol has called for "paradigmatic reorientation"[1] to address the fundamental problems existing in the state system, as modern scholars investigate the social, political and economic facets of the global state. Such concerns should explore how the state excludes women in all these sectors and how these problems should be resolved.

Nancy Fraser's interpretation of the welfare state sheds more light on the inadequacies of the dominant theories of the state. She argues that power, as elucidated by power and class theorists, is deeply rooted in the citizens who are part of the diverse state institutions: economic, social and political.[2] She contends that the study of citizenship explains power distribution in the state system, and whichever group possesses economic, social, and political power controls the state. According to Fraser, such power is concentrated in the hands of males. Therefore, the state's power is male power. Women as a group are not positioned equally with men. The state is structured into two spheres, the private and public. These sectors are intertwined and dependent on each other, and male supremacy is apparent in both. The male is the head of household, the "statesman," and also chief executive of diverse international political and economic organizations, including the United Nations, World Bank, International Monetary Fund, North Atlantic Treaty Organization, and the Organization of Petroleum Exporting Nations. Women are not positioned in the state as are men in terms of access to power structures. As a matter of fact, the contribution of women is devalued at the state level. Gender is central, therefore, in analyzing the global state, especially the minimal engagement of women. Again, the state cannot merely be reduced to class and interests as have been argued by Marxist and realist scholars.

Therefore, it is the duty of the women-centered theorists to eliminate bias in political philosophy and in conventional discourse. Alison Jaggar notes that there are many voices of women, and they have disparate policy prescriptions as to how the state relates to women.[3] The most significant articulations are their views on human nature, or on the nature of social order, and the nature of inequality (factors perpetuating sex inequality). Of importance, too, are their variant assessments of the good society, strategies for actualizing that goal, and finally, their prescriptions for sex role changes.[4] According to Jaggar, three major schools have emerged—liberal, radical, and socialist feminism—and are summed up below. Jaggar omitted the womanist standpoint—which is also discussed.

For the liberal feminist tradition, the state is perceived a neutral arbiter. This group of scholars is satisfied with the status quo and therefore desires to enhance women's situation by lobbying for laws that would protect women's interests. Instead of arguing for a complete transformation of the existing political system, the liberal feminists see their solution in a political process in which the federal government would increase its role in integrating women into the state system.[5] Their task is to extend to women the democratic political values of liberty, equality, autonomy, self-fulfillment and justice.[6] While the liberal feminists desire to use laws to resolve gender-based discrimination, they do not view the oppression of women as a structural feature of the capitalist system. Women's freedom, according to this school, would be brought about by the state itself, as limited legal reforms are directed at upgrading women's status.

Radical feminism, as the name suggests, adopts a different approach to settle the lack of integration of women into the system. The radicals argue that the operation of the capitalist system makes it impossible for the genuine establishment of liberal political values and allows only partial alterations. This ideology contends that capitalism supports values of individual competition which are inconsistent with the feminist values of interdependence and nurturance. The basic assumption of radical feminism is rooted in the liberal belief that sex roles stem from individual freedom of choice. Individuals possess the power to actualize themselves apart from societal conscription.[7]

Some radical feminist theorists believe that sexual division of labor is deeply rooted in biology. Women are perceived as essentially inferior to men due to their reproductive capacity, and women and children must depend on their male heads of households for survival. Furthermore, they argue that men's economic power gives them control of the state and allows them to use it to perpetuate the subordination of women in the society as a whole. The state is perceived as the instrument of patriarchy and, therefore, cannot safeguard women's interests. The election of a few women to policy-making positions does not negate this problem, as men still retain economic and political power.

Because women are depicted as being under sexual slavery, and as being forced into motherhood, and because men are seen as having control over women's bodies, women's liberation can be accomplished only by separate and autonomous women's organizations. Women as a class must unite to overhaul the status quo.[8] This analysis calls for the revolutionary demise of the existing order, and the establishment of a gender-free society.

Even though there is agreement on the need to restructure the state by various women-centered writers, the means of actualizing that objective differ. The radical reinstatement of the status quo promotes disorder, a deviation which has constantly plagued humankind for many generations. However, the change of consciousness fosters avenues for stable relations between genders in the state system. This is where socialist feminism comes into play. This framework purports an alternative means other than violent demise of the existing system.

Emerging in the 1970s, socialist feminism is still a developing perspective. It has as its basic objective the development of an eclectic political theory capable of synthesizing the most substantial contributions of radical feminism and traditional Marxism. Jaggar argues that this framework holds the prospect of establishing a unique advancement of political theory and practice for women's emancipation.[9] Like the radical feminists, the socialist counterparts address issues as varied as sexuality, and reproduction (mothering); however, the socialist feminists elucidate the traditional Marxist historical materialist approach in a mode that pertains to the insights of radical feminism. For instance, traditional Marxism posits that the struggle for feminism strongly corresponds to class conflict.[10] Radical feminism asserts that women's liberation must be primary to any other type of justice in the system. Socialist feminism disagrees. Nonetheless, it does not purport to substitute socialism for feminism, or vice versa. Rather, it juxtaposes these issues. For example, these writers see capitalism, male dominance, racism and imperialism as interchangeable. Any effort to address an aspect of this problem is incomplete unless such an attempt seeks to eradicate all forms of oppression in the system.

In addition, they acknowledge diversity by sex, age, class, nationality, racial and ethnic origins not only as part of modern-day phenomena, but as deeply intertwined with historical materialism. This concept, according to socialist feminist theory, depicts the dialectic relationship between sex and society which is gender based. Gender is socially derived.

The state, according to socialist feminism, is not a neutral arbiter between conflicting forces, but rather the condensation of a balance of forces. The strongest of these is male dominance. They recognize that the differences between women and men are not pre-socially conferred, but are socially fabricated and therefore socially modifiable. The abolition of capitalism and male dominance must be precursory to the attainment of freedom and equality in the state system. For instance, abolish capitalism and male dominance, and one creates an equitable society. They argue that the absence of women in the state's executive positions is a perfect example of alienation. They, therefore call for a society where all the members are able to freely and fully participate in every aspects of the state's apparatus. The socialist feminist framework seeks a society where masculinity and femininity no longer exist.

The vitality of this theory is in raising questions for other political traditions[11], which fully attracts attention. It calls for an ultimate democracy, a process in which all peoples' needs will be equitably addressed, and seeks a society where people can integrate their capacities for intellectual and hand-operated labor, for work, for sexuality, for art and for play, until those categories no longer describe and separate human activities. The weakness of this perspective stems from its failure to state exactly how the valid democratic procedures can be initiated to abolish all social ills including age-related prejudice, racism, sexism, socialism, capitalism and other forms of bias.[12]

The womanist theory is utilized by African-American scholars to evaluate the level of integration of men and women into the state system. They trace the root of racial and gender-based discrimination against the people of African descent back to the imperialist and colonial periods. They argue that the global state in those periods was exploitative and oppressive. Imperialist needs resulted in the trans-atlantic slavery that sapped Africa of millions of its precious human resources. Colonialism promoted the interests of the imperial powers to the detriment of Africa. The abolition of slavery produced millions of Africans in the diaspora who were oppressed and discriminated against. The struggles for integration manifested in the Civil Rights Movement did enhance the status of the minority group but in a limited form. Unlike the radical school, which calls for a complete overhaul of the state system, the womanists rely on the state apparatus to address change in relation to both black women and men, including women and members of minorities in general. The major difference between the womanist school and the other theories is that the former places strong emphasis on liberation of both black men and women and members of minorities being discriminated against under the state system. It also addresses the class distinction between women and men on the basis of racial distinction which had fueled oppression in the system.

Global feminism, even though at a developmental stage, acknowledges the fact that women are less viable actors on the global arena in the 20th and 21st centuries. It recognizes the part women have played as monarchs prior to the 20th century and puts emphasis on empowerment of women cross-culturally and the enabling of women to become highly integrated into the global system. It recognizes the fact that most state positions are occupied predominantly by men, and advocates the enhancement of the status of women through education and policy change.

The major difference is that all of these feminisms diverge as to the extent of women's alienation and how the state could better address their concerns. Nonetheless, there is a consensus among them that women's interests are not fairly articulated in the state system. They argue that sexism in the state system creates a kind of dualism where the elites are blinded by gender differentiation. The state is divided into two hierarchical spheres, the private and public. In the private sector, the male is the traditional head of the household and the female is the child bearer and rearer. In the public sphere, which includes the economic, social, and political, there is a tendency towards capitalist orientation and encouragement of individual competition at the expense of the less competitive group. In this carefully structured order, the male is the political and economic elite. This analysis is classified as the dialectical sex ordering, another terminology for capitalist patriarchy. Therefore, the workplace and the home are hierarchical and both re-enforce each other.

According to a United Nations report, women rarely account for 1 or 2 percent of senior management positions in the economic sector. The report stated that it will take a century of hard work and serious planning before women are fully integrated in the system.[13] Also, even if women represent nearly 50 percent of the global population, one-third of them are in paid labor force, and women receive only one-tenth of the world's total income, and own less than 1 percent of the world's resources.

On the other hand, men dominate the work force and the political arena. Men are better paid than women and, as some women are unemployed, women are described as the army of reserved labor. In any case where women are employed, they are found in the lowest rank of the labor pool. In a nutshell, the feminist theory of the state argues that the state is gendered. The female constitutes a separate class from the male. The female is the proletariat, whereas the male is the elite[14]. In the private sphere, as well as the public, the male, who is also the traditional head of household, is also head of a country, the secretary general of the United Nations, chairman of North Atlantic Treaty Organization, World Bank, the Organization of Oil Producing Countries, North American Free Trade Association, Asian Pacific Economic Organization, etc. Therefore, men dominate all the hierarchical structures of the state system both at the domestic and international levels.

Generally, in feminist thought, the concept of capitalist patriarchy is most frequently employed to denote a structure of masculine domination or a sexual system of power.[15] Even though their conclusions may differ, there seems to be a consensus among feminist theorists that the contemporary state system, whether socialist, traditional, or classist, is patriarchal.[16] Carole Pateman argues that the concept of "patriarchy" best "captures the specificities of the subjection and oppression of women, and distinguishes this form from other forms of dominations."[17] Such a concept has to be retained in any political philosophy of women; moreover, it addresses the problem of sexual domination in the state system, whereas the individualist and class theorists fail to address such issues. The contemporary liberal state system has evolved from the traditional to the modern, a progression which Carole Pateman has summarized as a transformation from a paternal version of patriarchy to a new, specifically modern or fraternal form, which she calls "patriarchal civil society."[18] The state at the primitive stage was patriarchal. With the onset of the industrial revolution, the state progressed from a simple to a more complex mode of political economy, still maintaining the patriarchal configuration. According to this view, the contemporary era is depicted by high technology and advanced capitalism. The state, as the arbiter, has not yet significantly altered its patriarchal structure. The actors in the state's arena are largely male.

While Pateman focuses on modern liberal civil society as a contract among men, Zillah Eisenstein argues that the contemporary liberal state system can best be classified as capitalist patriarchy on the basis of its transformation from feudal to capitalist modes of production.[19] Her analytical focus centers on changes undergone by America and England in the mid-19th and 18th centuries, respectively. Eisenstein contends that these eras mirrored the interchange and metamorphosis of patriarchy and industrial capitalism: the modes of production developed from a single farm-unit system to large-scale agriculture, and advanced to the complex industrial system. The current system, even if it appears to have division between public and private spheres, is actually a conglomeration of families and their modes of production and the politics emanating from such interactions. According to Eisenstein, patriarchy denotes a pattern of social interaction closely linked to hierarchical relations between men and women. This occurs in such a fashion that men benefit more than women in the system. Women are workers and reproducers. They sustain the system. Women are controlled at home and at work by men. In this sense, patriarchy is a system of male oppression of women. It is a system in which men control the labor of women and children in the family.

In addition, under capitalism, men extend the patriarchal techniques of hierarchical organization and control learned from the family structure to the economic sphere. This is manifested in the hierarchical sexual ordering in the work force: men dominate numerically in the work force and are better paid than women. As some women are unemployed or underemployed, they are viewed as the army of reserve labor, and are found in the lowest rank of the labor pool. Commitment to patriarchal structures, the hierarchical relation of the workplace, and capitalism also infiltrate the home on the most intimate levels. The domains of family and market structure each other, and subsequently filter through the political process. Because men are the prevalent actors in these sectors, modern states uphold this type of sex-order division of labor and wage labor system in the nature of prevailing social, political and economic institutions. Therefore, capitalist patriarchy does describe this politico-economic gender ordering.

The concept of capitalist patriarchy, according to Eisenstein, supersedes the "division of class, sex, private and public spheres, domestic and wage labor, family and economy, personal and political, and ideology and material conditions."[20] The woman is both a worker and mother, producer and reproducer. Capitalist patriarchy emphasizes the mutually reinforcing, dialectical relationship between capitalist class structures and hierarchical sexual structuring.[21] Women constitute a separate class from the men. The woman is the proletariat, whereas the man is the elite. Understanding the interdependence of capitalism and patriarchy, therefore, is essential in feminist political analysis. The family and the state are interrelated; one cannot separate the two. Each reinforces the other, but in both sectors, male power is supreme.

Sandra Goldberg argues that capitalist patriarchy is universal if one defines the concept to mean any system of organization—political, economic, industrial, financial, religious or social—in which the overwhelming number of top positions in the hierarchy is occupied by males.[22] If we adhere to Nancy Fraser's critique of the welfare state, she argues that capitalist patriarchy depicts an elaborate network at the state's disposal, whereby citizens are subjects positioned as economic and political agents competing against one another. The consequence is one group (men) dominating the other (women). Women in this case become citizens with limited rights.[23] The state in this regard has the responsibility to preserve life. The services provided by the state are supposed to reflect the interests of all its citizens, but women and men as citizens do not receive equal shares of the state's resources. Rather, women are expected to become passive laborers and to be submissive, while men are active participants. Women, thus, have no political base because of the nature of the state systems.

The socialist feminist perspective provides the most logical hypothesis to explain the relationship between the global state and the women, and how, despite the apparent contradictions, a few women have managed to make headway as policy initiators in the Third World. Insights on the problematic of gender and class on political behavior highlight the minimal participation of women as national leaders.

In gaining an understanding of these gender differences, women can change their consciousness of themselves, as well as their positions in the state system.

WOMEN AS NATIONAL LEADERS

While family affiliations have played a significant role for women to emerge as national leaders, especially in the developing economies, class distinctions are also crucial for emergence of women as national decision-makers in the advanced industrial economies. The system of government, especially democracy and monarchy, are the two political systems where women seem to stand a better chance as political leaders. Democratic regimes are the most likely environment for women to emerge as rulers because the masses have more access to the decision-making arena.

Although the numbers are on the increase, about 54 women have emerged as political leaders in the world. Table 1 shows countries of the Global South (encompassing Asia, Latin America and Africa) where women have presided, in no particular order of significance: Bangladesh's Khalida Zia (Mohammed Zia-ul-Haq's widow); Sri Lanka's Sirimavo Bandaranaike (Solomon Diaz Bandaranaike's widow); Chandrika Kumaratunga (Solomon Diaz Bandaranaike's daughter and Mr. Kumaratunga's widow)[24]; Pakistan's Benazir Bhutto (Ali Bhutto's daughter); the Philippines' Corazon Aquino (Benigno Aquino's widow), and Gloria Arroyo; Violeta Dona Barrios de Chamorro (Pedro Joaquin Chamorro's widow) in Nicaragua; Eugenia Mary Charles in Dominica; Haiti's Ertha Pascal Trouillot and Claudette Werleigh; Isabel Peron of Argentina (the wife of President Peron); Bolivia's Lidia Gueiler Tejada; China's Soong Ching-Ling, Burma's Aung San Suukyi, Netherlands Antilles' Maria Liberia-Peters and Susanne Camelia-Romer, Burundi's Sylvie Kinigi; Indira Gandhi (Jawaharlal Nehru's daughter) in India; Golda Meir of Israel; Tamsu Ciller of Turkey; Ruth Perry of Liberia, Janet Jagan of Guyana, Mireya Moscoso of Panama, Sheikh Hasina Wajed in Bangladesh, Elizabeth Domitien of Central African Republic, Senegal's Mame Madior Boye, Pamela Gordon and Jenny Smith of Bermuda, Mongolia's Nyam-Osoriyn Tuyaa, Megawati Sukarnoputri of Indonesia, and Agathe Uwilingivi Mana of Rwanda.[25]

While the Global South has had about 35 women leaders, about 19 women have also risen as heads of governments in the Global North including Australia, Europe and North America (Table 2). The presidents are as follows: Tarja Kaarina Halonen of Finland, Sabine Bergmann-Pohl of Germany, Vigdis Finnbogadottir of Iceland, Mary Robinson and Mary McAleese of Ireland, Vaira Vike-Freiberga from Latvia, and Switzerland's Ruth Dreifuss. The prime ministers include the United Kingdom's Margaret Thatcher, Portugal's Maria de Lourdes Pintasilgo, Hanna Suchocka of Poland, Gro Harlem-Brundtland of Norway, Milka Planinc of the former Yugoslavia, New Zealand's Helen Clark and Jenny Shipley, Malta's Agatha Barbara, Lithuania's Kazimiera Prunskiene, Edith Cresson of France, Kim Campbell of Canada and Reneta Indzhova of Bulgaria.

The relatively small numbers of women in executive positions are borne out by the data. For instance, in 1969, there were only four women in cabinet-level positions in the whole of Latin America. In March 1986, the president of Peru had no women in the cabinet. But 1995 ushered in a new era for Peru when 5 percent of members of Congress were women. Then, three women occupied important positions in Peru's Parliament with one of them becoming the president of Congress. Still, the number of female participants remains significantly small compared to the number of women in the country. To illustrate this point further, data from other parts of Latin America support our claim. President Sarney's Brazilian cabinet in February 1986 was exclusively male. Colombia and Chile successfully elected only two women, both serving as ministers of education.[26] In 1993, there was only one woman in the Chilean government, heading the Department of Women's Affairs.[27] In 1994, Guatemala nominated 19 women ministers and Honduras 11. For the Caribbean region in 1994, Bahamas had 23 female ministers, Dominica 9, Guyana 12,Trinidad and Tobago 19, and Jamaica 5.

In Africa, women constitute about 4 percent of national cabinet or equivalent posts.[28] Seychelles made history in 1994 when 31 women were nominated into the nation's cabinet offices. In the same year, the Central African Republic had 5 women ministers; Guinea Bissau had 4; Lesotho, 6; Niger, 5, Zimbabwe, 3; Seychelles, 27; Swaziland, 20, and South Africa, 25.[29] Over half of African states in 1994 had no women in the cabinet. Some of these included Libya, Morocco, Somalia, Sudan, and Comoros. Sylvie Kinigi and Agathe Uwilingiyimana made history in 1993 when they became the interim prime minsters of their respective countries, Burundi and Rwanda. (Table 5).

As Table 4 suggests, the situation is not different in Asia, where women have made slight progress towards occupying state positions. In 1994, women held less than 2 percent of the cabinet posts in the region. For example, Eastern Asia had 0.6 percent of women in chief executive positions; South-eastern Asia, 1.9; Central Asia, 0.0; Southern Asia, 5.7; Western Asia, 0.7; Oceania, 8.8.[30] China had 21 percent women's parliamentary representation; and Korea Democratic Republic, 20 percent. Women's representation at the highest levels of government was generally weakest when women presided as heads of governments. For instance, apart from Mrs. Gandhi, India had only one woman minister between 1952 and 1975. It was reported that eleven others were ministers in the union government and two were chief ministers in the state government.[31] During her first stint in government, only one woman was elected into Mrs. Gandhi's cabinet. However, women did not preside over the cabinet in Mrs. Gandhi's 1980 appointments. When Rajiv Gandhi succeeded his mother following her assassination in 1984, he nominated only Mrs. Moshina Kidwa in his 14-member cabinet. He later included two other women as cabinet members. According to Kearney, there were only four women ministers in Mrs. Bandaranaike's regime.[32]

The experiences of four women leaders in the Third World suggest an exception. These leaders are found in South Asia and Latin America: the Philippines, India, Pakistan and Nicaragua.[33] The four countries provide examples of different forms of political development, ranging from the open and democratic (but not entirely perfect) systems of India, the frequently authoritarian governments of Pakistan; to the democratizing systems in the Philippines and Nicaragua.

Mrs. Gandhi and Benazir Bhutto exemplify rare circumstances where daughters led their nations due to the loss of their fathers. Moreover, Benazir Bhutto was chosen due to her long involvement in Pakistan's political process and the resultant regime change following the death of her political enemy General Zia. Her emergence marked the first time, in the modern period, a woman had led a predominantly Moslem nation.

Aquino's unprecedented ascendance pointed to the Filipinos' frustration with the ills of Ferdinand Marcos' regime, highlighted by the murder of Benigno Aquino. It also revealed the extent of the Catholic Church's influence in the country. Chamorro's rise in Nicaragua, in Central America, is similar to that of Mrs. Aquino in the Philippines in the sense that both came to power as a result of the death of their husbands, neither of whom were heads of state or government. Nicaragua is crucial to this study due to Mrs. Chamorro's commitment to the formerly war-torn Nicaragua, and the role she played to bring democracy to the nation. As did Aquino's, Chamorro's emergence brought an end to an authoritarian leadership, and paved the way for the nation's transition to democracy.

One factor which characterizes the rise to power of these four leaders, as we see, is that their paths to national leadership were greased by family ties. Family affiliations have become of importance for women governing in the developing countries. A woman's status in the society is defined basically by the status of her male kin (father, husband, and brother). It is chiefly on this basis that women become politically involved or uninvolved at the national level. Hence, the hierarchical economic ordering simultaneously trickles down into the sexual political differentiation. The woman with a prominent male kin automatically belongs to a higher political class than a woman whose male kin belongs to a lower economic and political class; therefore, women with prominent male kin are not positioned equally with the majority of women who are at the bottom of the political ladder. Class differences between women in general and women possessing "superior family" backgrounds (who, due to their family names have emerged as heads of governments) further complicate gender/class analysis.

For instance, Fatton insists that "women have a contradictory insertion into the social structure. While women as a group suffer from the effects of patriarchy, they do not experience equally the ravages of class domination."[34] Their status in terms of class affiliation is accorded in terms of patriarchal relation to the means of production. This is to say that special material and social circumstances surrounding women's classification in the state system are to a greater extent influenced by women's family backgrounds.[35] Class division in the state system originates from the exploitative relationship between the owners of the means of production and the workers. Such a relationship structures male wage labor, which consequently affects social ordering in terms of power structures and, of course, class and gender divisions. The capitalist class or the elite group acquires resources, power and privilege in the society. Their status is passed down to their kin. Generally, women as part of the capitalist patriarchy acquire the socioeconomic status of their fathers, husbands or brothers.[36]

There are, however, ones who have achieved a different socio-economic status other than that inherited from their kin but this number has remained marginal. The Benazir Bhuttos, Corazon Aquinos, Indira Gandhis, and Violeta Chamorros typically adopted their male kin political legacies. Hence, the hierarchical political gender-based ordering. Therefore, just as there are class differentiation between men and women, there is a class distinction among women on the basis of economic and political success of their male relative. This kind of insertion further complicates gender analysis. Women's family backgrounds influence their economic and political classes, in terms of gender differences which enlist them to a separate class from their male kin and men in general. It is on the grounds of the contradiction that some women emerge as policymakers in the Third World.

Benazir Bhutto's father, Ali Bhutto, was the former prime minister of Pakistan. Her father's position in the political system enhanced her chances of participating in politics of that country, a predominant Islamic nation. During her campaign for election, after Ali Bhutto's brutal assassination, Benazir Bhutto constantly identified herself as the daughter of the martyr Shah Nawaz Khan Bhutto, and "I am your sister as well." When she was alienated from the country's politics during her first leadership, her campaign slogan read, "surrounded by conspiracies, is she not the daughter of Asia?" During her second attempt to govern Pakistan, her mother asked her to step down for her brother, a decision which was gender-based.

Corazon Aquino's husband, Benigno Aquino, was a popular senator and a presidential hopeful when he was brutally assassinated under President Marcos' leadership. This sudden death enlisted Aquino into politics and this factor in conjunction with gender, plus a number of other factors, paved the way for her leadership.

Jawaharlal Nehru, Indira Gandhi's father, was the prime minister of India, a patriarch who played a crucial role in India's independence drive. When he passed on his daughter was chosen by the syndicates, mainly from the desire to "have a Nehru in office." They also thought that, being a woman, Indira Gandhi would be easily manipulated. But, they were wrong and that caused problems for her.

Finally, Chamorro's husband, Pedro Joaquin Chamorro, was an influential political activist and a newspaper editor who constantly denounced the evils of the Somoza regime. When he was murdered for his political activities, Violeta bore his political mantle as she was voted into power. Part of her charm was her "saintly image," and the fact that she had the backing of the United States government.

These women's class affiliation are different from those of the majority in their countries. Their linkage to the capitalist patriarchy enlists to a different class from women they represent and this linkage immensely contributed to their ascendance and their decline. This claim is substantiated by Eisenstein's analysis of the ruling class. She insists that:

> The ruling class desire to preserve the family reflects its commitment to a division of labor that not only secures it the greatest profit but also hierarchical sex ordering of the society culturally and politically.[37]

Therefore, these women's presence in the political arena in the cases studied help reinforce the patriarchal structure, a structure threatened by instability as a result of these assassinations and national conflict.

According to Keohane, Rosaldo, and Gelpi, capitalist state systems treasure women's contribution according to male criterion, especially when women's presence satisfies the "needs of emergency, women then become men's equal, only to regress when the urgency recedes."[38] In order to stabilize the system due to turmoil precipitated in these states by the sudden departure (assassination) of their fathers or husbands, these women were elected into office to reinforce the interests of the ruling class. While they were in power, the gender difference constantly affected their performance as national leaders. Their presence does not suggest that the state is neutral; rather, it supports the capitalist patriarchal nature of the state.

As long as modern states exclude the interests of women, establishing the feminist standpoint is an epistemic device for reclaiming women's importance in the state system. Women's contributions to the states' structure as mothers and workers would then be acknowledged, not written off. The standpoint emanates from shared experiences and knowledge which are socio-politically derived. Women's roles as reproducers, mothers and wives have been used to justify their treatment as second-class citizens. The gender-based division extends to women's activity in the public sphere. Because of this gap, women emerge late in the political and economic sectors. Due to their late advent in the political and economic spheres, women constitute an exploited class. Women are underpaid, and serve as unpaid homemakers, and they are not fairly represented in the state positions because the political arena is contradictory. Consequently, women's interests are crippled by the state due to its patriarchal environment.

There are structural differences between genders and, as a result, women have been classified as less viable actors. To put it another way, the nature of sexual inequality in the global state system is one where women are poorly represented and their interests overlooked. Further, this palpable neglect lays the groundwork from which women as a group must struggle. The assumption here implies that the material world is structured into two spheres, masculine and feminine, which are essentially conflictual on the basis of an acquired tradition that presumes one gender's domination over another. The preeminence of men fosters the subjugation of women; hence the predetermined practice of hierarchy.

Moreover, the dominant group exploits and subjects the less viable one and imposes its world view on the latter. As a result, there are two perspectives: one, as perceived by the dominant group, which Nancy Hartsock dubs "surface appearance"; and the other, as perceived by the subordinate group, which she calls "deeper essence."[39] The deeper essence reflects the ways in which women work as producers and reproducers and the awareness that emerges from their experience as part of material reality, and their perception of being closely linked to nature. Women have been exploited as workers but are also conscious of their values as women, as well as of the incomplete but prevailing male supremacy; hence the duality which allows a sort of "triangulation."[40]

Triangulation in this context stems from the two world views created by the divergence and allows the development of a third world view, which is what feminists are purporting: the basic task of a feminist standpoint is a systematic uncovering of gender inequality and the rejection of the common masculine assessment of existence as authoritative. It is crucial to recognize this disparity, to call for a united voice among women on the basis of commonality of experience, in order to refute discrimination across class, race and gender. This evolution of woman is highly significant in the state system because it establishes a scale of justice capable of enhancing the system by incorporating the untapped potentials of women when they are granted full opportunity to actively participate as citizens of the state system.

ENDNOTES

[1]Theda Skocpol, "Bringing the State Back In: Strategies for Analysis in Current Research," in P.B. Evans, D. Rueschmeyer and T. Skocpol eds. *Bringing the State Back In* (Cambridge, England: Cambridge University Press, 1985), 3; Kathleen Lyn, "Uncovering the Political Impacts of Gender: An Exploratory Study," *Western Political Quarterly* 42 (1989): 397–42.

[2]Nancy Fraser, "Women, Welfare and Politics of Need Interpretation," *Hypatia* 2 (1986): 102.

[3]Alison M. Jaggar, *Feminism and Human Nature* (New Jersey: Rowman & Littlefield, 1988) 169-303.

[4]These topics comprised the divergent issues as presented by the variant scholars. This chapter only sums up significant points relevant to the discussion.

[5]Anne N. Costain, *Inviting Women's Rebellion* (Maryland: Johns Hopkins University Press, 1993).

[6]Juliet Mitchell, "Women and Equality," *Partisan Review* 42 (1975): 381.

[7]Anne Koedt, Ellen Levine, and Anita Rapone, eds., *Radical Feminism* (New York: Quadrangle Books, 1973); Shulamith Firestone, *The Dialectics of Sex: The Case for Feminist Revolution* (New York: William Morrow, 1970), 9–11 and 206.

[8]Montique Wittig, *Les Gueilleres* (New York: Avon, 1971); Also, *The Lesbian Body* (New York: Avon, 1973).

[9]Alison Jaggar, 123.

[10]Kate Millet, "Sexual Politics: A Manifesto for Revolution," in Anne Koedt, Ellen Levine, and Anita Rapone, eds. *Radical Feminism* (New York: Quadrangle Books, 1973).

[11]Maria Lugones, and E.V. Spelman, "Have We Got a Theory for You! Feminist Theory, Cultural Imperialism and the Woman's Voice," paper presented to the Tenth Anniversary Conference of the Eastern Division of the Society for the Women in Philosophy, Northampton, Massachusetts (October 1982), 7–22.

[12]Alison Jaggar, 344.

[13]United Nations, *The World's Women 1995: Trends and Statistics* (New York: United Nations Publications, 1995), 151.

[14]Christine Delphy, *Closer to Home: A Materialist Analysis of Women's Oppression* (Amherst: University of Massachusetts Press, 1984), 69; Zillah Eisenstein, ed., *Capitalist Patriarchy and the Case for Socialist Feminism and Political Theory* (Stanford, CA: Stanford University Press, 1989), 378.

[15]Sheila Rowbotham, *Dreams and Dilemmas* (London: Virago Press, 1983), 208-9; Lisa Disch, "Toward a Feminist Conception of Politics," *Political Science and Politics* 24 (1991): 501–04.

16Cheris Kramarae and Paula A. Treichler, *A Feminist Dictionary* (Boston: Pandora Press, 1985), 323-4; Timothy Bledsoe and Mary Herring, "Victims of Circumstances: Women in Pursuit of Political Office," *American Political Science Review* 84 (1990): 213–23.

17Carole Pateman, *The Disorder of Women: Democracy, Feminism, and Political Theory* (Stanford, CA: Stanford University Press, 1989), 35; Rita J. Simon and Jean M. Landis, "Women's Place and Men's Attitudes About a Women's Place and Role," *Public Opinion Quarterly* 53 (1989): 265–76.

18Karen van Wagner and Cheryl Swanson, "From Machiavelli to Ms: Differences in Male-Female Power Styles," *Public Administration Review* 39 (1979): 66–72.

19Zillah Eisenstein, ed., *Capitalist Patriarchy and the Case for Socialist Feminism* (New York: Monthly Review Press, 1979), 23.

20Ibid.

21Ibid, 5.

22Sandra Goldberg, *Male Dominance: The Inevitability of Patriarchy* (London: Abacus, 1979), 10; Susan Tenebaum, "Women Through the Prism of Political Thought," *Political Science Quarterly* 15 (1982): 90–102.

23Nancy Fraser, 106.

24"Troubled Sri Lanka Turns to a Woman," *U.S. News & World Report,* 29 August/ 5 September 1994, 14.

25"Woman Chosen to Run Rwanda," *Boston Globe,* 17 July 1993, A3.; Jone Johnson-Lewis, "Women Prime Ministers and Presidents: 20th Century Global Women Political Leaders," Women's History Guide <http:womenshistory.about.com> 7-6-2004.

26In 1979, three out of the twelve government members were women in Costa Rica. Therefore, Costa Rica was an exception to this rule. See the *Europa Year World Book,* 1987, 57.

27This comment was made by Ricardo Israel, Instituto de Ciencia Politica, Universidad de Chile, Santiago, Chile in 1993.

28Jane L. Parpart and Kathleen Staudt, *Women and the State in Africa* (Boulder, CO: Lynne Rienner, 1989), 5; *The World's Women 1995: Trends and Statistics* (New York: United Nations Publication), 152.

29*Women's Indicators and Statistics Database* (Wistat), Version 3, CD-ROM (United Nations Publication, 1994).

30*Worldwide Government Directory* (Washington, D.C.: Belmont, 1994).

31Vicky Randall, *Women and Politics* (Chicago: University of Chicago Press, 1987), 111.

32R. N. Kearney, "Women and Politics in Sri Lanka," *Asian Survey* 20 (1981): 205.

33Ifeyinwa E. Umerah-Udezulu, *The State as Capitalist Patriarchy: Women and Politics in the Developing Countries* (Unpublished Ph.D. Dissertation, May 1995).

34Robert Fatton, "Gender, Class and State in Africa," in Parpart and Staudt, 50.

35Rosalind Petchesky, "Dissolving the Hyphen: A Report on Marxist-Feminist Group," in Zillah Eisenstein, 378; Kathleen Howard-Mariam, "Egypt's Other Political Elite," *Western Political Quarterly* 34 (1981): 174-87; JoAnne F. Aviel, "Political Participation of Women in Latin America," *Western Political Quarterly* 34 (1981): 156–73.

36Zillah Eisenstein, 31.

37Ibid.

38Nannerl O. Keohane, Michele Z. Rosaldo and Barbara C. Gelpi, *Feminist Theory: A Critique of Ideology* (Chicago: University of Chicago Press, 1982), 8-9; Linda Reif,

"Women in Latin American Guerrilla Movement: A Comparative Perspectives," *Comparative Politics* 18 (1986): 147–69.

[39] Alison Jaggar, 277–8.

[40] Anne Ferguson, "Women as a Revolutionary Class," in Pat Walker, ed., *Between Labor and Capital* (Boston: South End Press, 1979), 279–312.

APPENDICES

Table 1: Women as Heads of State or Government: Global South

Country	Presidents/Prime Ministers	Years in Office
Argentina	Isabel Pe'ron	1974–1976
Bolivia	Lidia Gueiler Tejada	1979–1980
Bangladesh	Begum Khalida Zia Sheikh Hasina Wajed	1991–1996 1996–
Bermuda	Pamela Gordon Jennifer Smith	1997–1998 1998–
Burma	Aung San Suukyi	Won election in 1990, but never ruled
Burundi	Sylvie Kinigi	1993–1994
Central African Rep.	Elizabeth Domitien	1974–1976
China	Soong Ching-Ling	1981
Dominica	Eugenia Mary Charles	1980–1995
Guyana	Janet Jagan	1997–1999
Haiti	Ertha Pascal Trouillot Claudette Werleigh	1990–1991 1995–96
India	Indira Gandhi	1966–1977 1980–1984
Indonesia	Megawati Sukanoputri	2001–
Israel	Golda Meir	1969–1974
Liberia	Ruth Perry	1996–1997
Mongolia	Nyam-Osoriyn Tuyaa	1999
Netherlands Antilles	Maria Liberia-Peters Susanne Camelia-Romer	1984–86; 1988–93 1993; 1998–
Nicaragua	Violeta Barrios de Chamorro	1990–1996
Pakistan	Benazir Bhutto	1988–1990 1993–1996
Panama	Mireya Moscoso	1999–
Philippines	Corazon Aquino Gloria Macapagal-Arroyo	1986–1992 2001–
Rwanda	Agathe Uwilingivi Mana	1993–1994
Senegal	Mame Madior Boye	2001–
Sri Lanka	Sirimavo Bandaranaike Chandrika Kumaratunga	1960–1965; 1970–1977; 1994 1994
Turkey	Tamsu Ciller	1993–1996

Table 2: Women Head of State or Government: Developed Countries

Countries	Presidents/Prime Ministers	Years in Office
Bulgaria	Reneta Indzhova	1994
Canada	Kim Campbell	1993
Finland	Tarja Halonen	2000–
France	Edith Cresson	1991–1992
Germany (former Dem. Rep.of)	Sabine Bergmann-Pohl	1990
Iceland	Vigdis Finnbogadottir	1980–1996
Ireland	Mary Robinson Mary McAleese	1990–1997 1997–
Latvia	Vaira Vike-Freiberga	1999–
Lithuania	Kazimiera Prunskiene	1990–1991
Malta	Agatha Barbara	1982–1992
New Zealand	Jenny Shipley Helen Clark	1997–1999 1999–
Norway	Gro Harlem-Brundtland	1981; 1986–1989; 1990–1996
Poland	Hanna Suchocka	1992–1993
Portugal	Maria de Lourdes Pintasilgo	1979–1980
Switzerland	Ruth Dreifuss	1999
United Kingdom	Margaret Thatcher	1979–1990
Yugoslavia	Milka Planinc	1982–1986

Source: UN 2000: *The World's Women: Trends and Statistics.*

Table 3: Percentage of Women in National Parliament in Single or Lower Chambers

	1987	*1995*	*1999*
World Average	9	9	11
Africa			
Northern Africa	3	4	3
Sub-Saharan Africa	7	9	10
Latin America			
and the Caribbean			
Caribbean	9	11	13
Central America	8	10	13
South America	7	9	13
Asia	18	12	13
Eastern Asia	10	9	12
South-Eastern Asia	5	5	5
Southern Asia	..	8	8
Central Asia	4	4	5
Western Asia		24	3
Oceania			
Developed regions	2	2	3
Eastern Europe	26	9	10
Western Europe	14	18	21
Other developed regions	7	12	18

Source: UN 2000: *The World's Women: Trends and Statistics.*

Table 4: Women Representation in both Ministerial and Sub-Ministerial levels

	January	*1994*	*January*	*1998*
	Ministerial Level	*Sub-ministerial Level*	*Ministerial Level*	*Sub-ministerial Level*
African				
Northern Africa	2	4	3	6
Sub-Saharan Africa	6	7	8	10
Latin America and *the Caribbean*				
Caribbean	8	17	11	23
Central America	10	11	6	15
South America	5	6	10	14
Asia	2	1	..	..
Eastern Asia	3	3	4	7
South-eastern Asia	5	2	4	3
South Asia	3	4	5	5
Central Asia	2	1	2	3
Western Asia		5	5	10
Oceania	5	5	5	10
Developed Regions				
Eastern Europe	3	6	8	14
Western Europe	16	11	16	14
Other developed regions	11	19	12	21

Source: UN 2000: *World's Women: Trends and Statistics.*

Table 5. Women in Public Life in Africa

Country or area	% parliamentary seats in single or lower chamber occupied by women			% women in decision-making positions in government				Year of ratification of CEDAW	Whether national plan of action provided to the UN Secretariat
				Ministerial level		Sub-ministerial level			
	1987	1995	1999	1994	1998	1994	1998		
Africa									
Algeria	2	7	3	4	0	8	10	1996	Yes
Angola	15	10	15	7	14	2	10	1986	Yes
Benin	4	8	6	10	13	0	5	1992	..
Botswana	5	9	9	6	14	6	20	1996	Yes
Burkina Faso	..	4	8	7	10	14	10	1987	Yes
Burundi	9	..	6	7	8	0	0	1992	Yes
Cameroon	14	12	6	3	6	5	6	1994	..
Cape Verde	12	8	11	13	13	9	50	1980	Yes
Central African Republic	4	4	7	5	4	17	6	1991	..

Chad	..	16	2	5	5	0	6	1995	..
Comoros	0	0	..	0	7	0	0	1994	..
Congo	10	2	12	6	6	0	0	1982	Yes
Cote d'Ivoire	6	5	8	8	3	0	3	1995	..
Dem. Rep. of Congo	5	5	..	6	..	7	..	1986	
Djibouti	0	0	..	0	0	3	3	1998	..
Eygpt	4	2	2	4	6	0	4	1981	Yes
Equatorial Guinea	3	8	4	4	4	0	5	1984	..
Eritrea	..	21	15	7	5	13	6	1995	Yes
Ethiopia	1	5	2	10	5	10	16	1981	Yes
Gabon	13	6	8	7	3	12	9	1983	..
Gambia	8	..	2	0	29	7	17	1993	..
Ghana	..	8	9	11	9	12	9	1986	Yes
Guinea	..	7	9	9	8	8	20	1982	Yes
Guinea-Bissau	15	10	10	4	18	19	16	1985	..
Kenya	2	3	4	0	0	4	9	1984	Yes

Country or area	% parliamentary seats in single or lower chamber occupied by women			% women in decision-making positions in government				Year of ratification of CEDAW	Whether national plan of action provided to the UN Secretariat
				Ministerial level		Sub-ministerial level			
				6	6	21	15		
Lesotho	..	5	4	6	6	21	15	1995	..
Liberia	6	6	..	5	8	0	6	1984	..
Libyan Arab Jamahiriya	..	..	..	0	7	0	0	1989	..
Madagascar	1	4	8	0	19	4	8	1989	..
Malawi	10	6	8	9	4	9	4	1987	Yes
Mali	4	2	12	10	21	0	0	1985	Yes
Mauritania	..	0	4	0	4	6	6	..	..
Mauritius	7	3	8	3	..	7	..	1984	..
Morocco	0	1	1	0	0	0	8	1993	Yes
Mozambique	16	25	25	4	0	9	15	1997	Yes
Namibia	..	18	22	10	8	2	17	1992	Yes
Niger	..	4	..	5	10	19	8	1999	Yes

Nigeria	..	..	..	3	6	11	4	1985	Yes
Rwanda	13	17	17	9	5	10	20	1981	..
Sao Tome and Principe	12	7	9	0	0	20	33	..	..
Senegal	11	12	12	7	7	0	15	1985	Yes
Seychelles	16	27	24	31	33	21	16	1992	..
Sierra Leone	..	..	6	0	10	2	11	1988	..
Somalia	4	..	..	0	0	0	0	..	..
South Africa	2	25	30	6	..	2	..	1995	..
Sudan	8	8	5	0	0	0	0	..	Yes
Swaziland	4	3	3	0	6	6	16	..	Yes
Togo	5	1	..	5	9	0	0	1983	..
Tunisia	6	7	7	4	3	14	10	1985	Yes
Uganda	..	17	18	10	13	7	13	1985	Yes
United Republic of Tanzania	..	11	16	13	13	4	11	1985	Yes
Zambia	3	7	9	5	3	9	12	1985	Yes
Zimbabwe	11	15	14	3	12	25	6	1991	Yes

Source: UN 2000: *The World's Women: Trends and Statistics.*

Literature and the Global Society

F. Odun Balogun

INTRODUCTION: THE BASIC CONCEPTS

Literature is ideal in illustrating the meaning of the concept *global society* because of the manner in which it demonstrates the unity in diversity of the human race. Before I elaborate on this claim, however, let me share my understanding of the concept *global society*. I begin with the oxymoron "unity in diversity." Like all oxymorons, this one warns about the danger of allowing oneself to be misled by superficial surfaces, by that which appears to be contradictory, but in fact is not. Diversity, dispersal, and difference do not preclude unity. Though geographic locations and social structures, languages and religions, histories and politics, skin colors and cultural norms are different, paradoxically, human beings are united by these very same factors that superficially appear to separate them. Regardless of the placement of our locations, for instance, human beings all live on earth, the round solid sphere, the one globe on which we stand, physically linked together. And in these days of space flights, satallites, Concorde travels, instant news, computer and telephone communications, multinationals, global finance, and global warming, no one needs to be reminded of how closely we are united on this globe.

Studies in genetics have also revealed as superficial the racial differences we perceive between people because genetic data indicate that "all human groups are closely related" and that "genetic differences among human populations are small," indeed, as low as only 0.33% (Russell 722). In fact, as a result of the wide genetic variations within any given population, the genetic makeup of a Caucasian can more closely resemble that of a black person in Africa than that of the Caucasian's European next-door neighbor.[1]

Perhaps nothing underscores the truth of the notion *unity in diversity* more than language, the instrument, indeed the essence of literature. The ability to use language is one of the capabilities that differentiate humans from animals. Yet, even though all human beings use language, each linguistic group speaks a different language. Thus, language both unites and separates us.

What *global societies* studies are about then is the obvious: that despite the differences in geographical locations and cultures, history and politics, all human beings are closely connected. Furthermore, global societies studies stress the point that more than at any other time previously, there is an urgency in today's world to emphasize our unity as human beings without dismissing our differences. Perhaps the most dramatic change in modern history is that, beginning with the second half of the twentieth century, the manner in which human beings interact has been speeded up phenomenally. The efficiency of today's communication technologies has in effect broken down and eliminated virtually all the barriers that previously had existed because of geographic distances between peoples. Today, individuals communicate instantly, no matter how far apart they may be located on the globe. Digital telephone and computer e-mail link people together instantly without the need to surmount physical distances. Even when physical relocation is a necessity, this is accomplished with an amazing, previously unimaginable speed. For instance, it is not unusual these days for a traveler to eat breakfast in one continent, have lunch in another, and enjoy dinner in a third.

In other words, unlike in the past when humanity was separated into different societies because of distance and the slow pace of communication technologies, today we live closely interconnected in one global society, one community.

This historic and revolutionary development has its implications. The rapidity in the speed of modern interaction and inter-relationships requires a commensurate speed in the level of understanding between peoples who, so to speak, have suddenly woken up to find themselves as close, rather than distant, neighbors. If the speed of modern communication is not matched by a corresponding speed in human understanding, the consequences for humanity might be disastrous. For instance, unless the people of the world as a whole come soon enough to a common understanding about the global environment, it might be too late to take the needed, concerted actions to stem the dangerous progression in global warming with all of its possible tragic consequences. Also, solving the new phenomenon known as global terrorism requires that all people understand its underlying causes from a universal, rather than from a narrow nationalistic, perspective. Only such an understanding can achieve the universal collaboration needed to end global terrorism. Until such a time as both the industrialized world and the developing nations from the so-called Third World come to a mutual understanding of the real fundamental causes of global terrorism in their economic, political and cultural specificities, both sides will continue to pay avoidable heavy prices in human and material losses, as tragically happened on September 11, 2001, when the attack on the World Trade Center twin towers claimed victims from all parts of the world.[2]

This is where global societies studies come in. The objective is to promote human understanding on a global scale without prejudice to any peoples. Because of this objectivity, global societies studies question the analysis of world issues from narrow nationalistic perspectives, be they of the industrialized or developing nations. The fact that we have all suddenly found ourselves living in one global society does not mean that we have all automatically started viewing things from a global perspective. Unfortunately, all too often our individual histories, as well as the political, economic, religious, and social cultures that these histories have nurtured, seriously inhibit the task of objective analysis, such that in forums like the United Nations, opinions are usually sharply divided between the industrialized and the developing worlds. Given its compositional diversity, a typical university classroom is in certain respects like a United Nations forum. Therefore, a global societies class would be a challenge to both the professor and the student, each of who must be prepared to submit his or her personal views to the scrutiny of objective analysis, the very reason for which academic institutions exist.

The goal of global societies studies is to promote global understanding by, on one hand, insisting that we seek out and embrace the things that bind diverse peoples together. On the other hand, global societies studies demand that we acknowledge and respect our cultural differences and actively seek ways to reconcile the contradictions and conflicts that these differences create.

While the rest of this chapter demonstrates how literature is a pre-eminent discipline for illustrating the concept of global societies studies, it must be emphasized that every discipline, whether in the sciences or humanities, can serve the same purpose. International finance and banking, for instance, are today integral aspects of all national economies. History, on its part, is a record of the interactions and events within and between nations, as biology is a study of the human anatomy regardless of racial and cultural origin. Sociology is a comparative analysis of social behaviors in time and space, just as political science analyzes power relations within and between societies.

However, even though literature, compared to other disciplines, is not unique in having the capacity to demonstrate the unity of the human society, it is nonetheless pre-eminent in the manner in which it does it. This is because of the nature of the origin and history of literature as an art form, the manner of its preoccupation with human and social issues, and the functions it performs.

LITERATURE AND THE GLOBAL SOCIETY

(i) What Is Literature?

By literature, I do not refer to the broad identification of the body of works, fictional and non-fictional, that together help illuminate the meaning of a specific topic, such as, for instance, the *literature* on American tourism to the safari game reserves of East Africa during the northern winter months. Rather, I refer to fictional literature, a verbal art, which is defined by, as well as it defines, language, the primary medium of human communication. Just as the painter as an artist, for instance, works with canvas, paper, brush, color, pencil and oil, the writer as an artist works with language as his or her primary medium. The experience of oral literature has shown that paper, pen, pencil, typewriter and the computer are optional, dispensable tools for the creation of literature. In using language to create, the writer depends a lot on imagination; therefore, fictional literature is synonymously known as imaginative literature.

(ii) Our Common Literary Origin

The origin of literature predates modernity and the emergence of the technology of writing; therefore, literature should not be exclusively defined by written literature, which is a comparatively modern phenomenon. Literature had existed for centuries in the oral form before writing was invented, and as scholars of oral tradition, notably Albert B. Lord, Walter J. Ong, Isidore Okpewho, John Miles Foley and others, have shown, literature had invented and perfected highly sophisticated literary devices long before the emergence of wtiting.[3] In fact, the first literary use of writing consisted in the transcription of existing oral literature, and this was how most of the traditional epics like *The Iliad, The Odyssey, Gilgamesh, Beowulf, Popol Vuh, The Song of Roland, The Epic of Sonjara, Mwindo* and others came to us in the written form.

Oral literature in its various generic divisions, including, for instance, myth, legend, folktales, epic narratives, songs, and ritual drama, was a cultural practice that was common to all pre-modern societies. There is no single human society that does not have an oral literary tradition because every society has a language and it has always been a natural tendency for people to use language creatively, imaginatively.

There is also an amazing similarity in the manners in which different linguistic groups creatively use language; hence it came about that despite geographic distances and linguistic differences, various traditional societies developed similar types or genres of oral literature. The particular details in which each genre is realized, however, often differ because of the differences in languages. The character of poetry in the tonal languages of Africa, for instance, is different from that of the poetry constructed in the syllabic languages of Europe. Until this distinction was acknowledged, for instance, it was erroneously believed for a long time that Africa did not create epics, which was regarded as an exalted form of literary creativity. Had this misconception persisted, the world would have been denied knowledge of the literary wealth of African traditional epics of which there are numerous examples, the best known being *The Epic of Sonjara* from Mali and the *Mwindo,* an epic of the Bantu-speaking Nyanga people of Zaire.[4]

(iii) The Epics

In spite of the minor differences occasioned by cultural and linguistic differences, however, there is an amazing similarity in the manner in which different peoples create epics such that scholars have been able to identify the typical thematic and stylistic characteristics of the genre, irrespective of the place of origin. Usually, an epic narrates a story of national importance and celebrates the exploits of a hero. Because traditional societies were mostly male-dominated, an epic rarely had a heroine as the main character. The role was usually reserved for a man with a noble lineage or an ordinary person who was favored by the gods and given special abilities. Odysseus, the hero of the Greek epic *The Odyssey,* for instance, was often assisted in battles and difficult situations by his patroness, the goddess Athena. The hero of *Sonjara,* the African epic from Mali, was a man who in spite of disabilities was favored by the gods. Though a secondborn in a country where the firstborn was heir, Sonjara nonetheless became the ruler. Also in spite of the initial physical difficulty of not being able to walk as a child, Sonjara grew up to become a strong man with supernatural powers and a great empire builder. The epic hero sometimes does not only receive special favors and powers from the gods, he may actually share in divinity. Such was the case, for instance, with the hero of the Mesopotamian epic *Gilgamesh* who was two-thirds god and one-third man.

Also everywhere, epics are narrated in highly formalized styles and are quite predictable in their stylistic devices. They use opening formulas, they have episodic plot structures and the story is presented in the form of a quest. In the case of the Greek epic hero, Odysseus, the quest is a search for a way to successfully return home after the victorious conclusion of the Trojan war. In his own case, Sonjara, the Malian epic hero, is in search of victory over his adversaries in a military campaign that traversed far and wide in the land. Gilgamesh, whose journey was in search of eternal life, ended up discovering how to be a better ruler, one who is not as conceited as he was at the beginning, but who now cares for the welfare of his subjects. Everywhere, epic narratives use stock or fixed epithets which take the form of adjectives in *The Odyssey* and *Gilgamesh,* but appear also as praise names in *Sonjara.* Epic simile and epic digression occur almost uniformly in epics, as do what I term epic "prefabs." The latter are chunks of narrative information which are periodically repeated, often word-for-word, at certain places in the narration.

(iv) The Creation Myths

Just as we find similarities in the epics of the various peoples of the world, so do we also locate affinities between various cultural myths. One of the first preoccupations of the oral literary artist was the all-important question of how the universe, human beings, and all that exists first came into being. There is a fascinating similarity in how the oral literary artists all over the world answered this question. Their views of pre-creation topography, for instance, are almost uniformly the same. The Yoruba myth of creation recounts that when the deities who were sent from heaven to create the earth descended, they met only "a watery, marshy waste" (Idowu 19 and Beier 7). The account in the Native American myth *Popol Vuh* is similar:

> There is no yet one person, one animal, bird, fish, crab, tree, rock, hollow, canyon, meadow, forest. Only the sky alone is there; the face of the earth is not clear. Only the sea alone is pooled under all the sky; there is nothing whatever gathered together. It is at rest; not a single thing stirs. It is held back, kept at rest under the sky.
> Whatever there is that might be is simply not there: only the pooled water, only the calm sea, only it alone is pooled.
> Whatever might be is simply not there: only murmurs, ripples, in the dark, in the night. (Tedlock 3080-81)

The best-known text of creation, Genesis, says this:

> In the beginning God created the heaven and the earth. And the earth was without form, and void; and darkness was upon the face of the deep. And the Spirit of God moved upon the face of the waters. (text of the King James version in Lawall 56)

The manner in which the solid earth was created from the watery surface differs from myth to myth. As recounted by Bolaji Idowu, for example, the Yoruba myth has this to say:

> What moved Olodumare to think of creating the solid earth, no one knows. However, He conceived the idea and at once carried it into effect. He summoned Orisa-nla, the arch-divinity, to His presence and charged him with the duty: for material, He gave him a leaf packet of loose earth (some say that the loose earth was in a snail's shell), and for tools a five- toed hen and a pigeon (Idowu 19).

Genesis reports that on the second day of creation, God created the firmament to separate the waters above from the waters below, and on the third day, He willed the solid earth into being, using the power of the spoken word:

> And God said, Let the waters under the heaven be gathered together unto one place, and let the dry land appear: and it was so. And God called the dry land Earth, and the gathering of the waters together called the Seas." (56)

Native Americans conceived of a single god with multiple entities that are called thirteen different names in the *Popol Vuh* (3079–3082) where the god is appropriately referred to with the plural personal pronoun "they":

> And then the earth arose because of them, it was simply their word that brought it forth. For the forming of the earth they said "Earth." It arose suddenly, just like a cloud, like a mist, now forming, unfolding." (3081)

Whatever the differences that may exist in the practical methods of creating the earth, the myths uniformly acknowledge God as the ultimate creator. And despite the surface differences, the perception of God in the myths is amazingly similar. Ancient Egyptians perceived God as manifested in the sun, and in Akhenaten's "Hymn to the Sun," we first confront the idea of the single godhead, an idea that is repeated throughout the poem, which begins in this fashion:

> When in splendor you first took your throne
>   high in the precinct of heaven,
>   O living God,
>   life truly began!

This sun-god is accoladed as "overlord over all earth" and he is the "sole God, beside whom is no other!":

> You are the one God,
>   shining forth from your possible incarnations
>   as Aten, the Living Sun.
> Revealed like a king in glory, risen in light.
>   now distant, now bending nearby.
> You create the numberless things of this world
>   from yourself, who are One alone. . . .
>   (Foster 42-46)

While the Old Testament projects the Jewish concept of a single godhead, the New Testament soon restores the traditional concept of the multiple godhead: God the Father, God the Son, God the Holy Ghost. Most traditional cultures propose the idea of the multiple gods, often identifying one as supreme. *Zeus,* for instance, rules the lesser gods in the Greek cosmology and *Olodunmare* is lord among the Yoruba deities. The Yoruba myth of creation provides a fascinating explanation for the appearance of the multiple deities, an explanation that makes it possible for the Yoruba to reconcile the concept of the single god (monotheism) with the notion of the multiple gods (polytheism) without a sense of contradiction. *Olodunmare,* the undisputable supreme Deity for the Yorubas, stays up in heaven, but He has lesser divinities to assist Him. Idowu calls these deities, each of who has a designated department to supervise, the ministers *of Olodunmare* (62). Among these is the arch-divinity *Orisa-nla,* one of the three deities that *Olodunmare* sent down to create the earth. Long after this task had been accomplished, appeared Atowoda, a slave, who in revolt rolled a huge boulder that splintered his master, the arch-divinity *Orisa-nla,* into fragments. Each of *Orisa-nla's* fragments became a minor divinity, an *orisa,* in its own right; hence the proliferation of *orisas* on earth according to the Yoruba world view (Bolaji Idowu 58-60).

While all the myths identified God as the creator of humanity, each culture conceives of the execution of this task in different ways. According to the Jewish tradition recorded in *Genesis,* while God created everything else through the magical power of the word, He created man through physical exertion, molding him in His own image and likeness from the dust of the earth. On the other hand, according to the Native Americans in the *Popol Vuh,* white and yellow corn, discovered by animals, was the material from which the first humans were formed (3088-91). In the Yoruba myth, the task of creating human beings was carried out under the principle of division of labor. The primary mission of *Orisa-nla* when he was sent by *Olodunmare* to earth was to mold human forms, but *Olodunmare* reserved for Himself the secret power of transforming the clay molds into living beings. *Olodunmare* alone possessed the power to breathe life into *Orisa-nla's* works (Idowu 71-75).

Speculations abound as to the source of the similarities that exist between oral literary traditions and the myths of creation. Though travelling in ancient times was extremely slow, people still travelled and they carried along with them their cultural lores. It was thus possible that the similarities derived from importation and outside influence. It is not inconceivable too, that, confronted with the similar problem of solving the riddle of creation, individual traditional cultures independently arrived at similar speculations. After all, it is usual today that though located continents apart, individuals, faced with the same challenges of modern life and technology, simultaneously produce similar theories and inventions, a situation that often leads to disputed patent claims. Human beings, irrespective of geographical locations, have the same sensibilities and intelligence, and they consequently feel and think alike and respond to physical and intellectual challenges in similar ways. Moreover, the speculation is that all humanity originated in the same place and only dispersed afterward through migration. Thus, the different cultural creation myths could simply be variations of the same original common myth.

(v) Modern Literature

Unlike in traditional oral literature, the sources of similarities in modern literatures are easily placed. Forced migrations during slavery, cultural imposition on colonial subjects, modern publishing and the internationalization of book and magazine distribution, the uniformity of the international educational systems, and the more recent development of electronic publishing—these and others are the obvious causes of the similarities found in modern literatures. Literary movements and theories that originate in one part of the world soon find their way to other parts of the globe to be read and imitated. The novel is a typical illustration. Invented by Europeans and perfected in the nineteenth century, especially by the English and the Russians, the novel was subsequently exported by the British and the French as cultural artifacts to their colonial empires. The colonial subjects embraced it, and in less than half a century, they have so mastered, transformed and perfected the genre that the Europeans are now re-importing it because the great masters today like Chinua Achebe, Naguib Mahfouz, Simon Rushdie, V.S. Naipul and Gabriel Garcia Marquez are from the former colonies of Africa, India, Latin America and the Caribbean islands.[5] As recent Nobel laureates like the playwright Wole Soyinka and the poet Derek Wallcot show, what is true of the novel is also true of modern poetry and drama in terms of the patronage and renewal of the genres by the non-Europeans who had imported them.

(vi) Functions of Literature

The primary reason literature travels, though slower in ancient times but with an amazing speed today, is that everywhere it exists or goes, literature performs the same universal human functions—simultaneously teaching and entertaining. The thematic preoccupations of literature have consistently been the so-called eternal universal issues of life: birth, death, love, marriage, jealousy, anger, compassion, hunger, thirst, etc. Literature probes deep into our emotional sensibilities and exposes our souls. In the process, we come to the easy recognition of the universality of human emotions because, irrespective of differences in racial, ethnic and geographic identities, human beings experience in similar ways the emotions of joy and sadness, love and jealousy, anger and hate, generosity and kindness, faith and despair, etc. Characters in literature may bear names and wear clothes that are strange to us; they may speak in tongues and appreciate foods different from ours; they may live in geographic zones and occupy social statuses that distance them from us; however, when these same strange beings confront emotional situations such as we experience, they react the same way as we do. In other words, literature teaches us about our common humanity and through the vicarious experience of the lives of others, it teaches us how to be human.

Often because literature pleases and thrills us, we tend to think that all it exists for is to entertain us. The poet, irrespective of the linguistic medium, explores the resources of language to create aesthetic pleasure for the reader. This is done through auditory manipulation of sound to create rhyme, refrain, onomatopoeia and other sound effects. The pleasure is enhanced as the poet simultaneously sifts through and also pairs syntactic units of the sentence to create a regular rhythmic balance, calculated to soothe or agitate us. Invariably, the poet simultaneously does a third thing to boost our pleasure. Through the creation of mental images like simile, metaphor and irony, the poet imaginatively transports us to a new plane of perception that sheds new light on reality and thus thrills us to no end with its sometimes epiphanic revelations.

The playwright so dexterously manipulates dialogue and action on stage that we soon forget that we are witnessing, not a real but a contrived human tragedy or humorous situation. Meanwhile, the empathetic emotions that have been awoken move us to cry or laugh with abandon for the lives on stage whose experiences we have vicariously shared. And who among readers have been able to resist the carefully plotted snares of the well-woven story? Through artful description, characterization, plotting and the use of devices such as suspense, symbols, flashback and foreshadow, the novelist keeps us glued to the narration, making us anxious to know what happens next.

(vii) Conclusion

Given the universality of these poetic, dramatic and narrative devices, it is possible for a work originally written in Yiddish or Yoruba to be enjoyed in the original or translation by a reader whose first language is German or Spanish. In other words, because of its nature, origin, history, methods and purpose, literature perhaps more than any other discipline helps us to discover our common humanity.

NOTES

[1] See also Neil A. Campbell et al. who say that scientific studies confirm "the fossil evidence for humanity's African origin" (713-715). *Biology.* Fifth edition. San Francisco: The Benjamin Cummings Publishing Co., Inc. 1999. I am indebted to my colleague, Dr. Leonard Davis of the Biology Department, for bringing Russell's and Campbell's texts to my attention.

[2] An example of the works that have illuminated the problems of globalization and the realities of its current practice and direction is Tina Rosenberg's essay "The Free-Trade Fix," which first appeared in the August 18, 2002, issue of *The New York Times Magazine* (28-33, 50, 74–75) and is included in this collection.

[3] For further reading on the nature of oral literature, its devices, and relationship with written literature see, for example, the following works: Albert B. Lord's *The Singer of Tales* (Cambridge, MA: Harvard University Press, 1960) and his "The Gospels as Oral Traditional Literature" (in William O. Walker, Jr., ed. *The Relationships among the Gospels: An Interdisciplinary Dialogue.* San Antonio, TX: Trinity University Press, 1978. 33-91); Walter J. Ong's *Orality and Literacy: The Technologizing of the Word* (London: Routledge, 1988); and John Miles Foley's *The Theory of Oral Composition* (Bloomington: Indiana University Press, 1988).

[4] Isidore Okpewho discusses this issue in detail in his *The Epic in Africa* (New York: Columbia University Press, 1979).

[5] For examples of how former colonial subjects use indigenous literary resources to transform and renew the imported genre of the novel, see F. Odun Balogun's *Ngugi and African Postcolonial Narrative: The Novel as Oral Narrative in Multigenre Performance* (Quebec: World Heritage Press, 1997) and Eileen Julien's *African Novels and the Question of Orality* (Bloomington: Indiana University Press, 1992).

SUGGESTED FURTHER READING

Beier, Ulli. *Yoruba Myths.* Cambridge, England: Cambridge University Press, 1980.

Kelleher, Ann and Laura Klein. *Global Perspectives: A Handbook for Understanding Global Issues.* Upper Saddle River, NJ: Prentice Hall, 1999.

O'Meara, Patrick, Howard D. Mehlinger and Mathew Krain. *Globalization and the Challenges of a New Century: A Reader.* Bloomington: Indiana University Press, 2000.

Stromquist, Nelly P. *Education in a Globalized World: The Connectivity of Power, Technology and Knowledge.* Blue Ridge Summit, PA: Rowman & Littlefield, 2002.

Traylor, Eleanor W. and Alphonso Frost and Leota S. Lawrence. *Broad Sympathy: The Howard University Oral Traditions Reader.* Needham Heights, MA: Simon & Schuster, 1997.

WORKS CITED

Foster, John L. Translator. "Akhenaten's 'Hymn to the Sun.'" In Sarah Lawall. Editor. *The Norton Anthology of World Literature.* 2nd Edition. Volume A. New York: Norton, 2002. 42–46.

Idowu, Bolaji E. *Olodunmare: God in Yoruba Belief.* New York: Wazobia, 1994.

Rosenberg, Tina. "The Free-Trade Fix." *The New York Times Magazine.* August 18th, 2002. 28–33, 50, 74–75.

Russell, Peter J. *iGenetics.* New edition (6th). San Francisco: The Benjamin Cummings Publishing Co., Inc., 2002.

Tedlock, Dennis. Translator. *Popol Vuh.* In Sarah Lawall. Editor. *The Norton Anthology of World Literature.* 2nd Edition. Volume C. New York: Norton, 2002. 3079-3092.

English Rules

Madelaine Drohan and Alan Freeman

When the leaders of the European Union's 15 countries gathered in Amsterdam in June, 1997, it fell to their Dutch hosts to keep journalists covering the meeting posted on what was going on. Among them, the leaders spoke Europe's 11 official languages. Add reporters from Japan, Poland, Hungary and the Czech Republic and there were at least 15 languages represented in the room. But when Dutch Foreign Minister Hans Van Mierlo began to talk, he chose English.

A lone Dutch reporter protested. He was drowned out by cries of "English! English!" by the majority, who wanted to hear the facts delivered in the language they may not speak perfectly but could at least understand. And increasingly these days—not just in Europe but around the world—that language is English.

The British Empire might be in full retreat with the handover of Britain's last significant possession, Hong Kong. But from Bengal to Belize and Las Vegas to Lahore, the language that spread from Britain through military might, political power, technology and sheer coincidence is rapidly becoming the first global *lingua franca*. The reason is obvious: The American cultural and economic colossus.

Native Mandarin Chinese speakers still far outnumber those whose mother tongue is English. But English is No. 1 when those who speak it as a second, third or fourth language are counted.

A quick look at the nightly television news provides ample evidence of English's ascendancy:

• In Africa, residents of Kinshasa, Zaire, jeer as the motorcade of ousted strongman Mobutu Sese Seko passes on the way to the airport. "We don't have to speak French anymore!" they shout. Rebel leader Laurent Kabila, who speaks fluent

Reprinted by permission from the *Globe and Mail*, July 27, 1997.

English, decides he will not only change the name of the country to the Democratic Republic of Congo, he will also adopt English as an official language.

• In Asia, students at a technical institute in the Cambodian capital of Phnom Penh mount a street protest against mandatory French classes. Cambodia, like Zaire, was colonized by French speakers whose legacy was their language. The students want to learn English.

• In Eastern Europe, military officers in the Polish, Hungarian and Czech armies (which were invited to join NATO) are hitting the school books again in preparation for the expansion of the military alliance. It has 16 members but only one dominant working language: English.

There's much to be said for having a global language. It can cut down on misunderstandings, provide wider access to sources of knowledge and improve and speed up communications.

But it can also lead to arrogance and complacency on the part of native English speakers, and a sense of grievance and inferiority in other language groups. Canadians need look no further than Quebec to see a prime example.

The English juggernaut is often blamed for the death of minority languages. Half of the world's 6,500 languages are expected to disappear in the next century. English is not always the culprit. Many minority languages have been overwhelmed by dominant languages such as Chinese or Russian.

But because English is in wider use around the globe, it comes in for more blame. And because language and culture are closely intertwined, there is a danger of backlash. "We are very concerned that English could be perceived as damaging to other languages," says Caroline Moore of the British Council, a state-funded group that promotes Britain and British culture. Ms. Moore is part of a team that is looking into the future of English. It predicts that English will remain the biggest global language for the foreseeable future. "But we're mindful of what happened to French and Latin," says Ms. Moore.

There is nothing inherent in English to explain why it has spread so far, says British linguist David Crystal in his book, *English as a Global Language.* He dismisses the suggestion that it is popular because it is simpler to learn, has just a few nouns with gender (such as "ship," often referred to as "her") or that it is more democratic because it does not have a class-based structure. "A language becomes an international language for one chief reason: the political power of its people— especially their military power."

Prof. Crystal points to the spread of Greek, Latin, Arabic, Spanish, Portuguese and French by their respective armies and navies to illustrate his point. There have been exceptions, he admits. One of the most notable is the failure of the French-speaking Normans to force the English to speak their language after they invaded Britain in 1066. "Perhaps if the Normans had taken up residence in larger numbers, or if good political relations between England and France had lasted longer, or if English had not already been well-established since Anglo-Saxon times, the outcome might have been different. This book would then, in all probability, have been written about (and in) French."

Like the Roman legions who spread Latin through Europe, it was British colonial soldiers, explorers and traders who initially spread English. In the modern world, the British have been replaced by the Americans, who now run the world's remaining superpower—in English.

The collapse of the Soviet Union has suddenly meant that Russian has lost influence as a language of power. Throughout Eastern Europe, millions of Poles, Hungarians and Czechs who used to be forced to learn Russian have gratefully dropped that language in favour of English, which is not only the language of commerce and mass culture but of their future military allies.

"In this department, everybody speaks English," says Colonel Grzegorz Wisniewski, deputy director at the Department for NATO Cooperation at Poland's Defence Ministry in Warsaw. "It's a prerequisite." For military officers such as Col. Wisniewski, the collapse of the Warsaw Pact presented a linguistic as well as a geopolitical challenge. After years of studying Russian, they realized that without English their careers would go nowhere. "I didn't study English before 1989 because I didn't think I would use this language or travel widely," says Col. Wisniewski, who now speaks English fluently.

School children were told during Soviet times that Russian was a global language. Now, throughout Eastern Europe, Russian is definitely out. And while German has economic influence and French continues to have a certain status in Romania, English is clearly the second language of choice throughout the region. At the recent Warsaw Book Fair, the official poster was in English, and even German books were presented in stalls that carried English signs announcing, "Books from Germany."

Geopolitical changes elsewhere have served to strengthen English as well. In South Africa, the collapse of apartheid has undermined the official position of Afrikaans in favour of English. Elsewhere in Africa, the French language is in retreat as French influence wanes. It started when the Hutu-led government in Rwanda, allied with France, was replaced by a Tutsi-led force that invaded from English-speaking Uganda. In neighbouring Zaire, where France supported Mr. Mobutu until the bitter end, the Congolese have happily renounced French in favour of English.

"The fact is that the French language is identified by the majority of Africans with support for the worst dictatorships," says François-Xavier Verschave, president of Survie, a Paris-based non-governmental organization with an interest in Africa. He remembers hearing a speech by the newly installed president of Rwanda in late 1995. "He took out two versions of his speech, one in English and the other in French. He decided purposely to read the one in English. The French ambassador, who was sitting next to me, turned green."

In Asia, English has become the *lingua franca* of business, displacing French in such places as Vietnam, Laos and Cambodia. The desire to do business with the Americans and other English-speaking countries has been a powerful incentive. "Anyone will learn a language if it's going to pay them," says Prof. Crystal.

The move to English has been further encouraged by countries in ASEAN, the Association of South East Asian Nations, which is led by Indonesia, Malaysia and

Thailand. The foundations for English in the region were laid by the British through trade, which in some places, such as Hong Kong and Penang, Malaysia, led to the establishment of British schools.

One of Canada's most important foreign-aid projects in the Pacific Rim region provides training in English as a second language to a couple of hundred Indochinese officials a year at a base in Singapore. (The Canadian government is also contemplating a program to encourage executives from France to study English in Canada on the grounds that they will feel more comfortable in a country where French is also an official language.)

In Korea and Japan, English has become the second language of choice as well. "The fact of life is that when you sit down with a Japanese or Korean official, 95 per cent of them are reasonably proficient in English," says a Canadian diplomat. That proficiency in English has benefited the British because Japanese and Korean firms looking for a foothold in Europe have established their factories in Britain, where they feel comfortable with the language.

The British also gain to the tune of at least £800-million a year from foreigners travelling to Britain to study English or attend English universities. Teaching English to Asians has become a big source of foreign exchange in Australia as well. In many parts of the world, English prospers because it's perceived as a neutral language in the battle between national groups. That's the case in Belgium, where French and Flemish speakers increasingly refuse to speak each other's language, leaving English to prosper as an alternative. And it's the case in India, which is producing some of the world's best English-language literature. Two recent issues of *The New Yorker* (June 23, 30, 1997) were devoted entirely to English writing coming out of India.

English is also thriving in Spain, Portugal and Italy, which have traditionally had more linguistic affinity with French. Diogo Vaz Guedes, a Portuguese businessman who studied French at the Lycée in Lisbon, says he never gets to use it any more. He sends his children to the local British school.

Anyone who doubts that English has become the dominant language of business need only go to the World Economic Forum, which attracts the world's business and political elite to Davos, Switzerland, each year. If you want to network in the corridors or try to conduct international negotiations over dinner, no other language goes as far. In the first few years after the Berlin Wall came down, the countries of Eastern Europe required interpreters for their representatives to Davos. The representatives were soon replaced by more polished delegates who spoke fluent English.

Multinational companies, like multinational institutions, must establish a common language or languages, and English is usually chosen or figures in the mix. At the headquarters of Airbus—a consortium of French, English, German and Spanish companies—in Toulouse, France, the working language is English.

While America's victory in the Cold War can be credited to its economic and military might, it isn't just nuclear weapons and Stealth bombers that are winning the linguistic war for English. It is also the power of Hollywood and American popular culture.

English is the language of T-shirts, rap music, advertising and MTV. American culture is an export industry that outranks aerospace exports when it comes to global penetration. And every can of Coke, rock-music CD or McDonald's hamburger spreads that culture a little bit further. Berlin's recently opened branch of Planet Hollywood features a video of the superstar owners, including movie star Arnold Schwarzenegger, welcoming patrons to the restaurant. But the Austrian-born hulk doesn't speak a word of his native German. He speaks English.

In the world of advertising, the use of English is growing not just in the ads themselves but also in the contracts and correspondence between advertisers and agencies. "When I write letters in French or Dutch I still use the terms camera-ready or layout because they are the ones everyone understands," says Barbara Captijn, director of North American Media Experts, an agency based in The Hague with a transatlantic clientele.

In the world of technology, English is particularly pervasive perhaps because many of the advances have been made in English-speaking countries. Ms. Moore of the British Council points out that Britain controlled the telegraph in the early days, giving it a potent tool with which to spread its language far and wide. The first radio broadcast was made in English. The first telephone call took place in English. And now the Internet is dominated by English because so much of it was constructed by and for Americans.

The steady march of the English language hasn't come without opposition. In France, there are efforts to counter its use on product labels and on the Internet. A recent survey suggested that 84 per cent of all web sites are in English. French President Jacques Chirac has warned that if the trend continues, future French generations will be economically and culturally marginalized: "The danger exists of a loss of influence for other major languages and a total eradication of smaller languages," he said.

Losing linguistic ground globally is harder for the French than most, says Prof. Crystal, because French was a world language in the 18th century, unlike most other languages. "The French really are very, very upset about the world dominance of English." This adds an emotional element to the debate—as is the case in Quebec.

Like residents of a river valley desperately trying to plug the breach in a dam above them with a thimble of putty, Quebec's language bureaucrats are doing their best to stop the flood of English on the Internet. They recently ordered a Montreal-area computer store to translate an English-only web site into French, arguing that French-speaking Quebeckers have a right to advertising in their own language. The Quebec government has also encouraged computer buffs to develop an alternative vocabulary to compete with the English terms used on the Internet.

In Russia, President Boris Yeltsin and Moscow Mayor Yuri Luzhkov complained vociferously about the widespread use of English on store signs and advertising billboards. In a move that should be familiar to Canadians, the Moscow mayor introduced a law requiring that store signs be predominantly in Russian and that all imported food products carry a Russian-language translation of the ingredients.

In the Netherlands over the past decade language activist groups have complained they have had trouble finding Dutch product descriptions. The Dutch are open-minded about language and are considered the linguists of Europe, with 96 per cent of children in secondary school studying English. Even so, there are signs that the spread of English has gone too far for some. A billboard in The Hague advertising

Calvin Klein jeans was recently defaced. "Keep English in England," read the message scrawled in Dutch on the sign, "English has no place in Holland." Ms. Captijn, the advertising director, says she was shocked when she saw the graffiti. "I went home and told my husband: 'There's starting to be a backlash.'"

Even when people have a positive attitude toward speaking English, it can lead to misunderstandings. Sometimes the message gets garbled by people with an inadequate grasp of the language. And sometimes a perfect command of English masks the fact that the parties having the conversation come from different cultures. Didier Savignat, director of the Alliance Française in London, uses the example of the business lunch as a potential pitfall. "In France, lunches are longer and they are more leisure than business," he says. "In England, it's the reverse." The lesson: Executives need to learn each other's culture as well as their language to have smooth relations.

Widespread use of English by people whose proficiency doesn't match their enthusiasm can lead to distorted messages, such as when television reporters interview people in foreign countries for news items shown in English-speaking countries. "You rarely see a TV report where foreigners are speaking their own language and it's dubbed or has subtitles," complains Mr. Savignat of Alliance Française. Coverage of the coup in Zaire/Congo provided many such interviews. "People were speaking very broken English. And you wonder, did they say what they meant?"

It's easier and cheaper for reporters to talk to English speakers because they are immediately accessible and there is no cost for a translator. But it also leads to faulty perceptions. During the pro-democracy demonstrations in Serbia, viewers of CNN and other English-language TV networks would be forgiven if they thought that Vuk Draskovic was the most important leader of the opposition movement, rather than Zoran Djindjic. Mr. Djindjic led a larger and better-organized political party. But Mr. Draskovic speaks fluent English and so won the contest for air time.

Hardest to take for many non-English speakers is the way that adoption of English as a global language has divided the world into a new set of haves and have-nots: Opportunities for knowledge, jobs and advancement may be open to the English speakers and closed to the others. Career ads in French newspapers published in Belgium are often in English, because multinationals increasingly regard mastery of the language as a job prerequisite.

Since English is generally the language of the wealthy and better-educated in many countries, there is a danger that the language is seen as a hurdle to advancement rather than a key to a wider world.

The strength of English also threatens to leave English speakers complacent about learning other languages. Who hasn't heard English speakers on holiday in a foreign country seemingly under the impression that if they just speak loud enough the non-English-speaking hotel clerk, waiter or operator will understand them?

The minister in charge of education in Scotland had deplored the fact that only 12 per cent of Scottish students over the age of 16 studied a foreign language in 1996, compared with 36 per cent as recently as 1975. By contrast, the latest statistics show 96 per cent of German high-school students study English and another 25 per cent study French.

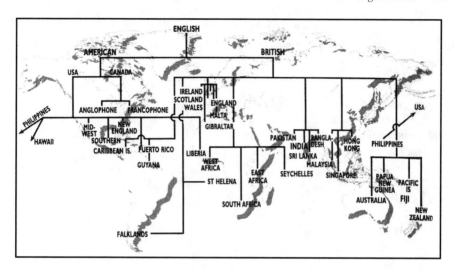

Prof. Crystal says he is heartened by evidence in the United States that businessmen are starting to realize that if they want to maintain their position in global markets they have to make a greater effort to speak to people in their native language. This, and the fact that the United Nations and the European Union have recently come out with statements on linguistic rights, has made him hopeful that English will not eventually bulldoze all other languages in its path.

But the danger is there. "The situation is undoubtedly pretty dire as far as linguistic diversity is concerned," he says. But if countries act now to strengthen minority languages so they can exist alongside a dominant language such as English, the future needn't be grim.

Those Canadians who have acquired a second language either through their parents or by dint of hard work know how much this broadens and enriches their lives. Languages are like windows on the world, each providing a slightly different view. Globally we will all be poorer if we opt for a unilingual future—viewing the world from a single perspective—when a multilingual future is still possible and, ultimately, desirable.

Turbulent Times

Lilianet Brintrup

Beautiful, smart, elegant, just lovely were some of the words I heard not long after I came to the USA for the first time in 1981 from Chile. These were the words I wanted to hear. But at twenty-five degrees below zero, they mixed with the cold weather my own fear and anxiety. There were more words. *Efficient, go for it, do it, just brilliant, intelligent, cool.* The words were unfamiliar to my heart, feelings, and mind. These new words were unexpected, with alien meaning, without transparencies. They were announcing my growing assimilation and acceptance into my foreign culture.

I had come to the U.S. to be a graduate student at the prestigious University of Michigan—Ann Arbor. I was to begin my Ph.D. in the Department of Romance Languages. I arrived in Detroit with my family—my husband and two children—a boy of five, Cosme Zvetan Andreas, and a girl of eighteen months, Colombina Mercedes. When I first arrived, it was the second of February and the winter was at its zenith, hard and implacable. People didn't smile. I supposed that they were in a hurry. I didn't see any sign of welcome, not even one small flag waving in the wind as a sign of welcome for foreign people. This lack of courtesy in a country of immigrants, many of whom had been exiled by brute force, really surprised me. I thought, "Well, it is just one P.M., people are having lunch or siesta, and the ones left here are showing their irritation and sadness." I wanted an explanation for this absence of courtesy.

Soon I became depressed and tired of waiting for somebody to explain to me what this oversight was all about. What I didn't know then was that in America, if you don't demand an explanation, no one will approach you to explain anything. But if you inquire directly about something, the accurate and precise explanations will

Reprinted from *Becoming American*, edited by Meri Nana-Ama Danquah, (2000), Hyperion Books.

be given to you immediately. In fact, one might even be overwhelmed with both the oral and written details of such responses.

The world that I had arrived in happened to be extremely structured, monolithic. Sometimes I thought it nice. Other times I saw this world as alienating because of its obsessions, its constant quest for knowledge and need for progress. I felt stuck. Not in mud, but in the pavement, walls, offices, elevators, and corridors. Only I was not entirely isolated. I was still able to hear the unpleasant noises of the city—the cars, the sirens of ambulances and fire trucks. Soon, in order to retain my already borderline health during my stint as a student, I developed a particularly necessary talent: I looked through the sealed windows to nature and its world outside—the birds, squirrels, and trees, the silent snow, the young and the mature people, the absence of children. And I learned that in places like this so-called university town, real life had very little space.

It seemed as if the people in this town were having a long, long, heartless sleep. So, in order for me to survive, I had to learn to "live" less, to have a minimal awareness of real life. This fragmentation would soon have a tremendous impact on me, my children, and my family as a whole. From the very first few months of my arrival, this disconnection between knowledge, people, and reality struck me vividly. Despite the seeming perfection of things, I sensed a big superficiality and arrogance in the academic world that I was to be a part of. When I established relations with all my wonderful and knowledgeable professors, they made me feel that if I were to sustain my presence in this academic world, the first principle that had to be learned was humility.

I had received the award of a fellowship, thus gaining the status of teaching assistant. Friends, professors, and Ph.D. classmates spoke about this wonderful fellowship that the American institutions gave to foreign students so that they would not be forced to work somewhere else. But, in truth, the only real support I received was the payment of my tuition and a very small salary. And the teaching assistantship was such a burden. It was an unbelievable amount of work, work, and more work. It was difficult to cope with everything, especially doing all of this with a family and no help at home. Things for me then were out of place. They were centered in the middle of constant stress. My mind was in incessant movement and I couldn't rest at all. Life became a turbulent race, leaving me ill-equipped to pay attention to my domestic world, much less to the other worlds around me.

I have never had as intense a sensation of chaos as I did in the midst of this supposed perfection to which I had immigrated. Even a duty like answering a phone call was a difficult and frustrating experience. Assimilation came most immediately to my son, who was five years old. My husband and I placed him in charge of answering all calls in English. He quickly learned how to get rid of calls from banks, offices, vendors, and other unwanted intruders. He was the tongue of the house, the role model of gestures and new ways of thinking. We looked to him as our permanent teacher. He brought in information about a variety of things. He taught us what to eat, how to buy it, when to eat it. He told us which people were our neighbors and educated us on the informality of dressing, the importance of sport, and the mentality of his teachers. I never felt more abandoned during the first year of our arrival than when my son was at school or when he went out to play with friends after school. Sometimes I would call him in because I had received a phone call that froze me, or sometimes simply because he was an American boy who seemed to gracefully understand and accept why we were in the USA. He, especially, always made me feel that I was in the right place. He had the capacity to erase all signs of my guilt. Many times, when I think of the ease with which he adapted, I believe that this country was built for children. He seemed to be so happy.

To be more effective and efficient academically, I received advice like this: "Don't cook and clean up your house every day. Buy food once a week and store it. Spend your spare time at the library or at your work." The most interesting advice I received was "Forget everything you have learned in the past and start again." How can someone just discard memory? The rupture of my academic tradition tore intensively at my soul. Yet I did not see any significance in discarding the memory of the process of my previous academic learning. Why this necessity of washing off my mind when the "new" information I was about to incorporate was only going to sustain the values of a society that seemed to value human relationships so little? Unlike my son, I was neither optimistic nor happy. I felt as if something had been taken away, like my skin and my verbal conception of the world. I was confused; I could see nothing more than contradictions. I even felt a little bit retarded in the midst of the intelligentsia. But I grew to realize that all this advice was coming from people who were actually a lot like me, and that the real problem was my lack of mastery of the English language. I became determined to communicate with and to hear the "Anglo-Saxon Americans."

I tried to find those Americans, but where were they? Where were the ones I came to see, to know—the Anglo-Saxon Americans? The only people that showed any interest in me were Latin-Americans, Greeks, Portuguese, Iranians, Chinese, Germans, Egyptians, and Arabs. Over time, I found that even what I had interpreted as genuine interest on their part was, in fact, a curiosity born of self-interest. After all, we all needed to learn how to survive, and we all looked to others who were somewhat like us to see and learn how they were doing it. In time, my English improved. Nevertheless, my inability to find those Americans for whom I had been searching was not only a question of lacking mastery of their language.

My dear Americans didn't show up. They were all basically too busy working from nine to five or in overnight shifts, or else they were in breakfast, lunch, or supper meetings, or in special training, or dating, or in some sort of professional development or skills workshops, or in seminars, in phone conferences, gardening, in their cars between bowling, football, or soccer, in their cars commuting to and from somewhere, or in their cars for the fun of it. I had entered into an incredibly mobile society where people were on the move all the time. This ceaseless mobility often brought to mind the image of an ocean where each of us swims and swims in order to go somewhere, although we always curiously come back to the point of our departure. We always come back avoiding deterioration, the passage of time, death. Moving, working, playing. The perfect ménage à trois in this territory. Such an alliance admits no divorce. One is always somehow vaguely attached to something or someone, a part of, not apart from. A foreign person can't help but feel confused, isolated, and paralyzed trying to figure out which road to take in order to avoid being mistaken.

I watched myself standing in the middle of this turbulent way of life with complete astonishment, trying to hold my family together, trying to save them from falling into an empty abyss. Food was a problem from the beginning. My daughter ran up and down the stairs of the house shouting and crying for the soup she used to eat in Chile. It was a simple vegetable soup. I made all efforts to reproduce it, but she kept on shouting for it for months until she discovered white bread, yellow cheese, and bologna. At the supermarket, I never knew what exactly to buy for them, so I let them choose. Doughnuts, white bread, and bologna invaded my refrigerator. White bread, that sponge of a food, was my children's favorite. For me, the only food I wanted during those first long winter months was food with a lot of calories. It was too cold to think about salad and fruit. At the time, I never read the food labels, which always looked so attractive and clever to me.

During the weekdays, the children had cold lunches (a sandwich or fruit) at school. I also adopted this form of nourishment and took from our refrigerator—that artifact which was now regulating our lives—anything I could eat at my desk. Not eating together in the dining room of our house made me feel that I was doing something completely wrong, illegal even. I had all but forgotten the "happy hour" of lunchtime. I was sure that we were going to fall into this way of life, into something similar to a black hole of nothingness, where everything was taking place all at once. So, firmly, I refused any job obligations and did not study after three P.M.—the moment my son arrived home from school and when I picked my daughter up from nursery school—in order to be there with them. Religiously, I served them tea between four and five P.M. I prepared them some Chilean pastry. I washed, cleaned, and didn't give up my white tablecloth that proudly covered the table every day at mealtimes.

I was terribly sad, and more than once I thought about quitting everything and returning to Chile, where my children would be surrounded by family, friends, their sensible and generous nanas. As a mother, I was suddenly living the painful experience of being a working mother of young children in a modern society. The dissolution of socializing as a way of being and also of eating disturbed me. I didn't know exactly how to move on and out from my domestic life without tearing apart my heart, customs, and manners. The inside of my home was a constant battle which took most of my energy and occupied all of my time. I seriously considered the idea of bringing over a maid from Chile. The cook we had before coming to the USA seemed to me to be the perfect one to solve all of my domestic problems. She was wise in anticipating the possible problems I would have in America. "Señora, how will you go away if you don't know how to cook? You don't know how to fry an egg the way your husband likes it." "I shall learn. Don't worry. I shall learn," I used to respond to her.

Being in a big university in a big country where everything looked so big, and on occasion, out of proportion, it was easy for me to connect the size of fruits and vegetables with the size of the territory and the size of the buildings. The supermarkets I visited reproduced this ideology of being "super," being "super superior," and therefore having a "super supper." Consequently, I admired the huge strawberries, the gigantic carrots, the enormous cucumbers, the immeasurable pumpkins, and the monstrosity of the apples. I would find myself with "the largest pear in the world," in the biggest and the best city with the tallest buildings imaginable and the most immense prairies on earth where the greatest cows grazed, where the most amazing and extraordinary people came up with super projects and ideas like the creation of Superman and Superwoman. It wasn't easy to adjust to a society with such extremes. It leads to confusion—of the same sort that I had been feeling, suggesting that one is always on the way to accomplishing some "mission impossible." Reproducing our Chilean domestic life was an inferno for the children.

Before too long, I became as busy as everyone else around me, always moving. I traded my siesta time for laundry time, my healthy leisure time for the unbearable workout time. I began to observe the women around me. They were strong, fast, competitive, efficient, even dominant and controlling. My husband was busy as well, too busy trying to get research done, and then, later, trying to get tenure at the university, to pay attention or even notice the details of our daily life. He and I felt then that getting tenure would not only ensure that we could stay in the country, but also that we would be able to relax and enjoy the life that other successful immigrants seemed to enjoy. Big mistake. We had so many projects on our minds that sometimes we found ourselves saying sadly, "We should have come earlier. We are not young enough to cope with the demands of this place." Just coping with the material acquisitions of a house, car, microwave, refrigerator, freezer, carpeting, television, Nintendo, CD player, computer, nice furniture, and practical clothes seemed a task unreachable. How much more coping before we reached a certain economic status, one which would allow us to buy a house in a "good" neighborhood, enable us to send our children to a "good" school. It took us a while to even realize that the really good schools in this country were not necessarily private or religious schools in rich neighborhoods. Surely immigrants, in this regard, are no different from many dedicated Americans who work from sunup till sundown to attain the luxuries of this country. But not coming from such a democratic party "par excellence" makes it harder to understand it.

I started buying all sorts of things in abundance. This exuberant way of life made me feel that I was rich and powerful. But, really, my mental health was in danger. The order of my previous domestic life was replaced by another order that I was unable to fully comprehend. My children cried, laughed, and complained too often. My husband's adjustment process was rapid and abrupt. He was always a warrior, a person determined to win any battle, to fight any obstacle, to blow up any insect near his shoulder. He had to take charge of America. As much as I admired him, his ambitious attitude and his combative behavior tired me. We were losing, little by little, through his activities, the feeling of being interrelated. He was too much like any other violent and ambitious creature. I recognized, though not without difficulty, that it was the only way for us to survive here. Because of him, I always had a place to live, food to eat, clothes to wear, and many other luxurious objects. He had, in vain, designed a prospectus for our life in order to save us from chaos. That dreaded chaos, which surfaced as the breakdown of our domestic life, came without us even noticing it. The university was a magnificent system, but it was like a headless monster unknown to me. I was scared to fail the demands. I was scared I would not be able to face the monster. Fear and competition had wrapped us both up. All the while that we were determined to become winners, we had forgotten what we were losing.

Assimilation was *the* major and overbearing task. To speak, to think, to eat, and to dream in more than one language. I became insensible and silly. To immigrate to the USA is to come to a mobile culture, where everything is changing, and where the immigrants are nothing special because the dominant style of life will ultimately absorb them. At first, I felt that Americans never appreciated my coming. Looking back now, I see that I was wrong in this belief. Over the years, I have witnessed the tremendous efforts on the part of Americans to celebrate diversity, minorities, and cultural differences. The opportunities that this place promises to immigrants are rather fantastic, but we don't know exactly where those opportunities are located. We think that they are everywhere—in the countryside, in the small village, in the big cities, even in the space at the very bottom of that ocean I so long imagined as a metaphor for life here in America. One has to seek out those opportunities in the midst of a profound disconnection between people, institutions, corporations, regular offices. In a place like this, where everything seems chopped, cut, fragmented; a place where there is no sense of community; a place where one is forced to move from place to place without a transition of any sort, one can become disoriented. There is something that has been difficult for me to understand: how Americans refuse to understand that we as immigrants cannot be "super" or "superior" to anything. Becoming American is an experience that cannot be the same for every immigrant. The experience of selling tacos in Los Angeles and being a professor at MIT or a researcher at NIH produces very distinct human beings.

So where am I in all this? I have never picked grapes or apples and I have never worked at the factories. I came as a Chilean white European with two German names. Now I am Hispanic. But not a "super" Hispanic of the nation. This transformation interests me. Instead of becoming just an American, I became a little part of America and a little piece of Hispanic-Latino-Chicano. Curiously, only my Chilean background has given me the feeling of roots. Roots that I do not find in that country. My little American portion has to do precisely with knowledge. I have been exposed to readings and dialogues produced by critical American minds. Reading and listening, I was able, and am able still, to observe the seriousness of their thoughts, the deep level of information, the rigor of the data based on extended studies. This is the portion of America that I want to be a part of: the process of dismantling myths, stereotypes, and lies. Being critical is one of the most relevant aspects of becoming American for me. What America gave me was a space to write, along with my developing abilities to clean a house, to cook, to select smart food, to be my own maid, to be a worker, to be personae.

When I went abroad and someone asked me where I came from, I answered in two parts: I am from Chile, but I am living in California. What I really want to say when I say, "I am living in California," is perhaps this: I came to this mythical and controversial place through effort, through hard work, and now I have a social security number, a driver's license, credit cards, status as a Hispanic and as a Californian. I have enough courage to deal with the USA. I have grown in this way—fighting stereotypes, and fighting to be a kind of quiet, conscious, and nonpassive Hispanic immigrant, a human being.

AHA!

Edwidge Danticat

AHA!

I'd like to tell you about an encounter I had a couple of months ago in a bookstore in Miami, Florida. I was doing a reading, and after the reading, a young man came up to me and asked me to sign a book for him. Before I could sign, he whispered, "Would you please write 'From one AHA to another'?" I stopped to ask him what he meant. What is AHA? "From one AHA to another" implied that I was one and he was one. What had I just become?

He said, "Well, AHA, spelled A-H-A, is an acronym for African-Haitian-American. That's what I am. That's what you are."

I had never heard that particular classification applied to either me or any of my friends before so of course I had tons of questions. He proceeded to tell me that this was a new way for young Haitians who had been in the United States for a while to define themselves, partly to combat all the negative labels they were bombarded with, among them "boat people" and "the AIDS people."

The term *AHA*, African-Haitian-American, had the following elements: African to acknowledge our ancestral roots deep in the African continent; Haitian, because of course most of us were either born in Haiti or were first generation born of Haitian parents; and American because we were from the Americas, living in the other "America," the United States of America.

1981

As I sat there in the bookstore, thinking about what this young man had said, I couldn't help but flash back to the time when I had just moved from Haiti to the

Reprinted from *Becoming American*, edited by Meri Nana-Ama Danquah, (2000), Hyperion Books.

United States in 1981. To catch you up with my life before that, I was born in Port-au-Prince, Haiti, in 1969. In a somewhat typical migration pattern, typical for many people I know, my father left Haiti when I was two years old. When I was four, he sent for my mother, and I was raised for the next eight years by an aunt and uncle.

I was twelve years old when I moved to the United States to be reunited with my parents. I came on a Friday night in the middle of March, not speaking a word of English. My father enrolled me in junior high school on Monday morning in a bilingual class. Now the spring of 1981, aside from being the time when Brooklyn, New York, and I discovered one another, was still a time of dictatorship in Haiti. Jean-Claude Duvalier (aka Baby Doc) was president. There was a swell of people coming by boat from Haiti to Florida to escape the dictatorship, the first large exodus of the 1980s. Every night on the six o'clock news, you could see dead, bloated bodies washing up on Miami beaches. This was often followed by some type of report on AIDS, still a fresh news topic then, too. Both items would keep all the members of my family anxious. The boat people, because coming from a poor Haitian family, any of those faces could have been one of our relatives. So we watched the television screen with great interest as the Coast Guard's white sheets were thrown over the dark, dead faces, already half buried in the Florida sand. And we watched with great interest those who had survived the boat journey to America and were able to walk away, only to be processed into detention centers in New York and Miami. We leaned in to observe their gait, their height, their body type, and we searched for traces of ourselves in them.

My parents belonged to a Pentecostal church in Brooklyn called Evangelical Crusade of Fishers of Men, which was very much involved in refugee work. So on Sunday afternoons after church, we would go and visit many of the refugees in confinement at the Brooklyn Navy Yard detention center. We would go to talk to them and pray with them, listen to their complaints, and, most important, get the names of relatives to contact on their behalf. After looking into their eyes and holding their hands, watching them cry and fully acknowledging once more how much they had sacrificed to come to the United States, I never understood why the children at school would shout their fate at us as a curse: "Get back on your banana boats, you dirty Haitians!"

As I said before, the spring of 1981 was also a time when AIDS hit the media in a major way. It was still a new disease, AIDS was, and there was a lot of speculation as to what the disease's origins were. All anyone seemed to know, all they seemed to be saying from the six o'clock news, was that there were only certain groups of people who got AIDS, among them homosexuals, hemophiliacs, heroin addicts, and Haitians. So the labels we were given in my Brooklyn neighborhood in the spring of 1981 were not very hip or self-assigned. They were like lashes from razored whips.

I am reminded of a particular day in the spring of 1981. After many taunts and fights with students who would continue to call us "boat people" and "AIDS people," a group of my fellow Haitian students decided to use a stereotype as our protection. We knew that among the many conceptions/misconceptions that the other students had about our culture was that we practiced a "dangerous" religion sensationalized in American films and denigrating political language as "voodoo." So the Haitian students all agreed to carry red handkerchiefs and spread rumors that the red handkerchiefs had spells and crippling powders in them. Soon whenever we were called names or taunted, up would go out handkerchiefs with a mumbling of some kind of abracadabra and our enemies would flee. Even those students who on other occasions had denied that they were Haitian participated in this wild scheme, reaffirming our solidarity.

Flash forward now some fourteen years, where my time spent in Haiti was at a deficit to the time spent in the United States. And in a bookstore unexpectedly someone is giving me this label that was part playful, part revolutionary in the way he presented it to me. And for some reason, it made me glad. I was glad about what this young man was calling me and was calling himself, because as he said, the moniker was "self-assigned" and self-assigned tags are always better than the ones other people holler as epithets against you.

Days after this encounter in the bookstore, I would think over and over about this meeting. Perhaps this AHA thing was a North Miami phenomenon. Maybe this was something this one particular person and his own group of friends called each other. I have never heard anyone use the term since. However this conversation left me with a sense of empowerment, given the many things that we have been called in the past.

DYASPORA

In Haiti, people like me are called dyaspora, meaning we are members of our country's Diaspora. We can also belong to something that is called the Tenth Department. Haiti has nine geographic departments, which are actual entities. The tenth department is not concrete land. It is not a specific place, but an idea to which Haitians can belong, no matter where we are in the world. We of the Haitian dyaspora maintain a very long umbilical cord with our homeland. People who live in the United States for twenty-five years still want to return to Haiti and run for government office.

I was once at the Haitian consulate in Manhattan with my mother when a man in his sixties walked in with his U.S. passport held high above his head. He marched up to the secretary at the front desk and denounced his United States citizenship so that he could run for parliament in Haiti. My mother, who has maintained her Haitian citizenship after more than twenty-five years of living in the United States, often says, "If I can't go to Haiti as often as I'd like, I might as well have my Haitian passport. At least I can look at it once in a while."

In spite of our own nostalgia, the term *dyaspora* can also be a painful epithet aimed at those of us who return to Haiti from abroad, acting as though we know all the answers to a country from which we had been absent during the most difficult times. Still, many of the well-intentioned dyaspora start businesses and build schools when they return to Haiti and, with their income capacity, are helping to bridge the huge gap between Haiti's majority poor and small elite.

MRS. CHÉ

In the building where I used to live in the spring of 1981, we all desperately tried to maintain the best of Haiti in our Brooklyn lives. The building had a very large population of Haitian families. On Sundays the families would exchange dinners and plates of sweets. Babysitting favors were taken for granted. If children were seen misbehaving on the street, any of the people in the building were allowed to scold them, and the minors would listen, knowing how much the adults trusted each other.

When I was teased at school, I would dream of that building and I would run home to it. It was a comforting leap into the most comforting elements of my life: social intimacy, community, kinship.

I remember there was an old woman who lived on the sixth floor of the building, Mrs. Chérubin; we called her Mrs. Ché. Mrs. Ché liked to say, "It is only my body that is here in America, but I am going to make the most of it." To Mrs. Ché, it was okay to look forward and back at the same time, to be melancholy about being away from home and joyful too, to have plantains with our Thanksgiving dinner, the proverbs of our language peek through the veil of our English sentences, to see the world with two eyes that do not always look in the same direction.

With Mrs. Ché, if something special was happening in the building, some party or special event that I couldn't attend, she would always say, "Edwidge, *map wè lonbraj ou la,*" meaning "Even if you can't be with us, I will see your shadow there."

The other night, I spoke to an uncle in Haiti whose seventieth birthday was coming up. I told him I was sorry I couldn't come for the small celebration he was planning, he told me he would look for my shadow there.

These days my shadow is more often in Haiti and my body in the United States. (There are times too when I am in Haiti for a long time that people tell me they see my shadow or feel my spirit at events in Brooklyn.) These days, I feel less like an immigrant and more like a nomad. I try to see as many different places and experience as many cultures as I can. The more cultures I experience, the more Haitian I feel, because it is my birthright as well as my chosen foundation, what I compare and contrast everything to, my floating banana boat, for which there is perhaps no longer a singular harbor.

A friend once told me, by way of a cautionary tale, the story of a woman who ran away from Haiti in her late teens to go live in Puerto Rico. In Puerto Rico, she picked up enough Spanish to get by but never really mastered the language. While in Puerto Rico, she never had a chance to use either one of our two official languages. *Kreyòl* or French, so she forgot both of them. After a while, she didn't speak either Kreyòl, French, or Spanish well. She moved to the United States later on in life, where she never learned English very well either. So when she had daughters in America, she and her daughters developed a potpourri language and a series of gestures in order to communicate.

After hearing that story, rather than feel pity for that woman, I envied her.

"Wow!" I remember thinking. Imagine, she gets to invent a language of her own out of her fragments of memory.

I have always had what Baudelaire called the grand malaise, secretly relishing the role of permanent outsider, never expecting to belong. That's why I don't agonize over being told to get back on my banana boat only to be called a dyaspora when my boat sets anchor. I don't want to be a culture-clash victim. Nor do I need to be. We live in a more and more migratory world. I don't know that many people these days whose bodies and shadows are exclusively anchored in the same harbor. However, these days I, too, call myself an AHA now and then. Peer-assigned and equally a-geographical as poly-geographical, it seems as good a harbor as any for both me and my shadow to temporarily reside.

A Road Still Becoming

Suheir Hammad

UTFO's "Roxanne Roxanne." I had heard other rap songs before, but this was the one which introduced me intimately to Hip-Hop. I was no more than ten years old and on my way home from school. Three fine Puerto Rican teenage boys were walking toward me down Fourth Avenue in Brooklyn's Sunset Park. One was carrying a flattened cardboard box under his arm, another, a boom box, and the last one was just smiling at the little girls who were admiring them. They were going to our now-empty schoolyard, the cardboard to be laid out on the concrete, so the boys could break-dance on top of it. The music from that huge radio could be heard from at least a block and a half away. But it wasn't until they were right in front of me that I heard the chorus to the song: "Roxanne, Roxanne, I want to be your man . . ." Word.

I rushed home, excited by the energy of the sound, and the smile the flyest boy had blessed me with. My mother was cooking fish. I loved the way she made fish—not breaded to death and served with tartar sauce, like in school. Mama would hook the whiting (forever to be called "ghetto fish" by my sisters and our friends who also grew up on it) up with some sumac and cumin, and the juice of a lemon. I put my books away, changed clothes, washed my hands, and came to help. I repeated the new chorus I'd learned under my breath as I placed olives and peppers on the table. Baba was home for lunch that day, a rare thing, so we had to set a proper table.

Smoking his cigarette while waiting for the food, Baba asked us what we had learned in school that day. My two sisters were two and four years younger than I, the first son was in kindergarten, and then there was the baby boy, who was spared the inquisition. We lined up in front of Baba as Mama took the fish out of the oil. As one of my sisters was reciting her ABCs, my pops heard me still humming to

Reprinted from *Becoming American*, edited by Meri Nana-Ama Danquah, (2000), Hyperion Books.

myself. "What are you saying?" he asked. And like an idiot, I rhymed the words for him. Pandemonium, as my brothers' favorite wrestling broadcaster would have said.

"What are you saying? This is what you learn in school? This is why we came to this country? So you can come home with filth in your mouth? No more. No more friends, no more music. Allah, what is this? What are we going to do with this? This music, this black music, rap, whatever it is, not in this house. We are not black, or Spanish. I'll break your teeth if I hear you repeat this trash again. Not in this house."

All this said at a decibel that made it clear Baba was more than a little upset.

*   *   *

My parents are of the first generation of Palestinians born and raised outside of their ancestral home. Both sets of my grands were evacuated, or forced, from their towns in 1948. Their homes were taken over by Jews who left Europe's horror to embrace my grandparent's land as their own. How many people were murdered during what the Palestinians call The Catastrophe, the creation of the state of Israel, no one knows for sure. Entire villages were killed off, the most famous one being Deir Yessin, where nearly three hundred people were massacred overnight. But the people I come from, those who survived and were violently uprooted from their land, were taken to emergency refugee camps set up by the United Nations.

My dad was born on the way out of Palestine and into Jordan, in the West Bank. A transit baby. Mom's family had already moved out of the camps when she was born, three years after the expulsion. Both were raised in Amman, my mother on the outskirts of the camps, my father in the heart of them. And both were raised in the shadow of the land just lost. My paternal grandfather carried the key to his house in Lydd with him until he died in 1985. The key hung like a rosary on the wall of his refugee home, a reminder and false hope, after his vow never to return until he was free to live in his own land. Never was.

I, too, have grown up under that shadow. When I was five years old, my parents left what they knew in Jordan and came to Brooklyn, looking for their American Dream. It was 1979. The Iranian hostage crisis was brewing, and oil was a precious thing at gas stations all over America. The country was on the verge of a Republican presidency, and the Sugar Hill Gang was recently famous and on top of the music charts for what was later called the first mainstream Hip-Hop jam, "Rapper's Delight."

My parents believed many beautiful things of America before they immigrated. *Amreeca* was the place where no one bothered you. Where your religion and race did not matter as long as you worked hard. It was the one true democracy in the world. The police here did not harass people or get away with murder, the way they did in Jordan or Lebanon. Money was to be made by anyone strong enough to work and smart enough to save.

This trip to a new land, the land of golden streets, was to be my father's first real chance at life. The camps had offered him no educational direction and no trade to learn. As the last-born child of his mother and the ninth out of his father's fifteen children, Baba had been raised in the unique position of being considered the baby and a middle child. As a man, he was expected to fully support his own growing family. Both of my parents graduated high school, my mother working as a teacher's aide briefly afterward, my father attending one year of college. But Baba left the university, as was in vogue during his youth, to join the popular resistance to Israeli rule. And like so many of his comrades, his dreams of a liberated homeland were eventually deflated and carried around as failure.

One of my paternal uncles had already been living in the States for a decade and had set up a business. My father was to come work for him and pay off the money my uncle spent on bringing me, my two younger sisters, my pregnant mother, and himself over to Amreeca. My brother was born a few months after we arrived, and with him came the first snow I remember.

Cold. My first memories of America are white, frozen over, magical, and cold. And I guess no matter what I have experienced here as a citizen, I more often than not come back to this same memory. I have a mean-ass cousin, who pushed me into that first snow, sticking snowballs into my ears and down my shirt. I got sick, but I didn't die. I became an American, accustomed to the cold.

* * *

I grew up, along with my brothers and sister, in a cramped two-bedroom apartment in Sunset Park, Brooklyn. At the time a predominately Puerto Rican neighborhood, Sunset was loud with salsa music and botanicas. The park the neighborhood is named after is a scraggly-looking city lot with some grass and scattered trees which goes on for five blocks in one direction and three avenues in another. I remember seeing my first crack vials in that park. The 1980s drug epidemic affected my neighborhood deeply. Crack especially, since it is so potent and cheap. It seemed as if it was over-night, but in over a year, I witnessed neighbors who'd been healthy, hard-working people become gaunt, haunted by the monkey on their back. Girls I had been at grammar school with, shiny, beautiful girls, became involved with and had babies with drug dealers, the same boys who'd been at school with us. The drug dealers became the ghetto superstars of our day. Many of them were shot, jailed, or killed.

My father busted his ass working off his debt and trying to feed his growing family. He worked in grocery stores all over the borough, always in poor neighborhoods. And poor neighborhoods most often translated into black neighborhoods. It's a phenomenon still alive today. You won't find many Arab, Asian, or Latino-owned business in white neighborhoods. And it seems rare to find black-owned businesses anywhere.

My father found himself in areas of Brooklyn, like East New York, Coney Island, Flatbush, which seemed to come right out of bad '70s gangster movies. Many of the stores he worked in were surrounded by broken-down, burned-out buildings. And more than once desperation, poverty, and substance abuse held my pops up at gunpoint. Robbed him of his pay. Pressed a revolver into his back and made him open up the cash register. For me, it was like Baba really was in a movie. He once came home with a bullet wound in his foot and blood dried on his forehead, evidence of where another bullet had grazed. As he carefully took his shoes off, he told us of how three masked men broke into the supermarket he was working in, with shotguns blazing. Drama. And the music to all of this? The first stages of Hip-Hop. No wonder he didn't appreciate my UTFO sound bite.

* * *

"We are not these people. We are Arab. We are not American or Spanish or black. *Ihna* Arab."

These sentences were a kind of mantra both of my parents used when they wanted to get across to us that we were not to dress, eat, do, talk, study, or simply be like anyone else. I always found it interesting whom my parents thought Americans were. When they said, "American, black, or Spanish," they were clearly differentiating between the "real Americans," and the others, the Africans, the Latinos, and, eventually, the Arabs. America was, and is, to my parents, still the frozen, white, and magical fantasy, with no room for us.

Being Palestinian in America has been a trip. Like my parents, I found no room available for this particular identity in mainstream America. The America of apple pies and Fourth of July picnics. Whether this America, the one of toothsome corn-bred beauty queens and football-playing patriotic blond boys even exists, I don't know. The America I witnessed, was shaped by, and am myself shaping, is carved out of concrete and soul. This is the Other America, and it is made up of the spaces we have created in order to survive. And the soundtrack to this notion of a nation for me is Hip-Hop.

The Black Nationalist–inspired lyrics of Public Enemy coming out of my headphones accompanied the television coverage I viewed of the popular Palestinian uprising of the late 1980s, the *Intifada*. This visual and aural climate created around me a new notion of identity. Chuck D's thick voice mouthing the condition of oppressed peoples in neighborhoods similar to my own, the images of young Palestinian kids throwing rocks at Israeli soldiers helped me to understand my place in the world, my place in America, and my place in my self. I was of more than one place. The shadow, which had followed my father out of his camp, merged with the shadow America had created for those citizens who didn't exactly fit.

These people, the ones who didn't fit, were not of one color, one religion, or one race. These people came from everywhere, and some of them came from here, before the United States was even an imperialist twinkle in the eye of some European. The ancestors of my friends all have different stories. Some were captured on their own land, sold, and shipped here as commodities. Others came on planes to find the financial opportunity promised them after America's Navy took control of their island. One of my friends' grandfather came here fleeing the Nazis, his hand tattooed with the numbers which replaced his name to make it easier for the keepers at the gas chambers to record.

My own people were affected by the Jewish Holocaust in a different way. Using the horrifying effects of Europe's "anti-Semitism" as a justification, Zionists and their supporters were able to fulfill their goal of creating a Jewish state in Palestine. I place the quotations there because history has found identity to be fluid. My grandparents, Semites by ancestral, cultural, linguistic, and geographical definition, found themselves on the receiving end of a racism intent on erasing them, or at best, relocating them for the convenience of European Jewry, who became the epitome of the word Semite. The West approved of and funded the state of Israel, and in that way, tried to forget about my people, about the people who were living off of, and for, that land.

Knowing the U.S. government has given aid to Israel for so long, and so unconditionally, has always created a tension within me. Especially recently, having just turned twenty-five years old in 1998, the fiftieth year of the Palestinian Diaspora. I find myself asking who would I be if things had transpired differently. I am an American now. My passport says as much, as does my Brooklyn tongue. But on my first trip to Palestine, I was treated as a straight-up terrorist at the airport. I had to remind the security people I was an American, not a threat to them. But I was the one needing to be reminded. I will always be of more than one place. And that can be threatening to some.

And that's what it often comes down to. Reminding people. Reminding myself where I come from. I will never be as American as apple pie. And thank Allah, 'cause I ain't never liked cooked fruit. I'll have some of my mom's ghetto-fried whiting with the Arab spices over fillet o fish, any day. But if being from a place is about where, and what, you have lived, I am from here, more than I am anywhere else. This is what I know. What I have lived. Being a citizen ain't only about paying taxes, although sometimes it feels like it.

So, with all of our histories, with all of the different paths taken to be here, we find ourselves together. Hip-hop is more than music, it is a culture and a mirror of the times for many of America's youth. Created in the Bronx, by DJs throwing block parties in burned-out lots and rhyming over beats, the music is now heard all over the world. In true oral tradition, MCs remind. Many, if not most, lyrics are somewhat autobiographical, and in that way, young urban people, who are not the recipients of the best educational programs nationally, use vernacular and rhythm to define themselves. My friends and I used rhymes to define and defend ourselves. We are the generation the media had called X, not after Malcolm, or a sense of righteousness, but to define us as unknown.

Some people threw graffiti up on the walls of their neighborhoods. What the police and most residents (including my parents who kicked my butt the time I pointed out my tag "Fresa Fresh" on the hallway banister) saw as vandalism, these artists saw as proof of their existence, for all to see. The use of the bright spray paints on city transport or depressing project walls has also been a try at bringing nature into areas where trees are sparse. A good piece is like a dance caught in the air, all movement, color, and open space. And the memorial walls, now famous, of neighborhood kids who died too young are a testament to the violence so many people have not survived. Faced with dehumanizing building design, kids beautified their hoods with the materials available. Survival.

B-Boying, the break-dancing those fine Puerto Rican boys were off to when they changed my life, has connections to African dance that are clearly visible to anyone who will care to look. Watch B-Boys dance alongside Capoiera players of Brazil and you will see amazing flexibility and similar movements. In Brazil, during the last century, enslaved Africans were not allowed to exercise their martial arts skills, but ingeniously, they did so as though they were dancing, right under the noses of plantation owners, who got off on watching captive people move. The fact that kids from Brooklyn and the Bronx brought the same movements to concrete and cardboard, one hundred years later and across the world, says as much about the conditions of poor neighborhoods in America as it does about the incredible retention capabilities of people. Survival.

Caribbean immigrants were the most popular DJs in the Bronx during the late '70s. Some of the best were young Jamaican men who had come to New York with their working-class parents to find a better life than the one in the Yard. These DJs were familiar with different sounds, Jamaica being well known for DJ clashes and different sound systems. By sampling beats from different music, the DJs brought the world to the streets of New York City. Punk, Ska, Rock, were all early influences on Hip-Hop, as much as Jazz and Bebop. Like my mother's best gumbo *(makluba)*, choice ingredients have gone into the pot. Survival.

Immigrants add as much to this culture as we gain from it. We have to remind ourselves that many of the things which are now popularly considered American were once marginalized as "the ways of colored folk." Jazz, Rock-and-Roll, Southern food. And now, what the media calls Rap. Survival.

And the MC. The front person, the face of Hip-Hop. The voice heard, the words memorized instead of homework. While all the elements are fundamental, each person has one that truly moves them. For me, it's the lyricist. The person who not only puts pen to paper, their heart on their sleeve, but also rhymes the words over a beat, to make you nod your head and think at the same time. It's about music, keeping an internal rhythm, and never missing it. My parents always told me the most perfect poetry was God's word. Between the Quran's teachings and Rakim's rhymes, I found myself in love with words, and wanting to record not only my story but the stories of those around me, so history would know we existed. Survival.

* * *

There is a huge part of me that thinks breaking down my lifestyle into parts is stupid. As though the experiences my sisters and I went through could each be boxed and checked off a list. The world doesn't work that way. Neither does being an American. The lens I look out of has been shaped by more than one movement, and many moments of tension, contradictions. All the "-isms" have played a part, including socialism, feminism, nationalism, and a racism not based on economic superiority but on limited contact with white Americans. My parents' religious beliefs and their cultural traditions have affected the way I walk in the world. Shit, just being a woman affects the way I walk down the street.

But I have to remind myself, I am more than a woman. I am more than a kid who grew up poor in Brooklyn. I am more than a type of hair or a way of wearing clothes. I am dynamic, as we all are. As America is. As this thing called Hip-Hop is. And I walk with a certain step. A particular one. Not the exaggerated hoodlum with the one-pant-leg-up-and-one-down walk Hollywood has decided is hip. Nor the head-held-high-and-shoulders-back walk I would wish for myself. Not yet. I walk with my ancestors in my bones. They are heavy. I walk with history on my shoulders. It is heavy. I walk with a beat in my head, usually a beat with a rhyme laced on top of it. Not too heavy, but deep. I am walking into the millennium. And America is walking alongside of me, many of her youth with the same step. No longer walking behind, not interested in leading the way, but together. Down a road still becoming. Nothing is static, and we change with every breath. I may never be apple pie, but more and more, America is becoming like me, like us.

Where Is the Globalized Me?

Long Yingtai

[The article is based on a speech delivered in Beijing by a well-known Chinese author who expressed mixed feelings about the cultural changes brought about by globalization particularly in the non-Western world.]

When preparing this topic, I kept thinking and tried to answer a question: to what extent has my life been "globalized"?

Usually I have my breakfast with milk, bread, plus butter and jam. If in big hotels, what I'm going to choose is basically between European and American styles. My breakfast is often accompanied with morning papers: Hong Kong's *Ming Bao*, Taibei's *Zhong Guo Shi Bao*, Singapore's *United Morning News*, or *Frankfurt Neue Press*, depending on which city I stay in. But there are some papers I always want to read and they are available wherever I am, such as *Asian Wall Street Journal* or *International Herald Tribune*. I also would like to listen to BBC or watch CNN.

After breakfast, I often take a morning shower. The shampoos I use are often made by a couple of the same international companies, and so is the bathroom paper. Sitting in front of vanity, I find cosmetics are bearing the same brands—French, American, Japanese—no matter which corner of the world I am in. Although I am not a fashion-monger, when I open the door of my closet, I always see those familiar names of the same fashion-makers.

EVEN THE APPEARANCE OF THE CITIES LOOK SIMILAR

If food and clothing have been globalized in the way I described, how about housewares, transportation, education and entertainment?

Speech delivered at the Modern Chinese Literature Center in Beijing, reprinted from the *United Morning Daily* (Singapore), excerpted and translated by Yinghong Cheng, January 2004.

Let's look at household stuff. Ikea has "unified" every apartment, whether it is in Mexico City, Shanghai, Helsinki or Los Angeles. When you drive or take a bus, you will see very few names of car manufacturers or bus makers. Even the trains in subways in different cities are made by just a few companies. Not only have furniture, cars, buses, and trains been globally identical, even appearances of cities look the same. Street lights, bus-stop signs, advertisement posters, and sidewalk designs, all of the so-called "street furniture," have become the products of global enterprises. A handful of global designers and developers bid against each other for the landscape and architecture of the cities, and that is why we now have so many cities with similar faces.

Then how about education and entertainment? After having an American breakfast, I drive a German car rolling through streets laid out by French planners, and arrive at a museum designed by British architects, to see a contemporary art exhibition.

It is possibly a multimedia art exhibition with pictures taken by cameras and camcorders. The grotesque and gaudy images convey a feeling of modern life, and may be pretty interesting at the first glance. But if you have seen too many similar exhibitions in Italy's Venice, Brazil's Sao Paulo, Turkey's Istanbul, Germany's Kahlsruhe and Korea's Kwangju, you can't help but ask yourself: why are the interpretations of "modernity" so similar to each other, despite being made by different artists from different locations and different cultures?

After the art exhibition, I might still have some time, so I walk into a bookstore. Right at the entrance, copies of *Harry Potter* are displayed. You see simplified Chinese versions if you are in China or Singapore, traditional Chinese versions in Hong Kong and Taipei, Spanish versions in Madrid, and German versions in Berlin.[1] No matter where you are, you will certainly see the same novel.

After dark, I often want to watch a movie. But how could you get rid of those Hollywood products? *Titanic* and *Crouching Tiger, Hidden Dragon* are shown everywhere, just as is McDonald's standard menu, whether in villages of Malaysia or downtown London. What will you see if you just stay home and watch TV like a coach potato? Well, I just recently moved to Hong Kong from Germany, and when I turned TV on and saw the very beginning of a soap opera, my kids shouted "I already saw that!" It was an American product and you see it in German if you are in Germany, in Spanish if you are in Spain and Cantonese if in Hong Kong.

Can't fall asleep? Want a sleeping pill? You will find you are taking the same pills you can get anywhere. Got a headache? You have the same pain-killer. Time to feed the fish? It's the same product of the fish-food from the same chain store. Want to send something to someone in another country? You have only either DHL or Federal Express to choose, no matter where you are, Beijing, Taipei, or Frankfurt, all the same process. Involved in lawsuit? Need life insurance? International law firm and global insurance companies are waiting for you at your door steps.

---

[1] Mainland China and Singapore underwent a reform and now use simplified Chinese characters while Taiwan and Hong Kong use traditional ones. One apparent difference between the two is the latter have more strokes.

Everything in your life—material, cultural and spiritual—has become commercialized under globalization. Every aspect of your life is penetrated by globally available goods. There is no way you can escape it.

One hundred years ago, in the time of Liang Qichao, Chinese intellectuals were talking about the sneaking Western thoughts.[2] It was a time western influence was just knocking the door and people were arguing whether to completely open the door and welcome it or to just narrowly open the door and let it creep in. With the passage of one hundred years, Western influence has invaded our world from all dimensions: the door, the window, and even the sewage system; it has penetrated our life from pure intellectual and abstract theoretical level to the most concrete and practical day-to-day needs and details.

99% IS WESTERN INFLUENCE

But what is "globalization"? This term is actually problematic and misleading. Whose influence? From where and to where? Who is "globalizing" whom? Is Indian or Arab influence penetrating my life? No. If you take a close look at your everyday life, you will find that so-called "globalization" is 99% westernization. If you take a close look at westernization, then 99% of it originated in the US. Therefore for us globalization is pretty much Americanization.

Because globalization is to a great extent Americanization, many Europeans have been very cautious and even fearful in face of it. Some radicals even appealed to violence against the symbols of globalization, such as Starbucks, global summit meetings, and McDonald's. They and people like them everywhere are deeply concerned about two things: one is monopoly of sources, for example in South Korea there were peasants committing suicide to promote the society's awareness of the difficult situations the South Korean peasants were facing when international agricultural companies began to control their country's market. Another thing is monopoly of values, because in globalization, wrapped in packages of commercial goods, foreign values are introduced into your countries and threaten the integrity and independency of native culture. When a German newspaper faced bankruptcy due to ill management and a British media group proposed to buy it, the German Chancellor exerted his influence to stop the transaction, because newsmedia is a culturally sensitive nerve system with functions of shaping public opinions and values. The Chancellor did not want to see foreign capital and international companies entering this field and manipulating public opinions and values.

Isn't this cultural arrogance?

In my growing-up years, the first time I came to be cautious about "globalization" was in 1975, when I first arrived the US.

Before I came to the US, I studied English in Taiwan. Our English teacher who came from the U.S. asked every student in her class to pick up an English

---

[2] Liang Qichao (1873-1929) was one of the earliest Chinese intellectuals who advocated introducing Western culture into China to enlighten Chinese, but many of his culturally conservative contemporaries were concerned about the negative impacts of Western culture.

name, because she could not recall all of those Chinese names. Therefore we came to be "Dick," "Tom," "Harry" overnight, and I picked "Shirley."

After I came to the US, I began to teach American students English composition. I had more than 20 students. I spent whole afternoon trying to match faces with names and I did it. At that moment I could not help asking myself: why couldn't the American teacher who taught me English sit down and spend a couple of hours to march Chinese faces with the names, instead she made us to change names for her convenience?

Isn't this cultural arrogance? After I came to realize this, "Shirley" disappeared and was replaced by "Long Yingtai." Note: it was "Long Yingtai," not "Yingtai Long."[3] I thought that since Americans could learn how to pronounce Chinese names and how to match Chinese names with their faces, why couldn't they also try to understand and accept the Chinese custom that puts last names first? That was in 1975 and I had not heard of the term "globalization," but I had already begun to be discontent with the fact that "cultural exchange" was actually a one-way channel.

As international enterprises grow everywhere, the trend of culture becoming commodities has become more apparent. When I attend meetings of international writers association, which is the occasion for writers from different countries to get together and discuss international peace and equal rights, I often find that you may talk about Shakespeare, Goethe, Thomas Mann, or Hemingway with anyone, but you can not discuss Chao Xueqing, Zhuang Zi, Han Fei or Zhang Ailing with the others, because cultural commodities are often imported or exported in one direction.[4]

One day in Frankfurt's largest bookstore, I was seeking a Daoist classics for my children. I could not find it in philosophy section, neither could I find it in literature or political science. Finally I found it in esotericism section, where Lao Zi and Zhuang Zi were put together along with Feng Shui, Japanese Zen Buddhism, zodiac, Qi Gong, and Tai Jie.[5]

Do our bookstores put Plato in the same section of Western astrology? Probably we do not. But we might put African novels in the same section with books introducing African animals or cannibalism, might we?

Globalization is both exciting and disturbing. Culture, including the basic values of life, is sent to your doorsteps as consumer goods unloaded from delivery trucks.

[3] The author emphasized the awakening of her cultural awareness against the U.S. "cultural arrogance" by keeping the Chinese order of her name—family name first and given name second—although she was living and working in the U.S. Most Chinese observe the Western custom and move their given names ahead of their family names when they study, work, or settle down in Western countries.

[4] Chao Xueqing (1714-1763) was a famous Chinese novelist whose *Dream of the Red Chamber* was a classic masterpiece. Zhuang Zi (399-295 B.C.) was one of Daoist founders whose literary style helped Daoism become popular. Han Fei (280-233 B.C.) was the founder of Legalism whose literary style helped Legalism be accepted by Chinese society. Zhang Ailing (1921-1995) was a famous 20th century Chinese female novelist who was particularly popular in Taiwan.

[5] Feng Shui is the ancient Chinese system of arranging environments by using existing settings in nature or positioning houses, furniture, tombs etc. to maximize the internal harmony thus benefit people. Zen Buddhism is a Buddhist variation in China and Japan emphasizing meditation and sudden enlightenment. Zodiac is a Chinese system associating people's years of birth with certain animals thus suggesting an influence of such animals' characters upon people's personalities. Qi Gong is a Chinese exercise for good health by controlling breath and absorbing "Qi," the natural energy. Tai Jie is a Chinese exercise and martial art.

We welcome it because suddenly we have more choices; we are apprehensive because such choices often come without alternatives, although in many occasions we are not aware of the hegemonic nature of such a cultural dumping. The goods imported by power are often not the most desirable ones to us. Furthermore, such enforced introductions frequently destroy the original order. For example, should the Iraqis welcome the culture and value brought in by American soldiers? Why some of them say yes while some others say no?

Such misgiving and ambiguity are common among Third World intellectuals. I once met an Indian writer. When we talked about the enlightenment in our youth, we found we were all "beneficiaries" of the US Information Agency[6]. In a time of both material and cultural shortage, the US government deliberately exported American values through its organizations and money. Was it bad? No, because such efforts contributed to our pursuit of democracy and openness. Was it good? Well, it came up with some hidden aims and it also limited our imagination of the future.

---

[6] The US Information Agency (1953-1999) was a federal foreign affairs agency supporting U.S. foreign policy and national interests abroad by conducting international educational and cultural exchanges, broadcasting, and information programs.

Transnational Crime:
A Growing Global Menace

Yaw Ackah

INTRODUCTION

When the French sociologist Emile Durkheim stated that crime is a normal aspect of every society he was not endorsing crime, rather he meant that crime occurs in all societies and therefore it is normal. The universal nature of crime makes it a global phenomenon that transcends both time and place (Albanese, 2002). Punishments like crucifixion, hanging, decapitation, imprisonment, fines and corporal punishment are also testimonies of the "normality" of crime in all societies and historical periods.

Most people are familiar with "index" crimes like homicide, rape, assault, arson, robbery, and burglary, which "indicate" the crime rate in the society. Index crimes of particular countries, however, may have limited local and national impact. On the other hand, the increased interdependence of events and actions of people and governments around the world in the last century has caused crime to take on a "global" face (Shelley, 2001; Arlacchi, 2001). Global or transnational crimes ("transnational crimes" will be used henceforth) consist of those criminal acts whose planning and execution transcend national borders and jurisdiction, and whose impact is felt in other countries (Albanese, 2002; Rush, 2000). To understand "transnational" crime, it must be perceived and approached as such, since no country can fight international crime alone. Besides, recent social and political events demonstrate *that what happens in one part of the world impacts all the rest.*

The advances in modern technology, banking, financial systems, transportation and telecommunication have had a double-edged-sword impact on transnational crimes. While they have speeded up interaction among people and countries and the movement of goods and services across the globe, they have also made the commission of crime much easier, hence the rapid growth in transnational crimes. There is no doubt that transnational crime has profited greatly from the process of globalization.

Transnational crime may be violent, or nonviolent. Violent transnational crimes include human trafficking, narcotics distribution, contraband smuggling (e.g., of firearms) and terrorism (including the acquisition of weapons of mass destruction). Nonviolent transnational crimes consist of corruption, counterfeiting and money laundering, intellectual property theft, depletion of national resources, environmental crime, and cyber crime. These crimes are however not mutually exclusive. Before discussing some transnational crimes, it is necessary to talk about organized crime, specifically its global aspect, in order to clear up some common misunderstandings.

TRANSNATIONAL ORGANIZED CRIME

Hollywood's romanticized depictions, albeit unrealistic and distorted, have attracted much attention to organized crime. Organized crime is defined as "those self-perpetuating, structured associations of individuals and groups combined for the purpose of profiting in whole or in part by illegal means, while protecting their activities through a pattern of graft and corruption" (Champion, 1997, p. 88). Organized crime is therefore not limited to any one specific criminal activity or individual(s). Transnational organized criminal groups operate across national borders. Their criminal activities include human trafficking, drugs (narcotics) and weapon distribution, trade in body parts, money laundering, cyber crime, and environmental crimes. A trademark of organized criminal groups is their readiness to use violence, including murder. In a 5-year period, 1995–2000, Russian Mafiya operatives murdered ninety-five Russian bankers, and hundreds of reform-minded business leaders and investigative journalists have been assassinated or kidnapped (Schmalleger, 2002). The Colombian drug cartels have murdered judges, law enforcement officers and witnesses. The Vietnamese, Japanese, Jamaican and Chinese crime mobs are also noted for extreme violence.

Transnational organized crime has thus emerged as one of the most pressing challenges of the early twenty-first century. The Ninth UN Congress on the Prevention of Crime and the Treatment of Offenders, which met in Cairo, Egypt, unanimously agreed that transnational organized crime is now a major force in world finance, able to alter the destinies of countries at critical stages of their economic development (Schmalleger, 2002). Participants identified the world's six major crime clans as the Hong Kong-based Triads, South American cocaine cartels, Italian Mafia, Japanese Yakuza, Russian Mafiya, and West African crime groups. Some equally dangerous organized crime groups operate from China, the Philippines, Vietnam, North and South Korea, Israel, the United States and Jamaica. In fact, no country can claim to be free of the tentacles of transnational organized crime. In our increasingly global economy, the threat to international networks and national economies should be seen as a collective economic problem.

The Russia "Mafiya" deserves special attention because it has gained the most notoriety since the collapse of the Soviet Union, and because of the rapid expansion of its influence into the US and other countries. Its discussion will also serve as a sampler of the degree of power, violence and influence of organized crime groups across the globe. The Mafiya has literally taken control of the Russian society and the fifteen newly independent republics. Intelligence reports from Russia estimate that the Mafiya consists of 100,000 members who owe allegiance to 8,000 stratified crime groups and control 70-80% of all private business and 40% of the nation's wealth. Additionally, the Mafiya controls Russia's banking system through the investment of ill-gotten gains, money laundering, intimidation, fraud, the outright purchase of financial institutions and murder. The Mafiya's annual black market value is worth over $18 billion (Perspectives, 2000). Other sources estimate that 80% of Russian businesses pay protection money to the mob (Schmallger, 2002). The remarkable sophistication and ruthlessness of the Russian Mafiya are largely traceable to the infusion of the expertise of former KGB agents and government functionaries into its ranks.

Although often ignored by the media, organized crime is very active in Western Europe. For example, the Italian Mafia is strongly involved in drug and human trafficking, money laundering, extortion, weapons and diamonds smuggling and environmental crimes such as illegal disposal of toxic waste. The biggest names in organized crime in Asia are the Chinese Triads and Big Circle Boys, the Japanese Yakuza, and Vietnamese gangs (Perspectives, 2000). Asian organized criminal organizations are particularly active in computer software piracy, credit card forgery and fraud and counterfeit identification and currency operations. In Italy and some South American countries, particularly those contending with weak economies and corrupt law enforcement, organized crime groups wield considerable power over national governments. Through the acquisition of innovative technology, organized criminal organizations are able to build their wealth, power and influence through alliances with counterparts across international borders (Shelley, 2001).

Corrupt law enforcement personnel and government officials, and the lack of fast and effective extradition laws have enabled transnational organized criminals to amass great wealth that is connected to major drug cartels and multinational companies. According to UN estimates, organized crime earns US$1.1 trillion per year. In fact, the international drug trade is reported to exceed the value of the international oil trade, and only international arms trade exceeds it by value (www.pctc.govph/edocs/updates, n.d.). According to Fields and Moore (1996), some organized criminals have appeared in the *Forbes* and *Fortune* lists of the world's wealthiest individuals. Columbian drug cartels, Japanese Yakuza and the Mafia have major stock and real estate holdings (ibid).

African organized crime groups are most noticeable in Nigeria and South Africa. Nigeria's crime organizations are widely involved in "advance fee frauds" or the infamous "419 scams," named for the article of the Nigerian criminal code that covers such operations. West Africa serves as one of the conduits for trafficking Southeast and Southwest Asian drugs into the US and Europe. In South Africa, some former members of the apartheid security forces are deeply involved in weapons smuggling, drug trafficking and diamond smuggling (Perspectives, 2000).

Organized criminal groups in South America, particularly in Colombia, Bolivia and Peru, are inextricably linked with drug trafficking. Colombia alone manufactures between 70 and 80 percent of the world's refined cocaine. In the past few years, however, Mexican cartels have snatched control of drug trafficking from the erstwhile dominant drug cartels, the Cali and Medellin (UNODC, 2003). The tri-border region of Argentina, Brazil and Paraguay is known as a magnet for organized crime (Perspectives, 2000).

In North America, organized crime is concentrated mainly in the US and Canada. The La Cosa Nostra (an offshoot of the Italian Mafia), the most notable group in the US, is involved in numerous criminal as well as legitimate businesses including construction, food retailing and trash disposal. Outlaw motorcycle gangs like Hells Angels, with over 180 chapters around the world, are also actively involved in drug trafficking, prostitution and money laundering. It is known that between 5 and 18 transnational criminal organizations are actively operating in Canada. This includes Asian triads, Italian and Sicilian Mafia groups, Russian/Eastern European mafiyas, and outlaw motor gangs (Perspectives, 2000).

A growing trend among transnational criminals is the pursuit of "legitimation" (involvement in legitimate activities), which enables them to "whitewash" their illegal activities. Many mafia bosses have successfully achieved at the minimum some semblance of public respect and civic legitimacy by making donations to community hospitals, charities, universities and political parties (Perspectives, 2000). The late New York mafia boss, John Gotti, made numerous cash donations towards community projects, hence the tremendous public outcry over the many unsuccessful attempts by the government to put him behind bars. In fact, his neighbors at Ozone Park perceived these as the "persecution" of a patriotic and philanthropic citizen (*www.newsday.com*, June 12, 2004).

Because globalization has increased global networks and reduced restrictions between international borders, opportunistic transnational organized crime groups have utilized these networks to maximize their profits and power as they share information, skills, costs, market access and relative strengths (Stephens, 1996, Dobriansky, 2001). Global organized crime can have damaging impact on political structures when criminals cooperate with insurgents or use intimidation, bribery and extreme violence to control elected officials, law enforcement personnel and businesses (e.g., drug cartels in Colombia and Peru, the Balkans, the Sicilian Mafia and Russian Mafiya). Now, we will discuss a few transnational crimes and their global impact.

TRAFFICKING IN HUMANS

> "Lydia was only 16 when she was lured to the house of a friend, drugged, and smuggled out of town . . . [The abductor] beat and raped her, and let his friends do the same. He told her that she owned his agency $35,000 and that she would repay the debt by servicing ten to twenty men a day in a brothel. He threatened to harm her family if she tried to escape. Addicted to drugs, scarred by sloppy abortions, suffering from STDs, and psychologically devastated, Lydia soon resigned herself to the nightmare that has become her life . . ." (Angert, 2003, p.1).

It is difficult to believe that in spite of our "modern" conceptions of democracy, abuse of individual rights and human dignity, slavery and bondage continue to persist in the 21st century. The sad truth is that there is a modern form of slavery ("white slavery") in which women and children are bought and sold, transported to other countries and forced into sexual and economic exploitation. Smuggling of persons is often confused with trafficking in humans. However, while the former is done with the migrant's consent and the relationship ends in the destination country, trafficking in humans on the other hand is often done without the victim's consent, or the consent is obtained through force, deceit or coercion, and involves a continual exploitation. The victims (mostly from Central and Eastern Europe and the poor, developing countries of Africa, southeast Asia, the Caribbean, South America, and the former Soviet Union) are lured with promises of education (in the case of children), glamorous jobs in modeling and fashion, and ordinary positions as housekeepers, nannies or hotel assistants. Others like Lydia are simply abducted (Angert, 2003). Upon their arrival at the destination country, their passports are confiscated, and they are either forced to pay back exorbitant fees or work as sexual or economic slaves, in sweatshops, for the traffickers, usually in the "three D-jobs": dirty, difficult and dangerous (UNODC, 2003).

The Internet has facilitated human trafficking through direct communication between potential suppliers and consumers (Albanese, 2002). As a result, human trafficking has grown into a significant global market in which more than 1 million women and children are trafficked annually across international borders (Arlacchi, 2001, Angert, 2003). This is in addition "to the already existing millions living under modern forms of slavery . . . 27 million by one expert's estimate, up to 200 million by another estimate" (Arlacchi, 3002, p. 3). The CIA estimates that between 45,000 and 50,000 women and children are trafficked into the United States alone each year. According to UNICEF, over 200,000 children are enslaved by across-border smuggling in West and Central Africa, annually. Regions of sudden political changes, economic collapse, civil unrest, internal armed conflict and natural disasters are rich sources of human trafficking because displaced persons are greatly vulnerable to exploitation, abuse and trafficking (OMCTP, 2003). This may explain why "up to 10 percent of Moldova's female population has already been sold into prostitution" (Angert, 2003, p. 6). International organized crime is deeply involved in human trafficking because it is a low-risk enterprise, and it is highly profitable. In the uncommon event that the trafficker is apprehended during transit, all he needs to do is disavow any knowledge of the existence of the victim or purposes of the trip. The UN estimates the human trafficking industry to be worth between $7 and $12 billion dollars a year. (Angert, 2003).

The attitude of both the source and destination countries helps perpetuate this crime. Source countries usually deny the existence of this crime within their borders. Destination countries, mostly European and North American, often treat the victims (who are also illegal aliens) as criminals, or with insensitive indifference. In some cases where the traffickers are prosecuted, and the victims have served their function as state witnesses, and therefore have outlived their usefulness, they are deported! Sometimes, because trafficked persons are placed in psychological situations similar to those of the victims of extreme torture, they become so submissive and terrified of their "masters" that they decline to cooperate with law enforcement officers even when they have the opportunity to do so (Jordan, 2001). The complicity of law enforcement officers in trafficking makes these victims reluctant to cooperate with police even though it is in their interest to do so.

Given that victims of human trafficking are forced into prostitution and other sex-related businesses, as well as exposed to rape, torture, HIV/AIDS, STDs, drug and alcohol addictions, this crime poses potentially disastrous public health problems of global proportions. In addition, by depriving source countries (particularly poor and developing economies) of potential human resources and revenue, the crime threatens sustainable development in those countries, while diverting revenue to feed transnational crime. Although globalization has spurned other transnational crimes, to the International Labor Organization human trafficking is truly "the underside of globalization" (OMCTP, 2003). It is also an indictment on the conscience of the international community.

TERRORISM

"Terrorism is a global threat with global effects" (Kofi Annan, UN Secretary-General, UNODC, 2003, p.1).

Although terrorism has been in existence since the dawn of recorded history, the September 11 attack, reportedly "the deadliest terrorist attack in history," was the catalyst that shocked and sharpened our awareness of the global relevance of terrorism. Countless and deadly terrorist attacks had been recorded in other parts of the world before and after the September 11 attack. A sample includes the bombing of the Federal building in Oklahoma City, the chemical agent attack on a Tokyo subway, attacks on American embassies in Kenya and Tanzania, the bombing of Flight 103, the bombings in Indonesia and Chechnya, the attacks on the Jordanian Embassy in Baghdad as well as bombings in Egypt, Algeria, Italy, Pakistan, Ireland, and the almost routine suicide bombings in Israel. After his arrest following the first bombing of the World Trade Center in 1993, Siddig Ibrahim Siddig-Ali, one of the suspects, declared ominously: "We can get you anytime" (Schmalleger, 2001, p. 676).

And predictably there have been several attacks since September 11. We have witnessed the suicide bombing of a busload of people, including children, in Israel, which resulted in the death of at least 20; an attack on the United Nations Headquarters in Baghdad; the bombing of a Najaf mosque, killing about a hundred people; and the beheading of two American civilians and a Korean. There was the fear that three Turkish nationals who were kidnapped would be beheaded also. These unexpected attacks demonstrate the ubiquitous, callous, thoughtless and vicious nature of terrorists.

It is paradoxical that although the world now appreciates that "terrorism" poses a clear threat to global peace and security, there is no universally accepted definition of "terrorism" because of the "relative" and subjective aspect of its conceptualization. Geographic location, historical period, and political, religious or moral orientation determine one's perception of what constitutes "terrorism" and, therefore, who is a "terrorist." It is in these contexts that Joan of Arc (France), Spartacus (ancient Roman empire), Che Guevara (South America), Nelson Mandela (South Africa), Ken Saro-Wiwa (Nigeria), Kwame Nkrumah (Ghana) and Mahatma Gandhi (India) were labeled as "terrorists" or "dangerous," and punished accordingly, even though others perceived these same individuals as "patriots," "heroes" or "heroines" and "revolutionary fighters." Therefore, one person's terrorist is another person's freedom fighter. Perhaps this is best illustrated in al-Qaeda leader Osama bin Laden's accusation that the United States commits "the highest degree of terrorism in the world" (Fagin, 2003, p. 18). In spite of the definitional nightmare, the consensus among criminologists is that "terrorism" is an act of violence usually perpetrated against noncombatant civilian targets to achieve political or social objectives (Schmalleger 2002, Albanese 2002, Rush 2000). Our discussion of terrorism in this chapter will be based on these considerations.

Terrorism, like many transnational crimes, has adopted a new face, a new sophistication in violence, audacity and choice of targets, that has increased the extent of the damage/harm it causes. For example, the collapse of the former Soviet Union has increased our concerns about terrorism because access to weapons of mass destruction and the capability to produce them are now readily available to the highest bidder. In two separate incidents, Lithuanian nationals were arrested for attempting to sell "Soviet-era, tactical nuclear weapons to Federal agents posing as arms brokers for drug cartels" (Schmalleger, 2002, p. 317). Recently, Abdul Khan, a nuclear scientist, admitted to selling nuclear technology to Libya, Iran and North Korea (*USA Today,* 2004). A further concern is that although modern weapons of mass destruction have lost their bulk and weight, they have gained unimaginable lethal power. In 1605, a would-be-terrorist named Guy Fawkes attempted to blow up the British House of Commons with 29 barrels of gunpowder (Schmalleger, 2002). Today the same objective can be accomplished with a small plastic charge concealed in a briefcase. Handguns can now be manufactured out of plastic polymers and ceramics capable of firing Teflon-coated armor-piercing bullets that cannot be detected with contemporary metal detectors (Schmalleger, 2001). In fact, the latest anti-aircraft rockets can be shoulder-fired. With a range of 5.2 km and impact time of few seconds, the potential threat this new weapon poses for air travel is obvious and frightening.

Contemporary terrorist groups are often categorized as either "nationalist" (the Irish Republican Army, Palestinian Liberation Organization, the Basque Fatherland and Liberty in Spain, and Kurdistan Workers' Party in Turkey) or "religious" (Osama bin Laden's al-Qaeda in Afghanistan, Hamas in Palestine, Hezbollah in Lebanon, the Baruch Goldstein in Israel, and the Aum Shinrikyo in Japan). The UN has identified "130 terrorist groups capable of developing homemade atomic bomb" (*Sunday Herald,* 2001). Some terrorist activities are sponsored by radical states to achieve political objectives through the use of surrogate warriors, mercenaries or "guns for hire." An example is the 1979 seizure of the American Embassy in Iran by "independent youths." Given that state-sponsored terrorists have access to more resources, they are potentially more deadly.

DRUG DISTRIBUTION

The drug phenomenon poses a threat not only to individuals but also to political and economic development, as well as the safety of our communities and stability of governments globally. Drug traffickers have taken advantage of the tremendous improvements in transportation and communication to maximize profit margins and refine their elusive skills in drug distribution. It is on record that traffickers sometimes ingeniously redesign the interiors of 727 planes to hold maximum amounts of cocaine (Stephens, 1996). They also have devised complex, tortuous, and complicated drug channels, "a spider's web of connection touching every part of the globe" (Fields and Moore, 1996, p. ix.). Drug profits are electronically transferred to dozens of banks around the world in less than 24 hours through falsified export documents and invoices for goods in order to disguise drug trafficking transactions (Stephens, 1996).

In the late 1990s, drug trafficking ranked as one of the world's most profitable enterprises with an annual income of between $200 and $300 billion (Lee, 1998). The huge profits allow drug cartels to consistently use bribes to buy respect and influence in their communities. It is estimated that the Colombian drug cartels spend over $100 million annually on bribes (Lee, 1998). In fact, Cali cartel leader Gilberto Orejuela has openly bragged, "We don't kill judges or ministers [state secretaries], we buy them" (ibid, p. 17).

Kaplan's (2001) tragic account of the activities of drug dealers in Rio de Janeiro, Brazil, illustrates the awesome power drug dealers can wield. In Rio de Janeiro drug dealers literally own several streets in the city in which the "law of the jungle" is the order of the day. The government simply does not exist in Rio de Janeiro's poorest slums, the "favelas." Here drug gangs rule—and they rule ruthlessly. The youth of inner cities in Brazil are twice the victims of drug distribution, either as addicts or as victims in the endemic drug turf wars. Drug distribution has destroyed lives, raised public health costs and contributed to the crime rate in Brazil's inner cities. This tragic picture is similar to others in many parts of the world where drug kingpins wield tremendous power.

MONEY LAUNDERING

By utilizing the advances in technology such as the Internet, organized criminal groups are able to tap into foreign stock exchanges and the global economy and threaten the security of the world's financial system. It has been estimated that individual money laundering cases are in the thousands of millions of dollars, larger than the gross domestic product of many countries. Organized crime groups are reported to have laundered at least US$7 billion in the South American region (Perspectives, 2000). In 1999 the Mafiya laundered about $10 billion through the Bank of New York (Arlacchi, 2001).

The strict banking secrecy laws, confidentiality laws and lax reporting regulations of International Banking Centers (IBCs) limit law enforcement investigations of money laundering. The International Monetary Fund (IMF) reported that funds in offshore accounts grew from US $3.5 trillion in 1992 to between US $8 trillion and US $10 trillion in 2000 (Perspectives, 2000). The diversion of money into the hands of drug traffickers disrupts currency and interest rates, distorts business decisions, increases the risk of bank failures and taints a country's economic reputation, as well as compromise the political stability of countries.

CYBER CRIME

Cyber crime (or computer crime) basically consists of using computers to engage in illegal activities. Computers become the "objects of crime" when, for example, an individual intentionally causes damage to computer hardware (machines) or software (programs). The physical or electronic damage to computers or computer programs constitutes the crime of computer as the object. Computers may also be used as "instruments/tools of crime" to steal: for example, the electronic looting of bank accounts. In a classic case, the controller at Halifax Technology Services embezzled $15 million by generating corporate checks to herself over a period of three years (Albanese, 2002).

Copyright infringement (e.g., software piracy) is probably the most prevalent cyber crime in the world. About 30% of all software in use globally has been pirated. The SIIA (Software Information Association Industry) reported that global losses from software piracy (known as "Warez" in the computer underground) totaled nearly $12.2 billion in 1999. North America, Asia and Western Europe account for 83% of worldwide revenue losses from software piracy. Some countries have especially high rate of software piracy. For example, 97% of software in use in Vietnam, 95% in China, and 92% in Russia are pirated (Schmalleger 2002). The growth and interconnection of global computerized financial networks have greatly contributed to the rise in cyber crime. A few weeks ago a teenager was arrested for creating the "blaster" virus that also infected over 500,000 computers globally. However, cyber crime is highly underreported because businesses are reluctant to report computer crime for fear of revealing their vulnerability to competitors and potential cyber criminals.

Perhaps, more importantly, the sensational media publicity that is usually accorded cyber crime (particularly creators of viruses) often enables the offenders to secure high-paying jobs. Given that the Internet is a global medium, the policing of cyber crime becomes an impossible law enforcement strategy. Besides, few countries have criminal statutes that deal specifically with cyber crimes. The Philippine government faced this problem when Onel de Guzman was arrested for creating the "ILOVEYOU" (or Love Bug) virus that caused havoc to computers worldwide and cost over $10 billion in damages. He was eventually released because none of the Philippines' existing criminal codes had specifically addressed computer crimes (Schmalleger, 2002).

ENVIRONMENTAL CRIMES (POLLUTION)

Environmental pollution includes the dumping of toxic materials and hazardous waste (chemical contamination) into the sea and rivers, air pollution, destruction of the forest, or extraction techniques such as surface mining. The illicit discharge of toxic and dangerous substances and wastes into water supplies and seas is not only a crime, but it also poses very serious threat to the life and health of people, as well as the world's eco-system. Serious environment pollution began with the advent of industrialization as we pursued profit and economic growth without due consideration for the long-term impact on the environment. The consequence of this profit-driven environmental exploitation is the "tragedy of the commons," that is, environmental changes that bring short-term benefits to a few individuals but long-term devastation to the majority (Hardin, 1968).

Environmental crimes evolved "out of a need to protect water supplies, soil fertility and human health in general, from the economic and social activities of man . . . and the increasing scientific understanding of the interdependence of eco-systems" (Robinson, 1993, p.1). Environmental crimes are considered transnational crimes because their impact on the environment transcends national borders. Plane-tary winds can transport air pollution from one country to another. For example, wildfires resulting from illegal logging in Indonesia created severe smog and atmos-pheric pollution that spread to neighboring Singapore, Malaysia, Brunei, Thailand and the Philippines (Buzan, www.pctc.gov.ph/edocs/updates, n.d.).

The combination of environmental pollution, racism and globalization mani-fests itself in a phenomenon known as "global environmental racism," which is the deliberate targeting of poor countries for the illegal dumping of toxic waste, and the abuse of environmental protection laws in these countries. The general pattern in global environmental racism is that waste disposal contractors in industrialized countries use bribery and other corrupt measures to procure rights to dispose haz-ardous waste for storage or destruction in underdeveloped countries (ibid, p. 2). Greenpeace has estimated that between 1989 and 1994 the Organization for Eco-nomic Cooperation and Development countries exported 2,611,677 metric tons of hazardous wastes to non-OECD countries (Robinson, 2001).

Typical examples of global environmental racism are: the Royal Dutch Shell oil pollution of Ogoniland in Nigeria; the dumping of waste rock into rivers by Freeport-McMoRan company in West Papua (Indonesia); the dumping of toxic byproducts in local rivers in Ecuador by Texaco; and the Exxon Valdez oil leak in the Prince William Sound in Alaska. Additionally, the half-hearted response to vic-tims and families following the Union Carbide explosion in Bhopal, India, in which thousands died and several suffered severe illness through toxic gas exposure, is an example of environmental racism.

Many reasons account for such global environmental racism as typified in the examples above. First, poor countries provide "pollution havens" for Western com-panies trying to escape the stringent laws in their own countries in return for "economic aid." Even developed countries like the US and Australia often provide "pollution havens" that companies utilize to "avoid stringent State laws" (Robinson, 1993, p. 3). Also, in Mexico where there are no "right to know" laws, " . . . both workers and communities are denied information about the toxins to which they are exposed. Companies pollute freely, degrading the border environment" (Robinson, 2001, p. 4). Multinational corporations rely on their tremendous economic and polit-ical power to blatantly violate environmental protection laws in poor countries. The use of bribery and "environmental blackmail" such as low environmental standards as preconditions for locating companies in the specific country are typical strategies. Additionally, poor countries "lack the political power, information and vital global strategies to take on powerful multinational corporations . . . " (Robinson 2001, p. 6). The unusually skewed global power relationship between rich and poor nations allows the former to violate numerous United Nations protocols and resolutions on the environment.

Attempts have been made to address the problem of global warming through the creation of an international treaty called the Kyoto Protocol. The 1997 Kyoto Protocol on Climate Change clearly sets emission standards for the developed countries and proposed projects like reforestation to ensure cleaner air (Kelleher and Klein, 1999). In 1992, the UN adopted the Declaration of the UN Conference on Human Environment in its continued efforts to slow the pollution and depletion of environmental resources. However, the effective implementation of these and other environmental "laws" depends solely on the goodwill of member nations. According to the *Earth Times* (2002), although by the end of 2000 there were over 500 environmental treaties, as of 2000, enforcement was so weak that few, if any, violations were punished. Countries that are best placed to monitor environmental laws (the rich industrialized nations) are invariably the most flagrant violators. A classic example is the Bush administration's refusal to support the Kyoto Protocol, claiming that " . . . reducing greenhouse gas emissions will hurt the US economy" (www.greenpeaceusa.org). More importantly, countries like the US and multinational corporations utilize their tremendous power in the media industry to disseminate information that downplays the critical need to maintain the complex but tenuous balance among people, the environment and economies. The former vice-president, Al Gore, failed to convince American voters of the importance of global warming, and as shown above, environmental issues do not rank high on President Bush's agenda. As a director at the Worldwatch Institute cautioned, "Pieces of paper don't frighten criminals. Unless governments start implementing the terms of these treaties, and put some teeth into enforcement, these lawbreakers will continue to ravage and pollute our planet" (*Earth Times*, 2002, p. 1).

It is now obvious that global environmental crime pays! In 2000, "the US imported an estimated $330 million worth of illegal timber from Indonesia" (ibid, 2002). Environmental crime like wildlife smuggling, poaching and illegal fishing and dealings in illicit hazardous waste reaped huge profits. We should be concerned that the world's resources are finite, and science has yet to devise strategies to reverse environmental destruction once it gets under way. Overutilization of the world's resources has the tendency to disrupt the balance between people, their economic activities and nature. We don't seem to appreciate that "Globalization is about to threaten our very existence through vast ecological criminality which, unless checked, would severely damage the food, water and clean air supply for all of us" (Fields and Moore, 1996, p. ix). These three are the three "critical resources" (Kelleher and Klein, 1999) which when destroyed could threaten the survival of life on this planet. The universal question we should ask is: What kind of environment are we going to bequeath to our children?

CONTROL OF TRANSNATIONAL CRIME

It is extremely difficult, but not impossible, to control transnational crime. The UN Office of Drugs and Crime (UNODC) was established to address all aspects of the drug problem, as well as the related problem of international terrorism. Between 1963 and 1999 (prior to the September 11, 2001, attack) the UN developed 12 universal conventions and protocols to combat global terrorism. These conventions and protocols obligated member states to penalize terrorism under their local laws so as to create "no safe haven for terrorists" globally. In response to the September 11 attack, the UN Security Council adopted Resolution 1373 on September 28, 2001, to combat terrorism on all fronts. In addition, Resolution 173 adopted the "Counter-Terrorism Committee of the Security Council . . . [that] has since become the UN's leading body to promote collective action against international terrorism" (UNODC, 2003, p. 2).

The United States responded to the September 11 attack with the creation of a cabinet-level Department of Homeland Security. The government has also put into effect an Executive Order on Terrorist Financing that aims at blocking property and prohibiting transactions with persons who commit, threaten to commit or support terrorism. It is encouraging to know that since September 11, 2001, the US has successfully blocked $34.3 million in assets of terrorist organizations, while other nations have blocked another $77.9 million (www.whitehouse.gov/response/financialresponse. n.d.).

In 2002 several countries attended a "Signing Conference for the United Nations Convention against Transnational Organized Crime" held in Palermo, Sicily, in 2000. Perhaps due to heightened appreciation of the need for a multifaceted approach to transnational crime, by the end of the three-day conference, 124 countries had signed the convention. The drafters agreed to cooperate, and exchange intelligence reports that would be incorporated into a state-of-the–art instrument to fight transnational crime. An equally practical response to transnational crime was the decision to adopt some principles of "inchoate or attempted crime," and prosecute the mere agreement to participate in the planning of an organized crime (i.e. conspiracy), whether or not the individual actually participated in the crime. In addition, the convention decided to criminalize money laundering, corruption, and obstruction of justice. To address the problem of money laundering and capital flight, banks will be required to release information that in the past was protected by "bank secrecy." There is little doubt that this bold decision "may prove to be one of the most effective elements of the Palermo convention, since organized crime loses much of its appeal if the profits from it cannot be safely held" (Arlacchi, 2001, p. 4). Finally, the convention adopted a "RICO" type provision to seize the property of organized criminals as well as the equipment used in the commission of the crime. The significance of the Palermo Convention is that it established standards for member countries to follow. The Interpol, UNICEF, Europol and several NGOs, including the European-wide organization La Strada, are cooperating to monitor and combat trafficking in human and firearms. In the USA, the Office to Monitor and Combat Trafficking in Persons operates globally through cooperating with other international bodies and organization. This body focuses on the "3 P's-Prevention [of trafficking], Protection [of victims] and Prosecution [of perpetrators]" (Angert, 2003, p. 6).

CONCLUSION

The global social fabric, political and financial systems are at the risk of deteriorating under the increasing power of transnational organized crime. The globe is "shrinking" through advances in telecommunication, transportation, and the exchange of information. On the other hand, transnational crime has gained awesome strength through global alliances. However, these alliances are also the source of its weakness, because its networks, though brutal, are fragile and easily penetrated. Therefore, coordination of international law enforcement strategies, coupled with UN commitment and leadership, should succeed in controlling transnational crime, and therefore at the minimum make the "global village" a safe place to live in.

REFERENCES

Albanese, J. (2002). *Criminal Justice*. 2nd ed. Boston: Allyn & Bacon.

Angert, A. (2003). "Sexual Bondage: The Slimy European Trade in Human Sex Slaves." *The Columbia Political Review*. February.

Arlacchi, P. (2001) "Nations Build Alliances to Stop Organized Crime." *Global Issues,* Aug.

Bonner, R. & O'Brien, T. (1999). "Activity at Bank Raises Suspicions of Russia Mob Tie." *New York Times,* August 19, p. 1.

Champion, D. *The Roxbury Dictionary of Criminal Justice: Key Terms and Major Court Cases*. Los Angeles: Roxbury Publishing C.

Dobriansky, P. (2001). "The Explosive Growth of Globalized Crime." *Global Issues.* Aug.

Economic Perspectives. (2003). *Trafficking in Persons Report*. US Department of Justice.

Fields, C. and Moore, R. (1996). *Comparative Criminal Justice: Nontraditional System of Law and Control*. Prospect Heights: Waveland Press, Inc.

Fagin, J. (2003). *Criminal Justice*. Boston: Allyn & Bacon.

Greenpeace USA: (2004). "U.S. Withdraws From Kyoto Protocol." Retrieved from *www.greenpeaceusa.org*, June 24, 2004.

Hardin, G. (1968). "The Tragedy of the Commons." *Science,* 162 (Dec. 13):1243–48.

Jordan, A. (2001). "Trafficking in Humans Beings: The Slavery that Surrounds Us." *Global Issues,* August.

Kaplan, D. (2002). "The Laws of the Jungle." *US News & World Report.* October 14.

Kelleher, A. & Klein, L. (1999). *Global Perspectives: A Handbook for Understanding Global Issues*. Upper Saddle River, NJ: Prentice Hall.

Lee, R. (1998). *Global Reach: The Threat of International Drug Trafficking*. Annual Editions: Drugs, Society, and Behavior. p. 15. Cluice Dock, CT: Dushkin/McGraw Hill.

McDowell, J & Novis, G. (2001). "The Consequences of Money Laundering and Financial Crime." *Economic Perspectives,* May.

OMCTP. *Trafficking in Persons Report*. Retrieved from *www.state.gov*, June 11, 2003

Perspectives. (2000). *Transnational Criminal Activity: A Global Context*. Canadian Security Intelligence Service, Report #2000/07, August 17.

Robinson, B. (1993). "The Nature of Environmental Crime." A Paper presented at the Australian Institute of Criminology Conference, on Environmental Crime. Sept.1–3.

Robinson, D. (2001). "Environmental Racism: Old Wine in a New Bottle." *Women in Action*, #2

Rush, G. (2000). *The Dictionary of Criminal Justice*. Long Beach, CA: Dushkin/McGraw-Hill.

Schmalleger, F. (2002). *Criminology Today: An Integrative Introduction*. Upper Saddle River, NJ.: Prentice Hall.

Schmalleger, F. (2001). *Criminal Justice Today: An Introductory Text for the Twenty-First Century*. Upper Saddle River, NJ: Prentice Hall.

Shelley, L (2002). "Crime Victimizes Both Society and Democracy." *Global Issues,* August.

Stephens, M. (1996). "Global Organized Crime." Paper presented at the Center for Strategic and International Studies Conference on Global Organized Crime, September 26, 1994.

UNODC. "Trafficking in Human Beings." Retrieved from *www.pctc.govph/edocs/updates.* August 05, 2003.

World Watch Institute. (2002). "International Environmental Crime Shouldn't Pay." *Earth Times*, September.

Science Directions:
Beyond Traditional Boundaries

Kraig A. Wheeler

Many advances in the physical sciences today originated as a direct response to the needs of our dynamic global community. Although significant efforts to develop new materials and improve on current resources remain a common theme, the approach to scientific study has evolved towards a more interdisciplinary approach that extends beyond the limits of institutional (i.e., academia and industry) and national boundaries.

As recently as a few decades ago, methods of scientific exploration seemed only to include the efforts of single investigators from the confines of traditional disciplines (e.g. biology, physics, and chemistry). The contribution of these isolated research events to science is undeniable and in many cases provided insight, with far-reaching implications, towards addressing important societal issues. Even so, because of the growing need for technological improvements, development of intellectual product from research must embrace new strategies to expedite the discovery process. Conventional studies that clarify fundamental scientific phenomena will still have a legitimate place in scientific exploration, but ultimately research efforts will be judged primarily on their relevance and impact to world issues. Thus, the investigative process of problem solving must transcend traditional boundaries and exploit the resources of the entire global community.

Presently, the merging of resources has the appearance of micro-communities consisting of multiple investigators with expertise in a vast collection of disciplines working toward a common goal. Since these communities operate under a goal-oriented umbrella, the inclusion of research participants spans scientific disciplines and the boundaries of nations and continents. Although the barriers to this model community once seemed insurmountable, technological advances in communication and travel have made these types of communities a reality. These communities often exist as collaborative ventures between investigators or as organized research cells within an academic or industrial setting.

The emphasis on "relevant research" has provided a wide avenue of reform for significant portions of the scientific community. Two of the most notable changes include sources of research funds and academic institutions. Funding agencies, such as the National Science Foundation and the Department of Defense, now heavily favor research proposals that include a strong "global relevance" component. Since funding for a significant portion of research conducted in academia originates from these agencies, the content of research projects often follows funding agency initiatives. In turn, the educational framework in the university setting has undergone a restructuring of the various branches of science to give a more interdisciplinary approach. The separation of scientific disciplines was once clear, but over the last few decades has slowly transformed to give, to some extent, indistinguishable borders. A few notable areas that emerged from this process include the National Nanotechnology Initiative (NNI) and Human Genome Project (HPG). The current NNI seeks to foster the emerging field of nanoscale science by exploiting engineering and other technological resources. The ability to operate at the molecular level, atom by atom, to construct practically useful structures provides the operational framework for NNI. While NNI is a fundamental science-based initiative, the primary goal is to transition science discovery into new technology. Progress from this research and development initiative is leading to unprecedented understanding and control over the basic building blocks and properties of all natural and man-made things. Credited to the coordination of ten federal department and independent agencies, NNI achievements include the development of single molecule electron devices, molecular motors, nanoscale fabrication using atomic force microprobes, microcantilevers to detect proteins, and enhanced medical imaging using nanoparticle-based probes. In a similar manner the HGP championed a multidisciplinary approach to solving real-world issues. The objectives of the genome project include:

- *identify* all the approximate 30,000 genes in human DNA,
- *determine* the sequences of the 3 billion chemical base pairs that make up human DNA,
- *store* this information in databases,
- *improve* tools for data analysis,
- *transfer* related technologies to the private sector, and
- *address* the ethical, legal, and social issues that may arise from the project.

Although originally designed as a 15-year undertaking, the entire human genome sequence was announced only a decade into the project. Much of the success of the HPG can be directly attributed to its interdisciplinary approach. HGP planners at the Department of Energy and the National Institute of Health emphasized the importance of using all available resources to complete program objectives. Some 18 countries have participated in the worldwide effort, with significant contributions from the Sanger Center in the United Kingdom and research centers in

Germany, France, and Japan. The unswerving commitment of HGP directors to support this enormous effort sets a clear standard of effective use of resources for years to come.

The NNI and HGP projects highlight the current trend of merging scientific disciplines to meet the technological needs of the global society. An additional indication of these developments in the scientific community is quite apparent from inspection of Nobel Prize winners. This yearly international award holds great significance, and undoubtedly is the greatest acknowledgment that can be given to scientists for their research. In the field of chemistry for example (Table 1), research honored by this award exemplifies the growth and acceptance of the interdisciplinary approach. Nobel Prize recipients in the last decade, including disciplines other than chemistry, illustrate this trend; whereas, awardees from several decades ago received this accolade due to research from the traditional confines of a specific discipline. A likely reason for this development is *societal impact*—all Nobel Prize recipients share one thing in common, their research is recognized as being significant to their discipline. Research programs that seek to make an important contribution to science must effectively use all available resources. Since, the resources of a single investigator are limited, the merging of assets (i.e., personnel and infrastructure) from research groups creates a community that is often more successful at solving problems than the sum of its individual parts.

Scientific exploration is indeed changing! At times, it appears to stall, and even resist the suggestion of change, but ultimately the wheel of science provides momentum and appropriately responds to the needs of the global community. The challenge to improve the methods of scientific discovery helped to precipitate the current interdisciplinary trend that spans our global community. Benefits from such communities continue to provide tangible answers to real-world problems and new and emergent technological resources for future generations.

Table 1. Nobel Laureates in Chemistry

1950	**Alder/Diels** (Germany)	Diene synthesis
1951	**McMillan/Seaborg** (USA)	Discoveryof transuranium elements
1952	**Martin/Synge** (UK)	Distribution chromatography
1953	**Staudinger** (Germany)	Macromolecular chemistry
1954	**Pauling** (USA)	Nature of the chemical bond
1955	**du Vigneaud** (USA)	Synthesis of a polypeptide hormone
1956	**Hinshelwood** (UK)/ **Semjonow** (Soviet Union)	Mechanistic chemistry
1957	**Todd** (UK)	Nucleotides and coenzymes
1958	**Sanger** (UK)	Protein structure
1959	**Heyrovsky** (Czechoslovakia)	Polarography
1960	**Libby** (USA)	Radiocarbon dating
1961	**Calvin** (USA)	Photosynthesis
1962	**Kendrew/Perutz** (UK)	Globulin proteins

Table 1. Nobel Laureates in Chemistry *(continued)*

1963	**Natta** (Italy)/**Ziegler** (Germany)	High polymers
1964	**Crowfoot-Hodgkin** (UK)	Biomolecule structure determination (X rays)
1965	**Woodward** (USA)	Syntheses of natural products
1966	**Mulliken** (USA)	orbital methodology
1967	**Eigen** (Germany)/**Porter** (UK)/**Norrish** (UK)	Fast chemical reactions
1968	**Onsager** (USA, Norway)	Thermodynamics of irreversible processes
1969	**Hassel** (Norway)/**Barton** (UK)	Chemical conformation
1970	**Leloir** (Argentina)	Sugar nucleotides
1971	**Herzberg** (Canada)	Structure of free radicals
1972	**Anfinsen** (USA)	Studies on ribonuclease
	Moore/Stein (USA)	ribonuclease active centers
1973	**Fischer** (Germany)/ **Wilkinson** (UK)	Metal-organic sandwich compounds
1974	**Flory** (USA)	Physical chemistry of macromolecules
1975	**Cornforth** (UK)	Stereochemistry of enzyme catalysis
	Prelog (Switzerland, Yugoslavia)	Chemical stereochemistry
1976	**Lipscomb** (USA)	Structure of boranes
1977	**Prigogine** (Belgium)	Theory of dissipative structures
1978	**Mitchell** (UK)	Biological energy transfer
1979	**Wittig** (Germany)/ **Brown** (USA)	Boron and phosphorous compounds
1980	**Berg** (USA)	Hybrid DNA studies
	Gilbert (USA)/**Sanger** (UK)	Nucleic acid base sequences
1981	**Fukui** (Japan)/**Hoffmann** (USA)	Frontier orbital theory
1982	**Klug** (UK)	Crystallographic methods/protein complexes
1983	**Taube** (Canada)	Electron transfer mechanisms
1984	**Merrifield** (USA)	Peptide and protein synthesis
1985	**Hauptman/Karle** (USA)	Determination of crystal structures
1986	**Polanyi** (Canada)/ **Herschbach** (USA)/**Lee** (USA)	Dynamics of chemical processes
1987	**Cram** (USA)/**Pedersen** (USA)/ **Lehn** (France)	Chemical specificity
1988	**Deisenhofer/Huber/ Michel** (Germany)	Photosynthetic reaction center
1989	**Altman** (Canada)/**Cech** (USA)	Catalytic properties of RNA
1990	**Corey** (USA)	Retrosynthetic analysis of chemical reactions
1991	**Ernst** (Switzerland)	High resolution NMR spectroscopy
1992	**Marcus** (USA)	Theories of electron transfer

1993	**Mullis** (USA)	Polymerase chain reaction
	Smith (Canada)	Site specific mutagenesis
1994	*Olah* (USA)	Carbocations
1995	**Crutzen** (Netherlands)/	
	Molina (Mexico)/	
	Rowland (USA)	Atmospheric chemistry
1996	**Curl** (USA)/**Kroto** (UK)/	
	Smalley (USA)	Fullerenes
1997	**Boyer** (USA)/**Walker** (UK)	Enzymatic mechanism of ATP
	Skou (Denmark)	ion-transporting enzyme Na^+, K^+-ATPase
1998	**Kohn** (USA)/**Pople** (UK/USA)	Computational methods
1999	**Zewail** (USA, Egypt)	Transition states/femtosecond spectroscopy
2000	**Heeger** (USA)/**MacDiarmid** (USA)/**Shirakawa** (Jp)	Conductive polymers
2001	**Knowles** (USA)/**Noyori** (Jp)	Chirally catalysed hydrogenation reactions
	Sharpless (USA)	Chirally catalysed oxidation reactions
2002	**Fenn** (USA)/**Tanaka** (Jp)	Mass spectrometry of biomolecules
	Wüthrich (Switzerland)	Three-dimensional NMR
2003	**Agre/MacKinnon** (USA)	Discovery cell membrane channels

Part III

Global Marketplace

The Free-Trade Fix

Tina Rosenberg

Globalization is a phenomenon that has remade the economy of virtually every nation, reshaped almost every industry and touched billions of lives, often in surprising and ambiguous ways. The stories filling the front pages in recent weeks—about economic crisis and contagion in Argentina, Uruguay and Brazil, about President Bush getting the trade bill he wanted—are all part of the same story, the largest story of our times: what globalization has done, or has failed to do.

Globalization is meant to signify integration and unity—yet it has proved, in its way, to be no less polarizing than the cold-war divisions it has supplanted. The lines between globalization's supporters and its critics run not only between countries but also through them, as people struggle to come to terms with the defining economic force shaping the planet today. The two sides in the discussion—a shouting match, really—describe what seem to be two completely different forces. Is the globe being knit together by the Nikes and Microsofts and Citigroups in a dynamic new system that will eventually lift the have-nots of the world up from medieval misery? Or are ordinary people now victims of ruthless corporate domination, as the Nikes and Microsofts and Citigroups roll over the poor in nation after nation in search of new profits?

The debate over globalization's true nature has divided people in third-world countries since the phenomenon arose. It is now an issue in the United States as well, and many Americans—those who neither make the deals inside World Trade Organization meetings nor man the barricades outside—are perplexed.

When I first set out to see for myself whether globalization has been for better or for worse, I was perplexed, too. I had sympathy for some of the issues raised by the protesters, especially their outrage over sweatshops. But I have also spent many years in Latin America, and I have seen firsthand how protected economies became corrupt systems that helped only those with clout. In general, I thought the protesters were simply being sentimental; after all, the masters of the universe must know what they are doing. But that was before I studied the agreements that regulate global trade—including this month's new law granting President Bush a free hand to negotiate trade agreements, a document redolent of corporate lobbying. And it was before looking at globalization up close in Chile and Mexico, two nations that have embraced globalization especially ardently in the region of the third world that has done the most to follow the accepted rules. I no longer think the masters of the universe know what they are doing.

The architects of globalization are right that international economic integration is not only good for the poor; it is essential. To embrace self-sufficiency or to deride growth, as some protesters do, is to glamorize poverty. No nation has ever developed over the long term without trade. East Asia is the most recent example. Since the mid-1970's, Japan, Korea, Taiwan, China and their neighbors have lifted 300 million people out of poverty, chiefly through trade.

But the protesters are also right—no nation has ever developed over the long term under the rules being imposed today on third-world countries by the institutions controlling globalization. The United States, Germany, France and Japan all became wealthy and powerful nations behind the barriers of protectionism. East Asia built its export industry by protecting its markets and banks from foreign competition and requiring investors to buy local products and build local know-how. These are all practices discouraged or made illegal by the rules of trade today.

The World Trade Organization was designed as a meeting place where willing nations could sit in equality and negotiate rules of trade for their mutual advantage, in the service of sustainable international development. Instead, it has become an unbalanced institution largely controlled by the United States and the nations of Europe, and especially the agribusiness, pharmaceutical and financial-services industries in these countries. At W.T.O. meetings, important deals are hammered out in negotiations attended by the trade ministers of a couple dozen powerful nations, while those of poor countries wait in the bar outside for news.

The International Monetary Fund was created to prevent future Great Depressions in part by lending countries in recession money and pressing them to adopt expansionary policies, like deficit spending and low interest rates, so they would continue to buy their neighbors' products. Over time, its mission has evolved into the reverse: it has become a long-term manager of the economies of developing countries, blindly committed to the bitter medicine of contraction no matter what the illness. Its formation was an acknowledgment that markets sometimes work imperfectly, but it has become a champion of market supremacy in all situations, echoing the voice of Wall Street and the United States Treasury Department, more interested in getting wealthy creditors repaid than in serving the poor.

It is often said that globalization is a force of nature, as unstoppable and difficult to contain as a storm. This is untrue and misleading. Globalization is a powerful phenomenon—but it is not irreversible, and indeed the previous wave of globalization, at the turn of the last century, was stopped dead by World War I. Today it would be more likely for globalization to be sabotaged by its own inequities, as disillusioned nations withdraw from a system they see as indifferent or harmful to the poor.

Globalization's supporters portray it as the peeling away of distortions to reveal a clean and elegant system of international commerce, the one nature intended. It is anything but. The accord creating the W.T.O. is 22,500 pages long—not exactly a free trade agreement. All globalization, it seems, is local, the rules drawn up by, and written to benefit, powerful nations and powerful interests within those nations. Globalization has been good for the United States, but even in this country, the gains go disproportionately to the wealthy and to big business.

It's not too late for globalization to work. But the system is in need of serious reform. More equitable rules would spread its benefits to the ordinary citizens of wealthy countries. They would also help to preserve globalization by giving the poor of the world a stake in the system—and, not incidentally, improve the lives of hundreds of millions of people. Here, then, are nine new rules for the global economy—a prescription to save globalization from itself.

1. MAKE THE STATE A PARTNER

If there is any place in Latin America where the poor have thrived because of globalization, it is Chile. Between 1987 and 1998, Chile cut poverty by more than half. Its success shows that poor nations can take advantage of globalization—if they have governments that actively make it happen.

Chile reduced poverty by growing its economy—6.6 percent a year from 1985 to 2000. One of the few points economists can agree on is that growth is the most important thing a nation can do for its poor. They can't agree on basics like whether poverty in the world is up or down in the last 15 years—the number of people who live on less than $1 a day is slightly down, but the number who live on less than $2 is slightly up. Inequality has soared during the last 15 years, but economists cannot agree on whether globalization is mainly at fault or whether other forces, like the uneven spread of technology, are responsible. They can't agree on how to reduce inequality—growth tends not to change it. They can't agree on whether the poor who have not been helped are victims of globalization or have simply not yet enjoyed access to its benefits—in other words, whether the solution is more globalization or less. But economists agree on one thing: to help the poor, you'd better grow.

For the rest of Latin America, and most of the developing world except China (and to a lesser extent India), globalization as practiced today is failing, and it is failing because it has not produced growth. Excluding China, the growth rate of poor countries was 2 percent a year lower in the 1990's than in the 1970's, when closed economies were the norm and the world was in a recession brought on in part by oil-price shocks. Latin American economies in the 1990's grew at an average annual rate of 2.9 percent—about half the rate of the 1960's. By the end of the 1990's, 11 million more Latin Americans lived in poverty than at the beginning of the decade. And in country after country, Latin America's poor are suffering—either from economic crises and market panics or from the day-to-day deprivations that globalization was supposed to relieve. The surprise is not that Latin Americans are once again voting for populist candidates but that the revolt against globalization took so long.

When I visited Eastern Europe after the end of Communism, a time when democracy was mainly bringing poverty, I heard over and over again that the reason for Chile's success was Augusto Pinochet. Only a dictator with a strong hand can put his country through the pain of economic reform, went the popular wisdom. In truth, we now know that inflicting pain is the easy part; governments democratic and dictatorial are all instituting free-market austerity. The point is not to inflict pain but to lessen it. In this Pinochet failed, and the democratic governments that followed him beginning in 1990 have succeeded.

What Pinochet did was to shut down sectors of Chile's economy that produced goods for the domestic market, like subsistence farming and appliance manufacturing, and point the economy toward exports. Here he was following the standard advice that economists give developing countries—but there are different ways to do it, and Pinochet's were disastrous. Instead of helping the losers, he dismantled the social safety net and much of the regulatory apparatus that might have kept privatization honest. When the world economy went into recession in 1982, Chile's integration into the global marketplace and its dependence on foreign capital magnified the crash. Poverty soared, and unemployment reached 20 percent.

Pinochet's second wave of globalization, in the late 1980's, worked better, because the state did not stand on the side. It regulated the changes effectively and aggressively promoted exports. But Pinochet created a time bomb in Chile: the country's exports were, and still are, nonrenewable natural resources. Chile began subsidizing companies that cut down native forests for wood chips, for example, and the industry is rapidly deforesting the nation.

Chile began to grow, but inequality soared—the other problem with Pinochet's globalization was that it left out the poor. While the democratic governments that succeeded Pinochet have not yet been able to reduce inequality, at least it is no longer increasing, and they have been able to use the fruits of Chile's growth to help the poor.

Chile's democratic governments have spread the benefits of economic integration by designing effective social programs and aiming them at the poor. Chile has sunk money into revitalizing the 900 worst primary schools. It now leads Latin America in computers in schools, along with Costa Rica. It provides the very low-income with housing subsidies, child care and income support. Open economy or closed, these are good things. But Chile's government is also taking action to mitigate one of the most dangerous aspects of global integration: the violent ups and downs that come from linking your economy to the rest of the world. This year it created unemployment insurance. And it was the first nation to institute what is essentially a tax on short-term capital, to discourage the kind of investment that can flood out during a market panic.

The conventional wisdom among economists today is that successful globalizers must be like Chile. This was not always the thinking. In the 1980's, the Washington Consensus—the master-of-the-universe ideology at the time, highly influenced by the Reagan and Thatcher administrations—held that government was in the way. Globalizers' tasks included privatization, deregulation, fiscal austerity and financial liberalization. "In the 1980's and up to 1996 or 1997, the state was considered the devil," says Juan Martin, an Argentine economist at the United Nations' Economic Commission for Latin America and the Caribbean. "Now we know you need infrastructure, institutions, education. In fact, when the economy opens, you need more control mechanisms from the state, not fewer."

And what if you don't have these things? Bolivia carried out extensive reforms beginning in 1985—a year in which it had inflation of 23,000 percent—to make the economy more stable and efficient. But in the words of the World Bank, "It is a good example of a country that has achieved successful stabilization and implemented innovative market reforms, yet made only limited progress in the fight against poverty." Latin America is full of nations that cannot make globalization work. The saddest example is Haiti, an excellent student of the rules of globalization, ranked at the top of the I.M.F.'s index of trade openness. Yet over the 1990's, Haiti's economy contracted; annual per capita income is now $250. No surprise—if you are a corrupt and misgoverned nation with a closed economy, becoming a corrupt and misgoverned nation with an open economy is not going to solve your problems.

2. IMPORT KNOW-HOW ALONG WITH THE ASSEMBLY LINE

If there is a showcase for globalization in Latin America, it lies on the outskirts of Puebla, Mexico, at Volkswagen Mexico. Every New Beetle in the world is made here, 440 a day, in a factory so sparkling and clean that you could have a baby on the floor, so high-tech that in some halls it is not evident that human beings work here. Volkswagen Mexico also makes Jettas and, in a special hall, 80 classic Beetles a day to sell in Mexico, one of the last places in the world where the old Bug still chugs.

The Volkswagen factory is the biggest single industrial plant in Mexico. Humans do work here—11,000 people in assembly-line jobs, 4,000 more in the rest of the factory—with 11,000 more jobs in the industrial park of VW suppliers across the street making parts, seats, dashboards and other components. Perhaps 50,000 more people work in other companies around Mexico that supply VW. The average monthly wage in the plant is $760, among the highest in the country's industrial sector. The factory is the equal of any in Germany, the product of a billion-dollar investment in 1995, when VW chose Puebla as the exclusive site for the New Beetle.

Ahhh, globalization.

Except . . . this plant is not here because Mexico has an open economy, but because it had a closed one. In 1962, Mexico decreed that any automaker that wanted to sell cars here had to produce them here. Five years later, VW opened the factory. Mexico's local content requirement is now illegal, except for very limited exceptions, under W.T.O. rules; in Mexico the local content requirement for automobiles is being phased out and will disappear entirely in January 2004.

The Puebla factory, for all the jobs and foreign exchange it brings Mexico, also refutes the argument that foreign technology automatically rubs off on the local host. Despite 40 years here, the auto industry has not created much local business or know-how. VW makes the point that it buys 60 percent of its parts in Mexico, but the "local" suppliers are virtually all foreign-owned and import most of the materials they use. The value Mexico adds to the Beetles it exports is mainly labor. Technology transfer—the transmission of know-how from foreign companies to local ones—is limited in part because most foreign trade today is intracompany; Ford Hermosillo, for example, is a stamping and assembly plant shipping exclusively to Ford plants in the United States. Trade like this is particularly impenetrable to outsiders. "In spite of the fact that Mexico has been host to many car plants, we don't know how to build a car," says Huberto Juarez, an economist at the Autonomous University of Puebla.

Volkswagen Mexico is the epitome of the strategy Mexico has chosen for globalization—assembly of imported parts. It is a strategy that makes perfect sense given Mexico's proximity to the world's largest market, and it has given rise to the maquila industry, which uses Mexican labor to assemble foreign parts and then re-export the finished products. Although the economic slowdown in the United States is hurting the maquila industry, it still employs a million people and brings the country $10 billion a year in foreign exchange. The factories have turned Mexico into one of the developing world's biggest exporters of medium- and high-technology products. But the maquila sector remains an island and has failed to stimulate Mexican industries—one reason Mexico's globalization has brought disappointing growth, averaging only 3 percent a year during the 1990's.

In countries as varied as South Korea, China and Mauritius, however, assembly work has been the crucible of wider development. Jeffrey Sachs, the development economist who now directs Columbia University's Earth Institute, says that the maquila industry is "magnificent." "I could cite 10 success stories," he says, "and every one started with a maquila sector." When Korea opened its export-processing zone in Masan in the early 1970's, local inputs were 3 percent of the export value, according to the British development group Oxfam. Ten years later they were almost 50 percent. General Motors took a Korean textile company called Daewoo and helped shape it into a conglomerate making cars, electronic goods, ships and dozens of other products. Daewoo calls itself "a locomotive for national economic development since its founding in 1967." And despite the company's recent troubles, it's true—because Korea made it true. G.M. did not tutor Daewoo because it welcomed competition but because Korea demanded it. Korea wanted to build high-tech industry, and it did so by requiring technology transfer and by closing markets to imports.

Maquilas first appeared in Mexico in 1966. Although the country has gone from assembling clothing to assembling high-tech goods, nearly 40 years later 97 percent of the components used in Mexican maquilas are still imported, and the value that Mexico adds to its exports has actually declined sharply since the mid-1970's.

Mexico has never required companies to transfer technology to locals, and indeed, under the rules of the North American Free Trade Agreement, it cannot. "We should have included a technical component in Nafta," says Luis de la Calle, one of the treaty's negotiators and later Mexico's under secretary of economy for foreign trade. "We should be getting a significant transfer of technology from the United States, and we didn't really try."

Without technology transfer, maquila work is marked for extinction. As transport costs become less important, Mexico is increasingly competing with China and

Bangladesh—where labor goes for as little as 9 cents an hour. This is one reason that real wages for the lowest-paid workers in Mexico dropped by 50 percent from 1985 to 2000. Businesses, in fact, are already leaving to go to China.

3. SWEAT THE SWEATSHOPS—BUT SWEAT OTHER PROBLEMS MORE

When Americans think about globalization, they often think about sweatshops—one aspect of globalization that ordinary people believe they can influence through their buying choices. In many of the factories in Mexico, Central America and Asia producing American-brand toys, clothes, sneakers and other goods, exploitation is the norm. The young women who work in them—almost all sweatshop workers are young women—endure starvation wages, forced overtime and dangerous working conditions.

In Chile, I met a man who works at a chicken-processing plant in a small town. The plant is owned by Chileans and processes chicken for the domestic market and for export to Europe, Asia and other countries in Latin America. His job is to stand in a freezing room and crack open chickens as they come down an assembly line at the rate of 41 per minute. When visitors arrive at the factory (the owners did not return my phone calls requesting a visit or an interview), the workers get a respite, as the line slows down to half-speed for show. His work uniform does not protect him from the cold, the man said, and after a few minutes of work he loses feeling in his hands. Some of his colleagues, he said, are no longer able to raise their arms. If he misses a day he is docked $30. He earns less than $200 a month.

Is this man a victim of globalization? The protesters say that he is, and at one point I would have said so, too. He—and all workers—should have dignified conditions and the right to organize. All companies should follow local labor laws, and activists should pressure companies to pay their workers decent wages.

But today if I were to picket globalization, I would protest other inequities. In a way, the chicken worker, who came to the factory when driving a taxi ceased to be profitable, is a beneficiary of globalization. So are the millions of young women who have left rural villages to be exploited gluing tennis shoes or assembling computer keyboards. The losers are those who get laid off when companies move to low-wage countries, or those forced off their land when imports undercut their crop prices, or those who can no longer afford life-saving medicine—people whose choices in life diminish because of global trade. Globalization has offered this man a hellish job, but it is a choice he did not have before, and he took it; I don't name him because he is afraid of being fired. When this chicken company is hiring, the lines go around the block.

4. GET RID OF THE LOBBYISTS

The argument that open economies help the poor rests to a large extent on the evidence that closed economies do not. While South Korea and other East Asian countries successfully used trade barriers to create export industries, this is rare; most protected economies are disasters. "The main tendency in a sheltered market is to goof off," says Jagdish Bhagwati, a prominent free-trader who is the Arthur Lehman professor of economics at Columbia University. "A crutch becomes a permanent crutch. Infant-industry protection should be for infant industries."

Anyone who has lived or traveled in the third world can attest that while controlled economies theoretically allow governments to help the poor, in practice it's usually a different story. In Latin America, spending on social programs largely goes to the urban middle class. Attention goes to people who can organize, strike, lobby and contribute money. And in a closed economy, the "state" car factory is often owned by the dictator's son and the country's forests can be chopped down by his golf partner.

Free trade, its proponents argue, takes these decisions away from the government and leaves them to the market, which punishes corruption. And it's true that a system that took corruption and undue political influence out of economic decision-making could indeed benefit the poor. But humans have not yet invented such a system—and if they did, it would certainly not be the current system of globalization, which is soiled with the footprints of special interests. In every country that negotiates at the W.T.O. or cuts a free-trade deal, trade ministers fall under heavy pressure from powerful business groups. Lobbyists have learned that they can often quietly slip provisions that pay big dividends into complex trade deals. None have been more successful at getting what they want than those from America.

The most egregious example of a special-interest provision is the W.T.O.'s rules on intellectual property. The ability of poor nations to make or import cheap copies of drugs still under patent in rich countries has been a boon to world public health. But the W.T.O. will require most of its poor members to accept patents on medicine by 2005, with the very poorest nations following in 2016. This regime does nothing for the poor. Medicine prices will probably double, but poor countries will never offer enough of a market to persuade the pharmaceutical industry to invent cures for their diseases.

The intellectual-property rules have won worldwide notoriety for the obstacles they pose to cheap AIDS medicine. They are also the provision of the W.T.O. that economists respect the least. They were rammed into the W.T.O. by Washington in response to the industry groups who control United States trade policy on the subject. "This is not a trade issue," Bhagwati says. "It's a royalty-collection issue. It's pharmaceuticals and software throwing their weight around." The World Bank calculated that the intellectual-property rules will result in a transfer of $40 billion a year from poor countries to corporations in the developed world.

5. NO DUMPING

Manuel de Jesús Gómez is a corn farmer in the hills of Puebla State, 72 years old and less than five feet tall. I met him in his field of six acres, where he was trudging behind a plow pulled by a burro. He farms the same way campesinos in these hills have been farming for thousands of years. In Puebla, and in the poverty belt of Mexico's southern states—Chiapas, Oaxaca, Guerrero—corn growers plow with animals and irrigate by praying for rain.

Before Nafta, corn covered 60 percent of Mexico's cultivated land. This is where corn was born, and it remains a symbol of the nation and daily bread for most

Mexicans. But in the Nafta negotiations, Mexico agreed to open itself to subsidized American corn, a policy that has crushed small corn farmers. "Before, we could make a living, but now sometimes what we sell our corn for doesn't even cover our costs," Gómez says. With Nafta, he suddenly had to compete with American corn—raised with the most modern methods, but more important, subsidized to sell overseas at 20 percent less than the cost of production. Subsidized American corn now makes up almost half of the world's stock, effectively setting the world price so low that local small farmers can no longer survive. This competition helped cut the price paid to Gómez for his corn by half.

Because of corn's importance to Mexico, when it negotiated Nafta it was promised 15 years to gradually raise the amount of corn that could enter the country without tariffs. But Mexico voluntarily lifted the quotas in less than three years—to help the chicken and pork industry, Mexican negotiators told me unabashedly. (Eduardo Bours, a member of the family that owns Mexico's largest chicken processor, was one of Mexico's Nafta negotiators.) The state lost some $2 billion in tariffs it could have charged, and farmers were instantly exposed to competition from the north. According to ANEC, a national association of campesino cooperatives, half a million corn farmers have left their land and moved to Mexican cities or to America. If it were not for a weak peso, which keeps the price of imports relatively high, far more farmers would be forced off their land.

The toll on small farmers is particularly bitter because cheaper corn has not translated into cheaper food for Mexicans. As part of its economic reforms, Mexico has gradually removed price controls on tortillas and tortilla flour. Tortilla prices have nearly tripled in real terms even as the price of corn has dropped.

Is this how it was supposed to be? I asked Andres Rosenzweig, a longtime Mexican agriculture official who helped negotiate the agricultural sections of Nafta. He was silent for a minute. "The problems of rural poverty in Mexico did not start with Nafta," he said. "The size of our farms is not viable, and they get smaller each generation because farmers have many children, who divide the land. A family in Puebla with five hectares could raise 10, maybe 15, tons of corn each year. That was an annual income of 16,000 pesos," the equivalent of $1,600 today. "Double it and you still die of hunger. This has nothing to do with Nafta.

"The solution for small corn farmers," he went on, "is to educate their children and find them jobs outside agriculture. But Mexico was not growing, not generating jobs. Who's going to employ them? Nafta."

One prominent antiglobalization report keeps referring to farms like Gómez's as "small-scale, diversified, self-reliant, community-based agriculture systems." You could call them that, I guess; you could also use words like "malnourished," "undereducated" and "miserable" to describe their inhabitants. Rosenzweig is right—this is not a life to be romanticized.

But to turn the farm families' malnutrition into starvation makes no sense. Mexico spends foreign exchange to buy corn. Instead, it could be spending money to bring farmers irrigation, technical help and credit. A system in which the government purchased farmers' corn at a guaranteed price—done away with in states like Puebla during the free-market reforms of the mid-1990's—has now been replaced by direct payments to farmers. The program is focused on the poor, but the payments are symbolic—$36 an acre. In addition, rural credit has disappeared, as the government has effectively shut down the rural bank, which was badly run, and other banks won't lend to small farmers. There is a program—understaffed and poorly publicized—to help small producers, but the farmers I met didn't know about it.

Free trade is a religion, and with religion comes hypocrisy. Rich nations press other countries to open their agricultural markets. At the urging of the I.M.F. and Washington, Haiti slashed its tariffs on rice in 1995. Prices paid to rice farmers fell by 25 percent, which has devastated Haiti's rural poor. In China, the tariff demands of W.T.O. membership will cost tens of millions of peasants their livelihoods. But European farmers get 35 percent of their income from government subsidies, and American farmers get 20 percent. Farm subsidies in the United States, moreover, are a huge corporate-welfare program, with nearly 70 percent of payments going to the largest 10 percent of producers. Subsidies also depress crop prices abroad by encouraging overproduction. The farm bill President Bush signed in May—with substantial Democratic support—provides about $57 billion in subsidies for American corn and other commodities over the next 10 years.

Wealthy nations justify pressure on small countries to open markets by arguing that these countries cannot grow rice and corn efficiently—that American crops are cheap food for the world's hungry. But with subsidies this large, it takes chutzpah to question other nations' efficiency. And in fact, the poor suffer when America is the supermarket to the world, even at bargain prices. There is plenty of food in the world, and even many countries with severe malnutrition are food exporters. The problem is that poor people can't afford it. The poor are the small farmers. Three-quarters of the world's poor are rural. If they are forced off their land by subsidized grain imports, they starve.

6. HELP COUNTRIES BREAK THE COFFEE HABIT

Back in the 1950's, Latin American economists made a simple calculation. The products their nations exported—copper, tin, coffee, rice and other commodities—were buying less and less of the high-value-added goods they wanted to import. In effect, they were getting poorer each day. Their solution was to close their markets and develop domestic industries to produce their own appliances and other goods for their citizens.

The strategy, which became known as import substitution, produced high growth—for a while. But these closed economies ultimately proved unsustainable. Latin American governments made their consumers buy inferior and expensive products—remember the Brazilian computer of the 1970's? Growth depended on heavy borrowing and high deficits. When they could no longer roll over their debts, Latin American economies crashed, and a decade of stagnation resulted.

At the time, the architects of import substitution could not imagine that it was possible to export anything but commodities. But East Asia—as poor or poorer than Latin America in the 1960's—showed in the 1980's and 1990's that it can be done.

Unfortunately, the rules of global trade now prohibit countries from using the strategies successfully employed to develop export industries in East Asia.

American trade officials argue that they are not using tariffs to block poor countries from exporting, and they are right—the average tariff charged by the United States is a negligible 1.7 percent, much lower than other nations. But the rules rich nations have set—on technology transfer, local content and government aid to their infant industries, among other things—are destroying poor nations' abilities to move beyond commodities. "We are pulling up the ladder on policies the developed countries used to become rich," says Lori Wallach, the director of Public Citizen's Global Trade Watch.

The commodities that poor countries are left to export are even more of a dead end today than in the 1950's. Because of oversupply, prices for coffee, cocoa, rice, sugar and tin dropped by more than 60 percent between 1980 and 2000. Because of the price collapse of commodities and sub-Saharan Africa's failure to move beyond them, the region's share of world trade dropped by two-thirds during that time. If it had the same share of exports today that it had at the start of the 1980's, per capita income in sub-Saharan Africa would be almost twice as high.

7. LET THE PEOPLE GO

Probably the single most important change for the developing world would be to legalize the export of the one thing they have in abundance—people. Earlier waves of globalization were kinder to the poor because not only capital, but also labor, was free to move. Dani Rodrik, an economist at Harvard's Kennedy School of Government and a leading academic critic of the rules of globalization, argues for a scheme of legal short-term migration. If rich nations opened 3 percent of their work forces to temporary migrants, who then had to return home, Rodrik says, it would generate $200 billion annually in wages, and a lot of technology transfer for poor countries.

8. FREE THE I.M.F.

Globalization means risk. By opening its economy, a nation makes itself vulnerable to contagion from abroad. Countries that have liberalized their capital markets are especially susceptible, as short-term capital that has whooshed into a country on investor whim whooshes out just as fast when investors panic. This is how a real-estate crisis in Thailand in 1997 touched off one of the biggest global conflagrations since the Depression.

The desire to keep money from rushing out inspired Chile to install speed bumps discouraging short-term capital inflows. But Chile's policy runs counter to the standard advice of the I.M.F., which has required many countries to open their capital markets. "There were so many obstacles to capital-market integration that it was hard to err on the side of pushing countries to liberalize too much," says Ken Rogoff, the I.M.F.'s director of research.

Prudent nations are wary of capital liberalization, and rightly so. Joseph Stiglitz, the Nobel Prize-winning economist who has become the most influential critic of globalization's rules, writes that in December 1997, when he was chief economist at the World Bank, he met with South Korean officials who were balking at the I.M.F.'s advice to open their capital markets. They were scared of the hot money, but they could not disagree with the I.M.F., lest they be seen as irresponsible. If the I.M.F. expressed disapproval, it would drive away other donors and private investors as well.

In the wake of the Asian collapse, Prime Minister Mahathir Mohamad imposed capital controls in Malaysia—to worldwide condemnation. But his policy is now widely considered to be the reason that Malaysia stayed stable while its neighbors did not. "It turned out to be a brilliant decision," Bhagwati says.

Post-crash, the I.M.F. prescribed its standard advice for nations—making loan arrangements contingent on spending cuts, interest-rate hikes and other contractionary measures. But balancing a budget in recession is, as Stiglitz puts it in his new book, "Globalization and Its Discontents," a recommendation last taken seriously in the days of Herbert Hoover. The I.M.F.'s recommendations deepened the crisis and forced governments to reduce much of the cushion that was left for the poor. Indonesia had to cut subsidies on food. "While the I.M.F. had provided some $23 billion to be used to support the exchange rate and bail out creditors," Stiglitz writes, "the far, far, smaller sums required to help the poor were not forthcoming."

Is your international financial infrastructure breeding Bolsheviks? If it does create a backlash, one reason is the standard Bolshevik explanation—the I.M.F. really is controlled by the epicenter of international capital. Formal influence in the I.M.F. depends on a nation's financial contribution, and America is the only country with enough shares to have a veto. It is striking how many economists think the I.M.F. is part of the "Wall Street-Treasury complex," in the words of Bhagwati. The fund serves "the interests of global finance," Stiglitz says. It listens to the "voice of the markets," says Nancy Birdsall, president of the Center for Global Development in Washington and a former executive vice president of the Inter-American Development Bank. "The I.M.F. is a front for the U.S. government—keep the masses away from our taxpayers," Sachs says.

I.M.F. officials argue that their advice is completely equitable—they tell even wealthy countries to open their markets and contract their economies. In fact, Stiglitz writes, the I.M.F. told the Clinton administration to hike interest rates to lower the danger of inflation—at a time when inflation was the lowest it had been in decades. But the White House fortunately had the luxury of ignoring the I.M.F.: Washington will only have to take the organization's advice the next time it turns to the I.M.F. for a loan. And that will be never.

9. LET THE POOR GET RICH THE WAY THE RICH HAVE

The idea that free trade maximizes benefits for all is one of the few tenets economists agree on. But the power of the idea has led to the overly credulous acceptance of much of what is put forward in its name. Stiglitz writes that there is simply no support for many I.M.F. policies, and in some cases the I.M.F. has ignored clear evidence that what it advocated was harmful. You can always argue—and American and I.M.F. officials do—that countries that follow the I.M.F.'s line but still fail to grow either didn't follow the openness recipe precisely enough or didn't check off other items on the to-do list, like expanding education.

Policy makers also seem to be skipping the fine print on supposedly congenial studies. An influential recent paper by the World Bank economists David Dollar and Aart Kraay is a case in point. It finds a strong correlation between globalization and growth and is widely cited to support the standard rules of openness. But in fact, on close reading, it does not support them. Among successful "globalizers," Dollar and Kraay count countries like China, India and Malaysia, all of whom are trading and growing but still have protected economies and could not be doing more to misbehave by the received wisdom of globalization.

Dani Rodrik of Harvard used Dollar and Kraay's data to look at whether the single-best measure of openness—a country's tariff levels—correlates with growth. They do, he found—but not the way they are supposed to. High-tariff countries grew faster. Rodrik argues that the countries in the study may have begun to trade more because they had grown and gotten richer, not the other way around. China and India, he points out, began trade reforms about 10 years after they began high growth.

When economists talk about many of the policies associated with free trade today, they are talking about national averages and ignoring questions of distribution and inequality. They are talking about equations, not what works in messy third-world economies. What economic model taught in school takes into account a government ministry that stops work because it has run out of pens? The I.M.F. and the World Bank—which recommends many of the same austerity measures as the I.M.F. and frequently conditions its loans on I.M.F.-advocated reforms—often tell countries to cut subsidies, including many that do help the poor, and impose user fees on services like water. The argument is that subsidies are an inefficient way to help poor people—because they help rich people too—and instead, countries should aid the poor directly with vouchers or social programs. As an equation, it adds up. But in the real world, the subsidies disappear, and the vouchers never materialize.

The I.M.F. argues that it often saves countries from even more budget cuts. "Countries come to us when they are in severe distress and no one will lend to them," Rogoff says. "They may even have to run surpluses because their loans are being called in. Being in an I.M.F. program means less austerity." But a third of the developing world is under I.M.F. tutelage, some countries for decades, during which they must remodel their economies according to the standard I.M.F. blueprint. In March 2000, a panel appointed to advise Congress on international financial institutions, named for its head, Allan Meltzer of Carnegie Mellon University, recommended unanimously that the I.M.F. should undertake only short-term crisis assistance and get out of the business of long-term economic micromanagement altogether.

The standard reforms deprive countries of flexibility, the power to get rich the way we know can work. "Most Latin American countries have had deep reforms, have gone much further than India or China and haven't gotten much return for their effort," Birdsall says. "Many of the reforms were about creating an efficient economy, but the economic technicalities are not addressing the fundamental question of why countries are not growing, or the constraint that all these people are being left out. Economists are way too allergic to the wishy-washy concept of fairness."

The protesters in the street, the Asian financial crisis, criticism from respected economists like Stiglitz and Rodrik and those on the Meltzer Commission and particularly the growing realization in the circles of power that globalization is sustainable for wealthy nations only if it is acceptable to the poor ones are all combining to change the rules—slightly. The debt-forgiveness initiative for the poorest nations, for all its limitations, is one example. The Asian crisis has modified the I.M.F.'s view on capital markets, and it is beginning to apply less pressure on countries in crisis to cut government spending. It is also debating whether it should be encouraging countries to adopt Chile's speed bumps. The incoming director of the W.T.O. is from Thailand, and third-world countries are beginning to assert themselves more and more.

But the changes do not alter the underlying idea of globalization, that openness is the universal prescription for all ills. "Belt-tightening is not a development strategy," Sachs says. "The I.M.F. has no sense that its job is to help countries climb a ladder."

Sachs says that for many developing nations, even climbing the ladder is unrealistic. "It can't work in an AIDS pandemic or an endemic malaria zone. I don't have a strategy for a significant number of countries, other than we ought to help them stay alive and control disease and have clean water. You can't do this purely on market forces. The prospects for the Central African Republic are not the same as for Shanghai, and it doesn't do any good to give pep talks."

China, Chile and other nations show that under the right conditions, globalization can lift the poor out of misery. Hundreds of millions of poor people will never be helped by globalization, but hundreds of millions more could be benefiting now, if the rules had not been rigged to help the rich and follow abstract orthodoxies. Globalization can begin to work for the vast majority of the world's population only if it ceases to be viewed as an end in itself, and instead is treated as a tool in service of development: a way to provide food, health, housing and education to the wretched of the earth.

Globalization—Losers and Gainers

Ismail Shariff

> Globalization will be panacea for all our ills, but only in favor of the developed countries of the north.
> —*Robert Reich, former*
> *U.S. Secretary of*
> *Labor/Human Services*

I

Globalization has been underway since the inception of the modern world system in the 16th century. The basic framework for globalization has been in place since the nineteenth century when the competitive system of states fostered the emergence of international agencies and institutions, global networks of communications, a standardized system of global time, international competition and prizes, international law, and internationally shared notions of citizenship and human rights. However, it is also a fact that since the end of World War II, and more particularly in the last decade, the world has undergone discernible changes both on political and economic fronts. To understand fully the ramifications posed of changes, we must more than ever, use imagination, tact, understanding, and, above all, a dynamic perspective in dealings with each other and with our problems in a global context.

Globalization means, in today's context homogenization of prices, products, wages, rates of interest, and profits to become the same all over. Thomas L. Friedman's book, *The Lexus and the Olive Tree*, is a celebration of the capitalistic way of freemarkets and the triumph of liberal democracy all over the world. Under the pretext of free markets, transparency and flexibility, the so-called "electronic herd," move vast amounts of capital in and out of countries to their political and economic merits from the Western vantage point. Countries wishing to attract foreign capital and gain the benefit of today's and tomorrow's technology have to do, in the words of Friedman, the "golden straightjacket."[1] Golden straightjacket refers to a package of policies including balanced budgets, economic deregulation, openness to investment and trade with a stable currency. In the end, the West decides which countries to reward and which to punish. In September 1997, at a World Bank meeting in Hong Kong, Malaysia's Prime Minister, Dr. Mahathir Mohammad complained bitterly that great powers at their instigation forced Asian countries to open their markets and had manipulated their currency in order to destroy them.[2] Friedman wonders what Mr. Robert Rubin, who was in the audience, (the then U.S. Secretary of the Treasury) might have said in response. He imagines it would have been something like this: "What planet are you living on?" Globalization is not a choice, it is a reality, and the only way you can grow at the speed your people want to grow is by tapping into the global stock and bond markets, by seeking multinationals to invest in your country and by selling into the global trading system. And the most basic truth about globalization is this: "No one is in charge."[3]

This is a far cry from the real truth, and because of this stance, globalization in general is encountering resistance from various interest groups, foremost among them are the environmentalists, labor leaders, cultural traditionalists, religious leaders of different persuasions, and the non-governmental organizations (NGOS). In spite of this growing resistance, under the leadership of the West and its economic power, globalization is proceeding relentlessly. Its apostles argue that the process has now sped up immensely and that the straightjacket allows little room to wiggle before completely redesigning the multidimensional relations unleashed by globalization.

Arguably, globalization involves the most fundamental redesign and centralization of the world's socio-economic interdependence since the industrial revolution. Yet, the profound implications of these changes have barely been exposed to serious public scrutiny or debate. Despite the scale of global reordering, neither the world leaders, educational institutions, nor the mass media, have made a credible effort to describe what is being formulated or even to explore the multidimensionality of its effects, particularly on the developing countries. It is true; the world economy is in a period of rapid change. Over the last decade, we have witnessed a series of unforeseen events: an end to the Cold War, ambitious market reforms in what were formerly planned economies, an acceleration of the process of economic integration in Western Europe, North America and East Asia, increased use of protectionist measures by the most major traders (particularly against the developing countries) and the growing rate of impoverishment of many developing countries burdened by staggering internal obligations. In a way, if the limits of rational reasoning do not doom Brettonwood's system, growing inequality across the world will. For the defining movement can be traced to the infamous Bretton Woods meeting in 1944, at which a

[1]Friedman, T.L. *The Lexus and the Olive Tree.* Anchor Books. New York, NY. 2000, p. 380.
[2]ibid 112
[3]ibid 112

dominant ideology of globalization—accelerated growth through global free trade and deregulations was institutionalized. At the opening session, U.S. Secretary of the Treasury Henry Morgonthau advocated "rapid material progress on an earth infinitely blessed with natural riches!"[4] He asked the participants to embrace the "elementary economic axioms"—that prosperity has no fixed limits. It is not a finite substance to be diminished by division.[5]

Since then as we look back fifty-six years later, we can see that economic growth has expanded fivefold, international trade has expanded by roughly fifteen times and foreign direct investment has been expanding at two to three times the rate of trade expansion. Yet, tragically, while the Brettonwood's institutions have met their goals, they have failed in their purpose of bringing prosperity to the people of the world. The world has more poor people today than ever before, (for a billion people in the developing countries, 1/5 of humanity unable to obtain the most essential element of social sustenance—food, clothing, jobs, education. Three million children are dying every year. One half million women, 99 percent of them living in the developing world, die in childbirth. 900 million are illiterate. 100 million are without shelter, radios, TV. and other amenities taken for granted in the developed world), all of them concentrated in the so-called developing countries, mainly due to policies enacted over the years to favor the developed countries.

The United Nations Development Program's annual Human Development Report (to underscore this imbalanced phenomenon) since 1992 has introduced 'a champagne glass metaphor' for an ongoing extreme economic injustice. The bowl of the champagne glass represents the abundance enjoyed by the 20 percent of the world population who live in the richest countries and receive 82.7 percent of the world's income. At the bottom of the stem, where the sediment settles we find the poorest 20 percent who barely survive on 1.4 percent of the total income. The combined income of the top 20 percent is nearly sixty times larger than those of the bottom 20 percent. Furthermore, this gap has doubled since 1960, when the top 20 percent enjoyed only thirty times the income of the bottom 20 percent. And the gap is widening. Perhaps even more startling expression of inequality is that the world now has more than 350 billionaires whose combined net worth equals the annual income of the poorest 45 percent of the world's population. Here also the gap is growing.

In his book, *The Work of Nations* (1992),[6] former U.S. Secretary of Labor under President Clinton, Robert Reich explained that under economic globalization, the Bretton Wood institutions have served the interest of the wealthy classes from a sense of personal and national interest and thereby from a lack of sense of concern for, and obligation to their less fortunate inhabitants of the developing world. A thin segment of the super-rich at the very tip of the champagne glass has formed stateless alliance that defines global interest as synonymous with the personal and corporate financial interests of its members, perhaps at the expense of the impoverished South or the so-called developing countries.[7]

[4]Isaak, Robert A. *Managing World Economic Change*. 2nd edition. Prentice Hall 1995. pp 64-65.
[5]ibid. p. 69.
[6]Reich, R.B. *The Work of Nations*, p. 33. Vintage Book. 1992.
[7]ibid. p. 67.

In the light of the above record, the emerging occasional descriptions under the guise of globalization, or the predications about the global economy are once again favoring the corporate leaders, their allies around the world, including the new powerful centralized global trade bureaucracy called The World Trade Organization (WTO). The vision they offer us unfailingly not only resembles the past in its positive outcomes, even utopian: Globalization will be a panacea for all our ills, but only in favor of the developed countries of the north.[8]

It is true that at the end of the Cold War, the certain victor was capitalism, and it won globally. But from a historical perspective this is neither the first victory of capitalism nor the first era of globalization as indicated in the beginning of this paper. The Economist, in its 1997 World Economic Survey, observed that, by most important measures, "the world was more closely integrated before 1914 than it is now, in some cases much more so." Everyone now recognizes that the first period of globalization confirmed the economies of Adam Smith: The economy, left alone, will produce the greatest wealth of nations and in the long-run the state will wither, or be pushed away, as though by an 'Invisible Hand'. Perhaps less appreciated in that it has also confirmed Karl Marx, in a most particular way: every system of power tends to develop its own ideology, and ideology guides and rationalizes the government policies that impose and sustain the system of power.

Contrary to Smith and Marx's way of thinking, it is not very hard to understand what happened in pre-1914 globalization that seems to echo very much at present. The operative word then was imperialism that led to exploitation through colonization. At the present it is exploitation through neo-imperialism or through global capitalism. So in a way global capitalism has effectively taken the place of colonization to continue to exploit the developing countries for the benefit of the few developed ones. As a result, it is within the realm of logical conclusion to observe that the on-going ideology of globalization perceived from any angle is nothing but another name for colonial domination which still opposes, as, in the past, the redistribution of wealth or status to place all on an equal footing.

II

If in the process of understanding the scope and significance entailed by the word globalization we venture to ask the question as to what is globalization, we may end up with a multitude of answers. From the diverse responses, we can discern one common pattern or what may be called the operating definition of globalization. Globalization has come to mean a complete reordering of international priorities, strategies, and values as all states are drawn ever more tightly in the interdependent global economic, technological, communications cultural and ethical web. But in a more realistic sense, at least to me, globalization can be defined in no more than one phrase "neo-colonialism." In order to understand the origins of the on-going process of globalization, it is imperative to understand in the historical context from where its origin started. From the middle of the 14th century through the first half of the

[8]ibid. p. 69.

20th century, European powers under the guise of the nation state sought to extend their political and economic influence throughout the world. This process of gaining control over other territories and nations in distant lands was referred to as imperialism and the establishment of direct control over the conquered or dominated territories was called Colonialism.

It is no secret that throughout modern history European states pursued imperial policies for more economic than political reasons. Economically, European empires sought to acquire raw materials markets for export commodities, and a source of cheap labor. In particular they sought to establish trade routes that would be commercially beneficial to the imperial state.

On the political front major powers competed for hegemonic leadership within the European continent by extending their control over foreign territories. Indeed, during the eighteenth and nineteenth centuries a major criterion of national power was the number, size and location of each power's colonial territories. Thus Britain, France and the Netherlands were actively engaged in extending their imperial control over territories throughout the world. For example, the British, through its East India Company, established control over the Indian Sub-Continent and South Africa, The Dutch in Indonesia, Sri Lanka and various territories in North America. The French, for their part, sought territories in North America and in the Caribbean in the Eighteenth Century and then extended their influence to Africa by establishing trading outposts in such territories as Mauritius, Madagascar, the Seychelles and Senegal. Only in the aftermath of World War II did the colonial system begin to disintegrate. Actually the process of decolonization began in 1947 when the British relinquished their hold on the Indian Sub-Continent. The decolonization process greatly accelerated in the late 1950s and during the 1960s more than 60 countries achieved political independence with three-fourths of them in Africa alone. More than a hundred developing countries from Asia, Africa, the Pacific and the Caribbean have joined the community of nations as a result of post-world war II decolonization. Today actually only Great Britain, to the chagrin of the Spanish and the Argentineans still control the Rock of Gibraltar and Falkland Islands as remnants of their past colonial hegemony.

Having lost control over greater parts of the world resources, the rulers of the colonial past, in the name of globalization, seem to have been successful in replacing the nation states with what is called a multinational corporation (MNC) to continue to exploit as before, the raw materials to markets for exports and a source of cheap labor. From the point of view of the western powers, nothing has changed except the vehicle of exploitation from colonization to the so-called Multinational Corporations, while shielding the ulterior motives behind the MNC, they successfully take pride in heralding the positive economic impact of the MNC on the developing countries. As such they systematically and falsely espouse that MNCs will accomplish the following in favor of the developing countries:

- Globalization provides considerable investment to both institutional and individual development.
- Globalization can provide increased employment opportunities to citizens of developing countries. (Employment of nationals is often used as a beacon

to allow the so-called multinationals to do business in developing countries, though this may not be the end result).

- The advocates of globalization point to the possibilities of improving the well being through education of the masses and also point out the contribution to infrastructure development (such as roads, transportation and other institutional facilities).
- Globalization further purports to share technology at no cost to the developing countries, thereby eventually leading to equalized working conditions, standards, attitudes, and values transnationally.
- Globalization further encourages foreign subsidiaries through increasing the activities of MNCs, thereby facilitating import substitution. This can be very important for those developing countries with sever balance of payments problems.
- Yet further globalization may generate a new source of revenue to the developing countries in the form of royalties and taxable income and finally,
- Globalization tends to encourage the creation of a more peaceful international environment, because the developing countries on their own cannot thrive if they have to deal with problems of multitude nature from feeding the growing population to trade barriers to financial and technological constraints.

But in reality they have accomplished the following to the contrary:

- Globalization has decapitalized the developing countries by taking out more money in profits than they invest in these countries.
- Rather than bringing in more investment, many multinationals simply borrow from local creditors, thus depleting capital resources that might have been used by indigenous businesses.
- The technological dependence so created by globalization by outside businesses means a developing country is less likely to develop its own innovative capacity. While borrowing technology is useful in the short-term, it does not help achieve the long-term national economic goals.
- With globalization, MNCs, through advertising, can encourage consumerism and the importation of luxury goods, thus undermining domestic investment that is vital to economic growth.
- Under globalization MNCs can counter mercantilist restrictions on trade by establishing subsidiaries abroad. In effect, this allows them to jump the trade barriers, continuing production and collecting profits at the expense of the developing countries in its own territory.
- Globalization does help MNCs to intentionally discourage industrialization for this would mean increased competition for them. They prefer instead the developing countries concentrate on supplying raw materials and cheap labor.
- Since developing countries are often forced to concentrate on primary and extractive materials for exports, they are denied the added value derived

from processing their own resources. The finished products must be imported, which adds to the costs of processing, transportation, and profits to the final bill.

- Under globalization, the profit orientation of MNCs works against progressive Socio-economic and political values.
- With globalization the MNCs are creating an elite class of wealthy individuals in developing countries like their rich counterparts in the developed countries, who are increasingly detached from the impoverished masses within their own societies.
- Globalization has made MNCs more footloose than ever, that is to rush to relocate in response to changing economic conditions
- MNCs are first and foremost, creatures of their home countries—think global, act local
- MNCs are bigger than their assets in their reach and influence, far greater than the offical statistics suggests
- MNCs are inherently exploitative, and
- Above all, globalization has vigorously promoted the homogenization of the consumer market the world over.

Thus the MNCs are propagating the above manifestations more than ever before in the world in general, and the developing countries, in particular. These trends are more evident among the more affluent population of the world. As a result, developments are evident in consumer tastes (particularly in the developing countries) created by global socio-economic pressures akin to keep up with the Joneses. Also, a new and materialistic international culture has taken root in these countries which people are saving less, borrow more, defer parenthood, and indulge in both affordable and unaffordable luxuries that are confined to international markets as symbols of styles and distinctiveness. This culture is easily and rapidly being transmitted at the present through the new telecommunications media, and it has been an important basis for transnational corporation's global marketing of products (such as German luxury automobiles, Swiss watches, British rain coats, French wines, American soft drinks, Italian shoes and designer clothes, Japanese consumer electronics). It is also a culture that has been easily reinforced through other aspects of globalization, including the internationalization of television, especially CNN, MTV, Star Television, and the Syndication of T.V. movies without any due consideration to the cultural or religious sensitivities in many countries of the world.

III

In a way the deeper ideological principle of globalization is not so new; it is only now becoming transparent when applied to the global economy. The basic principle revolves around the absolute primacy of exponential economic growth and an unregulated "free market" the need for free trade to stimulate the growth; the destruction of "import substitution", which tend to promote economic self-sufficiency in favor of export-import oriented economies accelerated privatization of public enterprises, and the aggressive promotion of consumerism, which combined with global development correctly reflects the western vision. Furthermore this guiding principle of the new economic structure also assumes that all countries—even those whose culture as diverse as, say, Egypt, India, China, Indonesia, Japan, Kenya, Sweden and Brazil to name a few, must now row their rising boats in unison. The net result being the emergence of a global monocultural life style and level of technological immersion, with the corresponding dismantling of local traditions and self-sufficient economies. In a way, we can summarize these outcomes of globalization on the world societies to three sinister policies expounded in the past and at the present by the west. They are:

1. Liberalism,
2. Mercantilism, and
3. Dependencism.

I. Liberalism: From a historical perspective the origin of economic liberalism can be traced back to the rise of capitalism in Great Britain in the late Eighteenth century;[9] Adam Smith, in his much celebrated book *Wealth of Nations,* published in 1776, advocated that the most effective way to foster national economic prosperity and promote individual welfare is through a market economy, in which people freely buy and sell goods and services to satisfy human needs and wants. Furthermore, he asserted that the best economic system is one in which government keeps its hands off of domestic and international activities. Thus, voluntary economic exchange should be practiced domestically through free enterprise and internationally through free trade.

In 1817, another British Economist, David Ricardo, put forth in his book, *Principles of Political Economy,* the theory of comparative advantage, which has served as the cornerstone of liberal trade theory. In a way Ricardo expounded on the theory of economic liberalism already made famous by Adam Smith. According to Ricardo, countries possess different productive endowments (e.g. national resources, labor technology, management) that lead to different relative productive capabilities. In order to maximize national economic output countries should specialize in producing commodities, which they have a comparative cost advantage and import those in which they have a comparative cost disadvantage.

In the 1930s, Eli Heckscher and Bertil Ohlin refined Ricardo's theory by arguing that national comparative advantages were based not only on different productive efficiencies but also on national factor endowments. Since the quality and quantity of resources differ among countries, a different factor endowment leads to different relative costs. In conclusion, they said as a result of differences in factor endowments in different countries, a country should export the output of their abundant resource and import the output of their scarce resource.

However, under the guise of globalization, the West is pushing economic liberalism, without qualifying the fact, that even Smith—Ricardo—Heckscher and Ohlin

[9] Bergsten, C.F. , Krause L.B. eds. *World Politics and International Economics.* Brooking Institution. 1975. Washington D.C. p. 179.

theories of international trade do not advocate the fact that all countries involved in foreign trade necessarily improve their relative economic welfare from unrestricted trade. Rather, it asserts only that trade provides potential absolute benefits for all states. Moreover, the doctrine does not assert that countries involved will benefit equally from trade. In other words, from this it is clear that the relative benefits are different, as Gilpin notes[10], that "it is not based on grounds of equity but on increased efficiency and the maximization of world wealth in favor of the West at the expense of the East"[11].

II. Mercantilism: was first adopted as a state policy in the Sixteenth century with the rise of nation-states. Mercantilism as a doctrine was successfully used by emerging nation-states of that time to consolidate and expand their power and authority through increasing control over foreign trade. Basically, mercantilism advocates that national economic welfares maximize the global economy when a state delivers greater economic wealth relative to other states. Relative economic gains are normally realized when a state achieves a trade surplus, that is, by exporting more than importing.

Mercantilism as a doctrine contradicts in its basic tenet with liberalism, for liberalism assumes that the interest of people, firms, and states are fundamentally complementary, whereas mercantilism assumes that states interests are basically competitive and conflictual and should be one-sided to triumph over others. This is exactly what the on-going globalization is trying to accomplish in favor of the west at the expense of the rest of the world.

In a way, under the guise of globalization, what is being practiced can be rightfully characterized as neo-mercantilism, meaning organized free trade by the Europeans and managed trade by North America. The goal of neo-mercantilism can be defined as trade policy whereby a state seeks to maintain a balance of trade surplus and to promote domestic production and employment by reducing imports, stimulating domestic production and promoting exports.

III. Dependencism: In general, the dependency theory recognizes the inequality in the relationship between the industrial west and the developing world[12]. Decisions made by business and governments in the industrial world affect the developing countries more than the other way around. This inequality can be rightly labeled as neo-imperialism or neo-colonialism, for developing countries though have achieved political independence but not economic independence. The way the world economic structure has evolved, at the present the developing countries need the developed West much more than vice versa. As such developing economies have come to depend on the Industrial West for markets for their exports, capital and capital goods, consumer goods, refined fuels, processed foods, and everything else that characterize a modern economy.

The west in contrast, import mostly primary and extensive commodities from the developing world, which adds only a small amount to their total production cost.

---

[10] Gilpin, R. *The Political Economy of International Relations*. Princeton University Press. 1997. p. 77.
[11] ibid. p. 103.
[12] Kelleher, A. and L. Klein. *Global Perspectives—A Handbook for Understanding Global Issues*. Prentice Hall. New Jersey. 1999. p. 88.

This imbalance of economic relationship has international socio-economic implications. A developing country does not have a bargaining position when negotiating on a political or economic basis. Nor is its leader consulted in the actions and policies of international government organizations (IGOs) such as the World Bank, IMF, etc.

IV

In recent years Muslim perception of global issues and hence, the very process of on-going globalization, has come under critical scrutiny. In a way, it has come to the realization that it is a preconceived plan by the West and its surrogates to undermine Islamic values: The pandemonium over the Salman Rushdie's novel Satanic Verses, the Gulf War, the ravages of the Muslim population in Bosnia and the merciless attack on the civilian population in Lebanon has convinced beyond suspicion the sinister plot. Even scholars in their pursuit to explain the current global science have resorted to partial characterization. For example Professor Samuel Huntington's essay entitled, "The Clash of Civilization,"[13] Francis Fukuyama's "The End of History and The Last Man"[14] and Felipe Fernandez, "Armesto's Millennium"[15] are interpreted as a part of the conspiracy against Islam. However, not all scholars share this view, for example the book entitled "A Sense of Siege: The Geopolitics of Islam and the West"[16] by Graham Fuller and Ian Lesser, and also the contention of Jean Baudrill[17] resorted to practical characterization. For example, the Harvard Professor, Samuel Huntington, in his essay "Clash of Civilization," argues vehemently that future global conflicts will be cultural, not ideological or economic in its ramifications. In a way, Professor Huntington comes close to identifying Islam as a potential enemy of civilization. It seems Huntington's thesis has been derived from established contemporary thinking. For example, Bernard Lewis writes that "We are facing a mood and a movement for transcending the level of issues and policies and the government that pursues them. This is no less than a clash of civilization."[18] "Islam has bloody borders,"[19] asserts Huntington.

Granted, the West and its protagonists are bent upon discrediting Islam, but the real blame lies within Islam itself, whether in the Middle East, Pakistan, Algeria, Egypt, or Afghanistan. The real culprits are in the Muslim leadership, for Muslims, unfortunately, their leadership has failed miserably. It is a sad commentary of plunder, and hidden illegal wealth looted from the people to be kept abroad and the rampant corruption contributing to the depth of their despair and helplessness and hence, their irrational response.

[13] Huntington, S. "The Clash of Civilization." *Foreign Affairs*. Vol. 72. No. 3. 1993. pp. 21-54.

[14] Fukuyama, F. *The End of History and the Last Man*. Avon Books. New York, NY.

[15] Fernandez, F.A. *Millennium: A History of the Last Thousand Years*. Scribner. New York, NY.

[16] Fuller, G. and I. Lesser. *A Sense of Seige: The Geopolitics of Islam and the West*. Westview Press. Boulder, Colorado. 1995.

[17] Baudrillard, J. *The Illusion of the End*. Oxford: Polly Press. 1994.

[18] Lewis, B. "The Roots of Muslim Rage." *Atlantic Monthly*. September. 1990. p. 37.

[19] Huntington, S. "The Clash of Civilization." *Foreign Affairs*. Vol. 72. No. 3. 1993. p. 29.

Furthermore, who annihilated large parts of Hamas in Syria to crush the Muslim brothers? Who slaughtered the Kurds in Halabja and the Shia in Southern Iraq? Bombs in bus stops and bazaars, which kill innocent people, are deplorable and not Islamic. But they will continue to take place as long as justice is denied.

If Huntington sees Islam as a world threat, Fukuyama reinforces it. According to him, Islam, which poses a threat to the triumphant liberal practice, consumerism, and democracy of the West, is a force of disruption in the tranquility at the end of history.

In a way, we ourselves are responsible for encouraging such criticism of Islam, for the simple reason we no longer are true Muslims. The first model for Muslim is the holy prophet. His life provides the balance between action and spirit, between this world and the next, he is the perfect person. Insane-e-Kamil[20]—we can promulgate theories based on the examples of prophets as an example for our Muslim leadership—rather than getting transfixed on off examples of Iran based on Shia culture and tradition. Whenever given a choice by polls, people have rejected religious parties in countries like Pakistan. The Jamat-I-Islami perhaps the best organized and the most coherent has never had more than a few members elected to the parliament. The answer to this mystery is simple, Islam does not encourage priesthood and there is no mockery in Islam, said the Prophet[21].

The second category is that of the military rulers and monarchies—of the former, General Zia in Pakistan used, Islam Saddam did not, until the Gulf War. The Shah did not, Saudis parade Islam. In reality so far all their efforts have backfired in one way or another.

The third category is the democratic one, which includes countries such as Bangladesh, Egypt, and Turkey. However, in these countries, stories of corruption, mismanagement and evident collapse of law and order have created a general disillusionment. Nonetheless, this category needs to be developed and strengthened for the future. For it reflects the Islamic spirit of egalitarianism, the need for tolerance in plural societies and larger global trends. In spite of its failure due to the misuses of democratic power by its leaders in running the nation state, this is the most viable category for our time.

In the final analysis, if the Muslim world were to wake up and see the damage that has been inflicted on its culture and economy by the on-going globalization they should in unison present a formidable opposition to the very basis of globalization in process. Failure to do so means that in the distant future the Muslim world is sure to lose its identity in the long run and its great values to the short-run exigencies of globalization, which do present an attractive life style. Therefore, it is imperative for the Muslim world to present the fact in no uncertain terms that the way the process of globalization is unfolding at the present can not be an answer to the growing problems of the Muslim world, in particular, and the developing world in general, unless the West recognizes and acts on the time honored principle of mutual economic interdependence among the countries of the globe in general and the Muslim world in

---

[20] Akbar, S.A. "Towards the Global Millennium: The Challenge of Islam." Annual Editions. *Global Issues.* Dushkin/McGraw. 1997–98. p. 193.
[21] ibid. p.193.

particular. *Anything less than this as it is permeating by the so-called globalization today* may not only undermine Islamic values but would lead to widening of the gap between the rich of the West and the poor of the East as never before.

V

Looked at from any angle, globalization represents the same old order with new means of control, new means of oppression, new means of marginalization. Under these concern:

It is dangerous for developing countries to embrace globalization. Its negative consequences are seldom mentioned; instead, lack of economic development is blamed on bad government, corruption and cronyism. A blind acceptance of an ideology is unacceptable, naïve and downright dangerous from the point of the developing countries.

Critics of globalization in general are not isolationists but are for better globalization. They want to not only bring forth the negative aspect of globalization, but also want to negotiate with those who favor this unfair arrangement. The critics turning to labor while agreeing to the ILO Labor Standards as reasonable, protest vehemently to the principle that wages should be equalized around the world without regard to the level of poverty, and unemployment as downright protectionist.

Developed countries erect obstacles to trade—in particular, barriers to trade in agricultural products and textiles. When the West, under the guise of globalization, pushes the developing countries to open their markets, they are erecting barriers of entry into their markets. This is paramount to not allowing the developing countries to sell what they produce. Globalization the way it is being unleashed, encourages unequal distribution of power and wealth, once again in favor of the West at the expense of the East.

Maintaining respect for traditional, local and national cultures is not something that is easy for economists to deal with. It is imperative that we not only maintain, but also nurture our international public good that values the diversity of cultures rather than let it be destroyed by the relentless homogenizing process of the current process of globalization.

To conclude, there are many valid concerns about the on-going process of globalization. Before we can defend it by heralding its benefits we must first make this process equitable beyond reproach. For this to happen in the words of Stanley Fisher, Deputy Director of International Monetary Fund (IMF), the policy makers of the advanced countries and the international institutions manage the process well and bring the developing countries into the process of globalization.[22]

Therefore, from the point of the both developed West and the developing East, the fact remains, that needs recognition of the importance of both by each side. No doubt international trade is binding the world increasingly in a common destiny. The world community as a whole must begin to realize that a more equitable international

---

[22] Fisher, Stanley. Overview—Global Economic Integration: Opportunities and Challenges—Symposium. Sponsored by The Federal Reserve Bank of Kansas City. Jackson. p. 318.

economic order based on trade and mutual interdependence is not only possible but also essential. Such a new order should be based on the fundamental principle that each nation's and each individual's development is intimately bound to the development of every other nation and every other individual in a global sense. In a way, the future of mankind is linked more closely today than ever before. All indications are that it will become more so in the coming decades.

Let us hope, therefore, that resources and good sense prevail so that the first, second, third, and now the fourth world's can truly become part of one world—forged together by a common destiny and guided by the human principle of peace, brotherhood, and above all, the mutual respect in international interdependence, hence, only than globalization becomes relevant to each and everyone on this planet, irrespective of national boundaries in ethnic religious differences.

SELECTED BIBLIOGRAPHY:

Ahmed, S. Akbar: "Towards the Global Millennium: The Challenge of Islam," Annual Editions, *Global Issues* 1997-98, pp. 191-95. Dushkin, McGraw, Guilford, Connecticut.

Baudrillard, J. *The Illusion of the End.* Oxford. Polly Press, 1994.

Economist, "White Man's Shame," *Economist,* September 25, 1999.

Freedom House, Freedom in the World, 1998-99, www.freedomhouse.org/survey99/tables/indeptab.html

Friedman, Thomas, *The Lexus and the Olive Tree* (New York: Farrar, Straus and Giroux) 1999.

Fuller G. and Lesser I, *A Sense of Seige: The Geopolitics of Islam and the West.* Westview Press, Boulder Colorado, 1995

Henderson, David, "The Changing International Economic Order: Rival Visions for the Coming Millennium," unpublished document, Melbourne Business School, Sept 1999.

Hirst, Paul, and Grahame Thompson, *Globalization in Question: The International Economy and the Possibilities of Governance.* Cambridge, UK: Polity Press. 1996.

Huntington, Samuel, "The Clash of Civilization?" *Foreign Affairs,* Vol. 72, no 3, 1993.

Kelleher, A. and L. Klein, *Global Perspectives—A Handbook for Understanding Global Issues.* Prentice Hall, NJ 1999.

Kennedy, Paul. *Preparing for the Twenty First Century.* Random House, NY. 1998.

Krugman, Paul, "Competitiveness: A Dangerous Obsession," In *The New Shape of World Politics.* New York: W.W. Norton and Foreign Affairs.

Lewis, B. "The Roots of Muslim Rage," *Atlantic Monthly,* September 1999.

Low, Patric, Marcelo Olarrega and Javier Suarez, "Does Globalization Cause a Higher Concentration of International Trade and Investment Flaws?" *World Trade Organization,* Staff Papers ERAD, August 1998.

World Bank. "Assessing Globalization: Does More International Trade Openness Increase World Poverty?" PREM Economic Policy Group and Development Economic Group, April 2000. www.Worldbank.org/html/extdr/ph/globalization/paper2.htm

World Bank, Social Indicators, www.worldbank.org/poverty/data/trends.

Weiss, Linda, *The Myth of the Powerless State: Governing the Economy in a Global Era.* Cambridge, UK: Polity Press, 1998.

Electronic Cash and the End of National Markets

Stephen J. Kobrin

Twenty-six years ago, Raymond Vernon's *Sovereignty at Bay* proclaimed that "concepts such as national sovereignty and national economic strength appear curiously drained of meaning." Other books followed, arguing that sovereignty, the nation-state, and the national economy were finished—victims of multinational enterprises and the internationalization of production. While sovereign states and national markets have outlasted the chorus of Cassandras, this time the sky really may be falling. The emergence of electronic cash and a digitally networked global economy pose direct threats to the very basis of the territorial state.

Let us begin with two vignettes. Fact: Smugglers fly Boeing 747s loaded with illicit drugs into Mexico and then cram the jumbo jets full of cash—American bills—for the return trip. Fiction: Uncle Enzo, Mafia CEO, pays for intelligence in the digital future of Neal Stephenson's novel *Snow Crash:* "He reaches into his pocket and pulls out a hypercard and hands it toward Hiro. It says 'Twenty-Five Million Hong Kong Dollars.' Hiro reaches out and takes the card. Somewhere on earth, two computers swap bursts of electronic noise and the money gets transferred from the Mafia's account to Hiro's."

The 747s leaving Mexico are anachronisms, among the last surviving examples of the physical transfer of large amounts of currency across national borders. Most money has been electronic for some time: Virtually all of the trillions of dollars, marks, and yen that make their way around the world each day take the form of bytes—chains of zeros and ones. Only at the very end of its journey is money transformed into something tangible: credit cards, checks, cash, or coins.

Hypercards are here. Mondex, a smart card or electronic purse, can be "loaded" with electronic money from an automatic teller machine (ATM) or by telephone or

Reprinted from *Foreign Policy* 107, (summer 1997), by permission of Stephen Kobrin.

personal computer using a card-reading device. Money is spent either by swiping the card through a retailer's terminal or over the Internet by using the card reader and a personal computer. An electronic wallet allows anonymous card-to-card transfers.

It is not just the current technology of electronic cash (e-cash) or even what might be technologically feasible in the future that presents policymakers with new challenges. Rather, policymakers must confront directly the implications of this technology—and, more generally, the emergence of an electronically networked global economy—for economic and political governance. As the U.S. comptroller of the currency, Eugene Ludwig, has noted, "There is clearly a freight train coming down the tracks. . . . Just because it hasn't arrived yet doesn't mean we shouldn't start getting ready."

ELECTRONIC MONEY

Many different forms of "electronic money" are under development, but it is useful to look at three general categories: electronic debit and credit systems; various forms of smart cards; and true digital money, which has many of the properties of cash.

Electronic debit and credit systems already exist. When a consumer uses an ATM card to pay for merchandise, funds are transferred from his or her account to the merchant's. Credit cards are used to make payments over the Internet. Computer software such as Intuit provides electronic bill payment, and it is but a short step to true electronic checks—authenticated by a digital signature—that can be transmitted to the payee, endorsed, and deposited over the Internet. Electronic debit and credit systems represent new, more convenient means of payment, but not new payment systems. A traditional bank or credit card transaction lies at the end of every transaction chain.

Smart cards and digital money represent new payment systems with potentially revolutionary implications. Smart cards are plastic "credit" cards with an embedded microchip. Many are now used as telephone or transit payment devices. They can be loaded with currency from an ATM or via a card reader from a telephone or personal computer, currency which can then be spent at businesses, vending machines, or turnstiles that have been equipped with appropriate devices. At this most basic level, a smart card is simply a debit card that does not require bank approval for each transaction; clearance takes place each day and the value resides in third-party accounts. There is no reason, however, that smart cards have to be limited in this way.

Banks or other institutions could provide value on smart cards through loans, payments for services, or products. The immediate transfer of funds between bank accounts is not necessary; units of value can circulate from card to card—and from user to user—without debiting or crediting third-party accounts. Assuming confidence in the creating institution, "money" could be created on smart cards and could circulate almost indefinitely before redemption.

Finally, electronic money can take true digital form, existing as units of value in the form of bytes stored in the memory of personal computers that may or may not be backed up by reserve accounts of real money. The money could be down-loaded from an account, supplied as a loan or as payment, or bought with a credit card over the Internet. As long as digital cash can be authenticated *and* there is confidence in its continued acceptance, it could circulate indefinitely, allowing peer-to-peer payments at will. These are big "ifs," but they are well within the realm of the possible.

Imagine a world where true e-cash is an everyday reality. Whether all of the following assumptions are correct or even immediately feasible is unimportant; some form of e-cash is coming, and we need to begin the process of thinking about its as-yet-unexplored consequences for economic and political governance.

The year is 2005. You have a number of brands of e-cash on your computer's hard drive: some withdrawn from a bank in Antigua, some borrowed from Microsoft, and some earned as payment for your services. You use the digital value units (DVUs) to purchase information from a Web site, pay bills, or send money to your daughter in graduate school. Peer-to-peer payments are easy: You can transfer DVUs to any computer, anyplace in the world, with a few keystrokes.

Your e-cash is secure and can be authenticated easily. It is also anonymous; governments have not been able to mandate a technology that leaves a clear audit trail. Public-key encryption technology and digital signatures allow blind transactions; the receiving computer knows that the DVUs are authentic without knowing the identity of the payer. Your e-cash can be exchanged any number of times without leaving a trace of where it has been. It is virtually impossible to alter the value of your e-cash at either end of the transaction (by adding a few more zeros to it, for example).

DVUs are almost infinitely divisible. Given the virtually negligible transaction cost, it is efficient for you to pay a dollar or two to see a financial report over the Internet or for your teenager to rent a popular song for the few minutes during which it is in vogue. Microtransactions have become the norm.

E-cash is issued—actually created—by a large number of institutions, bank and nonbank. Electronic currencies (e-currencies) have begun to exist on their own; many are no longer backed by hard currency and have developed value separately from currencies issued by central banks. DVUs circulate for long periods of time without being redeemed or deposited. Consumer confidence in the issuer is crucial; as with electronic commerce (e-commerce) in general, brand names have become critical.

The early 21st century is described as a world of competing e-currencies, a throwback to the 19th-century world of private currencies. The better known brands of e-cash are highly liquid and universally accepted. It is a relatively simple matter for you to set up filters in your electronic purse to screen out e-currencies that you do not want to accept.

GOVERNANCE IN THE DIGITAL WORLD

E-cash and the increasing importance of digital markets pose problems for central government control over the economy and the behavior of economic actors; they also render borders around national markets and nation-states increasingly permeable—or, perhaps, increasingly irrelevant. In a world where true e-cash is an everyday reality, the basic role of government in a liberal market economy and the relevance of borders and geography will be drastically redefined.

While at first glance this concern appears to reflect a traditional break between domestic and international economic issues, in fact the advent of e-cash raises serious questions about the very idea of "domestic" and "international" as meaningful and distinct concepts. The new digital world presents a number of governance issues, described below.

• *Can central banks control the rate of growth and the size of the money supply?* Private e-currencies will make it difficult for central bankers to control—or even measure or define—monetary aggregates. Several forms of money, issued by banks and nonbanks, will circulate. Many of these monies may be beyond the regulatory reach of the state. At the extreme, if, as some libertarians imagine, private currencies dominate, currencies issued by central banks may no longer matter.

• *Will there still be official foreign exchange transactions?* E-cash will markedly lower existing barriers to the transfer of funds across borders. Transactions that have been restricted to money-center banks will be available to anyone with a computer. Peer-to-peer transfers of DVUs across national borders do not amount to "official" foreign exchange transactions. If you have $200 worth of DVUs on your computer and buy a program from a German vendor, you will probably have to agree on a mark-to-dollar price. However, transferring the DVUs to Germany is not an "official" foreign exchange transaction; the DVUs are simply revalued as marks. In fact, national currencies may lose meaning with the development of DVUs that have a universally accepted denomination. Without severe restrictions on individual privacy—which are not out of the question—governments will be hard-pressed to track, account for, and control the flows of money across borders.

• *Who will regulate or control financial institutions?* The U.S. Treasury is not sure whether existing regulations, which apply to both banks and institutions that act like banks (i.e., take deposits), would apply to all who issue (and create) e-cash. If nonfinancial institutions do not accept the extensive regulatory controls that banks take as the norm, can reserve or reporting requirements be enforced? What about consumer protection in the event of the insolvency of an issuer of e-cash, a system breakdown, or the loss of a smart card?

• *Will national income data still be meaningful?* It will be almost impossible to track transactions when e-cash becomes a widely used means of payment, on-line deals across borders become much easier, and many of the intermediaries that now serve as checkpoints for recording transactions are eliminated by direct, peer-to-peer payments. The widespread use of e-cash will render national economic data much less meaningful. Indeed, the advent of both e-cash and e-commerce raises fundamental questions about the national market as the basic unit of account in the international economic system.

• *How will taxes be collected?* Tax evasion will be a serious problem in an economy where e-cash transactions are the norm. It will be easy to transfer large sums of money across borders, and tax havens will be much easier to reach. Encrypted anonymous transactions will make audits increasingly problematic. Additionally, tax reporting and compliance relies on institutions and intermediaries. With e-cash and direct payments, all sorts of sales taxes, value-added taxes, and income taxes will be increasingly difficult to collect. More fundamentally, the question of jurisdiction—who gets to tax what—will become increasingly problematic. Say you are in Philadelphia and you decide to download music from a computer located outside

Dublin that is run by a firm in Frankfurt. You pay with e-cash deposited in a Cayman Islands account. In which jurisdiction does the transaction take place?

• *Will e-cash and e-commerce widen the gap between the haves and the have-nots?* Participation in the global electronic economy requires infrastructure and access to a computer. Will e-cash and e-commerce further marginalize poorer population groups and even entire poor countries? This widened gap between the haves and the have-nots—those with and without access to computers—could become increasingly difficult to bridge.

• *Will the loss of seigniorage be important as governments fight to balance budgets?* Seigniorage originally referred to the revenue or profit generated due to the difference between the cost of making a coin and its face value; it also refers to the reduction in government interest payments when money circulates. The U.S. Treasury estimates that traditional seigniorage amounted to $773 million in 1994 and that the reduction in interest payments due to holdings of currency rather than debt could be as much as $3.5 billion per year. The Bank for International Settlements reports that the loss of seigniorage for its 11 member states will be more than $17 billion if smart cards eliminate all bank notes under $25.

• *Will fraud and criminal activity increase in an e-cash economy?* At the extreme—and the issue of privacy versus the needs of law enforcement is unresolved—transfers of large sums of cash across borders would be untraceable: There would be no audit trail. Digital counterfeiters could work from anywhere in the world and spend currency in any and all places. New financial crimes and forms of fraud could arise that would be hard to detect, and it would be extremely difficult to locate the perpetrators. The task of financing illegal and criminal activity would be easier by orders of magnitude. E-cash will lower the barriers to entry and reduce the risks of criminal activity.

Most of the issues raised in the recent National Research Council report on cryptography's role in the information society apply directly to electronic cash. Secure, easily authenticated, and anonymous e-cash requires strong encryption technology. Anonymous transactions, however, cannot be restricted to law-abiding citizens. Encryption makes it as difficult for enforcement authorities to track criminal activity as it does for criminals to penetrate legitimate transmissions. Should privacy be complete? Or should law enforcement authorities and national security agencies be provided access to e-cash transactions through escrowed encryption, for example? What about U.S. restrictions on the export of strong encryption technology? E-cash is global cash; how can governments limit its geographic spread? Can they even suggest that strong encryption algorithms be restricted territorially?

GEOGRAPHIC SPACE VS. CYBERSPACE

A recent U.S. Treasury paper dealing with the tax implications of electronic commerce argues that new communications technologies have "effectively eliminated national borders on the information highway." It is clear from the paper's subsequent discussion, however, that the more fundamental problem is that electronic commerce may "dissolve the link between an income-producing activity and a specific location."

The source of taxable income, which plays a major role in determining liability, is defined geographically in terms of where the economic activity that produces the income is located. Therein lies the rub: "Electronic commerce doesn't seem to occur in any physical location but instead takes place in the nebulous world of 'cyberspace.'" In a digital economy it will be difficult, or even impossible, to link income streams with specific geographic locations.

Digitalization is cutting money and finance loose from its geographic moorings. The framework of regulation that governs financial institutions assumes that customers and institutions are linked by geography—that spatial proximity matters. E-cash and e-commerce snap that link. What remains are systems of economic and political governance that are rooted in geography and are trying nonetheless to deal with e-cash and markets that exist in cyberspace. The obvious disconnect here will only worsen over time.

The geographical rooting of political and economic authority is relatively recent. Territorial sovereignty, borders, and a clear distinction between domestic and international spheres are modern concepts associated with the rise of the nation-state. Territorial sovereignty implies a world divided into clearly demarcated and mutually exclusive geographic jurisdictions. It implies a world where economic and political control arise from control over territory.

The international financial system—which consists of hundreds of thousands of computer screens around the globe—is the first international electronic marketplace. It will not be the last. E-cash is one manifestation of a global economy that is constructed in cyberspace rather than geographic space. The fundamental problems that e-cash poses for governance result from this disconnect between electronic markets and political geography.

The very idea of controlling the money supply, for example, assumes that geography provides a relevant means of defining the scope of the market. It assumes that economic borders are effective, that the flow of money across them can be monitored and controlled, and that the volume of money within a fixed geographic area is important. All of those assumptions are increasingly questionable in a digital world economy.

Many of our basic tax principles assume that transactions and income streams can be located precisely within a given national market. That assumption is problematic when e-cash is spent on a computer network. It is problematic when many important economic transactions cannot be located, or may not even take place, in geographic space.

The increasing irrelevance of geographic jurisdiction in a digital world economy markedly increases the risks of fraud, money-laundering, and other financial crimes. Asking where the fraud or money-laundering took place means asking Whose jurisdiction applies? and Whose law applies? We need to learn to deal with crimes that cannot be located in geographic space, where existing concepts of national jurisdiction are increasingly irrelevant.

The term "disintermediation" was first used to describe the replacement of banks as financial intermediaries by direct lending in money markets when interest rates rose. It is often used in the world of e-commerce to describe the elimination of intermediaries by direct seller-to-buyer transactions over the Internet. Many observers argue that e-cash is likely to disintermediate banks. Of more fundamental importance is the possibility that e-cash and e-commerce will disintermediate the territorial state.

To be clear, I argue that we face not the end of the state, but rather the diminished efficacy of political and economic governance that is rooted in geographic sovereignty and in mutually exclusive territorial jurisdiction. Questions such as, Where did the transaction take place? Where did the income stream arise? Where is the financial institution located? and Whose law applies? will lose meaning.

E-cash and e-commerce are symptoms, albeit important ones, of an increasing asymmetry between economics and politics, between an electronically integrated world economy and territorial nation-states, and between cyberspace and geographic space. How this asymmetry will be resolved and how economic and political relations will be reconstructed are two of the critical questions of our time.

WHAT IS TO BE DONE?

The question asked here is not What is feasible? but What are the limits of the possible? Whether the picture presented here is correct in all—or even some—of its details is unimportant. A digital world economy is emerging. Imagining possible scenarios is necessary if we are to come to grips with the consequences of this revolution.

The purpose here is to raise problems rather than to solve them and to imagine possible futures and think about their implications for economic and political governance. A digital world economy will demand increasing international cooperation, harmonizing national regulations and legislation, and strengthening the authority of international institutions.

The harmonization of national regulations will help to prevent institutions, such as those issuing e-cash, from slipping between national jurisdictions or shopping for the nation with the least onerous regulations. However, it will not address the basic problem of the disconnect between geographic jurisdiction and an electronically integrated global economy.

If it is impossible to locate transactions geographically—if the flows of e-cash are outside of the jurisdictional reach of every country—then the harmonization of national regulations will accomplish little. The basic problem is not one of overlapping or conflicting jurisdictions; it stems from the lack of meaning of the very concept of "jurisdiction" in a digitalized global economy.

The erosion of the viability of territorial jurisdiction calls for strengthened international institutions. It calls for giving international institutions real authority to measure, to control, and, perhaps, to tax. The Basle Committee on Banking Supervision—an international body of bank regulators who set global standards—could perhaps be given the authority to collect information from financial institutions wherever they are located and formulate and enforce regulations globally. Interpol, or its equivalent, may have to be given jurisdiction over financial crimes, regardless of where they are committed. That does not mean a world government; it does mean a markedly increased level of international cooperation.

The questions we must face are whether territorial sovereignty will continue to be viable as the *primary* basis for economic and political governance as we enter the 21st century and what the implications will be for the American economy—and Americans in general—if we refuse to cooperate internationally in the face of an increasingly integrated global economy.

Electronic Cash: A Glossary

Digital data: Information coded into a series of zeros and ones that can be transmitted and processed electronically.

Digital signature: A code that allows absolute authentication of the origin and integrity of a document, check, or electronic cash that has been sent over a computer network. A blind signature allows authentication without revealing the identity of the sender.

Disintermediation: The substitution of direct transactions for those that are mediated. The term originated when rising interest rates caused savings to be withdrawn from banks—whose interest rates were capped—and invested in money market instruments that were the direct debts of borrowers. Banks were disintermediated. In electronic commerce, the term refers to the rise of direct buyer-to-seller relationships over the Internet, disintermediating wholesalers and retail outlets.

Electronic money: Units or tokens of monetary value that take digital form and are transmitted over electronic networks. Digital Value Units are the basic units of denomination of electronic money; they may or may not correspond to units of national currency.

Encryption: The coding of information for security purposes, such as credit card numbers or electronic cash used over the Internet. Public-key encryption uses a mathematical algorithm comprising a pair of strings of numbers to encrypt and decrypt the data. For example, the sender would encrypt the data with the receiver's public key and the receiver would decrypt with his or her private key.

Internet: A global network of linked networks that allows communication and the sharing of information among many different types of computers. The World Wide Web is a graphical system on the Internet that allows rapid movement between documents and computers through the use of embedded (hypertext) links.

Smart card: A plastic card, similar to a credit card, containing a microchip that can be used to retrieve, store, process, and transmit digital data like electronic cash or medical information.

Economic Development

Ann Kelleher and Laura Klein

Modern technology offers the tantalizing prospect of enabling the world to produce enough food, shelter, clothes, clean water, and basic medical care for every person on the planet. Sadly, while this capability exists, its promise has not become a reality at the turn of the twenty-first century. Out of the world's population of well over five billion, about two billion people lead debilitating lives of desperation on the margin of survival. They seem to inhabit a different world from the planet's minority who enjoy a comfortable, consumer-goods lifestyle.

This chapter offers general explanations as to why a wide and growing gap exists between the world's rich and poor. This reality runs contrary to the image implied by *development*, which is supposed to provide an answer to the problem of poverty. Development is an economic process intended to enable increasing numbers of people to produce enough wealth to support an acceptable quality of life. Unfortunately, for those attempting to understand the process, this seemingly simple, straightforward definition masks major differences in strategy and in what an "acceptable lifestyle" actually means.

The dominant interpretation of development assumes that it means achieving a modern machine-based lifestyle, one measured by ownership of televisions, automobiles, and appliances, and characterized by plenty of food and leisure time. Yet an increasing number of people are adopting a different approach to development, one that emphasizes the fact that hundreds of millions of people on Earth have little hope of becoming part of a heavily industrialized society or of experiencing a consumer-goods lifestyle. These people must fulfill their basic needs for adequate shelter, food, clothes, and medical care by improving the productivity of their agricultural-based economies.

The industrial development strategy requires extensive economic growth. Such growth produces the extra earnings needed to invest in machines, the fossil fuel energy to run them, educated people to fix them, and the constant flow of new technology to update them. With industrial development, earnings from economic growth must be ongoing because energy and new technology costs continue as well. The alternative approach to development, however, does not accept economic growth as essential. It defines the process as one of "improvement" and "enrichment," of leading to a better life. Thus, achieving an acceptable lifestyle can mean having enough of life's basics without becoming part of a modern consumer-oriented, energy-guzzling, machine-dependent economy.

The two development strategies, one calling for economic growth and the other for fulfilling basic needs, propose different answers to the problems of the world's poor. Yet the adherents of both strategies decry the chronic, dispiriting, debilitating poverty that can kill hope and create desperation, disease, and dehumanization. One pitfall in analyzing development issues among the world's poor is that relevant information can seem too abstract, statistical, and unrelated to the actual lives of real people. Therefore, our discussion begins by introducing an individual whose lifestyle represents the majority of the world's population.

> Meet Lucia. She has good looks, not the prettiness of youth, but long-lasting, pleasant features with the high cheekbones typical of Andean peoples. It takes only a brief conversation to gain respect for this Quechua Indian peasant woman. She has a quiet confidence and speaks articulately. Choosing her words thoughtfully, she seems self-assured and refined. In her, life's hard experiences have produced a reflective composure.
>
> Lucia, her husband, and two children live in one of the farming sectors outside of Mollepata, a town about 9,000 feet high in Peru's Andes Mountains. Most of the over 900 town residents, and 3,000 people in its surrounding rural sectors, earn a living either directly or indirectly from subsistence agriculture. Potatoes, vegetables, grains, and some livestock are raised on slopes slanting often eight degrees or even more. The potato fields lie at the highest elevations allowing crop cultivation, around 11,000 feet. This food source was cultivated long before Europeans discovered it during their conquest. Dependent on what they raise themselves, Mollepata's residents remember well the drought beginning in 1982, when the seasonal rains did not come. Severe malnutrition was commonplace and starvation for many, but not all, was avoided only by the intervention of international relief agencies.
>
> In the early 1990s, Lucia organized a team from the women's committee in her sector to compete in a planting contest. Fourteen teams, twelve male and two female, entered the contest sponsored by a local non-governmental development organization. It took courage for the women to compete because in Quechua society men are responsible for raising the crops. The contest required three days of work. Not only did the teams plant a crop in their designated area of a large field, but also designed and dug irrigation channels. Lucia's team came in second. Upon receiving the prize of farm hand tools, she noted that her team's performance showed that women can contribute to the incomes of their families.

Lucia and her family are among the approximately three-quarters of the Earth's inhabitants for whom physical survival is a goal, not a given. Yet our short introduction to this peasant woman contradicts the assumption that the poor, out of necessity, always become beaten down, boorish, coarse, or devoid of hope and human feelings. If they can make decisions and meet their physical needs, low-income people can experience meaningful, useful, and fulfilling lives. People who live in poverty statistically may not always think of themselves as poor.

Poverty exists in virtually every country of the world and has common causes wherever it is found. Two worlds exist within the economies of most countries—one of privilege, the other of need. Statistics show that these worlds are moving farther away from each other in terms of living standards and productivity, but they remain intertwined economically in ways that most people do not realize. Even though rich and poor people live within the same state borders, the poor in industrialized countries are often obscured by a large middle class. Still, the overwhelming majority of the world's poor live in what can be called *developing countries* because of their desperate need for a successful development process. Industrial countries, in contrast, have achieved the economic growth it takes to move a majority of their people into the modern middle class. In these states, the poor live in pockets surrounded by people who, in global terms, live as part of the world's rich. Yet since most global poverty is located in states with primarily agricultural-based economies, tackling development as a global issue usually focuses on the situation of states in the *developing world.*

THE DEVELOPING WORLD

Many people first learn of the developing world through pictures of starving children in newspapers or on television. When a natural disaster, war, or both causes large-scale deprivation, the events make the nightly news. Such news stories often leave the impression that relief aid will fill the need until the unusual situation causing the problem works its way through. The episode is treated as an isolated emergency, with little attention focused on mitigating the underlying chronic poverty that allows one crisis to push large populations to the very edge of survival. The unspoken assumption—that such disastrous events are inevitable from time to time—is reinforced.

This sense of inevitability is strengthened by the data on global poverty, which make the problem appear so monumental that people reason nothing can be done to correct it in the foreseeable future. Such news articles typically begin by describing the differences between developing countries and industrialized countries in terms of economic performance. A key comparison uses the *per capita gross national products* of various countries. *Gross national product (GNP)* represents the total value (in US dollars) of all goods and services a country's economy has produced in a given year, including international transactions. The GNP then can be divided by the country's number of people to produce the *per capita GNP*. These admittedly very general figures, called *macroeconomic data,* provide a common measure of the relative wealth produced by each of the world's states.

One popular source of macroeconomic data, including per capita GNP, is the *World Development Report,* a book of comprehensive economic statistics published annually by the World Bank (an international governmental organization described in Chapter 1). The World Bank data shown in Table 1 report the per capita GNP for selected countries in 1995. In at least fifteen countries with low-income economies, per capita annual income was $300 or less in 1995. This represents very little purchasing power in any country. Overall, forty-two state economies with over three billion people were classified as having a low-income economy. High-income

234 Ann Kelleher and Laura Klein

Table 1
**PER CAPITA GNP FOR SELECTED STATES
AND GROUPS OF STATES, 1995**

		GNP per capita (in US dollars)
Low-Income Economies		
Average:		$430
Examples:	Tanzania	120
	Pakistan	460
	Honduras	600
Lower-Middle-Income Economies		
Average:		$1,670
Examples:	Egypt	790
	Jamaica	1,510
	Poland	2,790
Upper-Middle-Income Economies		
Average:		$4,260
Examples:	South Africa	3,160
	Hungary	4,120
	Greece	8,210
High-Income Economies		
Average:		$24,930
Examples:	New Zealand	14,340
	United States	26,980
	Japan	39,640

Source: World Bank, *World Development Report 1997* (New York:
  Oxford University Press, 1997).

economies included twenty-four states with a combined population of over eight hundred million.

Table 1 data show the wide disparity in wealth between the world's poorest and richest states. Many states that are classified as "middle income," are actually in the "lower-middle-income" range. While few middle-income states have experienced significant economic growth, Thailand and Botswana each had an average per capita GNP growth rate of over 6 percent a year in 1980–1993, while South Korea averaged over 8 percent during that time (World Bank 1995). Some states, such as Singapore, have moved from middle- to high-income status. While the economic growth of some countries has enabled them to move up in the income ranking, most states with small economies have not been as successful. In fact, a comparison of per capita GNPs shows that the disparity between high- and low- income countries has *increased* over time. Data from the *World Development Report* document the increase (World Bank, 1979, 1995). In 1977, the average GNP per capita was $170 for low-income states,

$1,140 for middle-income states, and $6,980 for high-income states. This meant the ratio of low-income to high-income stood at 2.4 percent, while the middle-income ratio was 16 percent. In 1993, the comparable figures were $380 for low-income, $2,480 for middle-income, and $23,090 for high-income states. Thus, the ratio of low to high income dropped to 1.6 percent and that of middle to high-income was 11 percent. These data show that both low- and middle-income countries produced less wealth in relation to that produced by high-income countries in the 1990s than they did in the 1970s.

Yet even in countries with the lowest per capita GNPs, a small percentage of the population maintains a lifestyle similar to that of the majority in high-income countries. Conversely, high-income countries, such as the United States, have pockets of poverty, some of them fairly large. The economic data for Native American communities illustrate this point: Their combined per capita income in 1989 was $8,328, whereas that of the United States as a whole was $20,910. The poverty rate for Native American families was 27 percent in 1989, up from 24 percent in 1979; but the overall US family poverty rate was 10 percent in both 1984 and 1979 (Paisano 1997:2,3).

The *World Development Report* also includes data more directly illustrative of the poverty issue, as indicated in Table 2. Poor people tend to have less access to nutritious food, medical care, and clean water, which is reflected in life expectancy and infant mortality rates.

Macroeconomic data thus tend to reinforce the unspoken resignation that little can be done to alleviate poverty in the world because the problem seems too large and continues to grow. Such a reaction could be interpreted as a contemporary version of the old aristocratic notion that "the poor will always be with us." To consider their condition as inevitable produces an attitude that is demeaning at best and debilitating at worst.

Using descriptive data to contrast the economic output of poorer countries with richer ones illustrates the problem, but does little to explain why poverty exists. The concept of development, discussed at the beginning of this chapter, is most usefully thought of as a process, not an end result. The key question is whether the process should aim to produce industrialization first, or whether it should initially concentrate on producing more food and other basic needs for daily living.

These objectives may not seem contradictory to development planners until they have to decide which projects to fund with chronically scarce investment resources. Should a large-scale project be built, such as a dam for electricity and irrigation, or should the money be used for projects that would enable villagers themselves to dig wells and irrigation ditches? One requires heavy machinery, the other shovels. If the industrial-based, heavy-machinery strategy is chosen, then those with access to large-scale financing get most of the benefits. If the pick-and-shovel-method is applied, poorer people can both participate in and have ownership of the project.

Both types of projects can be found in most countries, but the debate goes on as to what should be the primary or immediate goal of development—that is, improving the daily lives of poor people or investing in the means to industrialize.

Table 2
LIFE EXPECTANCY AND INFANT MORTALITY RATES
FOR SELECTED STATES AND GROUPS OF STATES, 1995

		Life Expectancy (in years)	Infant Mortality Rate (per 1, 000 live births)
Low-Income Economies			
Average:		63	69
Examples:	Tanzania	51	82
	Pakistan	60	90
	Honduras	67	45
Low-Middle-Income Economies			
Average:		68	41
Examples:	Egypt	63	56
	Jamaica	74	13
	Poland	70	14
Upper-Middle-Income Economies			
Average:		69	35
Examples:	South Africa	64	50
	Mexico	72	33
	Greece	78	8
High-Income Economies			
Average:		77	7
Examples:	New Zealand	76	7
	United States	77	8
	Japan	80	4

Source: World Bank, *World Development Report 1997* (New York: Oxford University Press, 1997).

The controversy, in turn, makes the problem of world poverty and the potential solutions to it difficult to analyze.

The dispute over development strategies exists in part because high-income countries historically have achieved their standard of living through industrialization. Thus, for many people planning and administering projects in the developing world, development means industrialization. Machine-based production may be expensive in the short term, but it is viewed as a proven path to reducing poverty in the long term. However, because it requires major economic growth and large-scale investments, advocates of the basic needs strategy alternative are increasing in number. Practitioners, academics, and some government and international aid agency personnel are coming to realize that for the world's poor majorities, the economic growth approach is not working. They focus on the need for a development strategy that will improve poor people's lives now, rather than later, when the industrial profits of the elite "trickle down." *Basic needs* development enables local people to produce more and better food and to provide basic medical care and literacy. These goals, it is argued, can be achieved in agricultural-based economies and are not dependent on industrial technologies.

The ongoing debate between advocates of the two general approaches of development—basic needs versus economic growth—recognizes that the two billion people living in poverty face a set of interrelated problems, which can be summarized as a *cycle of underdevelopment*. The leaders of many low-income countries oppose the use of the word *underdevelopment* arguing that it implies that their societies are "backward." Still, the term aptly summarizes the conditions that keep so many poor people from improving their lives.

Underdevelopment: A Vicious Cycle

As shown in Figure 1, a network of four interrelated, mutually reinforcing factors severely inhibit improvement in basic needs or economic growth in low-income and some middle-income countries. Breaking out of the cycle is extremely difficult, such that most low-income countries and communities have not been able to achieve a self-sustaining development process.

Dual Economy   A *dual economy* is one in which a small "modern" elite, comprised of people who live a consumer lifestyle, exists in a society where the vast majority of the population lives in poverty. The elite is composed mostly of large landowners, high-level government officials, a few businesspeople engaged in international trade and finance, and professionals such as physicians. A small middle class also exists, made up mostly of school teachers, managers, shopkeepers, and mid-level government workers. It remains virtually invisible when contrasted with the wealthy elite and the rest of the population, sometimes as high as 70 to 80 percent, who experience a very different way of life. Living in rural areas, most people eat what they grow themselves through backbreaking labor

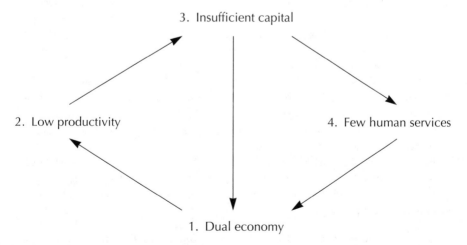

Figure 1   CYCLE OF UNDERDEVELOPMENT

performed without machinery. They lack social programs as a fallback in hard times. Economists refer to this lifestyle as *subsistence*, meaning people produce enough to live on and very little more.

Early economic growth development specialists in the 1950 and 1960s assumed a modern manufacturing sector would expand in low-income countries, albeit slowly, as the industrialization process became self-sustaining. As it had in industrialized countries, this process was expected to bring more jobs and educational opportunities to the poor in the subsistence sector. Yet steady growth has not occurred in most of the developing world. On the whole, countries with low per capita GNPs have experienced a few years of some economic growth but not enough to change the structure of their dual economies.

Low Productivity   A dual economy typically has low *productivity*, which economists define as the output of goods and services in relation to the number of work hours used to produce them. Low productivity results in low income and little savings because not much extra is produced beyond what people consume. This, by definition, is the case with those living a subsistence lifestyle. An economy with a large subsistence sector yields very little surplus and, therefore, does not grow. Hence, low productivity limits not only future growth but also the wages workers can earn, contributing in part to what economists call the *poverty trap*. Industrial development requires substantial economic growth over several years. Figures vary, but the countries increasing their per capita incomes have typically achieved growth rates between 7 and 14 percent during a five- to ten-year period. Such growth allows for the surplus produced as income and savings to be turned back into the economy as investment in capital.

Insufficient Capital   Economies with low per capita GNPs, large subsistence sectors, and low productivity have little capital. Physical capital, often called *infrastructure*, includes such things as factories, farms, roads, railroads, telephones, banks, and machinery, while financial capital includes bank deposits, earnings from international trade, and money. The goods an economy produces for immediate consumption, such as food, cars and clothes, are not capital. In sum, *capital* refers to the finances plus facilities needed to produce wealth. Wealth means goods and more capital.

Dual economy, productivity, and capital are closely related factors. As a result, the problems in low-income economies are interrelated and structural, meaning they are built into their situation. Such a mutually reinforcing combination of deeply rooted problems does not respond to a bit of tinkering here and there. A development project or two, however effective, will not change the basic structure of the economy. A subsistence economy with low productivity and little capital thus experiences great difficulty in generating enough growth to begin self-sustained development. It struggles with the cycle of underdevelopment, as indicated by the arrow closing the cycle in Figure 1.

Few Human Services   Low-income economies have little infrastructure and, by definition, lack the educational and medical care facilities of industrialized economies. Yet, as economists point out, "human capital" is needed for a successful development process. Schools, universities, clinics, and hospitals produce an educated and healthy population, which is needed for economic initiative and improved productivity to occur. Data reporting on people's access to education and medical care show the severe deficiencies in the world's poorer states as compared with richer ones. The figures in Table 3 are from the *1996 Human Development Report,* a compilation of statistics and explanatory narrative that is published each year by the United Nations Development Program (UNDP), an aid agency of the United Nations.

A lack of basic human services inhibits development and reinforces the existence of a dual economy. Thus the arrow that completes the cycle of underdevelopment in Figure 1 connects factor 4, "Few human services," to factor 1, "Dual economy." Without sufficient educational and employment opportunities the middle class remains very small, leaving virtually intact the polarized pattern of two main economic and social classes—namely, the high-income elites and the subsistence agriculturists. A dual economy lacks the large middle class that characterizes the industrialized world. A middle class is important because it provides not only a substantial domestic market but also new leadership and an educated voting public.

The cycle of underdevelopment presented thus far explains the unremitting set of obstacles faced by developing economies. Such problems would slow development even in a society with clearheaded and incorruptible leadership choosing enlightened public policies, a questionable standard even in countries with more productive economies. Advocates of both the economic growth and the basic needs development strategies recognize the problems associated with the vicious cycle of underdevelopment, but they diverge over what should be done about it. Economic

Table 3
POPULATION PER DOCTOR AND PUPILS PER TEACHER RATIOS FOR GROUPS OF STATES

	Population per Doctor (1993)	Pupils per Teacher (1992)	
		Primary	Secondary
High human development	1,661	25	17
Medium human development	3,454	27	19
Low human development	14,053	43	24
All developing countries	5,767	33	22
Least developed countries	18,496	45	26
Industrial countries	344	18	14
World average	4,968	30	20

Source: United Nations, *Human Development Report 1996* (New York: Oxford University Press, 1996).
"Human development" is a classification from a statistical index that compiles data on life expectancy, adult literacy, school enrollment, and per capita gross domestic product (GDP).

growth strategists generally rely on international interventions to begin the development process. Outside aid and investments, for example, are designed to make up for the internal lack of productivity and capital. In contrast, the basic needs approach addresses the problem of a dual economy head-on by attempting to change the subsistence lifestyle. Once people produce more food and other essentials of life, so the basic needs reasoning goes, they can perhaps produce a surplus to invest. Some of the investment may well be in human services, yet some could find its way, via a reliable banking system, into the industrial sector. Either way, the central problem should not be considered in terms of productivity and capital, but as providing a better quality of life for ordinary people.

It should be pointed out that some states classified as having low- or middle-income economies have had occasional growth years, although they have not reached the 7+ percent sustained growth needed for substantial development. Yet people in the developing world expect more. The model of a better lifestyle is tantalizingly flashed on television screens in villages around the world. Seeing US situation comedies or soap operas, the most frequently televised programs worldwide, can raise expectations as to what constitutes an acceptable lifestyle. Many people in the developing world, as well as in the industrial world, seek answers to the question of why a majority of the world's countries face the cycle of underdevelopment.

The Colonial Legacy

As noted in Chapter 1, most developing countries were at one time ruled directly or indirectly by an industrialized state during the age of imperialism. A strong case can be made that global European domination has contributed to the deeply entrenched dual economies of the developing world. In this context, the United States is considered as "European" because its dominant population originated in Europe. The United States dictated policies in Central American countries and Cuba for decades beginning in the late nineteenth century. It also became the colonial ruler in the Philippines and Puerto Rico after the 1898 Spanish-American War.

In many parts of the world, some of the precolonial rulers had initiated economic development. In the Middle East, for example, factories and shops producing textiles flourished during the early 1800s in Egypt, Beirut, and Damascus. Great Britain at that time was the world's leading exporter of fabric and clothing. From Britain's point of view, textile making in the Middle East posed a threat to one of its main foreign policies—that is, establishing new markets for its own manufactured products. When it became the dominant imperial power in Egypt and in other areas claimed by the Ottoman Empire, Britain dismantled the local textile industry.

While it may be unfair to blame colonial rulers for all of the problems facing the developing world today, colonialization did initiate some of the problems while doing little to mitigate others. Subsistence agriculture, for example, was not forced on an unsuspecting and powerless people. It was already the economic mainstay before Europeans arrived. Yet the flip side of a dual economy, the elite, was superimposed by the Europeans after the precolonial rulers were removed from power. Establishing a new elite illustrates the fact that "progress," like other kinds of change, often has both positive and negative consequences. The new European-trained elite did learn the languages, management, and communication skills essential in today's international system. However, today this elite controls government as well as business decisions using the language and governing style of the ex-colonial power, be it French in Senegal or English in India, for example. This results in a separation between the elite and the larger majority of people. The gap is made even larger by differences in lifestyle and education. The elite decision makers often have earned advanced degrees in an industrialized country and live with all the conveniences available to people in high-income countries. This lifestyle gap is not simply one of quantity but of quality as well. It represents differences in culture as well as in the number of modern consumer goods one can enjoy.

Many argue that colonial rule helped to provide a transition from a traditional society to a more modern one and to initiate infrastructure development. Transportation systems such as railroads were built, as were educational facilities, in the capital cities. Mines and port facilities were constructed, and banking plus other capital expenditures were made by the imperial powers in laying the basis for a modern economic sector. When they left, the facilities remained in the control of the local elites, who also benefited from them.

Those emphasizing the negative legacy of imperialism hasten to note that the infrastructure investments served, and continued to serve, the economic interests of Europe and the United States. The transportation systems linked the sources of raw materials inland with seaports. While useful for the movement of commodities from mines in the colony's interior to the "mother" country for processing, such railroads, canals, and roads did little to develop the economy of the colony itself. They did not interconnect income-producing internal regions with each other. Angola in southwest Africa provides a case in point. Three railroads were built by Portugal, the colonial ruler. Each one connected an interior region producing trade products with a port city on the coast. The northern line carried coffee and diamonds, the center line moved cooper ore from the Congo, and the southern line transported iron ore. All three lines traversed east and west, moving roughly parallel to each other. None of the three interconnected.

The colonial ruler intended to provide new markets and sources of raw materials for its own companies, and to accomplish this with the least possible political and military expense. Economic development of the local economy was incompatible with both objectives. Local competitors within the colony would threaten the colonial power's domination of the market, and mass education would risk raising local nationalism and undermine colonial rule. Disputes will continue over the positive and negative legacies of the imperial age, but the fact remains that local development was not the colonizers' primary objective.

Finally, colonizers in the developing world introduced new crops, not for food but for income. Literally called *cash crops*, they included sugar, coffee, cotton, tea, tobacco, bananas, and other commodities wanted in Europe and the United States. Cash crops also include natural resources as well as agricultural products, such as tin and tea. Economists use the phrase *primary commodities* when referring to cash crops because, unlike manufactured goods, they are traded unprocessed or in their natural state.

The imperial conquest consisted of massive land grabs by European settlers seeking to produce cash crops. They used the labor of the conquered peoples whenever possible, or turned to importing indentured servants or slaves. On English, French, and Spanish islands in the Caribbean, for example, most of the indigenous people died within a few decades of the conquest. They were replaced with slaves from West Africa. Unlike the Europeans, previous empires had not always taken over the land of peoples they ruled. China's tributary system and the Arab and Ottoman Empires, for example, extracted taxes or tribute and obedience, but often left the existing economic and social system virtually intact. Contrary to this practice, European conquest changed not only the political leadership, but also the society's religious, economic, and social status practices. The continuing cultural impact of imperialism is discussed in detail in Chapter 2.

Today, many developing countries still earn a large percentage of their international trade income by selling the cash crops introduced during colonial rule. As with other continuing effects of imperialism, exporting primary commodities stimulates opposing arguments over whether it has had positive or negative consequences. Copper, sugar cane, cattle, hemp, and potash, for example, provide developing countries with some income in the postcolonial era. Yet exporting unprocessed products while importing manufactured goods produces a trade deficit. A deficit results because the prices of unprocessed products tend to decrease over time in relation to the prices of manufactured goods. Thus, developing countries find themselves in an unfavorable position in trading with industrial countries.

Outside Interventions

Virtually all the world's national economies engage in ongoing international economic interactions. Since World War II, the volume of economic transactions that cross national borders has increased annually for both developing and industrial nations. Economic interactions with other states, international organizations, and private corporations can assist in the development process. Such relevant outside interventions occur in four categories: trade, foreign aid, private investment, and technical assistance. As Figure 2 indicates, these interventions can provide machinery, financing, and expertise, but each brings problems of its own.

Trade   Trade in primary commodities, a legacy of colonialism, can earn income for a developing state in the years when prices in the international market are high. Trade earnings, called *foreign exchange* by economists, are used to buy machinery as well as to build roads, buildings, factories, and other infrastructure. Because foreign exchange is used to buy products imported from other countries, it exists as accounts in large banks with worldwide operations. These accounts are in US dollars, British pounds, or another currency that businesses in other countries will accept in exchange for their goods. Such a currency is referred to as a *convertible,* or *hard, currency.* Some development theorists believe that good planning can make up for annual fluctuations in cash crop prices. Others point out that the amount of money earned by the sale of primary commodities depends on processing and markets located outside of the developing country. Processing plants

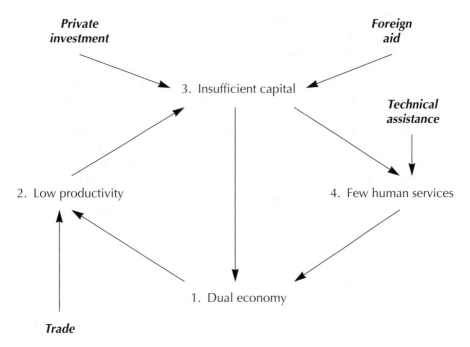

Figure 2   CYCLE OF UNDERDEVELOPMENT: OUTSIDE INTERVENTIONS

and market outlets are controlled by businesses in the industrial world, and it is their interest to keep the costs of raw materials as low as possible. They often play one source of primary commodities against another to keep prices down.

Foreign Aid   The second type of international economic transaction, *foreign aid,* is designed to provide capital directly in the form of loans. Except for a small percentage of aid provided by private international agencies, foreign aid comes from either another country's government or an IGO such as the World Bank. For decades the United States was the leading state aid donor. But according to *World Development Report* data for 1993, Japan provided over $11 billion in official development assistance, while the United States contributed $9.5 billion (World Bank, 1995). As a percentage of donor GNP, the United States has always ranked well behind other industrialized states, and its rating has steadily dropped since 1960. In that year, the United States provided 0.53 percent of its GNP in economic aid. By 1980 the figure was 0.27 percent and by 1993 it had dropped to 0.15 percent—the lowest among the world's eighteen major aid donors. The Scandinavian countries have always led in the percentage of their GNPs designated for foreign aid. Denmark was the highest in 1993, at 1.03 percent of GNP.

Opponents of economic aid often make the mistake of thinking it is a giveaway program. To the contrary, in virtually all cases foreign aid takes the form not of grants but of loans requiring repayment, often at commercial rates of interest. Missing loan payments affects a country's credit worthiness. Low credit ratings mean that subsequent loans (needed to finance international trade, for example) will cost more in interest because of the increased risk.

Foreign aid generally provides financing for specific development projects. Often a project will not produce income for some time, but loan payments come due right away. Also, the economic and political "strings" that accompany foreign aid can be a drawback. Most projects require the purchase of machinery, which generally must be made from companies headquartered in the country providing the aid. Thus, much aid financing never leaves the donor country. Not only does this practice help business in the industrialized country, but it also ensures continued earnings through a trade in spare parts. Foreign aid also produces a web of political strings, intangible but nonetheless real. Economic indebtedness brings with it political indebtedness, allowing aid donors to pressure governments in aid-recipient countries for diplomatic support.

Private Investment   As the third form of outside intervention, private investment has the virtue of avoiding government-to-government political ties and loan repayments. Investments by multinational corporations can bring income directly into a local economy through new employment opportunities. *Multinational corporations (MNCs)* are private businesses with holdings or operations in two or more countries. They are among the largest economic units in the world, as measured by a comparison of their revenues and the GNPs of states. A ranking of countries and MNCs according to the size of their annual product in 1991 showed the Sumitomo Corporation as the twenty-first largest producer of wealth, ahead of such states as Austria, Turkey, South Africa, and Israel. Mitsubishi was listed twenty-second and General Motors at twenty-fifth (World Bank 1994 and Mattera 1992: 704). Of the top seventy-five in 1991, twenty-seven were MNCs. Clearly, many of the world's largest businesses have much greater resources than most members of the United Nations.

The preponderant number of multinational corporations, and all of the biggest, are headquartered in the world's leading industrial countries: the United States, Japan, Germany, France, United Kingdom, Canada, and Italy. An MNC can exercise great policy-making influence on the government of a low-income country, especially when the MNC produces one of the few sources of foreign exchange earnings in a country. Multinational corporations are often promised a favorable business climate, such as low taxes, freedom from environmental restrictions, and suppression of unions. Like trade and foreign aid, private investment by MNCs is part of the dependent relationship the developing world has with the industrial world. Private companies bring in personnel with management and other skills needed for development; however, such people focus on work to be done to enhance the company's profitability and can be withdrawn at any time. They do not assist with projects prioritized to develop the local economy itself. Employing outside experts for this purpose is called *technical assistance.*

Technical Assistance   The fourth form of outside intervention, technical assistance makes up for the lack of local human resources by bringing in experts from other countries. Often these specialists do the planning and sometimes help make decisions as a project is carried out. Villagers, the intended beneficiaries of many projects, usually participate only as physical laborers. As a result, the villagers who are expected to carry on after the experts leave do not have a vested interest in the project and often are untrained in its upkeep. These "beneficiaries" may not even perceive the project as serving their needs because of their lack of participation in the planning. They did have to do the hard physical work to build the project, which meant less time in their fields. Such disregard for the human dimension of development has accounted for the failure of a large percentage of rural projects in past decades.

Other Factors

The factors contributing to the cycle of underdevelopment create structural problems that make development difficult. Outside interventions can either help or hinder the process. They can inadvertently reinforce the problems while purporting to provide solutions. Trade, aid, private investment, and technical assistance act positively on an economy when local elites have achieved stable economic and political decision-making processes. Such stability results from a social consensus. When people agree on the basics—for example, that they live in the same society and share a common future—they can develop ways of disagreeing without reaching an impasse. In extreme cases, an inability to work out problems can tear a country apart, as happened in Lebanon during the civil war of 1976–1989. Lebanon had achieved substantial economic growth and a relatively high standard of living and had become the banking center of the Middle East before internal violence destroyed its economy. Thus, in addition to economic factors, any analysis of developing world problems must account for the underlying social factors that may explain why some countries achieve ongoing growth and improved standards of living while others do not.

Overcoming economic deficiencies becomes much more difficult in a society pulled apart by people who do not share a common identity, value system, and commitment to an established political unit. Most states have multiple cultural groups within their borders. In some countries the groups share social and political commonalties, while in others they do not. Social cohesion enables people to continue on under one political authority in spite of severe economic downturns, resource depletion, and social tensions. When many groups are invested in one cohesive society, the country is more likely to survive the severe social and political dislocations of economic development.

Two other factors have proven important in providing a positive context for development: sufficient natural resources, either within a country's own borders or accessible through trade, and stable population growth (that is, growth that does not outrun an economy's ability both to sustain its population and produce capital investment). One caveat should be noted before moving into a discussion of each factor. All three do not apply in the same way to every country in the industrial world. Japan, the example most often cited, was relatively resource poor when it began industrialization, and this continues to affect the country's policies. Japan needs to sell industrial goods in order to make up for deficiencies in fuel by import-ing oil. The cohesiveness of Japanese society has helped the country compensate for being located on mountainous volcanic islands with little arable land and few natural resources.

Lack of Social Cohesion   The borders of developing countries often encompass various ethnic groups with no previous history of cooperation and, therefore, with no sense of common purpose prior to their colonial rule. When Europeans drew the borders of the present-day developing countries, they often forcibly brought together groups of people who had fought for generations. Even among groups who had interacted peacefully, tensions arose when they were merged into one state. Where they had been relative equals, now one was favored by the European ruler as its local elite. As a result, the country's identity, borders, and political institutions became sources of unresolved conflict when independence was achieved. The power of colonial rule had masked underlying tensions among ethnic groups, which surfaced with independence.

The postcolonial history of Nigeria provides an extreme example of intereth-nic problems subsequent to colonial rule. Like many other states in sub-Saharan Africa, Nigeria's borders date from the Congress of Berlin in 1884–1885, when European states met to settle disputes over the partitioning of Africa. No representa-tives of Africa's indigenous peoples attended the Berlin Conference, not even to pro-vide information. Great Britain and France were the contenders for areas that now are part of Nigeria. France had moved down the Niger River while the British had moved up. A boundary was drawn as a compromise between them. The British con-solidated their holdings around the delta of the Niger River and inland, calling the area Nigeria. It included many peoples speaking over two hundred languages, and three major cultural groupings with substantially different lifestyles and a history of conflict: the Hausa-Fulani in the north, the Yoruba in the west, and the Ibos in the east. The Ibos proved themselves the most adaptable to British practices and became civil servants and teachers, the core of a British-educated elite.

Nigeria became independent in 1960. By 1965, interethnic tensions had increased and were marked by a series of incidents resulting in Ibo deaths. Other factors contributed to the conflict, such as the fact that Iboland was rich in oil and Nigeria had virtually no economic integration among its internal regions. Conse-quently, many Ibos attempted secession. They declared their eastern region as the new state of Biafra. A brutal war ensued in 1966–1969, ending with Biafra's defeat. It is not possible to say with certainty that British colonial rule resulted in Nigeria's bloody war so soon after independence. Yet major factors contributing to the war derive from or were exacerbated by colonial policies.

When negative judgments about ethnic strife in the developing world are made by people in the industrial world, they ignore the fact that it took centuries of warfare for today's major European countries to arrive at a mutual consensus as to their borders. The United States has also fought wars—with Canada because it was part of the British Empire, with Mexico, with various indigenous peoples, and with itself in a bloody civil war—before its borders became unquestioned. It should not be surprising, then, that some developing countries have erupted in ethnic conflict to redraw international borders or to change which group rules within the existing borders.

Some commentators link the rampant corruption and government mismanagement in some developing states to their lack of social cohesion. Civic mindedness evolves from a sense of loyalty to the larger society. In its absence, rule becomes personalized, favorable to one ethnic group or the family and friends of the ruler. Vast amounts of capital have been diverted to personal use rather than invested in development projects. Mobutu, the former president of Zaire, renamed the Democratic Republic of the Congo, offers a glaring example of how a corrupt leader can drain and impoverish a state. Billions of dollars flowed out of Zaire and into personal accounts in international banks during the more than thirty years Mobutu was in power. Such "capital flight" and corrupt government policy making have proven formidable obstacles to development in several other developing countries.

Insufficient Natural Resources   This second factor contributing to development problems does not receive the attention it deserves. Most low-income countries lack the natural resources and moderate climates that industrialized countries possessed when they began a development process. Geographic location has much to do with the problems faced by today's developing nations. Almost all developing countries are located within the 37-degree latitudes north and south of the equator. Those outside of this region, such as Turkey, Argentina, Chile, and South Africa, are middle income or better. The heat in the planet's equatorial zone produces tropical, desert, or monsoon climates. Each of these climates presents problems for development. Deserts lack water, and tropical areas have thin topsoil that erodes quickly. In a monsoon region, rain comes down in destructive torrents during a short wet season, which alternates with many dry months. Such a rain pattern erodes and leaches nutrients from the soil. It contrasts sharply with the steady, easily absorbed precipitation of temperate zones. The bulk of Africa, for example, is located on both sides of the equator. Potential farmland makes up only one-fifth of the continent: 20 percent is desert and 57 percent is reddish, rain-washed, acidic soil. High in iron and aluminum, this soil does not produce thriving, cultivated plants (Harrison 1984:70).

Explosive Population Growth   Economists agree that optimum economic growth occurs when a population grows slowly and steadily. New markets are thus created at a pace that stimulates new production. Such a balance between economic expansion and population growth is not characteristic of the developing world. Overpopulation is a problem in low-income countries, where high population growth rates exist alongside low economic growth rates (see Table 4).

States with higher-income economies tend to have lower population growth rates. They also report relatively lower economic growth rates but, since their economies are already industrial, they do not need to sustain high growth. In the long run, major population growth and stagnant economies pose insurmountable problems for the agricultural and industrial sectors of a developing economy. One

Table 4
POPULATION AND ECONOMIC GROWTH RATES
FOR SELECTED COUNTRIES

	Population Growth Rate (1990)	Economic Growth Rate (1989)
Low-Income Economies:		
Tanzania	3.66%	1.8%
Nicaragua	3.36	–2.0
Bangladesh	2.67	3.5
Lower-Middle-Income Economies:		
Senegal	2.78%	2.2%
Bolivia	2.76	–0.4
Jamaica	1.21	.05
Philippines	2.49	1.8
Upper-Middle-Income Economies:		
South Africa	2.22%	2.2%
Uruguay	0.56	–0.2
Greece	0.23	1.2
High-Income Economies:		
New Zealand	0.87%	1.9%
United States	0.81	2.6
Japan	0.43	4.1

Source: Allen, *Student Atlas of World Politics* (Guilford, CT: Duskin Publishing Group, 1994).

result is a strain on the social fabric of several countries. A solution could be capital investment in new machinery to increase the productivity of existing land, but this is prohibitively expensive in most villages.

The problem of exploding population growth did not face the already industrialized world. During their first decades of development, the populations of Europe, the United States, and Japan grew roughly parallel to increases in productivity resulting from the new machinery. Then, after achieving advanced stages of industrialization, a demographic transition occurred. This transition, illustrated in Figure 3, included certain changes in population growth in every industrialized country. Whereas before industrialization population growth was checked by a high death rate, now it is held steady by a low birthrate.

Before industrialization, populations generally had high birth rates and death rates. Thus explosive population growth did not occur. This changed during industrial development's early stages because more food, better sanitation, and wider availability of medical care substantially lowered the death rate. Since birthrates stayed high, the population increased. As industrialization advanced, it produced a higher standard of living based on employment in the manufacturing and service sectors. Having many children became an economic burden rather than a necessity. In a subsistence

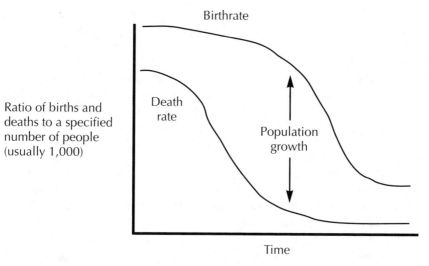

Figure 3   THE DEMOGRAPHIC TRANSITION

agricultural lifestyle, children are the work force needed to herd animals, carry wood, and take care of younger children. Industrial economies provide reasons for having fewer children as well as the technologies to achieve this result.

Unlike the population growth trends in the industrialized countries, developing countries find themselves stuck in the middle of the demographic transition with low death rates and high birthrates. In contrast to the past experience of today's high-income countries, economic growth in developing countries is not enough to absorb their growing populations. Colonial rule, and subsequent international aid programs, have brought lower death rates through increased sanitation and the eradication of some diseases. Ironically, the humanitarian work of missionaries and aid agencies has produced a long-term problem for the very people they have attempted to help. Using new medical practices, disease was attacked as the most visible cause of human suffering and the one most susceptible to an immediate solution. However, as discussed above, long-term development was not the objective, and even if it had been it would have taken longer to develop than it took to decrease the death rate. To put the problem in economic perspective, eradicating smallpox was relatively cheaper than building infrastructure. The present population explosion in low-income countries shows that unintended, secondary consequences can have major effects.

The problems facing developing countries can be summarized by contrasting their experience with that of an industrialized country. The United States, for example, began as a colony and after a successful war for independence became one of the world's leading economic powers in about a hundred years. Applying the factors explained in this chapter to analyze the US situation shows that most of the problems faced by developing countries today did not exist for the United States. Such an analysis points out why a similar development process has not worked for many developing states.

First, the territories that became the United States proved to be among the richest in the world, with arable land to feed a growing population and raw materials for an industrial economy. Second, the population and the economy grew roughly parallel to one another. Third, large-scale immigration and the existence of indigenous peoples did not, in the long run, threaten social cohesion. The peoples originally inhabiting lands ceded to the United States by Great Britain, Spain, France, and Mexico, proved weak opponents and only small numbers remained after their populations were decimated by new diseases, such as smallpox, for which they had no immunity. Generations of new settlers from Europe wanted to become US citizens and each contributed to the new country's economic growth. This process fostered stability. The one group brought by force, African Americans, was not able to make demands in the country's early decades since most of its members were slaves. This group was not allowed to assert political influence until the 1960s, when the United States was already industrialized and had a legitimized political system able to handle the stress.

Economic factors also favored US development. A dual economy never took root. Given the vast amounts of rich arable land, the frontier farmers who began with a subsistence lifestyle produced within a few years surpluses for sale in markets back east or in other countries. Such productivity allowed local communities to afford human services, schooling for their children, and health care. Investment capital, raised both domestically and from Britain in the early 1800s, built railroads and mines. The United States in its first decades had many advantages not characteristic of the typical developing country in the late twentieth century.

In spite of such a favorable situation, the country's population suffered a long civil war with a devastating loss of life. With over 500,000 casualties, the US Civil War was as grim as the internal conflicts experienced by developing countries in the late twentieth century. The extended struggle had its ethnic cause as well as deeply felt differences brought on by the process of economic development.

At the end of the twentieth century, the United States had the largest economy in the world, with a $6.4 trillion GNP in 1993 (World Bank 1995). In comparison, Japan's and Germany's second and third GNP rankings were reported at almost $4 trillion and $2 trillion, respectively, and the figure for all developing countries combined was $3 trillion. Despite such wealth, the United States still has pockets of developing economies in its rural areas and inner cities. The onrushing, ever-more complex industrial technologies have not swept every area of the United States onto the bridge to the twenty-first century, to say nothing of the majority of the world's population who remain poor.

THE INDUSTRIAL WORLD

The developing world and its problems are part of the international economic system. As the dominant states in the system, industrialized countries have had a different experience from that of developing countries as their high-income economies continue to become more interdependent by leaps and bounds. The international economic system, introduced in Chapter 1, has worked to produce startling growth. The

Industrial Revolution has greatly expanded world trade, producing surplus goods and an insatiable demand for raw materials. Refinements in machinery mean higher productivity and more goods, requiring larger markets. Thus the cycle continues. According to data provided by an international relations specialist, in 1913 world trade amounted to about $20 billion, but by the early 1990s about $3.7 trillion in goods were exchanged. The post–World War II era has brought a trade boom: Between 1948 and 1968, world trade increased from $53 billion to $350 billion, or 660 percent, and the pace in more recent years has not slackened (Rourke 1993:442).

A second category of international transactions, financial ties, have also greatly accelerated since World War II. Private bank lending in other countries totaled $4.78 trillion in 1990, with Japan as the largest lender at $666 billion and the United States the second largest at $527 billion. Another form of financial interaction is direct investment, or the purchase of capital in other countries. US international investments in 1950 amounted to $11.8 billion, which had mushroomed to $598 billion by 1990. The United States has also been the recipient of substantial investment capital, with direct foreign investment totaling $466 billion in 1990, (Rourke 1993:442). Unlike many developing states, increased trade and financial flows have contributed to the world's leading economies. They have achieved continuing economic growth over the long term and an ever-rising living standard.

A country's trade data and monetary transactions are totaled every year in its *balance of payments*. This summary of a state's international economic interactions with all other states shows credits minus debits in all categories of transactions: exports and imports, tourist travel and purchases, business investment and profits, loans and debt payments. If a country has to borrow heavily to bring its account into balance for several years in a row, doubts arise as to the future health of the economy. As with government budget deficits, investors tend to shy away from a country with chronic balance-of-payments problems.

Trade Issues

Trade generates about 15 percent of the world's total production of goods and services. For the United States and Japan, trade amounts to about 20 percent of GDP, whereas, for members of the European Union it averages about 50 percent (Balaam and Veseth 1996:113). Yet a basic, centuries-old policy argument within states goes on over whether and how to protect their own businesses from international competition. In their earlier stages of development, the leading industrialized states used *protectionism* to keep foreign companies from competing with their own "infant industries." Many of these policies are still in practice. They result in tariffs and other barriers to trade, including quotas and regulations on incoming products. Governments adopt a wide variety of regulations, such as subjecting imports to specific health and safety requirements, and limitations on where goods can enter a country.

In addition to restrictions aimed at keeping foreign goods out or increasing their price, a government may also use subsidies to make its country's products internationally competitive. The United States and some European countries, for example, buy selected agricultural products from their own farmers at a high enough price for the growers to make a profit. Then they sell these products in other countries at the lower prices dictated by international competition. Taxpayers take the loss. Subsidies can occur in other ways as well, such as in what is called parity payments in the United States. The US government pays farmers to keep land out of production and thus reduce the amount of corn, or wheat, or whatever the product. This can increase its price if sources for the commodity in other countries do not increase their production. Subsidies also exist for manufactured goods. One subsidy takes the form of government credits for overseas sale, which reduce the amount of interest that businesses pay for loans needed to finance trade. This, in turn, reduces the costs US companies must pass along to their customers in other countries, and they can charge lower prices than their competitors. The US Export-Import Bank handles such government-backed loans for US businesses.

Advocates of free trade disagree with protectionist policies. They say that mechanisms designed to enable a state to sell more than it buys cannot work in the long run because some countries inevitably have to be on the short end of the trade equation. In other words, everyone cannot sell more than they buy. Government policies that protect a country's businesses and markets have the effect of reducing the amount of goods flowing worldwide and thus limiting global economic expansion. Markets become constricted and economies of scale cannot be attained, so prices rise. On the other hand, if states adopt free trade policies, competition lowers prices for all consumers.

Free trade proponents argue that today's economies are so interlinked that for many industries it is outmoded to think of goods as from a single country. A decision made in one US town illustrates the point. Its local government decided to "Buy American" and chose a John Deere earth mover priced about $15,000 higher than one sold by Komatsu, a Japanese company. Unfortunately for the town's nationalistic objective, the John Deere machine was made in Japan, except for the motor, while the Komatsu was made in Illinois (Brown and Hogedorn 1994:162). A Boeing airplane provides another example of economic interdependence. Many of its important parts—rudders, landing gear, and computers—are made in Italy, Australia, Brazil, Japan, Korea, Canada, France, Ireland, Singapore, and the United Kingdom. Economists point out that because economic internationalization already exists, it should be allowed to become more efficient through free trade.

The debate over trade policy directly relates to people's daily lives because trade affects employment and living standards. A reduction in either exports or imports results in job losses. Fewer imports means some products become unavailable or more expensive and the standard of living drops. Also, ordinary people own shares in corporations in other countries through stock markets and mutual funds. In both the industrial and developing worlds, rural people produce cash crops, whether as laborers or landowners. Thus, their income fluctuates directly with the vagaries of international trade.

Monetary Issues

In addition to the exchange of goods through trade, states and their citizens interact in the world economy through the exchange of money for investments, aid, and personal transactions such as tourism and charity donations. The majority of these international financial flows are channeled through the world's largest private banks. They have subsidiaries in many countries and the size to handle billions of dollars worth of transactions every day. Each transaction requires the exchange of money, called *currency* by economists. Thus, the process of determining how much each state's currency is worth in relation to that of another state becomes very important, though it is often little understood by the general public.

News reports observe that the US dollar has become weaker or stronger. "Common sense" gives the impression that having a stronger currency is better, but such an assumption only sometimes proves true. Take, for example, a decline in the US dollar when compared to the German mark. This can be bad news for an American who intends to buy a German automobile actually made in Germany. But it would be irrelevant if the same person is going to buy a German automobile made in the United States. Or it could be good news if the American is working for a computer company that sells its products to Germany.

The worth of a country's currency in relation to that of another country is called the *foreign exchange rate*. This term is used when a person wants to know, for example, how many US dollars it takes at any point in time to buy how many British pounds, Japanese yen, Russian rubles, Ecuadorian sucres, Thai baht, Tanzanian shillings, Peruvian intis, Israeli shekels, or any other state's currency. To make the situation more confusing, exchange rates fluctuate, sometimes significantly, in relatively short periods of time. For example, Americans planning a trip to the United Kingdom months in advance may decide how many US dollars they will take based on the current exchange rate between the dollar and the British pound. Yet their trip could cost more if, upon arriving in London, they received fewer pounds for their dollars than they planned on because the exchange rate changed.

Applying the economic principle of supply and demand can help explain why the worth of a currency fluctuates. If Canada, for example, has a healthy economy, a growing demand for the Canadian dollar may well result. Banks and other multinational corporations would want to invest in a strengthening and stable economy. Since in the immediate term, the supply of Canadian dollars would stay about the same, their value will rise because demand for this currency has increased. It is not a coincidence that the four most internationally used currencies derive from four of the world's largest economies and more stable societies; namely, the US dollar, Japanese yen, German mark, and British pound.

A government's policies on interest rates and budget deficits can also have an effect on the worth of its currency. If a state's central bank raises interest rates, its currency often becomes more attractive because people in other countries will want to invest in an economy with higher rates. Thus, the currency becomes stronger when demand for it increases. Large, multiple-year government budget deficits, however, often have a downward influence on the worth of a currency. They cause investors in other parts of the world to question whether putting money into the economy of a government that cannot manage its own budget well is a sound, low-risk investment. High budget deficits mean large-scale borrowing. Demand for the currency sags, as does its worth. The United States, however, seems like an exception to this generalization because it continues to attract the foreign purchase of dollars for investment purposes. The reason is that the United States has been able to sustain huge budget deficits, larger than the whole economies of a majority of the world's countries. The gigantic size of the overall US economy, and thus the taxes paid to the government, has enabled it to afford paying the interest on the US national debt. Debt payments amounted to 15 percent of the 1995 US budget, or a little over $232 billion (Historical Tables, Budget of the United States Government, Fiscal Year 1997:103, 111). Actually, given the growth of the US economy over the years, the percentage of its budget deficit in relation to its annual GNP has actually decreased since 1992 and during most of the 1980s.

Economic internationalization has created a situation where an individual country, even one as wealthy as the United States, needs the help of other governments to establish effective economic policies. Take, for example, US efforts to steady the value of the dollar in relation to other currencies. A rising dollar means US imports are cheaper but exports drop because their prices rise. This occurs because it takes more of other currencies to buy fewer dollars, and the products valued in dollars. A falling dollar has the opposite effect. US exports increase but, since the dollar is worth less, imports cost more because it takes more dollars to pay for them. In the long run, economic transactions are aided by stable pricing and, therefore, stable currencies.

To steady the dollar, the US Treasury can buy and sell dollars. Buying dollars boosts their value by making them scarcer, whereas selling them puts more in circulation and thus decreases their value. The problem lies in the fact that the Treasury Department only has about $20 billion compared with the $750 billion to $1 trillion traded daily on the world's currency exchanges. This means the private currency exchanges have much more influence on the value of the dollar than any feeble response the US Treasury can afford. There is more hope of stabilizing the price of the US dollar if the world's leading countries together buy and sell dollars at the same time. Yet US citizens expect their government to manage the economy well and often do not realize this requires international cooperation.

Unfortunately for government policy makers in industrial states, their citizens often do not realize the extent to which their prosperity is connected to the international economy. Another complicating factor in establishing effective economic policy is the fact that a state's citizens exert opposite pressures depending, for instance, on whether they are employed by an importer or an exporter. They pressure government to act in their own interests. This can mean wanting the government to protect jobs by limiting imports of, say, automobiles. If quotas are set on car imports, or high tariffs levied to increase the prices of cars from other countries, such actions would invite retaliation from the countries affected. They could limit their imports from the protectionist state, thereby triggering a downward spiral of decreasing trade. In such a situation, everyone would suffer since trade wars produce economic declines in every country involved. Herein lies the paradox: Economies are internationally interdependent, yet their business and government leaders respond to demands from within their own country. Businesses must answer to stockholders, and democratic government officials must please voters.

A more sensible reaction would appreciate the delicate and difficult task of influencing trade and currency values. Many of the relevant factors remain outside of any single government's decision-making domain. Interdependence means mutuality. Whatever their position on their government's trade and monetary policies, citizens in states with high-income economies have difficulty realizing that the economic problems faced by their countries are not on the same scale as those impacting the developing world. Industrial states can do more to help themselves than can developing states. The consequences of economic downturns, enhanced by a global economy, have so much more destructive effects in developing countries that it sometimes seems as though they exist on a different planet.

Relations Between Industrialized and Developing Countries

As pointed out previously, increasing international trade and financial flows since the Second World War have fostered sustained economic growth over the long term in the world's high-income states. Some with middle incomes have prospered as well, but low-income economies generally have not made significant gains. The growing world economy has not produced balanced, healthy economic growth in the poorer states. Instead, the cycle of underdevelopment more aptly describes their plight. In the context of weak economies, the negative effects of international trade and foreign investments have been devastating. Issues of trade and currency values preoccupy the economic policies of states with low-income economies even more than those with high incomes because the downturns are far more debilitating. Government decision makers in weak economies have less ability to counter the negative effects. To be poor means having few choices for both individuals and governments.

One of the reasons low-income states suffer enhanced trade problems is that they produce mainly primary commodities. The prices paid for these raw material exports tend to increase more slowly over time compared with the prices of industrial goods. The problem is greater in the many low-income economies that produce only a few commodities for export. They are more vulnerable because an annual fall in the price of one commodity can cause a depression for that year. These states do not have the cushioning effect of income from a variety of other products.

In addition to trade difficulties, developing countries suffer severe monetary problems. Since their currencies are not in demand outside of their own borders, their governments and citizens wanting to make international transactions must buy another country's currency, one accepted on a worldwide basis. The value of these convertible currencies—the US dollar, British pound, Japanese yen, and German mark—generally increases in comparison to the developing state's currency. One of the reasons is that the poorer countries have chronic budget, trade, and balance-of-payments deficits. They borrow heavily from other governments, all in the industrial world, or from international aid organizations, whose policies are set by industrialized countries, or from multinational private banks, all of which are owned by people in the industrialized world. Borrowing by developing states incurs liabilities that even further undermine the worth of their currencies. Thus, they need to exchange more of their own money for the world's international convertible currencies to pay for imports and to repay loans. This puts additional inflationary pressure on the local currency, and the cycle continues its downward spiral.

Because they have little impact beyond their own borders, the problems of most developing economies do not inspire much concern in the industrial world, except for a few creditor banks. However, economic decisions made in the industrial world have direct effects in the developing world. This decision-making inequality, sometimes called *dependency*, may be illustrated by an example. The worth of the US dollar is not just an issue in the United States. More often than not, when businesses and governments want to buy and sell goods they use US dollars for the transaction since there are more of them available and acceptable around the world than any other currency. So stabilizing the value of the dollar is important to virtually all the world's countries, and vital to the indebted ones whose payments are calculated and paid in dollars. What the US does to strengthen or weaken its own currency can help or cost a country dearly. In the early 1980s, for example, the US government decided that fighting inflation deserved the highest priority. To strengthen the dollar, interest rates were set at their highest level since World War II. As the worth of the dollar rose, it added literally billions to the loan payments of the developing states. In contrast, the worth of the Ecuadorian sucre or Jordanian dinar, for example, has no measurable effect on the United States.

Citizens of industrial states are beneficiaries of their countries' favorable economic position. They should realize that their governments have worldwide economic responsibilities. Only the governments of the leading industrial states can set policies beneficial to the global economy in the long run. Interdependence means that income increases in the poorer regions will benefit the whole international economy. The United States, for example, sold over 40 percent of its 1993 exports in the developing world. If steady growth were achieved in more economies, markets and investments would expand for industrial world businesses.

Thus far, this chapter has introduced general concepts and analysis explaining international economic interdependence and development issues. In the process, it has pointed out the relationships between the industrial and the developing worlds. Now the discussion moves on to consider a case study of a specific, successful development project. It illustrates the applicability of many of the concepts introduced throughout this chapter. In so doing, the case study accomplishes two tasks. First, it makes real heretofore abstract concepts about the pressing global issue of economic development. Second, it demonstrates the fact that projects designed to improve the daily lives of the poor can succeed.

New Rules:
The American Economy in the Next Century

Lester C. Thurow

The global economic environment in which the United States participates is undergoing tremendous and rapid change, but not for the first time. At the end of the nineteenth century, the invention of electricity sparked what some have called the second industrial revolution. Inventions such as underground transportation and streetcars made large cities possible for the first time. New industries developed, including electrical power and telecommunications, and old industries were transformed. The elevator reversed traditional rent differentials and made the top floors of buildings more valuable than the bottom floors for the first time in history. Light bulbs replaced oil and gas lamps, allowing economic and leisure activities to take place around the clock. As electric motors replaced steam engines, distributed power meant that the old linear factory could be abandoned and replaced with very different configurations of production.

Similarly, future historians studying the end of the twentieth century will refer to the major changes we are witnessing as the third industrial revolution. These changes are often called the "information revolution," but it is more accurate to say that we are entering an era of man-made, brain-power industries, for this revolution has replaced natural resources with human skills as mankind's most productive asset. The symbol of this new era is at hand: today, for the first time in history, the world's wealthiest man, Bill Gates, is a knowledge worker and not a petroleum magnate, as had been the case for the past hundred years. The political and technical changes that define this third industrial revolution have important implications for the US economy and for US economic policy.

Reprinted from *Harvard International Review* 20, no. 1 (winter 1998).

THE ECONOMIC WORLD TO COME

The extent of this third industrial revolution far surpasses new information technologies. With the development of biotechnology, an era of partially man-made plants, animals, and even humans is dawning. New, custom-designed materials and intelligent, computer-controlled machines are rendering traditional production processes obsolete. Microelectronics and the computer are revolutionizing every sector of the economy—and not just the communication and information aspects of these industries. The oil industry, for example, harnessing acoustical sounding, deep-water production techniques, and horizontal drilling, has rapidly transformed itself into a knowledge-based industry. Some of the important new sectors that will develop from this revolution—computers, semiconductors, and electronic entertainment—are already visible. Others, such as electronic retailing, are in their infancy, and others have yet to be born.

A hundred years ago, local economies and local business gradually diminished in importance and were replaced by national economies and large national corporations. So today, national economies and national companies are gradually being replaced by a global economy characterized by multinational corporations. We are witnessing not only the expansion of world trade, but the emergence of an unprecedented global economy in which world trade will be a critical part of almost all business enterprise.

This transnational economy is already taking shape. Most national central banks are now irrelevant, as the world's money is essentially controlled by three key institutions: the US Federal Reserve Board, the Bank of Japan, and the German Bundesbank. Global capital markets, centered in London, Tokyo, and New York, are facilitating increased internationalization in every area of finance. Home mortgages from a local US bank, for example, are bundled with other home mortgages, securitized, and sold on global capital markets—perhaps to some foreign investment group. In this new, globalized financial world, even a local bank could thus find itself servicing international loans.

This globalization blurs national economic boundaries. Consider the accelerometer, a US$50 semiconductor chip that replaces about US$650 worth of mechanical sensors that control the air bags in cars. Today, accelerometers are assembled in the United States by skilled labor, shipped to the Philippines for testing, re-exported for packaging by mid-skill workers in Taiwan, and then sent to Germany where they are installed in BMW's, some of which are shipped to Singapore for final sale. By definition, an economy is the area over which captalists arbitrage prices and wages, looking to buy at the lowest possible costs and sell at the highest possible prices. The case of the accelerometer illustrates how businesses now conduct arbitrage in one huge global marketplace. BMW manufactures each component of its vehicles wherever it can be most cheaply produced, regardless of national boundaries.

THE EROSION OF NATIONALITY

Much of the sales and production of most of America's big corporations is now occurring overseas. Coca-Cola makes 80 percent of its sales outside of the United States. The meaning of "American corporation" changes when only one-fifth of the corporation's sales occur in the domestic market. Just as large national corporations once replaced small family businesses in the second industrial revolution, even larger multinational corporations are now replacing national corporations. These companies play a global game and, in many respects, regard countries in the same ways that large US corporations regard individual US states.

As corporations become increasingly mobile, countries will be forced to compete in order to encourage companies to establish headquarters and plants within their borders. Intel, for example, is receiving a huge subsidy from Israel in exchange for building a large semiconductor facility there. Such plants are essentially put up for bid; whichever country gives the company the best deal in terms of wages, skills, transportation costs, markets, taxes, and direct subsidies is rewarded by a corporate presence and the associated benefits. Though foreign companies do not yet negotiate directly with the US federal government to get anything beyond the normal level playing field, they have become very good at playing US states off against one another. Mercedes and BMW, for example, were able to negotiate large subsidies—hundreds of thousands of dollars in tax reductions and expenditures directed at their needs—with the states of Alabama and South Carolina.

Countries that once seemed uncompetitive have succeeded by offering special services to the global economy. The Cayman Islands, whose lax banking regulations have attracted customers weary of regulation in their home countries, have become the world's fifth largest banking center. Dummy corporations established in the Cayman Islands, for example, have allowed Taiwanese investors to pour money into mainland China despite official bans on such investment. And yet none of these businessmen ever goes to the Caymans—all the necessary transactions take place electronically.

Technology and globalization are rapidly changing the way businesses operate, limiting the ability of governments to restrict—or even control—economic activity.

ECONOMIC INTERDEPENDENCE

Put simply, globalization and multinationalization have reduced the powers of governments to regulate behavior and to set independent economic policies. Companies are no longer wedded to any one economy: they simply move their operations to locations where banking regulations, anti-trust policies, and the rules governing intellectual property rights are most favorable to their interests. Citibank, for example, does its investment banking in London to avoid US laws prohibiting banks from serving as both commercial and investment banks. European airlines buy large blocks of shares in US domestic airlines that would be illegal if the buyer were a US airline. Drug manufacturers move to India because it does not recognize patents on new drugs.

Americans have noticed this loss of governmental power less than others because it has been less real in the United States. As the United States has historically been the world's largest unified economy and most important power broker, the US government has retained more of its economic independence. The dollar is the world's unrivaled reserve currency. The United States holds the largest voting rights on the boards of global institutions such as the World Bank and the International Monetary Fund (IMF). US military protection was a valued commodity during the Cold War, and many countries were careful about crossing the United States economically to ensure the health of their alliance with Washington. But all of this is about to change: the United States will remain a large player in the world economic game, but it will soon be subject to the same limitations facing everyone else.

The Cold War is over, and other nations no longer have to defer to American economic views to ensure US support for the sake of their national security. Japan, no longer dependent on American protection against the Soviet Union, now finds it easier to withstand US pressure on economic issues. US influence is also declining at both the World Bank and the IMF. The United States is providing a smaller fraction of funding to both institutions, and eventually, its formal voting powers will be reduced to reflect this decreased involvement. The United States is no longer the world's biggest economy—it is the second, behind the European Common Market.

EURO-BLUES

The most noticeable change in the US position will come with the introduction of the Euro in 1999. For the first time since the Second World War, investors and financiers will have a viable alternative to the US dollar, and the venerable greenback will become just another currency. A few years ago, the dollar was falling dramatically against the yen (down from 112 to 78 yen to the dollar) and other currencies, but there was no run on the dollar, even as holders of dollar reserves were losing a third of their real purchasing power. Why not? The answer, of course, is that there was no place to go. Individual European currencies were too small to allow inflows of hundreds of billions of dollars, and the Japanese market was still too regulated and too closed for the yen to be a good alternative. As a result, holders of thousands of billions of dollars in international reserves were forced to sustain enormous losses in the real value of their reserves. With no better alternative, few investors redenominated their selling prices or disposed of their dollar reserves despite the dollar's problems. Had the Euro been in place when the dollar was plunging, more investors would have abandoned the dollar, perhaps precipitating a frenzied sell-off.

With the advent of the Euro, the rest of the world is apt to become much less interested in holding US dollars, making it more difficult for the United States to borrow the funds necessary to sustain a permanently large trade deficit. The risks of a deficit are simply much greater with the Euro in place. The events that put an end to the current pattern of large US trade deficits will not flow from actions taken in the countries that directly run large trade surpluses with the United States. For them, decreased lending would harm the US sales of their corporations. The shift is also not likely to begin with official government reserves because no one would deliberately shake the world trading system. It will most likely start when private companies and banks decide that they hold too many dollars. The advent of the Euro will represent the elimination of 14 European currencies. This, in turn, will reduce the need for foreign exchanges reserves, mostly held in dollars, for most banks and companies. Middle Eastern oil sellers will likely want to start denominating some of their oil sales and holding some of their reserves in Euros. Others will follow suit. Financial economists will make a lot of money running sophisticated mathematical models to determine the exact amounts that should be moved from dollars to Euros and how much redenominating of sales from dollars to Euros should occur, and traders eager for commissions will urge their customers to make the suggested revisions in their portfolios. The momentum of global currency markets away from the dollar will be considerable.

The bottom line is simple: the United States is unlikely to be able to run a large trade deficit for very long after the Euro comes into existence—the funds necessary to sustain this deficit will not be forthcoming. To the extent that US imports are redenominated in Euros, the United States will also become a normal economy in that import prices will rise when the dollar goes down—something that does not happen when import prices are denominated in dollars. In the future, a falling dollar will translate into rising inflation in the United States. The French have been forthright in stating that one of their key reasons for supporting the Euro is that it will force the United States to face the same constraints that limit France and most other countries.

ECONOMIC CHESS

In a global economy, competition resembles a three-dimensional chess game. First, the game is played at a national level. Americans pay taxes to the US government, and, in return, they receive a set of publicly provided benefits. A tax system out of line with the rest of the world may handicap US citizens, but government educational investments provide them with many of the skills they will later sell as individuals. The US government provides (or does not provide) the world-class infrastructure—telecommunications, transportation, and the like—that American companies need to be competitive, low-cost sellers. The government also finances the basic research that allows its citizens to build the new industries of the future, such as biotechnology, and to enjoy the economic benefits of being ahead of the rest of the world. Governments do not directly compete, but they build the platforms on which economic competition takes place. To the extent that the US government invests in education, infrastructure, and research, it is helping American companies and individual Americans compete.

Second, the game is played at the corporate level. If an Intel or a Microsoft can dominate the microchip or software markets and earn far above the average rates of return, those who work for such companies or own such companies share in the benefits. Corporations on the leading edge of technology are able to earn higher profits and pay higher wages. Any corporation's technical edge depends partly on its own skills, investments, and creativity, and partly on government investment. The success of the American biotechnology industry is a good example of the need for both. Government research investment created the knowledge base for the industry and paid for the training of the most highly skilled part of its work force, but the biotech companies used those skills and technology to create a multibillion dollar industry.

Even companies that successfully become multinational tend to keep far more than a proportional share of their very best jobs—top management, research, and product development—near their traditional home base. Phillips of the Netherlands is a good example: the company's foreign sales have resulted in a lot of good jobs for the Dutch. As headquarters for southern China, Hong Kong has become much richer than it was when it had a stand-alone economy prior to China's opening up in 1978. Countries and the individuals in them benefit from having successful multinational companies. Successful American multinational companies make it possible for more Americans to be successful individually.

Thirdly, the global economic game is played on an individual level, where personal skills are sold on domestic or global markets. Those skills are partly generated by government investment in education, but they are also derived from what we as individuals invest in our own skills and the experiences we acquire. To make maximum use of them, it pays to work for a good multinational company with a technical edge. For those with the right skills working for the right companies, a global economy opens opportunities for higher wages and more successful careers.

ONE WORLD, ONE WAGE

Not long ago, unskilled US workers enjoyed what might have been called an "American premium." They were paid more than laborers with the same skills in other parts of the world simply because, as unskilled Americans, they would work with higher capital-to-labor ratios, better raw materials, and larger numbers of highly-skilled fellow workers than their foreign counterparts. As a result, America's unskilled workers were relatively more productive and thus earned higher wages than similar unskilled workers elsewhere in the world.

The American premium for the unskilled has disappeared. With better transportation and communications, the superior complementary inputs that once gave unskilled Americans a competitive edge can today be harnessed anywhere in the world. Foreign businesses take advantage of these opportunities to cut costs and earn greater profits. As a result, wages for the unskilled in the United States are falling, and wages for the unskilled in foreign countries are rising to meet them. This phenomenon, referred to by economists as "factor price equalization," is steadily eroding the American premium.

In a global economy, the judgment that a country is competitively successful leaves a lot of important questions unanswered. Real per capita GDP in the United States rose 40 percent from 1970 to 1996. America was undoubtedly successful. Yet at the same time, 60 percent of the work force in 1995 was laboring for real wages below previous peaks. At the median, real wages for nonsupervisory workers were down 13 percent from peak 1973 levels. America was competitively successful, but a majority of Americans were not.

The problem is not, as some have suggested, that the US economy is witnessing the "end of work" and a lack of jobs. The US economy generated 12 million net new jobs in the last four years and has the lowest unemployment rates seen for a quarter of a century. The problem for most Americans is falling real wages. At the same time, with a booming stock market and the wage gains that the economy generated over the past three decades, the top 20 percent of the population has seen its earnings and wealth rise rapidly. For them, the global economy has been a golden opportunity.

America remains a competitive success, yet at the same time, it is running a record trade deficit of over US$200 billion. Some domestic producers—in the semi-conductor and software industries, for example—are gaining global market share, but even more firms, such as auto-makers and oil companies, are losing. Yet this market share may well have been lost to foreign producers owned by the same corporate parent. American capitalists are successfully hedging their positions, but the average American laborer is not.

The factor price equalization that accompanies globalization calls for wage reductions for the unskilled, wage increases for the skilled, higher returns to capital, and lower returns to labor. Other factors such as a technological shift toward skill-intensive industries may be contributing to this trend, but the forces that derive from arbitrage and the resulting factor price equalization are certainly present as well. These forces do not lead to societal equality. The resulting inequalities can be reduced with greater public investments in the skills of the lowest wage-earners, but they probably cannot be eliminated.

DEMOCRACY AND CAPITALISM

All of this creates a problem for democracies. Democracy and capitalism have very different core values. Democracy is founded on equality—one vote per citizen regardless of his intelligence or work ethic. Capitalism, however, is motivated by inequality: differences in economic returns create the incentive structure which encourages hard work and wise investment. Because investments in human or physical assets, and hence future income, depend on current income, wealth tends to generate wealth and poverty tends to be a trap. The economically fit are expected to drive the economically unfit out of existence: there are no equalizing feedback mechanisms in capitalism.

Historically, the social-welfare state and social investment in education have been used to reconcile capitalism and democracy. The state took actions to equalize market outcomes—implementing progressive taxes, pensions, health care, special tax benefits for home mortgages, and unemployment insurance—and helped the individual develop marketable skills by way of public education to insure that differences in living standards did not grow too wide. Regardless of the results of such policies, this system put the state visibly on the side of equality. Low-income individuals knew that the state was taking actions to raise their absolute and relative earnings.

Today, economic globalization and the overburdened US social security system are putting this system at risk. Ever increasing consumption expenditures on ever more numerous elderly voters have to be financed by reducing social welfare benefits for other groups, by cutting social investments in the future (education, infrastructure, and research), or by raising payroll taxes. Globalization has rendered this last option impossible. Higher payroll taxes simply drive industries and employment abroad—

Slowing Down?

The United States' Gross Domestic Product (or GDP, the total value of all final goods produced in an economy) as a fraction of the world's GDP total grew from slightly under 2% in 1820 to about 15% in 1900 to a remarkable 30% in 1951. Since the Second World War, however, not only has the rate of US GDP growth slowed, it has slowed relative to rates in other countries. As a result, US influence in world economic organizations like the World Bank is gradually diminishing. Starting in the late 1960s, GDP growth rates fell for countries around the world, but US growth rates fell even faster, slipping below those of many other countries.

According to Michael French's *US Economic History Since 1945,* three schools of thought exist to explain this slow-down. The first points to the persistence of an absolute US productivity advantage in many sectors and suggests that the growth slowdown was due to short-term factors, such as the recessions of the 1980s and the rising value of the dollar. A second perspective holds that the decline in relative US GDP growth is a result of exceptionally appropriate economic policies in foreign nations and not due to US failings. A third argument is that the United States is indeed losing its ability to compete with other economies because of its low savings rates and insufficient investment in education. Recently, though, economic difficulty in Germany and in Asia has raised the possibility that US productivity growth may again rise relative to that of other countries.

as is now dramatically visible in Europe. Lower social investment in education, skills, infrastructure, and research makes US companies and workers less competitive in world markets. With lower earnings, they are less able and less willing to pay the taxes necessary to finance expensive social programs.

As a result, the system that has held democracy and capitalism together for the last century has started to unravel. As earnings distributions widen due to factor price equalization and a skill-intensive technological shift, and as the US government seems unable and unwilling to do anything about it, that majority which faces lower real earnings will sooner or later become disaffected with democracy. Resolving this difficulty—finding a new method of linking democracy and capitalism symbiotically—will perhaps be the most critical economic and political problem facing the United States in the twenty-first century.

Part IV

Future Global Trends

Emerging Technologies:
What's Ahead for 2001–2030

William E. Halal, Michael D. Kull, and Ann Leffmann

Revolutionary innovation is now occurring in all scientific and technological fields. This wave of unprecedented change is driven primarily by advances in information technology, but it is much larger in scope. We are not dealing simply with an Information Revolution but with a *Technology* Revolution.

To anticipate developments in this Technology Revolution, the George Washington University Forecast of Emerging Technologies was launched at the start of the 1990s. We have now completed four iterations of our Delphi survey—in 1990, 1992, 1994, and 1996—giving us a wealth of data and experience. We now can offer a reasonably clear picture of what can be expected to happen in technology over the next three decades.

Time horizons play a crucial role in forecasting technology. Forecasts of the next five to 10 years are often so predictable that they fall into the realm of market research, while those more than 30 or 40 years away are mostly speculation. This leaves a 10- to 20-year window in which to make useful forecasts. It is this time frame that our Forecast addresses.

The Forecast uses diverse methods, including environmental scanning, trend analysis, Delphi surveys, and scenario building. Environmental scanning is used to identify emerging technologies. Trend analysis guides the selection of the most important technologies for further study, and a modified Delphi survey is used to obtain forecasts. Instead of using the traditional Delphi method of providing respondents with immediate feedback and requesting additional estimates in order to arrive at a consensus, we conduct another survey after an additional time period of about two years.

Finally, the results are portrayed in time periods to build scenarios of unfolding technological change. By using multiple methods instead of relying on a single approach, the Forecast can produce more robust, useful estimates.

Reprinted from the *Futurist*, (November–December 1997), by permission of the World Future Society, 7910 Woodmont Avenue, Bethesda, MD, 20814.

For our latest survey, conducted in 1996, we selected 85 emerging technologies representing the most crucial advances that can be foreseen. We then submitted the list of technologies to our panel of futurists for their judgments as to when (or if) each technological development would enter the mainstream, the probability it would happen, and the estimated size of the economic market for it. In short, we sought a forecast as to when each emerging technology will have actually "emerged."

The respondents include prominent futurists, forecasters, and technical experts, such as authors Marvin Cetron and Joseph F. Coates and mathematician Olaf Helmer, the co-inventor of the Delphi technique. Panelists only respond to questions when they feel confident that they know enough to render an informed judgment. Their responses have shown remarkable consistency: Overall, the average variance appears to be on the order of plus or minus three years.

INFOTECH TO LEAD PARADE

The results indicate that a wave of major technological advances seems likely to arrive during the next three decades. Highly important technological innovations are occurring in all fields, and most of the new technologies under study will arrive between the years 2003 and 2025. It seems clear that almost all fields of endeavor are undergoing a serious transformation that will, in turn, transform society.

The four information-technology fields—computer hardware, computer software, communications, and information services—appear to lead this wave of innovation by about five years.

This finding fits our theory that information technology serves as the principal factor now driving the Technology Revolution.

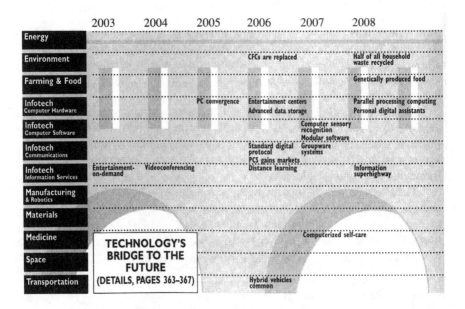

Space appears to be the lagging field. Some relatively simple space technologies are likely to arrive fairly soon, particularly the privatization of space efforts, but almost all serious technologies seem destined to wait about 30–60 years for their development and implementation. Space programs can be most readily postponed because the payoffs are uncertain and distant; furthermore, serious space exploration beyond the solar system will require technological breakthroughs that transcend our present knowledge of physics.

HIGHLIGHTS OF LATEST SURVEY

Information technologies may lead all others, but advances may be slower to come than conventional wisdom currently suggests. Entertainment-on-demand is not expected until 2003, and the time when half of all goods in the United States are sold through information services will not come until 2018.

Personal digital assistants will not be adopted by the majority of people until 2008. Personal computers may soon be able to incorporate television, telephone, and interactive video, but our panel did not see this or a Web-TV with telephone capabilities in wide use until 2005 or 2006.

Software also has a way to go. Although search engines are used on the Web, we will not see intelligent software agents in routine use until 2009. Expert systems, once heralded as the decision-making software for the 1990s, have a 72% chance of finding routine use by 2010. Computer programs that can learn and adjust their own programming will not be commonly available until 2012. Language translation has a similar fate, not achieving widespread use until 2012.

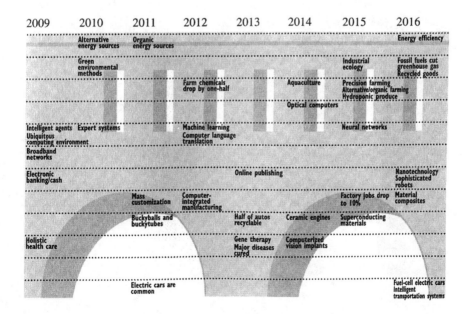

Computerized medical systems should be in common use by 2007. Two years later, holistic health practices will be well integrated into medicine. Gene therapy will be eradicating inherited diseases by 2013. Growing genetically similar or cloned organs is likely by 2018.

Automation and computer-integrated manufacturing should result in the proportion of factory jobs declining from 20% of the current work force to less than 10% by 2015. The helpful robot servants may arrive in 2016.

Promising advances in nanotechnology and microscopic machines could lead to the development of self-assembling and intelligent materials around 2026 or 2027. A form of carbon known as buckminster-fullerene, or "Buckyballs," will become significant in developing new materials by 2011.

Genetic engineering should allow the routine production of new strains of plants and animals by 2008. In 2015, the majority of farmers will have adopted organic or alternative farming methods, and the use of chemical fertilizers and pesticides will have declined by 2012 to less than half of current usage. However, automated farming and urban greenhouses will not appear until 2020.

By 2010 or so we should expect manufacturers to have adopted "green" methods, and a significant portion of energy will be derived from renewable sources and biomass. Improvements in fossil-fuel efficiency will reduce greenhouse-gas emissions by one-half by 2016.

The technologies that may have the most direct impact on daily lives are in transportation. By 2017, high-speed rail systems will connect major cities of the

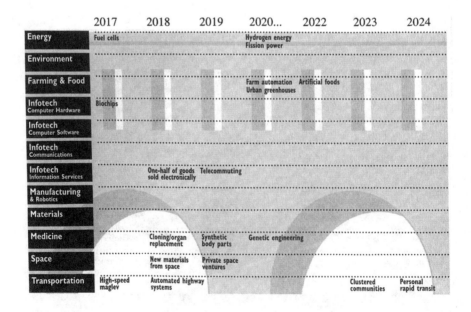

developed world. Around this time, we will see automated highway systems and intelligent transportation systems commonly used to reduce traffic congestion.

Space remains the most intriguing frontier, but advances here are the most difficult to forecast since they require massive project planning, coordination with the government, and, increasingly, international collaboration. The exploration of Mars will begin with the completion of a manned mission in 2037. Five years after that, in 2042, a spaceship or probe will be launched to explore a neighboring star system.

THE 2001–2010 DECADE

The data allow us to create a longitudinal scenario covering the first three decades of the new millennium.

In the first decade of the twenty-first century, the Information Revolution should mature, producing major advances in all fields. Multimedia interconnectivity will allow people to interact seamlessly across diverse information media and geographic borders. Virtual reality and large flat panel displays will take the place of the computer monitor, permitting simultaneous viewing of several applications at once, virtual meetings, and group collaboration.

Education, entertainment, commerce, and tourism will enter a new era of electronic access. Sophisticated software will aid consumers and professionals by providing intelligent agents to filter news and mail. Expert systems may see routine use as surrogate doctors, lawyers, and other professionals.

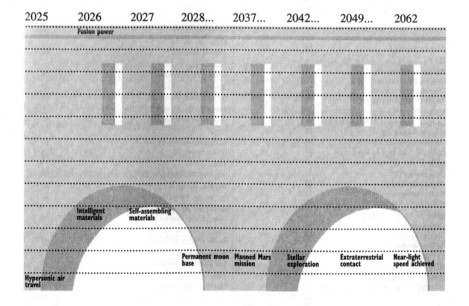

The Technological Road Ahead

Here is a chronology based on the George Washington University Forecast of Emerging Technologies.

The panel estimated the probability (in percent) of each forecast being realized by a given date as well as the likely market demand for it (in dollars). The number in parentheses indicates the technological category of each forecast in the list of 85 forecasts on pages 363–367.

Technology and Category (see pages 363–367 for details)	Probability (in percent)	Demand (in millions of dollars)	Technology and Category (see pages 363–367 for details)	Probability (in percent)	Demand (in millions of dollars)
2003			**2015**		
Entertainment-on-demand (7)	84%	$90 million	Neural networks (5)	61%	$28 million
2004			Alternative/organic farming (3)	57	76
Videoconferencing (7)	83	44	Superconducting materials (9)	56	43
2005			Industrial ecology (2)	55	48
PC convergence (4)	84	111	Hydroponic produce (3)	53	40
2006			**2016**		
Entertainment centers (4)	83	109	Nanotechnology (8)	66	31
Distance learning (7)	78	41	Recycled goods (2)	66	126
CFCs are replaced (2)	77	52	Sophisticated robots (8)	64	130
Advanced data storage (4)	75	44	Energy efficiency (1)	61	49
Standard digital protocol (6)	70	70	Fossil fuels cut greenhouse gas (2)	59	46
Hybrid vehicles common (12)	69	87	Fuel-cell electric cars (12)	58	116
PCS gains markets (6)	56	42	Intelligent transportation systems (12)	58	90
2007			Material composites (9)	53	100
Computerized self-care (10)	82	87	**2017**		
Groupware systems (6)	75	33	High-speed maglev (12)	58	120
Computer sensory recognition (5)	73	34	Biochips (4)	54	58
Modular software (5)	72	47	Fuel cells (1)	53	61
2008			**2018**		
Parallel processing computing (4)	80	64	New materials from space (11)	57	21
Information Superhighway (6)	78	74	One-half of goods sold electronically (7)	55	208
Genetically produced food (3)	75	67	Automated highway systems (12)	55	70
Personal digital assistants (4)	75	54	Cloning/organ replacement (10)	53	63
Half of all household waste recycled (2)	74	53	**2019**		
2009			Private space ventures (11)	62	60
Intelligent agents (5)	79	28	Synthetic body parts (10)	58	68
Ubiquitous computing environment (5)	75	32	Telecommuting (7)	56	468
Broadband networks (6)	70	103	**2020**		
Electronic banking/cash (7)	70	69	Farm automation (3)	60	82
Holistic health care (10)	61	55	Urban greenhouses (3)	53	55
2010			Genetic engineering (10)	53	21
Alternative energy sources (1)	77	46	Hydrogen energy (1)	50	102
"Green" environmental methods (2)	73	90	Fission power (1)	46	26
Expert systems (5)	72	59	**2022**		
2011			Artificial foods (3)	39	75
Mass customization (8)	73	330	**2023**		
Electric cars are common (12)	70	102	Clustered communities (12)	53	85
Organic energy sources (1)	60	43	**2024**		
Buckyballs and buckytubes (9)	59	20	Personal rapid transit (12)	43	62
2012			**2025**		
Computer-integrated manufacturing (8)	73	124	Hypersonic air travel (12)	48	91
Machine learning (5)	67	31	**2026**		
Computer language translation (5)	65	41	Intelligent materials (9)	57	66
Farm chemicals drop by one-half (3)	60	27	Fusion power (1)	50	113
2013			**2027**		
Gene therapy (10)	63	63	Self-assembling materials (9)	56	82
Online publishing (7)	60	66	**2028**		
Major diseases cured (10)	58	116	Permanent moon base (11)	55	32
Half of autos recyclable (9)	58	51	**2037**		
2014			Manned Mars mission (11)	59	30
Optical computers (4)	64	67	**2042**		
Ceramic engines (9)	58	49	Stellar exploration (11)	51	47
Aquaculture (3)	56	52	**2049**		
Computerized vision implants (10)	56	32	Extraterrestrial contact (11)	33	45
2015			**2062**		
Precision farming (3)	69	71	Near-light speed achieved (11)	43	75
Factory jobs drop to 10% (8)	67	150			

The medical community will have accepted the validity of holistic methods and computerized self-care. New genetic strains of plants and animals will provide designer foods and customized farming.

Alternative forms of energy, environmental management, and transportation will also seriously begin to alter lifestyles. Pollution control and highly effective recycling efforts will become normal in developed countries, which may allow developing countries such as China to leapfrog "dirty" industrialization in favor of "clean" and sustainable development.

THE 2011–2020 DECADE

The early 2010s will witness the most striking technological advances in terms of number, scope, and sophistication that civilization has ever seen.

Electronic working, learning, shopping, and publishing will become a way of life, much as automobiles became a way of life a few decades ago. More powerful computers incorporating optical technologies and biochips will begin to simulate the human brain in sensory recognition and thought processing.

This will be the decade of information-technology diffusion, transforming other fields. Academic research will be performed anywhere, at any library, with any colleagues. Travelers can know where they are or where their baggage is at any given moment through satellite global positioning networks, and much of travel itself will become virtual.

Information technology will allow parents to check on their kids, farmers to check on their crops, and states to check on criminals. Automated factories will translate personal details of a consumer's taste into mass-customized products that suit individual needs. Blue-collar jobs will dwindle to less than 10% of the work force.

Gene therapy will cure or prevent diseases, and genetic pioneers may try to improve the genome of normal humans who want to be smarter, stronger, or longer-lived. Farmers will genetically manipulate plants to improve yields and make crops resistant to pests and spoilage. The cloning and/or manufacture of body organs should help increase lifespans. Composite materials, nanotechnology, and a variety of other methods will permit the production of almost any physical object, while maglev trains, fuel-cell powered cars, and intelligent transportation systems should allow vastly improved mobility.

THE 2021–2030 DECADE

The third decade of the twenty-first century will see expansion into bold new frontiers, notably advanced materials, exotic forms of transportation, and space. The capabilities of intelligent and self-assembling materials, fusion power, artificial foods, and other advanced technologies will improve dramatically.

Nations will find their influence declining relative to multinational corporations and virtual or "clustered" communities. This trend is likely to create tension between local versus global concerns. A worldwide consensus will be needed for progress on complex, controversial problems of population, environmental sustainability, space development, and human bioengineering. No single nation can readily provide the resources necessary to mount huge projects such as an advanced space program or a planetary energy grid. If society wishes to pursue these goals, a profound restructuring of international relations lies ahead.

PLANS FOR FORECAST PROJECT'S FUTURE

The George Washington University Forecast has reached its current state of development by dint of continual improvements during and between four iterations covering almost an entire decade. More improvements are anticipated: We are in the process of refining the clarity and focus of the question series and of strengthening the panel through more rigorous selection methods. These plans should make the next forecast, to be conducted in 1998, significantly better.

An experimental Web site has been developed that allows individuals to access the latest results electronically and to enter their own estimates. We are now considering the possibility of using this idea to replace the biennial round-by-round approach to provide a continuous stream of data. Individuals on the Web could enter their estimates, and these would be compared with the expert panelists. The role of the research team would be to identify emerging technologies and serve as the system's gatekeepers.

With some support, we can easily envision this concept expanded to the point where it would become a national, or even international system that draws on the estimates of thousands of people to provide continually updated forecasts online. In addition to gaining far more sophisticated data, such a system would also serve the crucial purpose of engaging students, scholars, policy makers, and the public in a stimulating educational dialogue that raises the general level of understanding of technological change. We anticipate this advance by the end of 1998.

The authors have conducted the Forecast without funding. Sponsors are currently being sought to support more ambitious plans. We hope that the encouraging potential of our approach will prove attractive to interested foundations who wish to lend their resources toward improving the Forecast.

The study makes one overwhelming conclusion abundantly clear: The Technology Revolution seems destined to transform modern civilization. And because the wave of historic innovation is so unprecedented that it is likely to change continuously even as we move through it, there is little alternative but to constantly monitor and forecast progress in science and technology in order to guide progress more wisely.

The Emerging Technologies from the Forecast Project

Here is a summary of the 85 emerging technologies, grouped in 12 categories, together with the Forecast panel's consensus estimate of the year each will occur.

1. Energy

Alternative energy sources: A significant portion (10%) of energy usage is derived from alternative energy sources, such as geothermal, hydroelectric, solar/photoelectric. 2010

Energy efficiency: Energy efficiency improves by 50% through innovations in transportation, industrial processing, environmental control, etc. 2016

Fuel cells: Fuel cells, converting fuels to electricity, are commonly used (30%). 2017

Organic energy sources: Biological materials, such as crops, trees, and other forms of organic matter, are used as significant (10%) energy sources. 2011

Fission power: Fission nuclear power is used for 50% of electricity generation. 2020

Hydrogen energy: Hydrogen becomes routinely used in energy systems. 2020

Fusion power: Fusion nuclear power is used commercially for electricity production. 2026

2. Environment

CFCs are replaced: The majority of CFCs (chlorofluorocarbons) are replaced by materials that do not damage the ozone layer. 2006

Household waste: One-half of the waste from households in developed countries is recycled. 2008

"Green" manufacturing: Most manufacturers adopt "green" methods that minimize environmental pollution. 2010

Recycled goods: The majority of manufactured goods use recycled materials. 2016

Fossil fuels produce less greenhouse gas: Improvements in fossil fuel energy efficiency and greater use of alternative energy sources "greenhouse" gas emissions by one-half from current volumes. 2016

Industrial ecology: The majority of manufacturing facilities use industrial ecology (eco-industrial parks operating as a closed system) to reduce waste pollution. 2006

3. Farming & Food

Genetically produced food: Genetic engineering techniques are routinely used to produce new strains of plants and animals. 2008

Farm chemicals drop: The use of chemical fertilizers and pesticides declines by half. 2012

Alternative/organic farming: The majority of farming in industrialized countries incorporates alternative/organic farming techniques into traditional methods. 2015

Aquaculture: Seafood grown using aquaculture provides the majority of seafood consumed. 2014

Farm automation: Automation of farming methods, using technology such as robotics, is common (over 30%). 2020

Precision farming: Computerized control of irrigation, seeding, fertilizer, pesticides, etc., is common (over 30%). 2015

Urban greenhouses: Urban production of fruits and vegetables using greenhouses and/or other intensive production systems is common (over 30%). 2020

Hydroponic produce: Produce grown using hydroponic methods is common (over 30%). 2015

Artificial foods: Artificial meats, vegetables, bread, etc., are commonly (over 30%) consumed. 2022

4. Infotech Computer Hardware

Personal digital assistants: Hand-held microcomputers are used by the majority of people to manage their work and personal affairs. 2008

Parallel processing: Supercomputers using massive parallel processing are commonly used (30%). 2008

PCs include interactive television: Personal computers incorporate television, telephone, and interactive video transmission. 2005

Entertainment center: An entertainment center combining interactive television, telephone, and computer capability is commercially available for home use. 2006

Optical computers: Computers using photons rather than electrons to code information enter the commercial marketplace. 2014

Advanced data storage: More advanced forms of data storage (optical, non-volatile semiconductor, magnetic memory, etc.) are standard on multimedia personal computers. 2006

Biochips: "Biochips" that store data in molecular bonds are commercially available. 2017

5. Infotech Computer Software

Modular software: The majority of software is generated automatically using software modules (object-oriented programming, CASE tools, etc.). 2007

Expert systems: Routine use of expert systems helps decision making in management, medicine, engineering, and other fields. 2010

Computer sensory recognition: Voice, handwriting, and optical recognition features allow ordinary personal computers to interact with humans. 2007

Computer translation: Computers are able to routinely translate languages in real-time with the accuracy and speed necessary for effective communications. 2012

Intelligent agents: Knowbots, navigators, and other intelligent software agents routinely filter and retrieve information for users. 2009

Ubiquitous computing environment: Embedded processors in common objects are integrated into the workplace and home. 2009

Neural networks: Computations are commonly (more than 30%) performed by neural networks using parallel processors. 2015

Machine learning: Computer programs are commonly available that learn by trial and error in order to adjust their behavior. 2012

6. Infotech Communications

Personal communication systems: PCS has a significant (10%) share of the market for voice communications. 2006

Standard digital protocol: Most communications system (80%) in industrialized countries adopt a standard digital protocol. 2006

Information superhighway: Most people (80%) in developed countries access an information superhighway. 2008

Groupware systems: Groupware systems are routinely used for simultaneously working and learning together at multiple sites. 2007

Broadband networks: ISDN, ATM, fiber optics, etc., connect the majority of homes and offices. 2009

7. Infotech Information Services

Entertainment-on-demand: A variety of movies, TV shows, sports, and other forms of entertainment can be selected electronically at home on demand. 2003

Videoconferencing: Teleconferencing is routinely used in industrialized countries for business meetings. 2004

Online publishing: The majority of books and publications are published online. 2007

Electronic banking and cash: Electronic banking, including electronic cash, replaces paper, checks, and cash as the principal means of commerce. 2009

Electronic sales: Half of all goods in the United States are sold through information services. 2018

Telecommuting: Most employees (80%) perform their jobs at least partially from remote locations by telecommuting. 2019

Distance learning: Schools and colleges commonly use computerized teaching programs and interactive television lectures and seminars, as well as traditional methods. 2006

8. Manufacturing & Robotics

Computer-integrated manufacturing: CIM is used in most (80%) factory operations. 2012

Factory jobs decline below 10%: Due to automation, factory jobs decline to less than 10% of the work force. 2015

Mass customization: Mass customization of cars, appliances, and other products is commonly (30%) available. 2011

Sophisticated robots: Robots that have sensory input, make decisions, learn, and are mobile become commercially available. 2016

Nanotechnology: Microscopic machines and/or nanotechnology are developed into commercial applications. 2016

9. Materials

Ceramic engines: Ceramic engines are mass-produced for commercial vehicles. 2014

Half of all autos are recyclable: Recyclable plastic composites are used in making half of all automobiles. 2013

Superconducting materials: Superconducting materials are commonly used (30%) for transmitting electricity in electronic devices, such as energy, medical, and communications applications. 2015

Material composites: Material composites replace the majority of traditional metals in product designs. 2016

"Buckyballs": The form of carbon known as "Buckyballs" (or "Buckytubes") is instrumental in developing new materials. 2011

Self-assembling materials: Self-assembling materials are routinely used commercially. 2027

Intelligent materials: Smart materials are routinely used in homes, offices, and vehicles. 2026

10. Medicine

Self-care: Computerized information systems are commonly used for medical care, including diagnosis, dispensing prescriptions, monitoring medical conditions, and self-care. 2007

Holistic health care: Holistic approaches to health care, both physical and mental, become accepted by the majority of the medical community. 2009

Genetic engineering of children: Parents can routinely choose characteristics of their children through genetic engineering. 2020

Gene therapy: Genetic therapy is routinely used to prevent and/or cure an inherited disease. 2013

Organ replacement: Living organs and tissue produced genetically are routinely used for replacement. 2019

Synthetic body parts: Artificial organs and tissue produced synthetically are routinely used for replacement. 2019

Computerized vision: Computerized vision implants are commercially available to correct eye defects. 2014

Major disease cured: A cure or preventive treatment for a major disease such as cancer or AIDS is found. 2013

11. Space

Private space ventures: Private corporations perform the majority of space launches as private ventures. 2019

Manned mission to Mars: A manned mission to Mars is completed. 2037

Permanent moon base: A permanently manned moon base is established. 2028

Stellar exploration: A spaceship is launched to explore a neighboring star system. 2042

New materials from space: Chemicals, metals, etc., that cannot be created on Earth are developed in space, where conditions allow it due to such factors as the absence of gravity and air pollution. 2018

Spaceships travel at near-light speed: Spaceships or probes reach 80% or more of the speed of light. 2062

Extraterrestrial contact: Intelligent life is contacted elsewhere in the universe. 2049

12. Transportation

High-speed trains: High-speed rail or maglev trains are available between most major cities in developed countries. 2017

Hybrid vehicles: Vehicles that combine electric and internal combustion engines are commercially available. 2006

Electric cars: Battery-powered electric cars are commonly (30%) available. 2006

Fuel-cell cars: Electric cars powered by fuel cells are commonly (30%) available. 2016

Hypersonic planes: Aircraft traveling at more than five times the speed of sound are used for the majority of transoceanic flights. 2025

Automated highways: Automated highway systems are commonly (30%) used to control speed, steering, braking, etc. 2018

Intelligent transportation: Intelligent transportation systems are commonly (30%) used to reduce highway congestion. 2016

Personal rapid transit: Car-like capsules on guide rails or other personal rapid transit systems are installed in most metropolitan areas. 2024

Clustered communities: Clustered, self-contained communities in urban areas reduce the need for local transportation. 2023

William E. Halal, Michael D. Kull, and Ann Leffmann

Panel for Latest George Washington University Forecast

About 45 well-known futurists and technical experts have participated in George Washington University's Forecast of Emerging Technologies.

Among participants in the 1996 Forecast were **Marvin J. Cetron,** president of Forecasting International, Ltd.; **Joseph F. Coates,** principal of Coates and Jarratt, Inc.; **Jerome C. Glenn,** coordinator of the United Nations University's Millennium Project Feasibility Study; **Theodore J. Gordon,** retired chairman of The Futures Group; **Olaf Helmer,** co-inventer of the Delphi Technique; **Harold A. Linstone,** editor of the journal *Technological Forecasting and Social Change;* **Joseph P. Martino,** Technological Forecasting Editor of THE FUTURIST; and **John L. Petersen,** author of *Out of the Blue* and *The Road to 2015.*

The Promise of Genetics

Joseph F. Coates, John B. Mahaffie, and Andy Hines

Genetics will be a key enabling technology of the twenty-first century, rivaling information technology, materials technology, and energy technology in importance.

The effects of all of these enabling technologies will be far-reaching across business and society, but advances in genetics in particular will be fundamental to many science and technology areas and societal functions, including health and medicine, food and agriculture, nanotechnology, and manufacturing.

One benefit of genetics that is already highly visible is in forensics. DNA identification will significantly enhance criminology. It may contribute to declines in violent crime, the identification of deadbeat parents, and the prevention of fraud. It may even deter rape and murder, as potential perpetrators fear leaving their DNA "fingerprints" on the scene.

Rising public interest in genetics is tied to the growing realization that humanity is capable of directly shaping its own and other species' evolution. We will no longer have to wait for nature's relatively slow natural selection. Genetics will bring the capability of speeding and redirecting evolution along paths of our choice. Eliminating genetic diseases, for instance, might take centuries through natural selection but could be accomplished in decades through genetic manipulation.

This power will doubtless inspire a profound global debate about how genetics should and should not be used.

THE GENETIC ECONOMY

On the economic front, genetics could reward those who invest in it for the long haul. It is an industry for patient capital. Its spread over many industries will make it an increasingly important factor in the global economy.

Reprinted from the *Futurist*, (September–October 1997), by permission of the World Future Society, 7910 Woodmont Avenue, Bethesda, MD, 20814.

Genetics is not a typical industry, in that it is not measured as a separate entity. It will be a part of, or embedded in, so many industries that government statisticians will not attempt such a measure. A good guess is that genetics will account for about 20% of gross domestic product, or roughly $2 trillion in 2025.

The early emphasis on using genetics to improve human health and battle disease will be supplemented with more exotic applications, such as manufacturing and materials, human enhancement, energy, environmental engineering, and species restoration and management. The food and agriculture industries, for example, are steadily expanding their use of genetics. Advances will come from applying what seem like isolated breakthroughs into a systems framework. For example, researchers working on eradicating a species of locust may develop a microorganism useful in converting crop wastes into biomass energy.

GENETICS AND SPECIES MANAGEMENT

The genomes of many animals, fish, insects, and microorganisms will be worked out, leading to more refined management, control, and manipulation of their health and propagation—or their elimination.

• **Designer animals.** Routine genetic programs will be used to enhance animals used for food production, recreation, and even pets. Goats, for example, are especially well suited to genetic manipulation. In affluent nations, goats will be used for producing pharmaceutical compounds; in less-developed nations, goats will produce high-protein milk.

Livestock will be customized to increase growth, shorten gestation, and enhance nutritional value. Farmers will be able to order the genes they want from gene banks for transmission to local biofactories, where the animals with the desired characteristics will then be produced and shipped.

Transgenic animals, sharing the genes of two or more species, may be created to withstand rough environments. Genes from the hardy llama in South America, for example, could be introduced into camels in the Middle East—and vice versa—to greatly expand the range of each. Some species will be introduced into entirely new areas. Parrots may be modified to withstand cold North American temperatures, becoming a boon to bird watchers in the United States.

Transgenic pets may become popular: Genes from mild-mannered Labrador retrievers could be put into pit bull terrier genomes.

• **Pest control.** Genetics will play a central role in pest management. The arms race between insects and pesticides has been marked by humans winning battles, but insects winning the war. Genetics will turn the tide.

One method is to breed pheromones into surrounding plants to lure pests away from their intended prey. Pests will also be sterilized through genetic engineering to disrupt their populations. Genetically engineered resistance to pests will be common through such techniques as inducing the plants to produce their own protective or repellant compounds.

Insects that carry disease will also be targeted through genetic engineering to control their populations. It is hoped that malaria will soon be eliminated this way.

• **Boosting plants.** Future farmers may have near total control over plant genetics. Plants will give higher yields and be more resistant to disease, frost, drought, and stress. They will have higher protein, lower oil, and more efficient photosynthesis rates than ever before. Natural processes such as ripening will be enhanced and controlled.

Genetics will allow farmers to customize and fine-tune crops, building in flavor, sweeteners, and preservatives, while increasing nutritional value. [See box, "Future Foods: The New Genetic Menu," page 288.]

The first step in agrogenetics is to identify disease-resistant genes; the second step is to put them into plants. Eventually, plants will be genetically engineered to produce specific prevention factors against likely disease invaders.

Forestry will also benefit from genetics. Genetic manipulation will result in superior tree strains with disease resistance and improved productivity. Trees will be routinely engineered to allow nonchemical pulping for use in paper making. Genetic forests will also help in the global restoration of many denuded areas.

• **Engineering microorganisms.** Manufacturers will use engineered microorganisms to produce commodity and specialty chemicals, as well as medicines, vaccines, and drugs. Groups of microorganisms, often working in sequence as living factories, will produce useful compounds. They will also be widely used in agriculture, mining, resource upgrading, waste management, and environmental cleanup. Oil- and chemical-spill cleanups are a high-profile application.

The development of so-called suicidal microorganisms will be an important factor. Engineered microorganisms would self-destruct by expressing a suicide gene after their task is accomplished. These would be developed in response to fears of runaways—that is, harmful genetically engineered microorganisms that rapidly spread destructive power. They would be particularly useful in the bioremediation of solid and hazardous waste sites and in agricultural applications such as fertilizers.

GENETICS IN INDUSTRY

Genetics will first become a force in improving human health, food, and agriculture. But over the next few decades it will have a greater impact across many industries, such as chemical engineering, environmental engineering, manufacturing, energy, and information technology. It will even contribute to the burgeoning field of artificial life.

Chemical engineering, for example, has begun "biologizing"—i.e., incorporating an understanding of complex biological interactions. Genetics will help the chemical industry shift away from bulk chemicals to higher value-added products, such as food additives or industrial enzymes used as biocatalysts.

Genetic engineering will also help to clean the environment and may be used to create totally artificial environments, such as in space and seabed stations or even for terraforming Mars.

Manufacturing, too, will become "biologized" and more like breeding. Manufacturing applications of genetics will include molecular engineering for pharmaceuticals and other compounds, rudimentary DNA chips, biosensors, and nanotechnology based on biological principles such as self-assembly.

Genetics in 2025

Application	Genetics' Potential Impacts
Health	Eliminate almost 2,000 single gene diseases, such as Huntington's Chorea. Cut in half the diseases with genetic predispositions, including dozens of cancers.
Behavior	Substantial reduction of schizophrenia. Education overhauled to tailor learning to individual genetic/cognitive profiles.
Forensics	Reduction in auto thefts, kidnapping, fraud, and other crimes due to DNA identification and security systems.
Livestock	Revival of pork industry with custom-designed varieties, such as ultra-lean pork.
Fisheries	Overwhelmed natural fisheries supplemented by aquafarms specializing in transgenic specialty fish.
Pest management	Crop loss due to pests reduced by two-thirds in the United States; Lyme disease eliminated.
Crops	Intermittent blights eliminated, allowing record yields of Irish potatoes, Kansas wheat, and Japanese rice.
Food	The number of foods making up 90% of the typical human diet rises from six to 37; foods are customized according to consumers' taste, preparation, and storage needs.
Forestry	Superior strains of trees allow worldwide tree coverage to double.
Microorganisms	Specialty chemicals, medicines, and foods are produced in bioreactors, enhancing agriculture, mining, waste management, and other industries.
Chemical engineering	Databases of molecules allow more rapid and accurate design of chemicals.
Environmental engineering	Bioremediation becomes primary cleanup mechanism in many hazardous waste sites.
Materials	One-third of people in affluent nations use biosensors to monitor their health.
Manufacturing	Bioreactors exploiting biological processes approaching the nanoscale are in widespread use for manufacturing nondurable goods.
Energy	Conversion efficiency of biomass triples. Oil recovery is enhanced.
Infotech	Genetic algorithms are applied to software programming, enabling neural network computers that mimic the intelligence level of chimps.

Source: *2025: Scenarios of U.S. and Global Society Reshaped by Science and Technology.*

A key consideration in biologizing will be society's commitment to sustainability, which could drive a search for environmentally benign manufacturing strategies. Biological approaches, while slower than mechanistic ones, could prove more sustainable. In the future, all industrial enzymes may be produced by genetic engineering. Already, recombinant DNA is used in cheese making, wine making, textiles, and paper production. Bioreactors, in which engineered living cells are used as biocatalysts, will be used for new kinds of manufacturing, such as making new tree species.

Linkages may be found between genetics and information technology: Researchers are striving for ways to take advantage of the fact that genes are pure information. A whole new discipline is evolving: "bioinformatics" to manage and interpret the flood of new biological and genomic data. A science of biological computing is also likely to evolve and compete successfully with silicon-based computing.

Genetics and information technology would work together in advanced computers. Biophotonic computers using biomolecules and photonic processors could be the fastest switching systems ever built.

GENETICS AND GLOBAL DEVELOPMENT

Genetics could be a tool for igniting a second Green Revolution in agriculture. Synthetic soil supplements, crop strains that accommodate a land's existing conditions, and integrated pest management techniques could be a boon to developing countries, such as India, facing burgeoning population growth on increasingly tired and overworked cropland.

Another potential economic benefit of genetics may be in tourism. Kenya, for instance, could promote tourism associated with wildlife by strengthening its indigenous species. Genetics could be used to rescue lions and elephants from extinction by boosting their food supply or developing vaccines to prevent viral attacks.

Like Kenya, Brazil has an economic opportunity in protecting and enhancing its biodiversity. Brazil's niche would be in pharmaceuticals and other chemicals, and it could tap its lush tropical forests—storehouses of over half the world's plant and animal species. Genes that promote rapid growth could be engineered into the native rain-forest tree species, thus helping to save forests once thought to be lost forever.

GENETICS TO IMPROVE HUMAN HEALTH

Genetics will increasingly enable health professionals to identify, treat, and prevent the 4,000 or more genetic diseases and disorders that our species is heir to. Genetics will become central to diagnosis and treatment, especially to testing for predispositions and in therapies. By 2025, there will likely be thousands of diagnostic procedures and treatments for genetic conditions.

Genetic diagnostics can detect specific diseases, such as Down syndrome, and behavioral predispositions, such as depression. Treatments include gene-based pharmaceuticals, such as those using antisense DNA to block the body's process of transmitting genetic instructions for a disease process. In future preventive therapies, harmful genes will be removed, turned off, or blocked. In some cases, healthy

---

Future Foods: The New Genetic Menu

Restaurants and grocery stores will offer future diners far more exotic choices than ever before, thanks to genetics that permit flavors, textures, and other properties from one species to be introduced into another.

Some items on tomorrow's menu might include:

- "Protrout," super-protein trout.
- Ultra-lean "Pig-No-More."
- "Octo-squid."
- "Beetatoes."
- "Beefison," meat with venison's flavor and beef's bulk.
- "Shrimpsters," less-squishy oysters produced with shrimp genes.
- Swordfish-flavored tuna.
- Duck-flavored pork.
- Seaweed dip seasoned with spring onion genes.
- A quail–chicken transgenic fowl dubbed "quicken."

Ultimately, genetic chefs may produce crossover transgenics: plants with animal genes and animals with plant genes, giving new meaning to "chocolate milk" and "duck à l'orange."

Source: *2025: Scenarios of U.S. and Global Society Reshaped by Science and Technology.*

---

replacement genes will be directly inserted into fetuses or will be administered to people via injection, inhalation, retroviruses, or pills. These therapies will alter traits and prevent diseases.

Although genetics will be the greatest driver of advances in human health in the twenty-first century, it will not be a panacea for all human health problems. Health is a complex of interacting systems. The benefits of genetics will also be weighted more heavily to future generations, because prevention will be such an important component. Genetic therapies will ameliorate conditions in middle-aged and older people, but those conditions will not even exist in future generations. For example, psoriasis may be brought under control for many via gene therapy; if an effective prenatal diagnosis can be developed, then no future child would ever need be born with the condition.

GENETICS AND HUMAN DESTINY

The greatest genetic challenge of the twenty-first century will be human enhancement. The human species is the first to influence its own evolution. Already, we have seen the use of human growth hormone for more than its original intent as a treatment for dwarfism. In many instances, use of HGH has been cosmetic rather than medically indicated.

In the future, genetics may also be used for mental enhancement. Parents lacking math skills, for example, may shop for genes that predispose their bearer to mathematical excellence and have these genes inserted prenatally or postnatally into their children. Other parents may select traits such as artistic ability, musical talent, charm, honesty, or athletic prowess for their children.

Of course, some challenging social questions are bound to arise as genetics leads to increasingly talented and intelligent children growing up in a society in which they are in many ways superior to their parents, teachers, and government authorities. Optimists may anticipate a more informed and enlightened society. Pessimists would worry about older people being warehoused in communities or homes for the genetically impaired.

Contributors

Yaw Ackah is Professor of Sociology/Criminal Justice at Delaware State University in Dover, DE. He received his Ph.D. from Howard University in 1993. He has published on fear of crime among immigrants in the US, diabetes and hypertension among African-Americans, and the over-incarceration of minorities in America. His current research focuses on gender-specific violent crimes, and serial murders in Ghana.

George A. Agbango is Professor of Political Science and Public Administration at Bloomsburg University in Pennsylvania. He served as Chair of the Department of Political Science (1992–1996) and Chair of the Mass Communications Department (2003–2004), both at Bloomsburg University. Dr. Agbango was President of the North American Chapter of the African Association of Political Science (1994–1998). He is current President of the Pennsylvania Black Conference on Higher Education. His book *Issues and Trends in Contemporary African Politics* was published in 1997 by Peter Lang Publishers.

The Honorable Kofi Annan is Secretary-General of the United Nations.

Dr. F. Odun Balogun is Professor of English at Delaware State University and has taught previously at the University of Benin in Nigeria and at Southern University, Baton Rouge, LA. He has published two books of literary criticism, *Tradition and Modernity in the African Short Story* (1991) and *Ngugi and African Postcolonial Narrative* (1997); an award-winning book of short stories, *Adjusted Lives* (1995); and over forty book chapters and journal essays.

Lilianet Brintrup was born in the Province of Llanquihue in southern Chile. Since 1990, she has been Professor of Hispanic American Literature and teaches Spanish at Humboldt State University in Northern California. She is the author of the poetry collections *En Tierra Firme* (Santiago de Chile: Ed. El Azafran, 1993), *Amor y Caos* (Santiago de Chile: Ed. La Trastienda, 1994) and *El Libro Natural* (Santiago de Chile: Ed. La Trastienda, 1999). Presently she is at work on two other collections of poetry.

Yinghong Cheng is Assistant Professor of History in the Department of History, Political Science and Philosophy at Delaware State University. Dr. Cheng's expertise is world history, specializing in comparative revolutionary movements. He has written articles on the Chinese, Cuban and Russian experiments in political and social transformation.

Joseph F. Coates is President of the futures consulting firm Coates & Jarratt, Inc. He is adjunct faculty at George Washington University in Washington, DC, and teaches courses on the future and technology.

Edwidge Danticat was born in Haiti and came to the United States when she was twelve years old. She is a gradute of Barnard College and Brown University and is the author of *Breath, Eyes, Memory; Krik? Krak!* and *The Farming of Bones.*

Madelaine Drohan works for the European Bureau of the Toronto *Globe and Mail* and is based in London.

Alan Freeman works for the European Bureau of the Toronto *Globe and Mail* and is based in Berlin.

Asgede Hagos, Ph.D., is Professor of Communications at Delaware State University and author of *Hardened Images: The Western Media and the Marginalization of Africa.* He served as Director of the Department of Mass Communications at Delaware State from 1977 to 1999. Prior to joining Delaware State University, he taught at Howard University from 1986 to 1984.

William E. Halal is Professor of Management in the Department of Management Science at the School of Business and Public Management, George Washington University. He most recently co-edited the book *Twenty-First Century Economics: Perspectives of Socioeconomics for a Changing World* (1999).

Suheir Hammad is the author of the poetry collection *Born Palestinian, Born Black,* and the memoir *Drops of This Story,* both published by Harlem River Press. She has been the recipient of numerous awards, including the Audre Lorde Poetry Award, and her column, "Psalms 26:7," appears regulary in *Stress* magazine. She lives in New York.

Andy Hines, a former associate at the consulting firm Coates & Jarratt, Inc., is a contributing editor on emerging technologies to *The Futurist.*

Stephen J. Kobrin is William H. Wurster Professor of Multinational Management and Director of the Joseph H. Lauder Institute of Management and International Studies at the Wharton School, University of Pennsylvania, in Philadelphia.

Michael D. Kull is a doctoral fellow in the Department of Management Science at the School of Business and Public Management, George Washington University.

Ann Leffmann is a doctoral candidate in George Washington University's Department of Management Science.

John B. Mahaffie is Vice President at the futures consulting firm Coates & Jarratt, Inc. He has authored numerous futures studies for corporations, government agencies, and nonprofit groups, and is a speaker on the future of science and technology, health and medicine, work and worklife, and other futures topics.

Dr. Akwasi Osei is Associate Professor and Chair of the Department of History, Political Science and Philosophy at Delaware State University. He is also Director of the Global Societies Program at DSU. Dr. Osei's areas of expertise are Africa in the international system, the African diaspora, and global studies.

Tina Rosenberg writes editorials for the *New York Times.*

Dr. Ismail Shariff is the Philip J. and Elizabeth B. Hendrickson Professor of Business and Chair of the Department of Economics, and Professor of Urban and Regional Studies at the University of Wisconsin-Green Bay. He is an authority on Third World economic development whose expertise has been sought by institutions such as the World Bank.

Lester C. Thurow is the Lemelson Professor of Management at the Sloan School of Management, Massachusetts Institute of Technology.

Ifeyinwa E. Umerah-Udezulu is Associate Professor of Political Science at Delaware State University. Her research interests include issues pertaining to gendered access to politics and health-care concerns and disparities among women cross-culturally. She has authored several book chapters and journal articles on these areas.

Jim Valle is a Professor of History at Delaware State University.

Kraig Wheeler received his bachelor's degree in chemistry from the University of Minnesota in Minneapolis in 1987 and his Ph.D. degree in organic chemistry from Brandeis University in Waltham, MA in 1992. He then accepted a postdoctoral fellowship at the University of Texas at Austin and subsequently joined the Department of Chemistry at Delaware State University, where he has risen to the rank of full professor. Dr. Wheeler's research interests include a wide variety of topics such as chemical transformations, materials design, hydrogen bonding, molecular topology, crystal engineering and X-ray crystallography.

Long Ying Tai, a known Chinese essayist and cultural critic. Long grew up in Taiwan, studied in the U.S., married a German and living in Germany for years, once being the director of Cultural Division of Taipei municipal government in the 1990s, and now living and teaching at a Hong Kong university. Long has been a popular author in the Chinese world, including China, Taiwan, Hong Kong, Singapore, and Chinese communities worldwide.

Maps

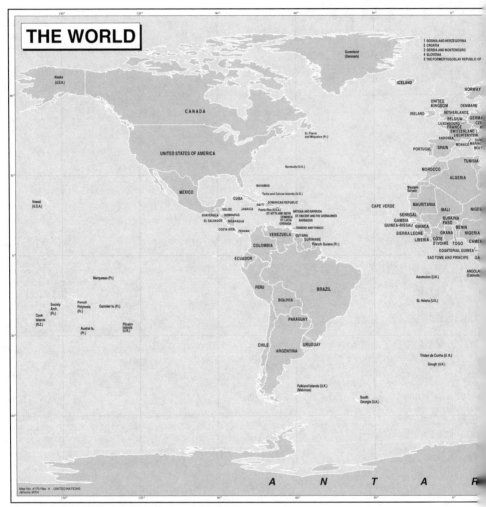

THE WORLD

1 BOSNIA AND HERZEGOVINA
2 CROATIA
3 SERBIA AND MONTENEGRO
4 SLOVENIA
5 THE FORMER YUGOSLAV REPUBLIC OF

Courtesy of the United Nations Cartographic Section.

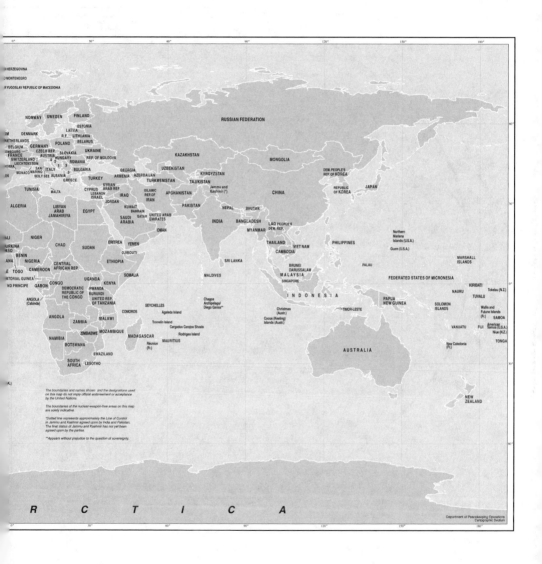

B HERZEGOVINA

O MONTENEGRO

R YUGOSLAV REPUBLIC OF MACEDONIA

NORWAY SWEDEN FINLAND

RUSSIAN FEDERATION

ESTONIA

M DENMARK LATVIA

NETHERLANDS R.F. LITHUANIA

BELGIUM GERMANY POLAND BELARUS

MBOURG CZECH REP. UKRAINE

FRANCE AUSTRIA SLOVAKIA

SWITZERLAND HUNGARY REP OF MOLDOVA

LIECHTENSTEIN ROMANIA

DORRA SAN ITALY BULGARIA GEORGIA UZBEKISTAN

MONACO MARINO ARMENIA AZERBAIJAN KYRGYZSTAN

IN HOLY SEE ALBANIA TURKEY TURKMENISTAN TAJIKISTAN

GREECE SYRIAN

CYPRUS ARAB REP. ISLAMIC

TUNISIA LEBANON REP.OF AFGHANISTAN Jammu and

MALTA ISRAEL IRAQ IRAN Kashmir (*)

JORDAN KUWAIT PAKISTAN

LIBYAN BAHRAIN NEPAL BHUTAN

ALGERIA ARAB EGYPT QATAR UNITED ARAB

JAMAHIRIYA SAUDI EMIRATES INDIA BANGLADESH

ARABIA OMAN MYANMAR

KAZAKHSTAN

MONGOLIA

DEM.PEOPLE'S

REP OF KOREA

REPUBLIC JAPAN

OF KOREA

CHINA

LAO PEOPLE'S

DEM. REP.

ALI NIGER CHAD ERITREA YEMEN THAILAND VIET NAM

URKINA SUDAN DJIBOUTI CAMBODIA PHILIPPINES

ASO BENIN SRI LANKA BRUNEI

ANA NIGERIA CENTRAL ETHIOPIA MALDIVES DARUSSALAM

E TOGO CAMEROON AFRICAN REP. MALAYSIA

ATORIAL GUINEA GABON CONGO UGANDA SOMALIA SINGAPORE

ND PRINCIPE DEMOCRATIC KENYA INDONESIA

REPUBLIC OF RWANDA

ANGOLA THE CONGO BURUNDI

(Cabinda) UNITED REP. SEYCHELLES

OF TANZANIA COMOROS

ANGOLA ZAMBIA MALAWI

NAMIBIA ZIMBABWE MOZAMBIQUE MADAGASCAR

BOTSWANA SWAZILAND

SOUTH LESOTHO

AFRICA

Northern

Mariana

Islands (U.S.A.)

Guam (U.S.A.)

PALAU

MARSHALL

ISLANDS

FEDERATED STATES OF MICRONESIA

KIRIBATI

NAURU Tokelau (N.Z.)

TUVALU

PAPUA Wallis and

NEW GUINEA SOLOMON Future Islands

ISLANDS (Fr.) SAMOA

America (U.S.A.)

VANUATU FIJI Samoa

TIMOR-LESTE Niue (N.Z.)

New Caledonia TONGA

(Fr.)

AUSTRALIA

Chagos

Archipelago/

Diego Garcia**

Agalega Island

Cargados Carajos Shoals

Tromelin Island

Rodrigues Island

Réunion MAURITIUS

(Fr.)

Christmas

(Austr.)

Cocos (Keeling)

Islands (Austr.)

NEW

ZEALAND

The boundaries and names shown and the designations used

on this map do not imply official endorsement or acceptance

by the United Nations.

The boundaries of the nuclear-weapon-free areas on this map

are solely indicative.

*Dotted line represents approximately the Line of Control

in Jammu and Kashmir agreed upon by India and Pakistan.

The final status of Jammu and Kashmir has not yet been

agreed upon by the parties.

**Appears without prejudice to the question of sovereignty.

R C T I C A

Department of Peacekeeping Operations

Cartographic Section

World

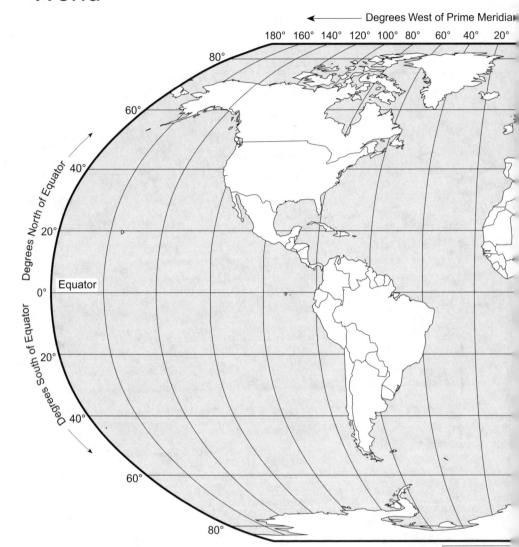

Degrees West of Prime Meridian

180° 160° 140° 120° 100° 80° 60° 40° 20°

80°

60°

Degrees North of Equator

40°

20°

Equator 0°

Degrees South of Equator

20°

40°

60°

80°

Degrees East of Prime Meridian ⟶

20° 0° 20° 40° 60° 80° 100° 120° 140° 160° 180°

Prime Meridian

0   1000   2000   3000 Miles

0   3000 Kilometers

Projection: Robinson

Courtesy: Arizona Geographic Alliance
Department of Geography, Arizona State University
Terry Dorschied

Courtesy of Tim Ridley/Dorling Kindersley.

AFRICA

Scale 1:51,400,000

Azimuthal Equal-Area Projection

0 —— 800 Kilometers

0 —— 800 Miles

Boundary representation is
not necessarily authoritative.

Courtesy of the U.S. Central Intelligence Agency.

803002AI (R02109

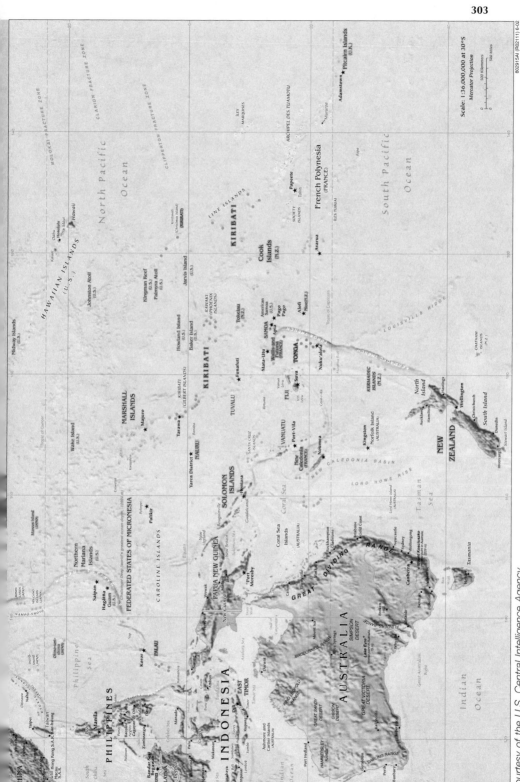

304

ANTARCTIC REGION

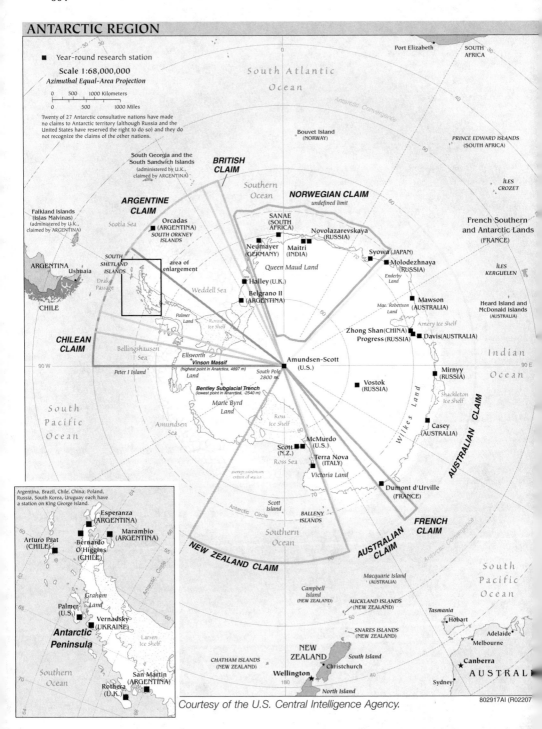

- ■ Year-round research station

Scale 1:68,000,000
Azimuthal Equal-Area Projection

0   500   1000 Kilometers
0   500   1000 Miles

Twenty of 27 Antarctic consultative nations have made no claims to Antarctic territory (although Russia and the United States have reserved the right to do so) and they do not recognize the claims of the other nations.

South Georgia and the South Sandwich Islands (administered by U.K., claimed by ARGENTINA)

BRITISH CLAIM

NORWEGIAN CLAIM
undefined limit

Port Elizabeth   SOUTH AFRICA

South Atlantic Ocean

Bouvet Island (NORWAY)

PRINCE EDWARD ISLANDS (SOUTH AFRICA)

ÎLES CROZET

French Southern and Antarctic Lands (FRANCE)

ARGENTINE CLAIM

Southern Ocean

SANAE (SOUTH AFRICA)

Novolazarevskaya (RUSSIA)

Falkland Islands (Islas Malvinas) (administered by U.K., claimed by ARGENTINA)

Scotia Sea

Orcadas (ARGENTINA)
SOUTH ORKNEY ISLANDS

Neumayer (GERMANY)   Maitri (INDIA)

Syowa (JAPAN)

Molodezhnaya (RUSSIA)

ÎLES KERGUELEN

ARGENTINA   Ushuaia

SOUTH SHETLAND ISLANDS

area of enlargement

Queen Maud Land

Enderby Land

Heard Island and McDonald Islands (AUSTRALIA)

CHILE

Drake Passage

Weddell Sea

Halley (U.K.)

Belgrano II (ARGENTINA)

Mawson (AUSTRALIA)

Mac. Robertson Land

Palmer Land

Ronne Ice Shelf

Amery Ice Shelf

CHILEAN CLAIM

Bellingshausen Sea

Ellsworth Vinson Massif (highest point in Anarctica, 4897 m) Land

Zhong Shan(CHINA) Progress (RUSSIA)   Davis(AUSTRALIA)

Indian Ocean

90 W

Peter I Island

South Pole 2800 m.

Amundsen-Scott (U.S.)

Mirnyy (RUSSIA)

90 E

Bentley Subglacial Trench (lowest point in Anarctica, -2540 m)

Marie Byrd Land

Vostok (RUSSIA)

Shackleton Ice Shelf

South Pacific Ocean

Amundsen Sea

Ross Ice Shelf

Casey (AUSTRALIA)

Wilkes Land

McMurdo (U.S.)

Scott (N.Z.)

Terra Nova (ITALY)

AUSTRALIAN CLAIM

Ross Sea

average minimum extent of sea ice

Victoria Land

Dumont d'Urville (FRANCE)

Scott Island

BALLENY ISLANDS

FRENCH CLAIM

Antarctic Circle

NEW ZEALAND CLAIM

AUSTRALIAN CLAIM

Southern Ocean

Antarctic Convergence

Macquarie Island (AUSTRALIA)

South Pacific Ocean

Argentina, Brazil, Chile, China, Poland, Russia, South Korea, Uruguay each have a station on King George Island.

Campbell Island (NEW ZEALAND)

AUCKLAND ISLANDS (NEW ZEALAND)

Tasmania

Hobart

Esperanza (ARGENTINA)

Arturo Prat (CHILE)

Marambio (ARGENTINA)

Bernardo O'Higgins (CHILE)

Adelaide

Melbourne

SNARES ISLANDS (NEW ZEALAND)

Palmer (U.S.)

Graham Land

Vernadsky (UKRAINE)

Antarctic Peninsula

Larsen Ice Shelf

CHATHAM ISLANDS (NEW ZEALAND)

NEW ZEALAND

South Island

Canberra

AUSTRAL

Southern Ocean

San Martin (ARGENTINA)

Rothera (U.K.)

Wellington

North Island

Christchurch

Sydney

Courtesy of the U.S. Central Intelligence Agency.

802917AI (R02207

305

ASIA

Scale 1:48,000,000
Azimuthal Equal-Area Projection

Boundary representation is
not necessarily authoritative.

ourtesy of the U.S. Central Intelligence Agency.

803057AI (R02105) 3-04

NORTH AMERICA

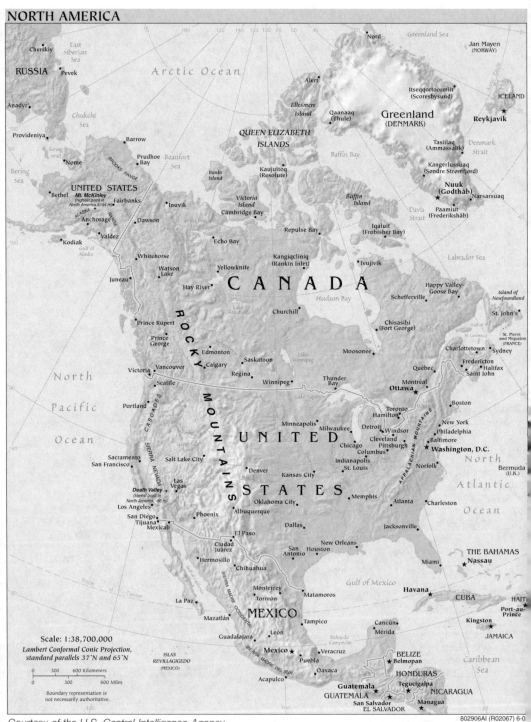

Courtesy of the U.S. Central Intelligence Agency.

802906AI (R02067) 6-0

SOUTH AMERICA

803053AI (R02108) 3-04

EUROPE

Scale 1 : 19,500,000
Lambert Conformal Conic Projection,
standard parallels 40°N and 56°N

300 Kilometers

300 Miles

Boundary representation
not necessarily authorita

Courtesy of the U.S. Central Intelligence Agency.

803055AI (R01083)

Physical Map of the World, June 2003